4QINSTRUCTION

Society of Biblical Literature

Wisdom Literature from the Ancient World

Leo G. Perdue, General Editor
Reinhard Gregor Kratz, Associate Editor

Area Editors

Bendt Alster
Pancratius C. Beentjes
Katharine Dell
Edward L. Greenstein
Victor Hurowitz
John Kloppenborg
Michael Kolarcik
Manfred Oeming
Bernd U. Schipper
Günter Stemberger
Loren T. Stuckenbruck

Number 2

4QINSTRUCTION

4QINSTRUCTION

By

Matthew J. Goff

Society of Biblical Literature
Atlanta

4QINSTRUCTION

Library of Congress Cataloging-in-Publication Data

Goff, Matthew J.
    4QInstruction / Matthew J. Goff.
        p. cm. — (Wisdom literature from the ancient world ; number 2)
    ISBN 978-1-58983-782-9 (paper binding : alk. paper) — ISBN 978-1-58983-783-6 (electronic format) — ISBN 978-1-58983-784-3 (hardcover binding : alk. paper)
    1. 4QInstruction. 2. Wisdom literature—Criticism, interpretation, etc. I. Title.
    BM488.A15G635 2013
    296.1'55—dc23
                                                               2013005788

For Meegan

בת חכמה ישמח אב

Proverbs 10:1 (with some modification)

Contents

Acknowledgments

This book has had a rather long process of gestation. I was originally asked to write this volume in 2004. In 2009 the book, and the series of which it is a part (Wisdom Literature from the Ancient World), came under the auspices of the Society of Biblical Literature press. I began work on the project in this context. I am grateful for the SBL's commitment to this volume and the series to which it belongs.

My work on this book has received extensive support. The Council on Research and Creativity of Florida State University facilitated the project with a Planning Grant and a COFRS Grant (a Committee on Faculty Research Support regular summer award). In 2011 I received a Faculty Travel Grant from the Office of the Provost that enabled me to attend the International Meeting of the Society of Biblical Literature in London, where I presented research from the present project.

Along the way I received help and encouragement from many people. Special thanks go to Leo Perdue, who created the Wisdom Literature from the Ancient World series and led the effort to have this volume included in it. Loren Stuckenbruck also deserves enormous credit for helping the volume reach the publication stage. John Collins, who sparked my interest in 4QInstruction when I was in graduate school, also steadfastly encouraged me during my work on this project. I thank John Kampen for sending me a prepublication form of his *Wisdom Literature* (Eerdmans, 2011), which was helpful in the later stages of the writing process. Hanan Eshel (ז"ל) deserves credit for informing me, at his house in Jerusalem in the summer of 2009, that he had identified a small Qumran fragment as belonging to 4QInstruction. Jean-Sébastien Rey, who has written a very good book on 4QInstruction (*4QInstruction: Sagesse et eschatologie* [Brill, 2009]), answered numerous computer questions of mine about how to present the text of this composition. Conversations and correspondence with numerous other people assisted me in the writing of this book. They include Sam Adams, Torleif Elgvin, Weston Fields, Gregory Goering,

Armin Lange, Eibert Tigchelaar, and Benjamin Wold. I am also grateful to the many people who edited and provided feedback on drafts of chapters: Seth Bledsoe, Eric Naizer, Kyle Roark, Elizabeth Scott, J. Andrew Sowers, Robert Williamson, and Matthew Woodard. Bob Buller at the SBL press did an excellent job in seeing this project to its completion, and I thank him for his efforts.

Unless otherwise noted, translations of Ben Sira and the Hodayot are from, respectively, Alexander di Lella and Patrick W. Skehan, *The Wisdom of Ben Sira* (AB 39; New York: Doubleday, 1987), and Hartmut Stegemann, Eileen Schuller, and Carol Newsom, *Qumran Cave 1.III: 1QHodayot^a with Incorporation of 1QHodayot^b and 4QHodayot^{a-f}* (DJD 40; Oxford: Clarendon, 2009).

My wife Diane has been unstinting in her support of my work, and I am enormously grateful. I am lucky to have her in my life. Our two children, Meegan and Liam, have been a continuous source of delight and inspiration during my work on this project. I dedicate this book to Meegan, who asked me if it was about unicorns. The next one will be for Liam.

Tallahassee, Florida
July 2, 2013

ABBREVIATIONS

AB   Anchor Bible
AGJU   Arbeiten zur Geschichte des antiken Judentums und des
            Urchristentums
ATM   Altes Testament und Moderne
BAR   *Biblical Archaeology Review*
BETL   Bibliotheca ephemeridum theologicarum lovaniensium
BInS   Biblical Interpretation Series
BJS   Brown Judaic Studies
BN   *Biblische Notizen*
BSIH   Brill's Studies in Intellectual History
BZAW   Beihefte zur Zeitschrift für die alttestamentliche Wissen-
            schaft
CBQMS   Catholic Biblical Quarterly Monograph Series
CBR   Currents in Biblical Research
CHANE   Culture and History of the Ancient Near East
CPJ   *Corpus papyrorum judaicorum*. Edited by V. Tcherikover. 3
            vols. Cambridge: Harvard University Press, 1957–1964.
DCLS   Deuterocanonical and Cognate Literature Studies
DJD   Discoveries in the Judaean Desert
DJD 1   *Qumran Cave 1*. Edited by Dominique Barthélemy and Józef
            T. Milik. DJD 1. Oxford: Clarendon, 1955.
DJD 34   *Qumran Cave 4.XXIV: Sapiential Texts, Part 2. 4QInstruc-
            tion (Mûsār Lě Mēbîn): 4Q415ff. With a Re-edition of 1Q26.*
            Edited by John Strugnell and Daniel J. Harrington. DJD 34.
            Oxford: Clarendon, 1999.
DJD 36   *Qumran Cave 4.XXVI: Cryptic Texts and Miscellanea, Part
            1*. Edited by Stephen J. Pfann. DJD 36. Oxford: Clarendon,
            2000.
DMOA   Documenta et Monumenta Orientis Antiqui
DSD   *Dead Sea Discoveries*

DTT	*Dansk teologisk tidsskrift*
EvT	*Evangelische Theologie*
FRLANT	Forschungen zur Religion und Literatur des Alten und Neuen Testaments
GDNES	Gorgias Dissertations in Near Eastern Studies
GKC	*Gesenius' Hebrew Grammar.* Edited by E. Kautzsch. Translated by A. E. Cowley. 2nd ed. Oxford: Clarendon, 1910.
HALOT	Koehler, L., W. Baumgartner, and J. J. Stamm. *The Hebrew and Aramaic Lexicon of the Old Testament.* Translated and edited under the supervision of M. E. J. Richardson. 4 vols. Leiden: Brill, 1994–1999.
HS	*Hebrew Studies*
HSS	Harvard Semitic Studies
HTR	*Harvard Theological Review*
JANESCU	*Journal of the Ancient Near Eastern Society of Columbia University*
JAOS	*Journal of the American Oriental Society*
JBL	*Journal of Biblical Literature*
JESHO	*Journal of the Economic and Social History of the Orient*
JJS	*Journal of Jewish Studies*
JLA	*The Jewish Law Annual*
JNES	*Journal of Near Eastern Studies*
JQR	*Jewish Quarterly Review*
JSJ	*Journal for the Study of Judaism in the Persian, Hellenistic, and Roman Periods*
JSJSup	Supplements to the Journal for the Study of Judaism
JSOTSup	Journal for the Study of the Old Testament Supplement Series
LASBF	*Liber annuus Studii biblici franciscani*
LSTS	Library of Second Temple Studies
NES	Near Eastern Studies
NovT	*Novum Testamentum*
OTL	Old Testament Library
PAAJR	*Proceedings of the American Academy of Jewish Research*
PAM	Palestinian Archaeological Museum
RB	*Revue biblique*
RevQ	*Revue de Qumran*
RHPR	*Revue d'histoire et de philosophie religieuses*
SB	Subsidia Biblica

SBLEJL	Society of Biblical Literature Early Judaism and Its Literature
SBLSP	*Society of Biblical Literature Seminar Papers*
SBLSymS	Society of Biblical Literature Symposium Series
STAC	Studies and Texts in Antiquity and Christianity
STDJ	Studies on the Texts of the Desert of Judah
TAD	*Textbook of Aramaic Documents from Ancient Egypt.* Edited by B. Porten and A. Yardeni. 3 vols. Jerusalem: Hebrew University, 1986–1993.
TBN	Themes in Biblical Narrative
TSAJ	Texte und Studien zum antiken Judentum
VT	*Vetus Testamentum*
WBC	Word Biblical Commentary
WDSP	Wadi Daliyeh Samaria Papyri
WUNT	Wissenschaftliche Untersuchungen zum Neuen Testament
YJS	Yale Judaica Series
ZNW	*Zeitschrift für die Neutestamentliche Wissenschaft*

A NOTE ON THE CRITICAL TEXT

This commentary offers a critical text of the major fragments of 4QInstruction. Two factors complicate this effort: the physically degraded nature of the material and the fact that there are several copies of the composition, which often overlap. The second issue means that text which is missing or illegible in one fragment of 4QInstruction can be reconstructed with material from another fragment. While people in the field of Qumran studies will be familiar with the system I have adopted in the presentation of the text in this commentary, for the sake of clarity I explain it to the general reader.

- A line over a *yod* or *waw* (ⅰ) designates that the orthography of these two letters is very similar and that I understand the letter in question as one of these two, while acknowledging that it could be the other.
- A dot over a letter (א̇) indicates that the letter in question is not fully extant and that I regard it as a probable, but not fully certain, reading.
- A circle over a letter (א̊) means that the letter in question is very poorly preserved and that my reading is possible but far from certain.
- A circle (○) in the main text (not above another letter) denotes that there is a letter at the location in question but not enough of it survives to identify it.
- Text in brackets indicates that it is not in the fragment at hand. The material within the brackets for the most part comes from overlapping fragments of 4QInstruction. Any text that overlaps with material from other fragments of the composition is marked with a type of underlining. This format is explained at the outset of each critical text of the book.

- Any letter within brackets that is in a shadow font (א) is not based on physical evidence but is rather supplemented on semantic grounds. In the translation this material is in italics.

The diacritical remarks explained above are present in the critical text and textual notes sections of each chapter. For the sake of simplicity, they are not retained when I cite the Hebrew of 4QInstruction in the main body of the commentary.

The critical text of each chapter is accompanied by instances in which one or more of the major editions of 4QInstruction texts (e.g., DJD 34, Tigchelaar, Rey) offer a different reading than the one offered here (in the textual notes section). Because of the fragmentary nature of the composition, there will inevitably be texts that qualified scholars transcribe in different ways. People should consult the images of the original fragments and decide for themselves how to transcribe a given word or letter of 4QInstruction. After the writing of this book was completed, Google launched a project in collaboration with the Israel Museum to make new high-resolution images of the Qumran scrolls readily available online. This is an exciting development, and it will be interesting to see how this resource can enable advances in the study of 4QInstruction.

Introduction

1. Manuscripts and Discovery

4QInstruction (1Q26, 4Q415–418, 4Q423), also known as *musar le-mebin*, is the longest sapiential text found among the Dead Sea Scrolls. There has been a great deal of interest in this composition in recent years.[1] 4QInstruction was officially published in 1999 in DJD 34 by John Strugnell and Daniel Harrington.[2] 1Q26 was originally published in DJD 1, which appeared in 1955.[3] Strugnell correctly suggested in August 1955 that 1Q26 might be part of a larger sapiential text, perhaps written by the Qumran sect, which is represented by four manuscripts from Cave 4, now numbered 4Q415–418.[4] By 1959 the basic form of the text was understood. Its manuscripts had been transcribed for the card index of the preliminary concordance of the Qumran scrolls, and its fragments had been photographed.[5] Strugnell's work on 4QInstruction took on renewed focus in 1992 when Emanuel Tov, as the new editor-in-chief of the Dead Sea Scrolls, appointed Daniel Harrington to become a partner with Strugnell to see the official edition of 4QInstruction to completion.[6] The first publication of 4QInstruction texts also occurred in 1992, in the works of Wacholder and Abegg, and Eisenman and Wise, both well known in the history of the Dead Sea Scrolls.[7]

---

1. Major studies include Rey 2009; Wold 2005b; Goff 2003b; Tigchelaar 2001; Elgvin 1997a (an important study that remains unpublished). For additional scholarship, consult Goff 2009b, 376–416; Harrington 2006, 105–23.

2. Strugnell and Harrington (1999) gave the name *musar le-mebin* to the text. Before this edition appeared, the document was often called Sapiential Work A.

3. Barthélemy and Milik 1955, 101–2.

4. Strugnell 1956, 64–66. According to Strugnell and Harrington (1999, xiii), when Strugnell joined the editorial team in September 1954, Milik had already begun to assemble some of the fragments of 4Q418. See also Tigchelaar 2001, 5–13. For the relation between 4QInstruction and the Dead Sea sect, see §10 below.

5. Strugnell and Harrington 1991, xiv; Tigchelaar 2001, 6–8.

6. Shanks 2002, 33; Strugnell and Harrington 1991, xv.

7. Wacholder and Abegg 1992, 44–154, 166–71; Eisenman and Wise 1992, 241–

4QInstruction is a lengthy composition, of which only fragmentary remains survive. It has been proposed that one copy of the work, 4Q418, was as lengthy as the Temple Scroll or the Hodayot, two of the longest texts from Qumran.[8] DJD 34 presents over 425 fragments as from 4QInstruction. Most of them are quite small. Since the composition's official publication, three minor texts of 4QInstruction have surfaced (XQ7; 4Q416 23; PAM 43.674 frg. 7).[9] The large number of fragments associated with the composition prevents this commentary from treating all of them in depth. Instead, this book examines in detail the largest and most important fragments of 4QInstruction:

1. 4Q415 2 ii
2. 4Q416 1
3. 4Q416 2 ii
4. 4Q416 2 iii
5. 4Q416 2 iv
6. 4Q417 1 i
7. 4Q417 1 ii
8. 4Q417 2 i

---

55. Wacholder and Abegg reproduced the transcriptions of texts of 4QInstruction based on the preliminary concordance. Eisenman and Wise based their work on the photographs of the scrolls at the Huntington Library in San Marino, California. For evaluation of the former work, see Tigchelaar 2001, 14–15; for the latter, see Harrington and Strugnell 1993, 491–99. For the story of the scrolls' publication in the early 1990s, consult VanderKam 2010, 233–40.

8. Strugnell and Harrington 1999, 2.

9. Puech and Steudel 2000, 623–27; Eshel and Eshel 2007, 277–78. The first fragment was published by Armin Lange in DJD 36 as XQ7, "XQUnidentified Text." The text is small, preserving remnants of thirteen words. A Finnish pastor purchased the scrap from an Arab in 1960. Upon the death of the pastor, the fragment was bequeathed to the state of Israel and became the possession of the Israel Antiquities Authority. John Strugnell was never informed of the text's existence during the years he worked on the edition of 4QInstruction (personal correspondence in 2002). The fragment published by the Eshels is even smaller than XQ7, with only two legible words surviving. They classify it as belonging to 4Q416 as fragment 23 of this copy. (Strugnell and Harrington in DJD 34 attribute 22 fragments to this manuscript.) PAM 43.674 frg. 7, which appears in Pike and Skinner 2001, has recently been identified by Tigchelaar and should be placed at the left end of 4Q416 2 i 10–12. See Tigchelaar 2001, 125; 2011, 317–22; Pfann 2000, 492–93; Kampen 2011, 189–90; Pike and Skinner 2001, 70.

9. 4Q418 55
10. 4Q418 69 ii
11. 4Q418 81
12. 4Q418 103 ii
13. 4Q418 126 ii + 122 ii
14. 4Q423 1
15. 4Q423 5

The vast majority of the extensive scholarly interest in this composition has focused on these texts, in particular 4Q416 1 and 2, 4Q417 1 and 2, and 4Q418 81.

The fragments of 4QInstruction derive from seven or perhaps eight copies of the work. They are: 1Q26, 4Q415, 4Q416, 4Q417, 4Q418, 4Q418a, and 4Q423.[10] This number of copies rivals that of major Qumran texts such as the War Scroll (seven) and the Damascus Document (eight). The multiple copies of 4QInstruction often produce a synoptic situation, in which several versions of the same passage are attested.[11] This allows poorly preserved passages to be reconstructed through other attestations of the same text, as is evident in the commentary that follows.

The major characteristics of the manuscripts of 4QInstruction are as follows:

1Q26

One of the smaller manuscripts of 4QInstruction, only five small fragments are attributed to it. 1Q26 1 overlaps with 4Q423 4 and 1Q26 2 with 4Q423 3.[12] The handwriting of the manuscript is classified as "rustic semi-formal" and dated to the early or middle Herodian period.[13]

4Q415

Thirty-two fragments are associated with this manuscript, most of

---

10. The determination of the number of manuscripts depends on the assessment of the material attributed to 4Q418, as discussed below.

11. Tigchelaar 2001, 148–50.

12. As mentioned above, this text was published originally in DJD 1. It is republished in Strugnell and Harrington 1999 (535–39). 1Q26 is at the Bibliothèque Nationale in Paris. The others manuscripts of 4QInstruction are in Jerusalem at the Israel Museum. See also Tigchelaar 2001, 146–47; Kampen 2011, 189.

13. For overviews of these script styles, see Cross 1961, 133–202; Yardeni 2002.

which are quite small.[14] The most substantial are fragments 2 ii, 9, and 11, which all deal in various ways with marriage and childbirth (see chapter 1). The overlap between 4Q415 11 and 4Q418 167a + b confirms that the manuscript is a copy of 4QInstruction. The handwriting is early Herodian and similar to 4Q418 and 4Q418a. The editors of DJD 34 suggest that the fragments of 4Q415, on the basis of their paleographic affinities with 4Q418, may stem from sheets that were once part of the latter manuscript but then removed from it.[15] 4Q415 is the only text of 4QInstruction that is opithsographic, meaning that its leather has writing on both sides. On the *verso* is 4Q414 (4QRitual of Purification A), a liturgical text.[16] It is written in a different hand from the *recto* and, in relation to 4Q415, is upside down. This suggests that the manuscript was reused at a later date by the author of 4Q414.[17] It is possible that 4Q415 was considered at that time a discarded or unnecessary manuscript.

4Q416

Twenty-two fragments comprise this copy.[18] Most of them are minor, but two of the most important texts of 4QInstruction belong to 4Q416: 4Q416 1, widely considered to be the beginning of the composition (see §2 below), and 4Q416 2, the longest and arguably most important fragment of 4QInstruction. It preserves a substantial amount of text from four columns. 4Q416 2 overlaps with material in 4Q417 2 and 4Q418 7–10. The paleography of 4Q416 suggests that it was written in the late Hasmonean or early Herodian periods (early to mid-first century B.C.E.). The editors

---

14. Strugnell and Harrington 1999, 41–71; Tigchelaar 2001, 28–41; Kampen 2011, 84–94.

15. Strugnell and Harrington (1999, 1) do not endorse this view consistently. See, for example, pp. 42 and 214. Tigchelaar (2001, 30) grants the similarities between 4Q415 and 4Q418 but is skeptical of the proposal in Strugnell and Harrington 1999 for explaining them.

16. The editor of 4Q414 is Esther Eshel. See Baumgarten et al. 1999, 135–54.

17. Strugnell and Harrington 1999, 41–42. Elgvin argues that 4Q414 was written before 4Q415. Tigchelaar (2001, 28–30) points out, in addition to arguments given above, that the *recto* or hair side of the leather (the 4Q415 side) was the side normally used for writing. See Eshel in Baumgarten et al. 1999, 135; Elgvin 1995a, 577.

18. Strugnell and Harrington 1999, 73–141; Tigchelaar 2001, 42–50; Kampen 2011, 60–83. 4Q416 has twenty-three fragments according to Eshel and Eshel 2007, 277–78, as discussed above.

of DJD 34 suggest that 4Q416 is the oldest copy of 4QInstruction, being perhaps twenty-five years older than 4Q415, 4Q417, and 4Q418.[19]

4Q417

Twenty-nine fragments belong to 4Q417.[20] As with 4Q416, most of these are quite minor, but 4Q417 1 and 2 are important fragments of 4QInstruction. They are crucial for understanding core topics of the work, such as its eschatology, creation theology, and financial advice. The handwriting of the manuscript is early Herodian formal. The numbering of 4Q417 1 and 2 was switched by the official editors of the composition. In pre-DJD 34 scholarship 4Q417 1 is called 4Q417 2 and vice versa.[21]

4Q418 AND 4Q418A–C

A vast number of fragments are associated with 4Q418.[22] They present more problems than the other manuscripts of 4QInstruction. The handwriting of 4Q418 is late Hasmonean or early Herodian (early to mid-first century B.C.E.). In DJD 34 the enumeration of 4Q418 fragments goes from 1 to 303, but several of these numbers are null and do not represent distinct fragments of 4QInstruction.[23] 4Q418 includes several well-known

---

19. Strugnell and Harrington 1999, 76.

20. Strugnell and Harrington 1999, 143–210; Tigchelaar 2001, 51–60; Kampen 2011, 94–118.

21. Tigchelaar 2011, 51. In Strugnell and Harrington (1999) the sequence of some of the other fragments of 4Q417 was rearranged. For example, 4Q417 11 was originally fragment 5. Five other small texts of 4Q417 were reclassified as 4Q468l–p. They are available in Pfann 2000, 422–25.

22. Strugnell and Harrington 1999, 211–474; Tigchelaar 2001, 61–125; Kampen 2011, 118–75.

23. For example, 4Q418 12 and 21 are now understood as belonging to fragment 8 (classified as 4Q418 8d and 8c, respectively). 4Q418 213 has been joined to fragment 2 and is now identified as 4Q418 2c. 4Q418 125 is an empty number since the fragment in question is now fragment 116. 4Q418 256–58 no longer have fragments associated with them since they have been joined to other manuscripts. Additional null numbers are discussed below. Strugnell and Harrington (1999, 474) doubt whether fragment 303 actually belongs to 4Q418. It is published by Ernst and Lange in Pfann 2000 (420–21) as 4Q468k (4QHymnic Text B?). Strugnell and Harrington (1999, 474) also include a list of over fifty small fragments that are presented as part of 4Q418, about which they express doubt as to whether they are actually from this manuscript. See also Tigchelaar 2001, 70–72.

and much-discussed fragments, such as fragments 55, 69 ii and 81. Several texts of 4Q418 overlap with other fragments of 4QInstruction.[24]

DJD 34 also describes three other manuscripts, classified as 4Q418a–c. Twenty-five small fragments are attributed to 4Q418a and two and one, respectively, to 4Q418b and 4Q418c.[25] On the basis of physical differences between the two groups of fragments, the 4Q418a fragments are considered in DJD 34 to come from a copy of 4QInstruction that is separate from 4Q418.[26] The editors hesitatingly suggest that 4Q418b and 4Q418c may be from still other copies of 4QInstruction.[27]

The classification in DJD 34 of the fragments that comprise 4Q418 has been criticized. Elgvin argued that several fragments (1, 2, 2a, 2b, 2c, 4, 286, 296, 297) of 4Q418 are actually from a separate manuscript, which he designates "4Q418b"[28] Strugnell and Harrington agree with Elgvin that the fragments which comprise 4Q418 1–2 are different from the rest of

---

24. 4Q418 1–2, for example, overlaps with 4Q416 1; 4Q418 7–10 overlaps with portions of 4Q416 2 and 4Q417 2; 4Q418 43–45 i (which are joined to comprise a single text) corresponds to 4Q417 1 i and 4Q418a 11; 4Q418 69 ii overlaps with 4Q417 5; 4Q418 77 with 4Q416 7; 4Q418 81 with 4Q423 8; 4Q418 167a + b with 4Q415 11; 4Q418 188 with 4Q423 9.

25. Strugnell and Harrington 1999, 475–503; Tigchelaar 2001, 124–39. Tigchelaar never endorses the separation of 4Q418b and is critical of some of the classifications and joins of fragments in the 4Q418a material as presented in Strugnell and Harrington 1999, 138–39.

26. The 4Q418a material consists of four multi-layered wads of fragments, most of which are quite thin. Also the 4Q418a fragments are in general much darker in color than those associated with 4Q418. See Strugnell and Harrington 1999, 475; Tigchelaar 2001, 126–30.

27. 4Q418b 1 and 2 were originally classified as fragments 116 and 112 of 4Q418, respectively. 4Q418c was originally 4Q418 161. The column length of 4Q418b is much narrower than that of the 4Q418 and 4Q418a fragments, suggesting it does not stem from these manuscripts. Strugnell and Harrington suggest that 4Q418c is not part of 4Q418, because of their differing column heights and the use in 4Q418c of geographical terms (i.e., Mount Carmel in l. 10), which are not found elsewhere in 4QInstruction. The editors grant that such arguments are not overwhelming, but nevertheless separate 4Q418c from 4Q418. Tigchelaar sees no convincing reason to endorse this separation. See Strugnell and Harrington 1999, 498, 501; Tigchelaar 2001, 124–25.

28. Elgvin 1995a, 570–71. Elgvin's 4Q418b should not be confused with the 4Q418b of Strugnell and Harrington 1999. Also, he classifies the rest of 4Q418 as "4Q418a" (referring to material classified in Strugnell and Harrington 1999 as 4Q418, not 4Q418a).

4Q418.[29] They dismiss, however, the possibility of a separate manuscript. Instead, they suggest that 4Q418 1–2 represents a sort of patch or repair sheet that was appended to 4Q418, because its original beginning page had become damaged. Tigchelaar suggests that 4Q418 1–2 represents the beginning of another copy of 4QInstruction, which he terms 4Q418* (to distinguish it from 4Q418 and 4Q418a), the rest of which has not survived.[30] The poorly preserved condition of the 4Q418 fragments prevents firm conclusions regarding the number of copies they contain. It is entirely possible that 4Q418 1–2 are remnants of a manuscript aside from 4Q418. These debates do not have a major impact on the interpretation of the surviving content of 4QInstruction (see §2 below).

4Q423

Twenty-four fragments belong to this manuscript.[31] Fragments 3 and 4 overlap, respectively, with 1Q26 2 and 1. 4Q423 5 has text that accords with 4Q418a 3.[32] 4Q423 1 depicts the *mebin* as entrusted with the garden of Eden, an important motif for understanding the nature of his elect status. Several texts of 4Q423, in particular fragment 5, help establish that at least some of the intended addressees were farmers (see chapter 15). The hand of 4Q423 is middle or late Herodian (first half of the first century C.E.), placing it, along with 1Q26, among the latest copies of 4QInstruction. One small fragment that was once part of 4Q423 was reclassified by the editors of DJD 34 as 4Q468q.[33]

2. THE STRUCTURE OF 4QINSTRUCTION

Considerable effort has been made to determine the sequence of the texts of 4QInstruction in its original form. Elgvin made a proposal of the work's original structure in his 1997 dissertation, and the editors of DJD

---

29. The 4Q418 1–2 material is much darker and thicker than is normally the case in 4Q418. See Strugnell and Harrington 1999, 226–27; Tigchelaar 2001, 62.

30. Tigchelaar 2001, 61–64. See p. 16, for a table that helps explain the nomenclature regarding copies of 4Q418 material used by Elgvin 1997a, Strugnell and Harrington (1999), and himself. Consult also Rey 2009a, 3.

31. Strugnell and Harrington 1999, 505–33; Tigchelaar 2001, 140–45; Kampen 2011, 182–89.

32. 4Q423 8 overlaps with 4Q418 81, 4Q423 9 with 4Q418 188, and 4Q423 11 with 4Q418 184.

33. Ernst and Lange in Pfann 2000, 423, 425–26.

34 report a (still unpublished) reconstruction of 4Q418 by Annette Steudel and Birgit Lucassen.[34] The most secure data point in this endeavor is that 4Q416 1 represents the beginning of the composition. This, however, is not a fact, but rather a reasonable explanation of its wide right margin (approximately 3 cm.).[35] Also, the column's emphasis on divine judgment would be fitting as an introductory text since it would establish an eschatological horizon for the rest of the composition (not unlike 1 Enoch 1).

Beyond the identification of 4Q416 1 as the beginning of 4QInstruction, relatively little can be plausibly inferred about the original structure of the composition. It is also not evident that there is a great deal at stake regarding this issue. The composition is generally, and reasonably, considered a wisdom text (see §4 below). Other sapiential texts, such as Proverbs and Ben Sira, are characterized by the often seemingly haphazard sequence of their contents. In terms of reconstructing narrative texts, such as the fragmentary Book of Giants, how one arranges the fragments is an important issue, since it reflects one's understanding of the sequence of events in the narrative. There is, by contrast, no narrative in 4QInstruction. It appears to be, like other wisdom texts, a loose collection of didactic teachings. Were a reconstruction of its original sequence possible, it is not clear that this would be of great assistance for the interpretation of the text.

However, in some cases a "relative reconstruction" of 4QInstruction texts is possible.[36] At times one can determine the placement of a given text not in relation to the original structure of the composition but to another text of 4QInstruction. For example, 4Q418a 15 and 18, which both derive from the same wad of texts, overlap respectively with 4Q418 167 and 4Q416 2 iv. Understanding the layers of the wads that intervene between the two fragments of 4Q418a as preserving actual revolutions of the physical scroll, one can infer that text which corresponds to 4Q418 167 was between three and five columns to the left of material that accords

---

34. Strugnell and Harrington 1999, 18–19; Elgvin 1997a, 29–31; 1995a, 564.

35. Strugnell and Harrington 1999, 73. Elgvin is exceptional in viewing 4Q416 1 as not from the beginning of the work, understanding it as from column 7 of the work, although he has since disavowed this view (personal correspondence). See also Tigchelaar 2001, 156–57. This issue is discussed in more detail at the beginning of chapter 2.

36. Tigchelaar 2001, 161.

with 4Q416 2 iv.[37] Such inferences are interesting but do not have a significant impact on the interpretation of 4QInstruction.

3. LANGUAGE AND STYLE

The Hebrew of 4QInstruction has several notable features. There are several words that are characteristic of the document.[38] They include:

- רז נהיה. This is the most distinctive term of the composition (see further §5 below). The term *raz* is a Persian loan-word and *nihyeh* is a *niphal* participle of the verb "to be."[39] It is often translated "the mystery that is to be." The expression signifies supernatural revelation that has been disclosed to the addressee.
- מבין. A *hiphil* participle that means "understanding one." It is the composition's preferred term for the addressee (consult §4 below).
- אוט. This enigmatic term probably refers to material resources that are available to the addressee, the exact nature of which cannot be recovered. See further the commentary on 4Q416 2 ii 1.
- המשיל. This *hiphil* verb denotes "to give dominion." It is often used in 4QInstruction, typically in the perfect with a second person singular suffix. At key points of the document this verb signifies that God has given the addressee a form of elect status. For example, 4Q423 1 2 employs the term to claim that he has been entrusted with the garden of Eden. In 4Q416 2 iii 11–12 the term helps convey that the deity has bequeathed to the *mebin* an "inheritance of glory" (see further the commentary on this text and 4Q418 81 3).
- חפץ. This term, which is attested over twenty times in the composition, refers to one's "desire." The term normally signifies in

---

37. Tigchelaar 2001, 163.

38. Several surveys of the distinctive terminology of 4QInstruction are available. See Kampen 2011, 46–54, Rey 2009a, 33–38, Tigchelaar 2001, 237–44, Strugnell and Harrington 1999, 31–32.

39. Morphologically, נהיה could be a perfect verb, but syntax suggests this is not the case. While I understand the term as a participle that modifies the word "mystery," it could be a nominal participle, in which case the two terms have a construct relationship, "the mystery of that which is." For the Persian background of the term *raz*, see Thomas 2009, 245–51. Consult also Rey 2009a, 287.

4QInstruction a person's (typically the addressee's) desire to meet his material needs. The word may refer to God's desire in 4Q416 1 2 (see commentary on this text). More detail on חפץ is provided in the commentary on 4Q418 126 ii 12.

- מחסור. The word denotes "lack" in a material sense and is important for conveying that the addressee is at times unable to meet his basic needs. Additional discussion of this word is offered in the commentary on 4Q417 2 i 17.

- מולד. This term is translated here as "birth time." In 4Q186 (4QHoroscope) the term has an astrological sense, signifying the "sign" under which one is born. While 4QInstruction shows no knowledge of astronomical lore, it has a deterministic conception of the natural order. It follows that the timing of human birth occurs according to a divine plan. The text urges the *mebin* several times to "seize the birth times" (4Q415 11 11, 4Q416 2 iii 20; 4Q417 2 i 11; 4Q418 202 1). This probably refers to the process of determining whether the prospective wife of the addressee (or his children) is among the elect, but some of the relevant texts are ambiguous. See further the commentary on 4Q417 2 i 11.

- פקודה. Meaning "visitation," this word denotes eschatological judgment several times in 4QInstruction, as discussed in the commentary on 4Q417 1 i 7–8. The term can also signify the divinely structured nature of the created order (4Q416 1 9).

In terms of style, several features are prominent in 4QInstruction. One is the work's preference for the second person singular, referring to the addressee. This is the case even though the composition is designed for a group of *mebinim* rather than a single individual. This is indicated by the fact that the word appears several times in the plural (4Q415 11 5; 4Q418 123 ii 4; 4Q418 221 3). 4Q418 81 17 suggests that there was more than one teacher as well. It is reasonable to think of the preference for the second person singular as a rhetorical device, intended to convey instruction to each *mebin* more personally and directly. However, it is possible that, while the document was produced for a group of people, instruction took place on a one-to-one basis. Very little can be determined about how instruction actually took place in the community to which 4QInstruction is addressed. Some texts prefer the second person plural, most notably 4Q418 55 8–12 and 4Q418 69 ii 4–15 (see commentaries on these texts; cf. 4Q417 1 i 20; 4Q423 5 10).

4QInstruction often begins new topics of discourse with the term *mebin* in an exhortation that urges him to acquire knowledge. A common formula is ואתה מבין plus an imperative (4Q416 4 3; 4Q417 1 i 1, 13, 18; 4Q417 2 i 28; 4Q418 69 ii 15; 4Q418 81 15; 4Q418 123 ii 5; 4Q418 126 ii 12; 4Q418 168 4; 4Q418 176 3). Parallelism is another common feature of 4QInstruction, as is often the case in ancient Hebrew literature.[40] A clear example is in the call for filial piety in 4Q416 2 iii 15–16: "Honor your father in your poverty and your mother in your lowly state, for as God is to man so is his father, and as Lord is to a person so is his mother" (cf. 4Q417 1 i 8–9; 4Q418 55 4; 4Q418 123 ii 4–5).

Regarding the syntax of 4QInstruction, several items should be noted. 4QInstruction is rather unusual in its preference for the phrase ואז ("and then"). In the Hebrew Bible the conjunction is almost always used without a *waw* (for exceptions, see, e.g., Exod 12:48 and Jer 32:2). This is also the case in Ben Sira (50:16, 20). Aside from 4QInstruction, ואז is found in the scrolls but is relatively rare (e.g., 1QS 3:11; 1QM 1:16).[41] 4QInstruction uses the expression several times with the verb ידע (second person singular) to convey what the addressee can learn if he follows the text's advice to study constantly. 4Q417 1 i 6–7 reads, for example, "[... day and night meditate upon the mystery that] is to be and study (it) constantly. And then (ואז) you will know truth and iniquity, wisdom [and foll]y" (cf. ll. 8, 13; 4Q416 2 iii 9). 4QInstruction also prefers וגם ("and also") over גם.[42] וגם begins a new section several times in the composition (e.g., 4Q416 2 ii 21; 4Q417 2 i 28). Another distinctive syntactic feature of 4QInstruction is the construction אל תקטול... ...פן ("do not X ... lest ..."; e.g., 4Q416 2 ii 16, 18; 4Q416 2 iii 4), which is quite rare elsewhere in the Dead Sea Scrolls.[43] The work also several times uses למה in the sense of פן ("lest"), as does Ben Sira (e.g., 1Q26 1 5; 4Q416 2 ii 14; Sir 8:1; 12:5).

---

40. For more on parallelism, see Reymond 2011; Berlin 2008.

41. For a fuller treatment of this issue, see Tigchelaar 2001, 237.

42. וגם is used in various constructions in the Hebrew Bible and Early Jewish literature. See for example Gen 6:4; Zech 9:11; Neh 5:8; Ezek 16:28; Sir 3:13; 7:32; 12:11; CD 5:11; 15:1; 1QM 11:3. Consult also Rey 2009a, 34.

43. Rey (2009a, 18–19, 334) points out that this construction is also found consistently in Ben Sira and should be viewed as a stylistic element that is distinctive to both works. This forms part of his argument that the two works not only have a common milieu but that their authors debated one another. As discussed in sections 9 and 10 below, both texts were written during the second century B.C.E., but their notable differences in terms of social class problematizes the extent to which one can posit that

4. Genre: 4QInstruction as a Wisdom Text

The wisdom tradition of ancient Israel comprises pedagogical literature, written by teachers for students, that is eudemonistic and didactic,
provides instruction on specific topics, and intends to foster in them a
desire to learn and seek knowledge.[44] Sapiential texts contain teachings
about practical topics that pertain to ordinary life, such as marriage or the
payment of debts. They also engage more speculative topics such as God's
creation of the world or theodicy. The wisdom tradition is represented in
the Hebrew Bible by Proverbs, Job, and Ecclesiastes and in the Apocrypha
by Ben Sira and the Wisdom of Solomon. Aside from 4QInstruction, there
are several other Qumran texts that are widely considered wisdom texts.[45]

4QInstruction is considered a sapiential text primarily because of its
explicit and insistent pedagogical nature. The addressee is often referred
to as a *mebin* ("understanding one"), a term that portrays him as someone
who is learning and thinking.[46] By contrast, virtually nothing is said in the
text about the speaker. Due to the didactic nature of the text, the speaker
can reasonably be understood as the teacher who instructs the addressee.
The teacher figure of 4QInstruction never emerges as a distinct person-
ality. In principle more than one person could have assumed the role of
teacher in the circles in which 4QInstruction was produced.

The term *mebin* is typically used in the singular, but several attestations in the plural help establish that 4QInstruction was written with a
particular community in mind, as discussed above. The term elsewhere
often refers to students and signifies a person who wants to learn. In Proverbs the term describes someone who wants to attain knowledge and
understanding.[47] The word is parallel to "scribe" (סופר) in 1 Chr 27:32

---

their authors interacted with one another. See also Rey 2008, 155–73; Adams 2010,
555–83.

44. Crenshaw 2010, 12; Perdue 2008.

45. For a review of the Qumran texts often identified as sapiential, see Kampen
2011; Goff 2007; 2010c, 286–306; Harrington 1996b.

46. The term occurs approximately twenty times in 4QInstruction (not including
instances in which it is reasonably supplemented). See, e.g., 4Q417 1 i 1, 14, 18; 4Q417
1 ii 8; 4Q418 81 15; 4Q418 102a + b 3; 4Q418 123 ii 5; 4Q418 158 4; 4Q418 168 4;
4Q418 227 1. Consult Kampen 2011, 51–52.

47. Prov 17:24: "Wisdom is before the face of the perceptive man (מבין) while
the eyes of the dolt are in the ends of the earth." This translation is from Fox (2009,

and describes courtiers trained in "every branch of wisdom" in Dan 1:4.[48] In the Hodayot the word denotes the elect community who has received revealed knowledge from their teacher (1QH 10:20). In the wisdom text 4QBeatitudes the term occurs in an exhortation that urges a student to listen to a teacher: "And now, understanding one, listen to me" (4Q525 14 ii 18; cf. 4Q303 1). The prominence of this term in 4QInstruction exemplifies its devotion to the education of students and helps establish it as a wisdom text.

In terms of content there is much in 4QInstruction that resonates with the wisdom tradition. 4Q418 221 2–3 explains that the work is intended to make both the simple (פותיים) and the intelligent ones (מבינים) understand (cf. 4Q418 81 17). A variant of the term "simple" is in the pedagogical prologue of the book of Proverbs, which, like the 4Q418 passage, calls for the instruction of both the uneducated and the learned.[49] 4QInstruction shows a marked interest in the ordinary life of the addressee, dispensing ample advice on commonplace topics. There are lessons, for example, on marriage and filial piety (e.g., 4Q416 2 iii 15–21). The composition gives extensive advice on financial topics, urging the *mebin* to pay debts promptly and avoid going surety (as in 4Q416 2 ii 4–6). The view that indebtedness poses grave risks and should be remedied as soon as possible fits not only with the low economic status of the *mebin* but also with traditional wisdom.[50] Proverbs and 4QInstruction give compatible financial advice using common imagery. Proverbs 6:4, for example, urges the addressee to go without sleep, as part of a teaching that emphasizes the risks of going surety. 4Q416 2 ii 9 uses this same image as part of its instruction for a debt slave and 4Q417 2 i 21–22 urges that a borrower should give his soul no rest until the debt is paid. One should not simply imagine 4QInstruction as influenced by the wisdom tradition in a vague or abstract sense. Rather, the author of the document, as part of his own education, was exposed to the study of teachings preserved in the book

---

635–36), who explains that the "understanding one" of the verse does not yet possess wisdom but has the potential to acquire it (cf. 8:9; 17:10).

48. The word occurs twenty-seven times in the Hebrew Bible. For a more in-depth study of the term, see Lange 2008, 274–77.

49. Prov 1:4–5: "to teach shrewdness to the simple (פתאים) … let the wise (חכם) also hear and gain in learning" (cf. v. 22; 8:5; 4Q185 1–2 i 14).

50. The poverty of the addressee and the fact that Proverbs and 4QInstruction show comparable caution towards borrowing are discussed in §9 below.

of Proverbs. In this respect, he can be compared to Ben Sira, in that both figures are teachers whose pedagogy is steeped in the traditional wisdom of Israel, as represented by Proverbs.

5. Revelation, Eschatology and Determinism in a Qumran Wisdom Text

While there is much in 4QInstruction that accords with Proverbs, the work contains important material that is alien to biblical wisdom. This is most evident in the theme of revelation. 4QInstruction's most important expression is רז נהיה, an enigmatic phrase that is normally translated "the mystery that is to be."[51] To underscore the importance of this expression, Menachem Kister has suggested that an appropriate title for the work would be חכמת רז נהיה ("the Wisdom of the Mystery That Is to Be").[52] The expression *raz nihyeh* is not in the Hebrew Bible and elsewhere in ancient Jewish literature is attested only three times—twice in the book of Mysteries (1Q27 1 i 3–4 [par. 4Q300 3 3–4]) and once in the Community Rule (1QS 11:3–4). In the former instance the *raz nihyeh* is associated with eschatological judgment (the wicked who will perish do not know it), and in the latter text it signifies supernatural revelation given to the elect.[53] 4QInstruction uses the expression over twenty times.[54] The phrase normally signifies something that should be studied, fronted with the *bet* preposition and accompanied by an imperative that encourages contemplation, as in, for example, 4Q417 1 i 6–7: "[… day and night meditate upon the mystery that] is to be (ברז נ[היה]) and study (it) constantly. And then you will know truth and iniquity, wisdom [and foll]y …" (par. 4Q418 43 4).[55] Several texts remind the addressee that the mystery that is to be

---

51. Goff 2007, 51–79; Thomas 2009, 150–60; Collins 2003, 287–305.

52. Kister 2009b, 1.304.

53. 1QS 11:3–4: "For from the source of his knowledge he has disclosed his light, and my eyes have observed his wonders, and the light of my heart the mystery that is to be."

54. 4Q415 6 4; 4Q416 2 i 5 (par. 4Q417 2 i 10); 4Q416 2 iii 9, 14, 18, 21 (par. 4Q418 9 8, 15; 4Q418 10 1, 3); 4Q417 1 i 3, 6, 8, 18, 21 (par. 4Q418 43 2, 4, 6, 14, 16); 4Q417 1 ii 3; 4Q418 77 2, 4; 4Q418 123 ii 4; 4Q418 172 1; 4Q418 184 2; and 4Q423 4 1, 4 (par. 1Q26 1 1, 4). The phrase is reconstructed in 4Q415 24 1; 4Q416 17 3; 4Q418 179 3; 4Q418 190 2–3; 4Q418 201 1; 4Q418c 8; 4Q423 3 2; 4Q423 5 2; and 4Q423 7 7.

55. The expression is joined to the *mem* preposition in 4Q416 2 iii 21. It is unaccompanied by any preposition in 4Q416 2 iii 14. He is to "gaze upon" (נבט; 4Q416 2 i

has already been disclosed to his ear (1Q26 1 4; 4Q416 2 iii 18; 4Q418 123 ii 4; 4Q418 184 2; cf. 4Q418 190 1).[56] He has access to this mystery and should study it.

4Q417 1 i 8–9 makes the striking claim that God created the world with the mystery that is to be (ברז נהיה). This assertion evokes Prov 3:19, according to which God fashioned the world by means of wisdom (בחכמה).[57] The mystery that is to be is the means by which the addressee obtains wisdom. It is supernatural revelation disclosed to him, upon which he is to reflect and contemplate. This "mystery" has pedagogical potential because of its association with the created order, as 4Q417 1 i 8–9 suggests. The composition makes several deterministic statements, indicating that reality is orchestrated according to a divine plan that the *mebin* can know. 4Q417 1 i 18–19, for example, associates deterministic knowledge of the natural order with the mystery that is to be: "And now, understanding son, gaze upon the mystery that is to be and know [the path]s of all life and the manner of one's walking that is appointed over [his] deed[s]" (cf. ll. 10–12). The mystery that is to be signifies a comprehensive divine scheme that orchestrates the cosmos, from creation to judgment, presented to the addressee as knowledge that can be ascertained through the study of supernatural revelation.

This meaning of the mystery that is to be accords with other early Jewish texts. The term *raz* (unaccompanied with *nihyeh*) denotes revealed knowledge in apocalyptic literature. The term is used eight times in Daniel 2 in reference to Nebuchadnezzar's dream, which God discloses to Daniel, who in turn praises the Lord as a "revealer of mysteries" (2:29; cf. vv. 18–19, 27–28, 30, 47 [2x]; 4:6). In the Aramaic Enoch scrolls the term signifies angelic revelation: "I know the mysteries that the holy ones have revealed and shown to me, and that I have read in the tablets of heaven" (106:19 [4QEn^c 5 ii 26–27]; cf. 8:3 [4QEn^a 1 iv 5]; 4Q203 9 3). Numerous other Qumran texts employ the term to denote supernatural revelation.[58]

---

5 [par. 4Q417 2 i 10]; 4Q417 1 i 3, 18 [par. 4Q418 43 2, 14]), "examine" (דרש; 4Q416 2 iii 9 [par. 4Q418 9 8], 14), "meditate" (הגה; 4Q418 43 4 [cf. 4Q417 1 i 6]), "grasp" (לקח; 4Q418 77 4) the mystery that is to be. 4Q415 6 4 urges him to "test (בחן) these things" with the mystery that is to be.

56. Mysteries are also revealed to one's "ear" in 1QH 9:23 (cf. 6:13; 22:26; 25:12).

57. Goff 2003a, 163–86.

58. See, e.g., 1QS 4:18; 1QH 12:28; 17:23; 19:19; 1QpHab 7:4–5; 4Q300 1a ii–b 2. For a good recent survey of the relevant material, consult Thomas 2009, 136–86.

The "mystery" of the mystery that is to be conveys that the knowledge in question originates from heaven. The participle that is part of this phrase conveys that the revealed mystery (the *raz*) pertains to the entire chronological order, from beginning to end.[59] While in the Hebrew Bible the *niphal* participle of the verb "to be" often denotes a closed action (e.g., Prov 13:19), the form appears in early Jewish texts in a variety of ways, often with an emphasis on the entire scope of time.[60] The Treatise on the Two Spirits, for example, declares: "From the God of Knowledge comes all that is and all that will be (כול הויה ונהייה)" (1QS 3:15). The *niphal* participle here strictly speaking denotes the future but is used to convey that all things, in the present and the future, are established by God. Elsewhere in the Community Rule the participle expresses that the cosmos which he created endures "in every age that exists" (בכול קץ נהיה; 10:4–5; cf. 11:17–18). The Hodayot and the Songs of the Sabbath Sacrifice employ the participle in a way that denotes the past, present and future (4Q402 4 12; 1QH 19:17; cf. 5:29; 21:13). The meaning of this participle in 4QInstruction accords with its usage in these texts. The *niphal* participle in 4QInstruction is associated three times not only with the mystery that is to be but also a tripartite division of time. The knowledge of what was, is, and will be is obtainable by the *mebin* through this revelation (4Q417 1 i 3–5 [2x]; 4Q418 123 ii 3–4).

The mystery that is to be is not the only indication of influence from the apocalyptic tradition in 4QInstruction. The work teaches the *mebin* that eschatological judgment is inevitable.[61] Two judgment scenes are preserved in 4QInstruction, in 4Q416 1 and 4Q418 69 ii. Both texts describe judgment in theophanic terms, with elements of the natural order, such as the seas and sky, quaking before the overwhelming power of divine judgment. Both texts also pinpoint the demise of wickedness to this event. 4Q418 69 ii 8 asserts that the "foolish of heart" and the "sons of iniquity" will be destroyed, and 4Q416 1, most likely the beginning of the composition, proclaims that all "iniquity" will be no more (l. 13). There are also reminders about the final judgment throughout the work. The vision of

---

59. Rey 2009a, 291; Schoors 2002, 87. Consult also the commentary on 4Q417 1 i 3–5.

60. Rey 2009a, 284–90.

61. Goff 2003b, 168–215; Collins 2004, 49–65; Macaskill 2007.

meditation passage (4Q417 1 i 13–18), for example, stresses that this event is an ordained and established feature of the natural order.[62]

6. THE ELECT STATUS OF THE *MEBIN*, THE LOT OF THE ANGELS AND THE PROSPECT OF ETERNAL LIFE

Also in keeping with apocalypticism, 4QInstruction shows a genuine interest in the angelic world, although the text never mentions a specific angel by name. The addressee is a member of a group with elect status that has special affinity with the angels. God established the *mebin* in the "lot" (גורל) of the angels (4Q418 81 4–5). Core Qumran documents use the same term to describe the *yaḥad* as in the lot of the angels (1QS 11:7–8; 1QH 19:14–15). 4Q418 81 affirms that God has separated the addressee from the "fleshly spirit" (ll. 1–2). This phrase probably encompasses not only the wicked but the non-elect in general—anyone who does not possess the potential to attain life after death. The judgment scene of 4Q416 1 affirms that the fleshly spirit will be destroyed in the final judgment (l. 12). The vision of meditation passage centers around a distinction between the fleshly spirit and the spiritual people, who were created in the likeness of the holy ones (4Q417 1 i 17; see chapter 6). The *mebin*, in his reflection upon this teaching, was likely supposed to identify with the spiritual people, and thus realize that he is like the angels, not the fleshly spirit. The addressee has affinity with the angels, which distinguishes him from the rest of humankind, those who are not in his elect community.

Being like the angels allows the *mebin* two core benefits that humans cannot normally obtain. First, this status provides an explanation as to why heavenly revelation was disclosed to him. 4Q417 1 i teaches that God has given the vision of meditation to the spiritual people but not to the fleshly spirit.[63] Second, the addressee has the potential to attain a blessed afterlife. This is not stated explicitly in 4QInstruction, but it can be reasonably inferred. The text affirms that the angels have eternal life (4Q418 69 ii 12–13). 4Q417 2 i 10–12 teaches that the *mebin* should not "rejoice" (תשמח) in his mourning and that there is "eternal joy" (שמחת עולם)

---

62. See also 4Q417 1 i 24; 4Q417 1 ii 11; 4Q417 4 ii 4; 4Q418 68 2–3; 4Q418 77 3; 4Q418 121 1; 4Q418c 5; 4Q423 4 3a and 4Q423 6 4.

63. As I discuss in chapter 6, this vision should probably be understood not as a disclosure that is distinct and separate from that of the mystery that is to be, but rather as an allusion to it.

established for those who mourn. The passage portrays the current life of the *mebin* as one of mourning. This characterization is consistent with the ethics of 4QInstruction, which emphasizes that the addressee should be humble (consult the commentary on 4Q417 2 i 10–14). This also accords with the text's assumption that his life can be filled with material hardship (see §9 below). If mourning is a cipher for the present existence of the *mebin*, "eternal joy" is reasonably understood as a reference to the eternal life he can obtain after death. In the Treatise on the Two Spirits. the phrase "eternal joy" (with עולם in the plural) is allocated to the elect, and denotes eternal life (1QS 4:7). In a wordplay in the Hebrew, this text describes one of the punishments established for the wicked as the "eternal pit" (שחת עולמים), a reference to their death and subsequent transfer to Sheol (4:12). 4QInstruction uses this same language to assert that the wicked will go to the eternal pit (4Q418 69 ii 6; with עולם in the singular). The wisdom text does not describe the nature of the eternal life which the addressee can acquire. However, given the composition's emphasis on his affinity with the angels, one can plausibly assert that he will join them after death. Obtaining this goal is a powerful incentive for the addressee to remain devoted to the pedagogy advocated by the composition.

7. The Elect Status of the *Mebin* and Genesis 1–3

4QInstruction turns to Gen 1–3 to teach the *mebin* about the nature of his elect status.[64] 4Q423 1 makes the remarkable claim that he is entrusted with the garden of Eden. He is to "till" and "guard" it—an assertion that draws directly from Gen 2:15. 4Q423 1 emphasizes that all of the trees of the garden provide wisdom. There is no sense that any of the trees are prohibited. Being appointed to work in Eden metaphorically describes the elect status of the *mebin*. His stewardship over the garden signifies that the special knowledge he acquires through the mystery that is to be entails toil, denoting the text's emphasis on the study of this mystery.

The vision of meditation passage asserts that the revealed vision has been given not only to the spiritual people but also to אנוש, an enigmatic term that probably signifies Adam (see chapter 6). The fleshly spirit is denied this vision because it does not possess the knowledge of good and evil, implying that the spiritual people do (4Q417 1 i 17–18). This trope

---

64. For the use of the Torah in 4QInstruction, see §8.

evokes Adam. Elsewhere 4QInstruction asserts that the knowledge of good and evil can be obtained by the *mebin* through the study of the *raz nihyeh* (ll. 6–8). This suggests that through this revelation the addressee can obtain knowledge originally possessed by Adam in the garden.

8. 4QInstruction: A Wisdom Text with an Apocalyptic Worldview

The prominence of supernatural revelation and other themes that fit with apocalypticism in 4QInstruction, such as eschatology and life after death, has profound consequences for assessing its status as a wisdom text.[65] Such themes are alien to the book of Proverbs. The expression "revealer of secrets" (גולה־סוד) has negative connotations in this book, describing a gossip who cannot be trusted to keep secrets (20:19; cf. 11:13). Ben Sira, as is well known, dismisses the value of esoteric knowledge ("hidden things"; נסתרות), which he contrasts with the importance of Torah (3:21–24). While some elements that are compatible with apocalypticism are present in both Ben Sira and the Wisdom of Solomon, 4QInstruction illustrates to an extent not evident before the emergence of the Dead Sea Scrolls that an early Jewish wisdom text could incorporate themes that accord with the apocalyptic tradition.[66] This Qumran text is the best example available of a sapiential text with an apocalyptic worldview.

4QInstruction's relationship to the wisdom tradition has been understood in various ways. Armin Lange has argued that the composition should be seen in direct continuity with the book of Proverbs. He empha-

---

65. Note, however, that the theme of revelation in 4QInstruction is not exactly the same as is often found in the apocalypses. In Daniel and 4 Ezra, for example, the reader watches a vision unfold, along with the seer himself, that is then interpreted by an angel (e.g., Dan 7:23–27; 4 Ezra 13:21–50). 4QInstruction, by contrast, contains no accounts of visions and there is no *angelus interpretus*. The composition emphasizes not the revelation of the *raz nihyeh* but rather the importance of studying it. The emphasis on the study of revelation can be understood as a combination of the text's pedagogical emphasis with influence from the apocalyptic tradition. See Goff 2005b, 57–67.

66. Both Ben Sira and the Wisdom of Solomon, for example, emphasize divine judgment (e.g., Sir 23:16–21; Wis 3:10). For an overview of the apocalyptic tradition, see Collins 1998. Studies that discuss the interplay between wisdom and apocalypticism in 4QInstruction include Collins 1997f, 265–81; Elgvin 2000a, 226–47; and Bro Larsen 2002, 1–14.

sizes the "präexistenten weisheitlichen Urordnung," the ordered structure
of the world established at the moment of creation that is, he argues, proclaimed in 4QInstruction and other wisdom texts such as Ben Sira and
Proverbs.[67] In his view, 4QInstruction endorses the older sapiential view
that God fashioned the world with a rational, intelligible structure through
appeal to the mystery that is to be, whereas it is knowable from empirical
observation in traditional wisdom.[68] Lange understands this development
as a consequence of a putative "crisis of wisdom" represented by the critique of conventional wisdom in Job and Ecclesiastes. By endorsing traditional sapiential themes through supernatural revelation, 4QInstruction
confirms for Lange the thesis of Gerhard von Rad that apocalypticism
should be viewed as an eschatological outgrowth from the sapiential tradition.[69] Elgvin, by contrast, understands the mystery that is to be as testify-
ing to 4QInstruction's decisive break from traditional wisdom.[70] The work,
he argues, replaces the figure of Woman Wisdom (who never appears in
the text) with the mystery that is to be. In his view 4QInstruction is a composite work, comprising an earlier work of practical wisdom that has been
heavily redacted by people with an apocalyptic worldview.[71]

It is better to understand the sapiential and apocalyptic traditions as
combined in 4QInstruction rather than set them against each other. Like
Proverbs and Ben Sira (e.g., Prov 3:19; Sir 1:9), 4QInstruction has no problem asserting that God has wisdom. Indeed, 4Q417 1 i 8–9 not only claims
that God created the world with the mystery that is to be, but then asserts,
in parallel language, that he did so with wisdom: God "m[ade (it) with wis]-
dom (חכ[מה) and for everything [with cleve]rness he fashioned it" (cf. Sir
42:21). 4Q418 126 ii 4–5 extols God's use of wisdom in his creation of the
world: "He has spread them out, in truth he has established them [... From
God nothing] is hidden. Moreover, nothing exists without his good will
and apart from [his] wis[dom] ([ומחוכ]מתו) ..." (cf. 4Q417 1 ii 10; 4Q417
2 i 19–20). 4QInstruction exhorts the addressee to observe regular, orderly
aspects of the cosmos (4Q418 69 ii 3–4; 4Q423 5 6). This is fully in keeping with the view, prominent in traditional wisdom, that God endowed the
world with a discernible, rational structure (Prov 8:22–31; Sir 42:15–43:33).

---

67. Lange 1995, 40. Consult further Lange 2010, 454–78.
68. Lange 1995, 62, 91.
69. Lange 1995, 301–6. See also Collins 1997e, 385–404; von Rad 1965, 2.306.
70. Elgvin 1997a, 61; 2000a, 239.
71. Note also Elgvin 2009, 162. Consult Nitzan 2005a, 257–79.

Like Ben Sira, 4QInstruction teaches that the nature of God and his creation is not fully attainable through empirical observation (Sir 43:32). The structured nature of the created order is also a major theme in apocalyptic literature (e.g., the Enochic Astronomical Book). 4QInstruction asserts that the world has a knowable structure by stressing God's creation of it (4Q417 1 i 8–9) rather than by expounding upon the motion of heavenly bodies or providing a detailed account of the heavenly world, as one often finds in the apocalypses. 4QInstruction's appeal to the beginnings of creation to thematize the structured nature of the world is in continuity with classic wisdom texts such as Prov 8 or Sir 24. As Lange stresses, the Qumran sapiential text differs from older wisdom in that it offers a way, beyond rational observation, to understand God and his creation. 4Q417 1 i 27, for example, exhorts that one should *not* rely on his own heart and eyes. Rather, the best way for the *mebin* to understand the world is by studying the mystery that is to be. The prominence of supernatural revelation in 4QInstrution reflects influence from the apocalyptic tradition. Lange and Elgvin are both right to stress that the term *raz* denotes heavenly revelation and constitutes a significant departure from Proverbs. But there is little reason to understand this as a response to Job and Ecclesiastes in the manner of Lange, since 4QInstruction shows scant interest in these works.[72] 4QInstruction is a product of complementary influences from the wisdom and apocalyptic traditions. This problematizes the view promoted by Elgvin that 4QInstruction should be divided into two strata, an earlier layer of practical wisdom and a later, apocalyptic layer.

As a wisdom text with an apocalyptic worldview, 4QInstruction should probably not be understood as an outlier among early Jewish wisdom texts. Rather, it is the best example available of a broader type of sapiential literature that is characterized by extensive influence from the apocalyptic tradition. Both the Treatise and the book of Mysteries, while they reflect scant engagement with traditional wisdom, can be understood as didactic instructions that prominently utilize apocalyptic themes such as revelation, eschatological judgment, life after death and determinism.[73] Moreover, these two works show extensive terminological similarities

---

72. Note, however, that 4QInstruction may show some engagement with the book of Qoheleth. See the commentary on 4Q418 69 ii 4–5.

73. Goff 2007, 69–103; Lange 1995, 121–70; Frey 2007, 40–45. Knibb (2003, 193–210) emphasizes the "shared thought-world" between 1 Enoch, 4QInstruction and the book of Mysteries.

with 4QInstruction.[74] This work and Mysteries invoke the mystery that is to be (1QS 11:3–4). The Treatise and 4QInstruction both employ the divine epithet "the God of Knowledge" (אל הדעות) in deterministic contexts (4Q417 1 i 8; 1QS 3:15; cf. 4Q299 35 1; 4Q299 73 3). All three of these works use the term "plan" (מחשבה) to describe God's deterministic scheme guiding the cosmos (4Q417 1 i 12; 4Q299 3a ii–b 11; 1QS 3:15–16). While the same community most likely did not produce all three of these works, 4QInstruction, the Treatise and the book of Mysteries can be viewed as attesting one strand of early Jewish wisdom literature that is distinguished by extensive engagement with the apocalyptic tradition.[75] This mode of wisdom literature may have influenced the later Sayings Source utilized by the gospels of Matthew and Luke.[76]

The kind of wisdom represented by 4QInstruction can be contrasted with that of Ben Sira. His instruction can be understood as exemplifying a type of early Jewish sapiential literature characterized by a rich combination of the sapiential and covenantal traditions. Ben Sira not only appropriates much of the instruction in Proverbs but also utilizes material from the Torah, famously portraying the personified wisdom of Prov 8 as a tree that takes root in Israel, the fruit of which is the Torah (Sir 24:23). The association of Torah with wisdom is not unique to this composition. It is also found in Baruch (4:1; cf. 11QPsᵃ 18:3, 12). The Dead Sea Scrolls include other texts that attest this development, such as 4QBeatitudes and 4QSapiential Work (e.g., 4Q185 1–2 ii 4; 4Q525 2 ii + 3 3–4). While it uses the Torah extensively, 4QInstruction never thematizes it in the manner of Ben Sira. The Qumran text does not share the Torah piety of Ben Sira. The surviving fragments of the work never even attest the word "Torah."[77] Ben Sira and 4QInstruction draw upon the same fount of traditional wisdom but they appropriate it in different ways and in combination with different influences. This complements the stark contrast between the two works in

---

74. Tigchelaar 2001, 194–203.

75. Neither Mysteries nor the Treatise emphasizes the poverty of their addressees, and they do not give financial instruction for someone who could fall into dire straits economically, whereas both of these points are prominent in 4QInstruction. This argues against positing a common provenance for these three texts. In terms of 4QInstruction vis-à-vis the Treatise, see the discussion below of the composition in relation to the Dead Sea sect.

76. Goff 2005a, 657–73.

77. Note, however, the phrase "by the hand of Moses" (ביד משה), which occurs in two unfortunately fragmentary texts of 4QInstruction (4Q418 184 1; 4Q423 11 2).

terms of social location, in that Ben Sira is a sage operating in an upper-class milieu, whereas 4QInstruction presupposes an addressee who is poor, or at least may easily become so.

9. The Poverty and Social Location of the *Mebin*

The poverty of the addressee is one of the distinctive features of 4QIn-struction.[78] The composition repeatedly reminds him that he is poor, employing the phrase "you are poor," using either אביון or ראש/רש (4Q415 6 2; 4Q416 2 ii 20; 4Q416 2 iii 2, 8, 12, 19; 4Q418 177 5; cf. 4Q418 148 ii 4; 4Q418 249 3). 4Q416 2 iii 19 places the "you are poor" formula in a conditional clause, the only explicit evidence of this usage of the expression in 4QInstruction. For this reason Tigchelaar has proposed that the *mebin* is not necessarily poor but could become so.[79] The members of the audience to which 4QInstruction is addressed undoubtedly had a range of professions, and not all of them were necessarily destitute. However, the text consistently suggests an addressee with a low social and economic status. Several texts assume that the *mebin* could be a farmer (see the commentary to 4Q423 5 5–6). 4Q418 81 15–20 is designed for a crafts-man who earns enough to survive from his trade. Other texts present the addressee as engaged in various sorts of business relationships, but they are not arrangements that yield a great deal of wealth or power. 4Q418 126 ii 12–13 gives instruction regarding trade between the addressee and another person.[80] Both parties are engaged in this transaction to meet basic material needs. The text addresses the possibility that the trade may not be successful in this regard. What is being traded (probably agri-cultural produce, as suggested by the word "basket" in l. 12) is relatively modest. The envisioned addressee is often not destitute but rather has suf-ficient, if not extensive, means of support.

The intended audience of the composition comprises people at vari-ous levels of poverty. The parade example for this issue is 4Q417 2 i 17–20. Lines 17–18 teach the *mebin* that his basic material needs can be met by assembling his "surplus," presumably a reference to agricultural produce that he can trade. The next lines (ll. 19–20) recommend that, when he is

---

78. Wold 2007, 140–53; Wright 2004a, 101–23; Goff 2007, 127–67; Fabry 2003, 145–65; Murphy 2002, 163–209.

79. Tigchelaar 2000, 62–75.

80. 4Q417 2 i 12; 4Q418 81 18–19; 4Q418 107 4.

without money, he borrow from God. This is presented as an alternative to borrowing from creditors. One should show a radical reliance on God for his sustenance. Such an ethic portrays his inability to be self-sufficient as an opportunity to practice an extreme form of piety. 4Q417 2 i 17–18 assumes that the addressee may experience lack but has the means to solve the problem. Ll. 19–20 are designed for someone who no longer has the means to support himself.

The variable financial status of the envisioned addressee is consistent with 4QInstruction's teachings on borrowing and surety. These are frequent topics of the work. This implies that the members of the intended audience were often in need of credit. One should be respectful and honest towards one's lenders and pay off the debt promptly (4Q417 2 i 20–24). The creditor may not show the same attitude towards the *mebin*. 4Q417 2 i 25–27, for example, indicates that the lender could have the addressee flogged. Amidst such treatment, the exhortation that one show honesty and dignity towards the creditor is notable, and reflects the importance of maintaining good relations with creditors. This also suggests that the *mebin* has a somewhat regular need for credit. Indebtedness is considered a problem, and is treated as a dangerous situation which one should stridently try to alleviate. Lines 21–22 of 4Q417 2 i state that one should go without sleep and have no rest until the debt is removed. 4Q416 2 iii 5–7 also encourages prompt payment of debts. Surety, the practice of pledging an item of value to guarantee the loan given to another, is also treated as a serious problem (e.g., 4Q416 2 ii 4–6).[81] 4QInstruction's wary attitude toward borrowing resonates with the sapiential tradition. Proverbs shows mistrust regarding borrowing and surety (e.g., 20:16; 22:7; 27:13).[82] Ahiqar also stresses the burdensome nature of debt (45–46 [sgs.]), as do other sapiential texts of the Ancient Near East, such as the Egyptian Instruction of Amenemope and the Mesopotamian Instruction of Shuruppak.[83]

---

81. Cf. 4Q415 8 2; 4Q416 2 iii 3–5; 4Q418 87 7.

82. The two compositions use similar language when giving financial instruction. See the discussion of Prov 6:1–4 and 4Q417 2 i 21–22 in §4 above.

83. The key passage from the Egyptian text is: "If you find a large debt against a poor man, make it into three parts; forgive two, let one stand, you will find it a path of life" (16.5–8); the Mesopotamian composition reads "Do not be a security. ... Then you [will be] a security" (12–13 [obverse]). See Goff 2007, 134.

It is common in the wisdom tradition, and throughout the Hebrew Bible, to show sympathy for the poor.[84] Proverbs 22:22, for example, teaches "Do not rob the poor because they are poor, or crush the afflicted at the gate."[85] Ben Sira espouses the same attitude: "My son, do not cheat the poor of their living" (4:1; cf. v. 8; 7:32; 31:4; 34:25). In contrast to both of these texts, 4QInstruction shows surprisingly little interest in the poor as an economic class. There is almost no advice recommending that one not abuse the poor.[86] There is, however, intense concern for the addressee as a poor person. The traditional sapiential instruction on borrowing and surety is applied to the addressee.

To return to Tigchelaar's skepticism regarding the poverty of the envisioned *mebin*, the point is not whether he is poor or not. The text repeatedly asserts that he is. The question is what is meant by such assertions. While in principle the intended audience could be from a range of financial levels, not a single teaching of the work unambiguously depicts the *mebin* as wealthy. Rather, the variation in economic levels of the intended audience moves from an addressee who is self-sufficient but with a modest income to one who has lost his means of self-support. The issue is not just the economic diversity of the intended audience but also that the envisioned *mebin* has means of support that can fluctuate and are not consistently reliable. This fits perfectly with the view that the addressee is a farmer or a petty tradesman, as discussed above. In the Second Temple period, as in most traditional societies, there was no middle class in the modern sense, and most people were small landholders and subsistence farmers (see the second excursus of chapter 3). Such individuals were exposed to the vagaries of the season, and at times, through no fault of their own, were forced to borrow to make ends meet.

4QInstruction also appeals to poverty in a metaphorical sense.[87] The *mebin* is encouraged to act like a "poor" or "humble" man (עני; 4Q417 2 i 14). When encouraging filial piety, the composition urges the addressee to honor his father with his poverty and his mother with his lowly status (4Q416 2 iii 15–16). A few lines later the composition associates pov-

---

84. Pleins 2001, 452–83.

85. Also note, for example, Prov 10:15: "The wealth of the rich is their fortress; the poverty of the poor is their ruin." See also 14:20–21; 18:11; 19:17; 21:13.

86. Note the reconstruction of 4Q418 146 2: "You shall n[ot] defraud the w[age of a laborer]" (cf. 4Q418 137 3).

87. Goff 2007, 163–66; Wold 2007, 153.

erty with taking a wife. The theme of poverty does not denote exclusively financial concerns. It can represent an ethical ideal.[88] This realization helps explain 4QInstruction's use of the "you are poor" formula. The envisioned addressee could easily suffer material hardship. One can presume that he was aware of his poverty. Yet the composition insistently reminds him that he is poor. This becomes intelligible if one understands poverty as signifying not just the economic reality of the *mebin* but also the ethical attitudes espoused by the composition. The refrain "you are poor" means not simply that he is materially poor but also that he should live in a way which is humble, simple and reverent.

The addressee's precarious financial situation suggests that, despite the emphasis on studying and teaching in the work, the *mebin* is not in training to become a scribe who serves the upper class.[89] 4QInstruction should thus be sharply distinguished from Ben Sira, a sage who does teach in an aristocratic milieu.[90] The social locations of both texts influence their teachings. Ben Sira never stresses the poverty of his students, but rather assumes that they have the wherewithal to show kindness to the poor, which he encourages (Sir 29:12). Whereas 4QInstruction teaches the *mebin* to be an ethical borrower who does not lie to those who lend to him (4Q417 2 i 22–23), Ben Sira encourages his students to be ethical creditors who should lend money to those in need, even though the loan may not be repaid (Sir 29:1–13). 4QInstruction never gives instruction regarding etiquette at banquets or proper speech before the powerful. Both topics are in Ben Sira (e.g., 13:9; 32:9; cf. Prov 23:1–3). The Qumran wisdom text illustrates that not all instruction and scribal activity in the Second Temple period took place in elite, aristocratic circles.[91] There is also a debate as to whether the *mebin* should be considered a priest (see the commentary on 4Q418 81 3). The low social setting of the work argues against this position, as do the facts that the work shows relatively little interest in cultic

---

88. In several sayings Proverbs associates the behavior it advocates with the poor and not with the wealthy. Proverbs 15:17, for example, reads, "Better is a dinner of vegetables where love is than a fatted ox and hatred with it" (cf. 17:1; 18:23).

89. *Contra* Strugnell and Harrington 1999, 21.

90. Adams 2010, 582–83.

91. Van der Toorn 2007. While Ben Sira praises the scribe over menial professionals, he does grant that some poor people are intelligent (10:23; 38:24–34; cf. Qoh 10:15).

issues or ritual purity, and that the intended audience includes women (4Q415 2 ii).

10. The Composition's Date and Relation to the Dead Sea Sect

The social setting of the intended audience of 4QInstruction provides insight into the nature of the community that produced the work. The group to which the document is directed is most likely not the Dead Sea sect.[92] The composition shows no awareness of offices that are important for the *yaḥad*, such as the *maskil* or *mebaqqer*. Other key epithets of that group, such as the Teacher of Righteousness or Wicked Priest, are never used. 4QInstruction presupposes that the addressee is free to make his own decisions. There is no sense that his behavior regarding marriage or finances is rigidly controlled, as one finds, for example, in the Damascus Document.[93]

The community to which 4QInstruction is addressed can, however, be understood as a sect. The group's members were taught that they have been separated from the rest of humankind, in that God has ordained the *mebin* to have an elect status that makes him like the angels (4Q418 81 1–5). Since this status includes access to supernatural revelation and life after death, both of which are construed as not widely available to people outside the group, the classification of the circle of *mebinim* in which 4QInstruction was produced as a sect is not unreasonable. But it is one with a much looser form of organization than that of the *yaḥad*.

The rationale for the formation of the group responsible for 4QInstruction can be reasonably sought in the low financial status of the *mebin*. The composition contains a striking contrast between the incredible claims made about the addressee in terms of his elect status, such as his stewardship over Eden, and the lowly position he actually had in society. The community responsible for 4QInstruction offered a way for a poor person to find dignity and self-worth amidst potentially degrading and humiliating circumstances.

---

92. For an argument that the text does stem from this community, see Jefferies 2002, 59–61. Kister (2009b, 1:305–7) also argues that 4QInstruction stems from the Dead Sea sect.

93. The notable affinities between 4QInstruction and major texts of the Dead Sea sect are discussed below.

4QInstruction was, like Ben Sira, probably written in the second century B.C.E. Elgvin advocates an early, pre-Maccabean date in that century,
in part because the text shows no awareness of the Antiochene crisis.[94] The
editors of DJD 34 propose that it was written in the Seleucid period but
grant that an earlier date, perhaps in the Ptolemaic or even Persian periods, is possible.[95] A *terminus ad quem* is provided by the manuscripts of
4QInstruction, the earliest one (4Q416) being written between 100–50
B.C.E. The prominence of features in the work that resonate with apocalypticism (reviewed above) suggests that it was written when the apocalyptic
tradition was flourishing and had become popular. This favors the second
century B.C.E. and argues against the earlier range of the time frame proposed by Strugnell and Harrington.

Another factor in assessing the date of 4QInstruction is its relationship to core documents produced by the Dead Sea sect. It has already been
established that the wisdom text is not a composition authored by the
group centered on the Teacher of Righteousness. Nevertheless, there are
striking affinities between core writings of the *yaḥad* and 4QInstruction.
As was mentioned above, the Community Rule describes heavenly revelation to the elect as the mystery that is to be (1QS 11:3–4). The Hodayot and
the wisdom text have the same phrase verbatim.[96] They also have numerous other thematic and terminological affinities.[97] The vision of meditation (Hagu) is prominent in 4Q417 1 i 14–18, and invites comparison
to the title of the enigmatic Book of Hagu, described in the rulebooks as
a volume with which leaders of the sect should be familiar (CD 13:2–3;
14:6–8; 1QSa 1:6–7). 4QInstruction was probably read and utilized by
members of the Dead Sea sect. This position is supported by the ample
number of manuscripts of the document found at Qumran. 4QInstruction
would thus be earlier than these core writings of the *yaḥad*. The origins
of this group have traditionally been placed in the early to mid-second

---

94. Elgvin 2004, 83–84.

95. Strugnell and Harrington 1999, 21. Stegemann (1998, 100) has argued for a
fourth or third century date for this text and the Qumran wisdom literature in general.

96. The phrase is דעתם יכבדו איש מרעהו; "[according to] their knowledge they
are glorified, each one more than his neighbor" (1QH 18:29–30; 4Q418 55 10).

97. As discussed in chapter 14, for example, both 4Q423 1 and 1QH 16 describe
the special revealed knowledge disclosed to their addressees as a garden that can
fall into ruin, both using "thorn and thistle" language from Gen 3:18. See Goff 2004,
263–88.

century B.C.E.[98] This would suggest that 4QInstruction was written at the beginning of the second century, as Elgvin has argued, or perhaps the late third. This remains a valid possibility. However, in recent years serious proposals have been put forward, based both on archaeological features of the Qumran site and on the scrolls themselves, to move the date of the Dead Sea sect to the early first century B.C.E.[99] Later dates for the composition of 4QInstruction in the early and middle portion of the second century thus become possible. The lack of reference to the Maccabean events does not require the pre-Maccabean dating proposed by Elgvin. Numerous compositions written after the revolt do not mention it. The author of 4QInstruction can be understood as roughly contemporary with Ben Sira, whose instruction was written ca. 180 B.C.E. But which figure appeared earlier cannot be established with certainty.

---

98. See, for example, Cross 1995, 100–120.
99. Magness 2002, 65; Wise 2003, 84.

1.

4Q415 2 II

TEXT[1]

[	כאב כבדי ח[ות]נֹֿ[ךֹ]	1
[	אל תמישי מלבבֹ[ך זֹעֹ]	2
[	כול היום וֹבחיקוֹ בֹרֹ[י]יֹתֹך	3
[	פן תפרעי ברית קוֹ[דש]	4
[	ואוֹיבת לנפשך זֹמֹ[	5
עוד לוא תשבֹי]	אֹ[י]שה עד לעֹ[ולם] [אֹ]	6
תהיֹ]	בבית מכוֹ[ר]וֹתיך [ובבריתך תֹ[אמנֹי	7
[	תהלה בֹפֹי כיל אנשים]	8
[	מֹבֹית מולדים] [לֹ[ ]	9

TRANSLATION

1 Like a father honor your fa[ther-in-l]aw. ...
2 Do not depart from his heart and ...
3 all the day long and in his bosom (is) [your] cove[nant ...]
4 lest you neglect a ho[ly] covenant ...
5 And one who is hostile to you (lit. "your soul") and ...
6 a w[i]fe fore[ver ... *You will no longer live*]
7 in the house of [your] ori[gins]. Rather in your covenant you [*will be faithful ... You will become*]
8 an object of praise in the mouth of all men ...
9 ... from the house of (your) birth ...

_____

1. Strugnell and Harrington 1999, 47–49; Tigchelaar 2001, 32–33; Rey 2009a, 138–43; Wold 2005b, 85–89. The textual notes section refers to these works.

TEXTUAL NOTES

2. מלבבך. This reading follows Rey. Tigchelaar, the editors of DJD 34, and Wold read בלבבך. A crease in the manuscript partially obscures the first letter of the expression, making it appear like a *bet* (see PAM 42.561; 43.549). 4Q417 2 i 9 also combines the verb מוש with "heart" prefaced by a *mem*. There appears to be a scribal hand replacing the final *kaf* with a *waw*, with a correction dot over the *kaf* in 4Q415 2 ii 2.

6. [לעֿ[ולם]. The editors of DJD 34 read לשֿ[, granting that the reading endorsed here is possible.

7. [מכוֿ]רותיך. Tigchelaar questions if there is enough space in the lacuna for this reconstruction. The issue is produced by the slightly awkward placement of the two pieces of the column on PAM 43.549. Consult the placement of the scraps in pl. VII of Rey 2009a.

COMMENTARY

Little of 4Q415 2 ii survives except for a portion of the right side of the column. The fragment is nevertheless highly significant. Among the Qumran wisdom compositions, or even ancient Jewish literature in general, it is one of the few texts that directly addresses a woman.[2] The female in question is probably the wife of the *mebin* or perhaps his daughter. She is given instruction on marriage.

4Q415 2 II 1

The first line of 4Q415 2 ii begins with the phrase "like a father honor." The word for "honor" (כבדי) is understood as a feminine singular imperative on the basis of the feminine forms elsewhere in the column (ll. 2, 4–5).[3] The emphasis on marriage in 4Q415 2 ii is also compatible with a female addressee. 4Q416 2 iii 15–17 uses the root כבד with regard to honoring one's parents. In 4Q415 2 ii 1 a woman is told to honor someone in the same way she would her own father. Unfortunately, the object of the imperative has survived only in traces. It is not fully clear whom she should honor. Wold suggests that she is to respect her husband like her father.[4] This is semantically attractive and consistent with the theme

---

2. Goff 2007, 49–53; Wright 2004b, 252–53; Wold 2005b, 85.

3. Orthographically it is possible to read כבדו. This could be a masculine imperative with a suffix ("honor him)." See Rey 2009a, 140.

4. Wold 2005b, 200.

that the wife moves from under the authority of her father to that of her husband (see commentary to 4Q416 2 iv). One would then have to supplement the phrase "your husband," reconstructing אישך or בעלך. However, the extant traces in 4Q415 2 ii 1 are not compatible with either of these words. Most commentators, as in the above edition, tentatively reconstruct "your fa[ther-in-l]aw" (ח[ות]נך) or at least suggest this as a possibility.[5] This reading is far from certain, but it is compatible with the traces. So understood, the line clarifies the position of the female addressee in relation to two significant men in her life—her father and the father of her husband. She should regard them both as having the same status. 4Q415 2 ii would also then indicate that the woman is married.

Marriage and Women in 4QInstruction

Marriage is a prominent issue in 4QInstruction.[6] Aside from 4Q415 2 ii, this topic is important in fragments 9 and 11 of 4Q415 and 4Q416 2 iv. The overriding concern is not simply that the bond of marriage be respected by the man and the woman, but also that dominion over the female be smoothly transferred from her father to her husband. This topic is explicit in 4Q416 2 iv (ll. 3–7). This is also the case in 4Q415 9 (ll. 7–8). This column also underscores the importance of childbirth, understanding the body of the woman as owned by the husband. It is *his* womb that conceives (4Q415 9 2; cf. 4Q415 2 i + 1 ii 5–7). 4Q416 2 iv 4, reworking Gen 2:24, claims that the wife is "one flesh" with the male addressee. 4Q415 11 is about the marriage of the daughter of the *mebin* (cf. 4Q416 2 iv 4). The addressee is to inform the prospective groom of her blemishes or bodily defects (מומיה; l. 6).[7] There is a similar recommendation in the 4QD material (4Q271 3 7–9). In 4Q415 2 ii the overall theme is that the woman should remain loyal to her marriage (l. 4) and that she is no longer under the control of her father, in whose house she was born (l. 9).

4QInstruction urges the male *mebin* to respect important women in his life. 4Q416 2 iii 15–16 recommends that he honor his mother and that

---

5. Rey 2009a, 139; Tigchelaar 2001, 33; Strugnell and Harrington 1999, 48.

6. The second excursus in this chapter is on women and divorce.

7. The defects in question may relate to her ability to bear children (cf. 4Q415 11 11). In the Mishnah a betrothal is rendered invalid if "defects" are found in the woman (m. Qidd. 2:5). For more on 4Q415 11, see Rey 2009a, 146–56; Wold 2005b, 226–30; Strugnell and Harrington 1999, 57–62. Consult also Ilan 1996a, 44–96.

she, along with her husband, be regarded "like a god" by her son because they gave him life. The association of taking a wife with "poverty" in 4Q416 2 iii 20 suggests that the man is to approach this endeavor with humility and dignity (see the commentary on this text). 4Q423 4 (par. 1Q26 1) is addressed to a farmer and stresses that a woman, presumably his wife, should understand that the success of a bountiful harvest should be attributed to God, not her husband. The column strives to ensure that the wife understands accurately how God's power affects their daily lives.

Ben Sira also shows interest in women who are significant in the life of his male students, including wives, mothers, and daughters (e.g., 25:13–26:27; 42:9–14).[8] He shows outright disdain for women.[9] One should refrain from reaching similar conclusions about 4QInstruction, despite its repeated emphasis of the husband's control. 4Q415 2 ii establishes not only that the elect male *mebin* is married but that instruction can also be given to his wife (or his daughter).[10] The men to whom the composition is oriented have been separated from the "fleshly spirit," a term that denotes people who are not among the elect (see commentary on 4Q418 81 1–2). It would have been unacceptable to marry a woman who was considered among the "fleshly spirit." The emphasis on the control of women takes place *within* the elect community to which 4QInstruction is addressed. The text never states that the female elect do not have access to the mystery that is to be or that they are not among the lot of the angels (4Q418 81 4–5), restrictions that are more in keeping with the fleshly spirit (see the commentary on 4Q417 1 i 13–18). The composition's assertion of conservative patriarchal norms takes place in the context of a rather radical situation—the women of the group were considered to have a status before God that was far superior to that of the vast majority of men (the non-elect). This makes understandable the mindset of 4Q416 2 iv that the elect male must be reminded of the female elect's lower station in relation to him. The repetition of 4Q416 2 iv on this point suggests that there was some confusion regarding the matter among community members (e.g., ll. 2, 3, 6). Since the composition stresses the elect status of the

---

8. Collins 1997c, 63–72; Camp 1991, 1–39; Trenchard 1982. See also Balla 2011. For a general survey, consult Schuller 2011, 571–88.

9. The parade example of Ben Sira's misogyny is 42:14: "Better a man's wickedness than a woman's goodness" (cf. 25:24).

10. This is the case whether one understands the female addressee as the wife or the daughter of the *mebin*. The latter option would also indicate that he is married.

male *mebin*, the insistence that the wife is a virtual extension of his body should not be understood solely in terms of patriarchal oppression but also as another indication of the wife's elect status.

4Q415 2 ii 2

This line contains an incomplete vetitive (an exhortation with a negation) addressed to a woman. Line 2 encourages her to remain faithful to her husband, but the extant phrase is somewhat ambiguous. The line originally referred to the heart of the female addressee, but was altered to mention instead "his heart," referring to her husband. With these revisions, line 2 encourages her not to let her love or devotion cease from his heart (cf. Prov 2:10). The masculine suffix is consistent with line 3, which mentions "his bosom."

4Q415 2 ii 3

Line 3 is also about marriage. The phrase "all the day long" concluded a phrase that began at the end of line 2, which has not survived. The whole statement probably stressed to the woman that her devotion to marriage and to her husband should be constant (cf. l. 6). The line attests חיקו. I understand this as "his bosom," but it could be read as חוקו, "his decree." The "bosom" reading is preferred because this word is prominent in other marriage texts of 4QInstruction. 4Q416 2 iv 5 refers to the wife of the *mebin* as "the wife of your bosom" (אשת חיקכה; cf. 4Q416 2 ii 21). The term, as I argue in the commentary on that text, helps convey the husband's dominion over his wife. In 4Q416 2 iv 5 the word "bosom" helps describe the woman as of 'his' bosom, referring to the *mebin*, conveying the view that the woman's body belongs to the man.

After the phrase "his bosom" 4Q415 2 ii 3 reads בר[. The editors of DJD 34 suggest that one could reconstruct ברית, "covenant," a prominent word in the column referring to the covenant of marriage (ll. 4, 7).[11] They do not, however, adopt this phrase in their translation, asserting that such a reconstruction would be "banal." Wold recommends reconstructing בר[א] ("to crea[te]"), suggesting that the line originally stated "he created you."[12] He understands the line as alluding to the Adamic motif that the woman was created from the rib of the man (Gen 2:21–22). Marriage

---

11. Strugnell and Harrington 1999, 34, 48.

12. Wold 2005b, 201. He also speculates that one could reconstruct "[your] crea[tion]" (בר[א]ך) or "at [your] beg[inning]" (בר[אשיתך]).

is indeed connected to Genesis in 4Q416 2 iv (see commentary below). 4Q415 2 ii, by contrast, contains no unambiguous allusions to Genesis. For this reason I prefer reconstructing ברית, "covenant." Although perhaps banal, this would produce a plausible understanding of the line—"in his bosom (is) [your] cove[nant]."[13] Line 3 would then emphasize the woman's devotion to her marriage. The covenant of matrimony resides, in a sense, in the bosom of the husband. This description of their marriage underscores the unequal status of the woman in relation to her husband. It is also compatible with the idea, prominent in 4QInstruction's marriage advice (e.g., 4Q416 2 iv), that the body of the wife is essentially an extension of the husband's.

In the Hebrew Bible, the word "covenant" can signify some sort of formal agreement made by two parties (e.g., Gen 26.28). Marriage is one such arrangement, and it can be described by this word. This is explicit, for example, in Ezek 16:8. Proverbs 2:17 claims that the "strange woman" forsook her spouse and "forgets the covenant of her God" (ברית אלהיה). The misdeed of the "strange woman" of Proverbs may be adultery or, less likely, divorce.[14] Malachi 2:14–16 is a difficult and ambiguous text, but it uses language that is strikingly similar to Prov 2:17 in a polemic against priests who divorce.[15] This material supports reading the word "covenant" in 4Q415 2 ii 4 as a reference to marriage.

4Q415 2 ii 4

The word "covenant" is also attested in this line. Line 4 encourages the woman not to neglect her covenant.[16] As discussed about the above line, the covenant in question is marriage, although an allusion to the Torah may well be implied. It is also possible that lines 3–4 refer to divorce. The emphasis on constancy in line 3 ("all the day long"; cf. l. 6) and not neglecting the covenant (l. 4) may be intended to encourage the wife not

---

13. Note that another possible reading is [בחוקי בר]יתך ("in the regulations of [your] cov[enant]").

14. Fox 2000, 121.

15. Proverbs 2:17 refers to the woman abandoning her husband, "the companion of her youth" (אלוף נעוריה). Mal 2:14–15 refers to the wife of the priest as אשת נעוריך, "the wife of your youth." See Hill 1998, 240–54; Collins 1997d, 123, 156.

16. The text in question is a "lest" clause. It is unfortunate that the preceding statement is not extant, since it would have clarified what the wife should (or should not) do, lest she neglect her covenant.

to divorce her husband. So understood, she has a right to initiate divorce, which 4QInstruction does not want her to exercise. Other lines of 4Q415 2 ii could be interpreted in the context of divorce, although this topic is never explicit in the column. Line 5 refers to a woman who hates the female addressee. Divorce may be the context for the tension between the two women.

Women and Divorce in Early Judaism

The right of divorce is endorsed in biblical law as an act initiated by the husband, not the wife (Deut 24:1–4; cf. 22:13–20). Ben Sira affirms divorce as a male right. This is also the case in rabbinic literature (Sir 25:26; m. Giṭ. 9:10; m. Qidd. 1:1; m. Yeb. 14:1).[17] The divorce bills from the Elephantine papyri present divorce as being initiated by women (*TAD* B2.6; B3.3; B3.8).[18] There is some evidence in Philo that women could divorce their husbands (*Spec.* 3.30).[19] This evidence, taken with the Elephantine material, suggests that it was possible for Jewish women to initiate divorce, at least in Egypt. There is some support for Jewish women having had this right in Palestine, but the evidence is not clear cut. Josephus mentions two women who divorced their husbands, Salome and Herodias (*Ant.* 15.259; 18.136; cf. Mark 10:12; 1 Cor 7:10–11). In both cases, Josephus understands these women as diverging from Jewish tradition. There are a few references to women initiating divorce in the Jerusalem Talmud, but it is not clear that the material in question preserves traditions from the Second Temple period (y. Ket. 5:10 [30b]; 7:7 [31c]).[20] Tal Ilan has claimed that an ancient Judean document from Naḥal Ḥever, classified as Papyrus Ṣeʾelim 13, is a bill of divorce written by a woman.[21] The letter was composed by a female named Shelamṣion (through a scribe) in either 134 or 135 c.e. According to Ilan, in lines 6–7 the woman asserts to her husband (Eleazar ben

---

17. Satlow 2001, 214; Brody 1999, 230.

18. Porten and Yardeni 1986–1999, 2.30–33, 60–63, 78–83. See also Botta 2009, 59–60.

19. The key text reads, "If a woman, after parting from her husband for any cause whatever, marries another ..." See Brewer 1999, 354. Consult also Sly 1990; Brooten 1983, 466–78.

20. Satlow 2001, 353; Friedman 1969, 33. See also Friedman 1981, 104–5.

21. Ilan 1996b, 195–202; 1999, 253–62. The official edition of this text is in Cotton and Yardeni 1997, 65–70. See also Brewer 1999, 352.

Ḥananiah), "this is from me to you a bill of divorce and release." This understanding of the text, however, has been questioned.[22] Even if one were to grant Ilan's interpretation of Papyrus Ṣe'elim 13, the early Jewish evidence in Palestine for women's right to divorce is not widespread or abundant.[23] There are examples of women initiating divorce, but the evidence suggests that the act is more the exception than the rule. Whether the wife was thought to have the right to divorce or not, divorce probably would have been discouraged by the author of 4QInstruction. The emphasis of 4Q415 2 ii on the woman honoring her marriage is not an endorsement of divorce. The view that husband and wife are "one flesh" also provides no foundation for divorce (see the commentary on 4Q416 2 iv 1, 4). The exhortation in 4Q415 2 ii 4 to a woman not to neglect her covenant need not necessarily be interpreted as discouraging her from divorcing her husband, although this option remains a possibility. A simpler interpretation is that the line urges her to respect her marriage and remain devoted to it.

4Q415 2 ii 5

The theme of divorce may also be in the background of 4Q415 2 ii 5. The line attests a brief but intriguing phrase: ואויבת לנפשך. The core question is whether the first word, a feminine participle of the verb "to treat hostilely," refers reflexively to the female addressee or another woman.[24] The editors of DJD 34 favor the former option.[25] However, no extant mate-

---

22. Greenfield and Yardeni, in the preliminary publication of this Aramaic text, suggest that it is a receipt of payment for money promised (the *ketubba* money) at the time of marriage to be paid in the event of divorce. Brody (1999, 232) understands Papyrus Ṣe'elim 13 as detailing the annulment of claims after the divorce has already happened. For Ilan's reading of the text one must read מנה of l. 7 as "from me," with the first person suffix marked with a *he*. This unusual reading is accepted by Brody (1999, 233). See also Cotton and Yardeni 1997, 69. Reading מנה as the more conventional "from him" is possible but would require that one posit an awkward change of speakers in l. 7 ("from her" is also possible). Shelamṣion writes to the man (e.g., l. 5), but, if one reads "from him" in l. 7 the wife is given a divorce bill *from him* (her husband). If the key phrase is read as "from me," Shelamṣion gives her husband ("to you") the divorce bill. See Yardeni and Greenfield 1996, 197–208; Schremer 1998, 193–202; Collins, 1997d, 120–21.

23. Satlow 2010, 352–53.

24. The word is probably not passive, *contra* DJD 34, 49, since one would then expect איובה, not איובת. The term is not in construct.

25. Strugnell and Harrington 1999, 49; Rey 2009a, 141.

rial in 4Q415 2 ii provides a clear rationale as to why the woman would treat herself in a hostile manner. The line is better understood as attesting some form of conflict between her and another woman. One could posit either polygamy or divorce as the underlying problem. There is no clear reference to polygamy anywhere in 4QInstruction.[26] Divorce may be at issue in line 4, as mentioned above. The verb "to hate" (שנא) is a technical term that signifies divorce; the word in line 5, "to express hatred" (איב), may have similar freight, although admittedly there is scant evidence elsewhere for this opinion.[27] I am inclined to understand divorce as the root of the problem between the two women, but there is not enough evidence to assert this view conclusively.[28] Line 5, if interpreted in terms of divorce, would provide a rationale as to why a woman hates the female addressee. Since she is married, the one who hates her could be a woman her husband had previously divorced.

4Q415 2 ii 6

The surviving words of this line accord with the theme that the wife remains steadfast in her marriage. The reference to being a wife "fore[ver]" suggests that the female, addressed in the second person, is to uphold the ideal that a woman should remain with her husband for her entire life (cf. l. 8).

---

26. The practice is allowed in biblical law (Deut 21:15) and was probably acceptable in Palestine during the time of the composition. See also CD 4:20–21; 11QT 57:15–19. See Satlow 2001, 189–92.

27. The verb שנא ("to hate") denotes divorce in the Hebrew Bible and in the Elephantine divorce contracts, perhaps overlapping to some extent with the verb "to change" (שנה; Deut 24:3; *TAD* B2.6 l. 23). Ben Sira provides some support for the view that איב could similarly refer to divorce. Sir 25:14, which is part of an extended section on wives, reads: "Any affliction but one from foes (μισούντων), any vengeance but one from enemies (ἐχθρῶν)." This verse is not extant in Hebrew. But given the context, the key "enemy" terms have been reasonably understood as originally feminine forms (cf. 7:26). Presumably one of these terms derives from שנא, suggesting that the verse refers to tension between two women, either in a context of bigamy or divorce. The Hebrew of Sir 25:14 may have relied upon the parallelism of שנא and איב. So Trenchard 1982, 69. Segal (1953, 145) reconstructed the Hebrew of the verse using the pair שנא and צר. See also Collins 1997d, 118–19.

28. Ben Sira 26:6 is generally understood as describing a conflict between women married to the same man: "A wife jealous of another wife is heartache and mourning" (cf. 37:11). See Di Lella and Skehan 1987, 349.

4Q415 2 ii 7

This line contains another attestation of the word "covenant," which probably refers to marriage, as in lines 3–4. The editors of DJD 34 also reconstruct "in the house of [your] ori[gins]" (בבית מכו[רותיד]).[29] Rey presents the text as follows: "[reste fidèle] dans la maison de [tes] or[igines] et dans ton alliance tu [demeureras]."[30] The second part of this statement makes sense, and informs the supplement used above. But the two phrases in the quotation are not in synonymous parallelism. Given the probable claim in line 9 that the woman moves from the house of her birth (see below), and the prominence in 4Q416 2 iv of the transfer of authority over her from her father to her husband, 4QInstruction probably did not teach the woman to remain faithful in the house where she was born. She left this domicile upon marriage. The reconstruction used above reflects this idea.

4Q415 2 ii 8

Line 8 mentions "an object of praise" (תהלה) in the mouth of men. The female addressee, if she follows the instruction that is given, will be praised by men as a good wife. Ben Sira extols the virtues of a wife who is modest (literally, "shameful"; ביישת) and chaste (26:15).[31] 4QInstruction, by contrast, does not emphasize the demure comportment of the ideal wife.[32] The composition stresses instead that she understands her status in relation to her husband. 4Q415 2 ii 8 celebrates the wife who accepts that she is ruled by her husband rather than her father.[33]

4Q415 2 ii 9

Line 9 describes the wife leaving the house in which she was born, that of her father. The line attests the phrase "from the house of (your) birth" (מבית מולדים).[34] The word מולד is significant elsewhere in 4QInstruc-

---

29. Strugnell and Harrington 1999, 49.

30. Rey 2009a, 139–41.

31. Contrast Prov 19:14, which praises a wife who is "thoughtful" (משכלת). See Di Lella and Skehan 1987, 350.

32. In contrast to Proverbs and Ben Sira, 4QInstruction never warns the male addressee about the "bad wife" or promiscuous women (e.g., Prov 21:9; Sir 25:16–26). See Wright 2004b, 253.

33. Ben Sira 36:24 (Eng. v. 29) presents the woman as a prized possession of her husband (קנין).

34. The words מכורות (l. 7) and מולדות are in parallelism in Ezek 16:3. Both this text and 4Q415 2 ii 9 probably attest the plural of abstraction, which can denote a state

tion, denoting human birth (see the commentary on 4Q417 2 i 11). The phrase בית מולדים occurs nowhere else in 4QInstruction, but is attested in the book of Mysteries. There the expression is associated with birth, but clearly has a broader cosmological significance. 4Q299 3a ii–b 13 proclaims a deterministic understanding of the world and that the "[p]lan of the time of birth" (חשבת בית מולדים[מ]) has been revealed.[35] The phrase occurs in a fragmentary context in 4Q299 5, which mentions astral phenomena such as the stars and light (l. 5; cf. 4Q299 1 4). It has been argued that בית מולדים has an astronomical sense in the book of Mysteries.[36] The terms בית and מולד do not occur together in 4QHoroscope (4Q186), but in this text both words have an astronomical sense.[37] Wold has argued that in 4Q415 2 ii 9 the phrase similarly alludes to the created order, providing a cosmological context for the text's instruction on marriage.[38] The author of 4QInstruction probably did think that a woman's devotion to her husband was in harmony with the natural order of things. But, in contrast to the book of Mysteries, 4Q415 2 ii never explicitly connects the phrase to deterministic or cosmological themes. The *mem* preposition that accompanies the expression in line 9 suggests it refers to an actual house—the abode in which the woman was born, *from* which she moved when she married. This is a prominent issue in 4Q416 2 iv (e.g., ll. 3–4). Lines 7–9 of 4Q415 2 ii probably envision what the author considers an ideal marriage—the shift of authority over the woman from her father to her husband, to whom she remains devoted for the rest of her life. Line 8, which asserts that the female addressee will be an object of praise among men, supports this interpretation (cf. l. 6).

---

or stage in a person's life such as "adolescence" (בחורים; Num 11:28). Consult Joüon and Muraoka 2008, 471 (§136h).

35. Goff 2007, 80–82.

36. Tigchelaar 2003, 87–88; Morgenstern 2000, 141–44; Elgvin 2004, 71–72.

37. See, for example, 4Q186 1 ii 7–9: "His spirit has six (parts) in the house of light and three in the house of darkness. And this is the sign (המולד) in which he was born: the period of Taurus." Consult Popović 2007.

38. Wold 2005b, 85.

2.
4Q416 1

Parallel texts: 4Q418 1–2c (underline); 4Q418 209 (dashed underline), 4Q418 212 (dotted underline) 4Q418 229 (double underline)

Text[1]

כֹ]וכבי אור	כֹּל רֹוחֹ[	1
ירוצו מעת עֹולם[	לֹתֹכן חפצֹי[	2
ואין להדמות בכול עת ילכו[	מועד במועד וֹ[	3
למֹמלכה[תֹ	לפי צבאם למשֹ]זר במשׂורה ולֹ○	4
[	וממלכה למדֹ]ינֹה ומדינה לאיש ואיש	5
[	לפי מחסור צבאם [ומשפט כולם לֹו	6
ומאֹורות[	וצבא השמים הכֹין מֹ[עת עולם	7
יגידֹו[	לֹמופתיהמה ואתות מוֹ[עֹדֹיהֹמה	8
[	זה לזה וכל פקודתמה יֹ[שֹׁלֹימֹוֹ וֹי]ספרו[	9
[	בֹשֹׁמים ישפוט על עבודֹת רֹשֹׁעה וכל בני אמתֹז ירצוֹ לֹ[פֹניו	10
קצה ויפתחו ויריֹעו כל אשר התגללו בה כי שמים יראֹו תֹ[רֹעֹשֹׁ מֹמֹקֹוֹמֹה ארץ[		11
יֹ]מים ותהמות פחדו ויתערערו כל רוח בשר ובני השמיֹ]ם בֹיוֹם[		12
מֹשֹ]פֹטֹה וכל עולה תתם עוד ושלם קץ האמֹ]ת לעולם ○○כֹל		13
לֹ[	בכל קצי עד כי אל אמת הוא ומקדם שנֹי] עולם	14
אֹ]	להבֹין צדק בין טוב לֹרֹעֹ לֹ[○]]רֹ כל משפֹט]	15
ל ל	יֹ]צר בשר הֹואֹה ומביניֹ]ֹם	16
[	בֹראתֹיֹזֹ כֹּיֹ הֹ[	17
[	]זֹד[	18

---

1. Strugnell and Harrington 1999, 81–88; Tigchelaar 2001, 42–44, 176–91; Puech 2005, 90–98; Rey 2009a, 228–34; Elgvin 1997a, 237–46. The textual notes section refers to these works.

Translation

1   every spirit [... *s*tars of li*ght*,]
2   to arrange the delights of [... they run on for*ever*,]
3   season by season and [... *and without* ceasing, in eve*ry period they move*]
4   according to their host to have dom[inion with authority and to ... *for kingdom*]
5   and kingdom, for pro[*vince* and province, for man and man ...]
6   according to the need of their host. [And the regulation of all of them belongs to him ...]
7   And the host of heaven he has established f[*orever* ... and luminaries]
8   for their wonders and signs of [*their*] se[*asons* ... they *proclaim*]
9   one after another. And all their assignments [they] c[omplete *and*] make known ...
10 in heaven he will judge over the work of wickedness. But all the sons of his truth will be favorably accepted b[*efore him* ...]
11 its end. And all those who polluted themselves in it (wickedness) will be terrified and cry out, for heaven will be afraid; [*earth*] wi[ll shake from *its* place;]
12 [*s*]eas and depths are terrified. Every fleshly spirit will be laid bare but the sons of heav[en ... *on* the day of]
13 its judgment. And all iniquity will come to an end forever and the period of tru[*th*] will be completed [*forever* ...]
14 in all the periods of eternity, for he is a god of truth. From before the years of [*eternity* ...]
15 to make a righteous person understand the difference between good and evil to ... every judgme[*nt* ...]
16 it is a fleshly [in]clination and understanding [*ones* ...]
17 his creatures, for ...
18 ...

Textual Notes

1. כּוֹכְבֵי אוֹר. Commentators generally reconstruct this phrase, following Tigchelaar, which is from 4Q418 229 (e.g., Puech; Rey). This reconstruction is plausible, but there is a clear space after אוֹ on this fragment.

10. בְּשָׁמִים. Some commentators read a *mem* instead of a *bet*. See DJD 34 and Puech. For explanation of the issue, see Rey.

10. כֹל; 4Q418 2 2: כול.[2]

11. כֹל; 4Q418 2 3: כול.

11. ויריעו; 4Q418 2 3: רֹעֹו[.

12. ותהמות; 4Q418 2 4: ותהום.

12. ויתערערו; 4Q418 2 4:]תֹרֹי.

12. השמֹי[ם]; 4Q418 2 4: שמים.

13. כֹל; 4Q418 2 5: כול.

13. עוֹד; 4Q418 2 5: עד.

13. לְעוֹלם. After this reconstructed text Puech and Rey read [ה]תהל[ו] ("[and] prai[se]") in the parallel text 4Q418 2 5. Not enough text survives to reconstruct plausibly any words.

14. כֹל; 4Q418 2 6: כול.

14. כֹי; 4Q418 2 6: כיא.

15. להבֹין. The editors of DJD 34 and Tigchelaar read להכֹון ("to be established"). I follow Rey and Puech. The flourish on the left top stroke of the third letter of the word is more in keeping in this fragment with *bet* than *kaf*. The parallel text 4Q418 2 7 reads להבין.

15. צדק; 4Q418 2 7: צדיק.

15. רֹ[ ]ֹל. Rey reconstructs לֹדֹ[ֹב]רֹ. Puech suggests לה[כֹי]רֹ.

16. ומבינֹי[ֹם]. One could also reconstruct ומבינֹו[תֹ].

COMMENTARY

4Q416 1 is generally considered the opening text of 4QInstruction. This would explain its unusually wide right margin (approximately 3 cm.). 4Q416 1 consists of two sections. Lines 1–9 discuss the orderly nature of the structure of the cosmos. Lines 10–17 contain a scene of eschatological judgment. These two themes complement one another and establish a theological framework for the rest of the composition that stresses eschatological recompense as an expression of God's dominion over the natural order.[3] Ben Sira's instruction likewise opens with an assertion of divine mastery over the world (Sir 1:1–10), but the combination of eschatological

---

2. For the sake of simplicity, I refer here to the composite text of 4Q418 2, 2a, 2b, and 2c as 4Q418 2. 4Q418 2a was originally classified as frg. 213. The fragment in question is sometimes identified as 4Q418 2c. See, for example, Tigchelaar 2001, 74; Strugnell and Harrington 1999, 225.

3. Rey 2009a, 261–75; Macaskill 2007, 99; 2008, 217–45.

judgment and cosmological order has a closer parallel in the apocalypse
1 Enoch, which also begins with these two themes (chs. 1–5).

The text of 4Q416 1 is intact mainly on the right-hand side of the
manuscript. Editors have been able to reconstruct additional parts of the
column. Much of this material is from 4Q418 1 and 2, which correspond
to 4Q416 1. Tigchelaar has proposed that 4Q418 2 can be somewhat
expanded by joining other fragments of 4Q418 to it.[4] His more important
and generally accepted joins involve 4Q418 212 and 229.[5] The expanded
text clarifies the prominence in 4Q416 1 of the theme of the cosmos's
orderly regulation (see the commentary on l. 3). This is a prominent theme
in early Jewish literature. 4Q416 1 can be profitably compared to texts such
as 1 Enoch 5, 1QS 10, 1QH 9 and Sir 42:15–43:33. Tigchelaar has also
suggested that 4Q418 238 be placed before the text of 4Q416 1 1. In this
case the first visible word of 4QInstruction would be *maskil*, the term for
instructor that denotes an important sectarian office in the Qumran rulebooks (e.g., 1QS 9:12–26; CD 12:20–23).[6]

4Q416 1 1–3

Only a few words are extant in these lines. Some of the lost material
can be reconstructed through the overlapping fragment 4Q418 229. Heavenly phenomena mentioned in lines 1–3 include stars (l. 1) and seasons
(l. 3). Line 7 refers to the luminaries. The focus on elements of the natural
world suggests that the expression כל רוח of 4Q416 1 1 could be understood as a reference to winds rather than spirits.

The phrase לתכן חפצי, "to arrange delights of …" (l. 2), is difficult.[7] It
could be rendered "to arrange his delights" (לתכן חפצו). The word חפץ
("desire") is frequent in 4QInstruction, often with a financial sense (e.g.,
4Q417 2 i 18; see the commentary to 4Q418 126 ii 12). In 4Q416 1 2 the
term apparently refers to God's desires. The phrase likely conveys the

---

    4. Tigchelaar 2001, 175–81; 2002, 99–126.

    5. The smaller fragments Tigchelaar joins to 4Q418 2 include fragments 217, 218
and 224 of 4Q418. See Tigchelaar 2001, 74.

    6. Tigchelaar 2001, 183. Elgvin has proposed that the beginning of 4Q416 1 be
reconstructed with fragments 73 and 201 of 4Q418. The beginning section of the
column would then mention the disclosure of revelation to Noah. The claim has not
held up to scrutiny. Elgvin himself has retracted this reading. See Tigchelaar 2001, 43;
Goff 2003b, 5; Strugnell and Harrington 1999, 422–23. For his older view, see Elgvin
1997a, 237–40; 1996, 148–49. Consult also Elgvin 1995a, 64–68.

    7. Strugnell and Harrington 1999, 84; Macaskill 2007, 94–95; Puech 2008b, 150–51.

idea that the structure of the cosmos is an expression of God's desire for order. One could reconstruct the phrase "the delights of [his will]" (חפצי [רצונו]), as in CD 3:15 (cf. 4Q418 127 5). The statement of line 2 that they "run on forever" (literally "from eternal time") emphasizes that the motion of heavenly bodies is regular and ongoing (cf. l. 7; 4Q418 69 ii 3–4; 4Q418 126 ii 1). The surviving and reconstructed material of line 3 stresses this point as well.

4Q416 1 4–5

These lines, though fragmentary, discuss the universal scope of God's dominion. The term "host" (צבא) is prominent in 4Q416 1, occurring in lines 4, 6, and 7. In the Hebrew Bible the word often denotes heavenly bodies such as the stars (e.g., Deut 4:19; Isa 34:4). It can also signify the angelic retinue who stand beside God's throne (1 Kgs 22:19). The phrase "their host" is in Gen 2:1, in the context of the creation of the cosmos (see also below on ll. 7–9). In the Dead Sea Scrolls צבא can denote angels. Note, for example, the phrase צבאות מלאכים ("hosts of angels") of 1QM 12:1 (cf. l. 8; 4Q381 1 10). The word probably refers to angels in 4Q416 1. The antecedent of the repeated expression "*their* host" (ll. 4, 6) is probably the stars (cf. "their wonders" in l. 8). So understood, the phrase "their host" may imply that God has assigned angels to guide the direction of the stars in their heavenly courses.[8] A similar system is given much fuller expression in the Enochic Astronomical Book (e.g., 1 Enoch 75).

The phrase "their host" is used in line 4 with the obscure expression [במשורה [ור]למש, translated above as "to have dom[inion with authority"]. The form "to rule" (למשור) is difficult grammatically but may be an Aramaizing form of an infinitive of the root שרר or שרה, both of which mean "to rule."[9] The term משורה can mean "measure" in the Hebrew Bible (e.g., Lev 19:35; 1 Chr 23:29), and in 4Q416 1 4 it surely conveys the structured and orderly nature of the cosmos (cf. 4Q418 81 9).[10] The expression probably also reflects angelic dominion over the stars. This meaning is suggested by the variant משורה in the Isaiah Scroll for MT

---

8. 4Q418 69 ii 9 may associate the angelic host with thunder (see commentary below).

9. Strugnell and Harrington, 1999, 84. Rey (2009a, 232) suggest the word derives from שור.

10. Kister 2005, 169.

משרה ("authority") in Isa 9:5 (1QIsaᵃ 8:23; cf. 1QM 13:4; 17:6–7).[11] The
expression למש]ור במשורה conveys the regulation and propriety of the
stars, under the authority of the angels who guide them. The phrase "[for
kingdom] and kingdom, for pro[vince and province, for man and man]"
of lines 4–5 highlights the universal nature of God's rule and asserts that it
affects all aspects of human society.

4Q416 1 6

This line discusses "their host" (l. 4) and continues the theme of God's
control of the cosmos. Here, however, the full expression is "need of their
host," which is difficult to interpret. The term מחסור is found often in
4QInstruction, occurring over twenty-five times, typically denoting material poverty (see the commentary on 4Q417 2 i 17). It is not clear, however,
that this is the case in 4Q416 1 6. מחסור could be an error for מסחור,
which can have the sense of "commerce."[12] So understood, the term would
denote not the "going around" of merchants, but would instead convey
an astronomical meaning, i.e., the circuits of heavenly bodies. The term
מחסור as written, however, seems to accord with the rest of 4Q416 1 6,
which asserts that the "regulation" (משפט) or orderly arrangement of the
angels belongs to God.[13] He controls all aspects of the celestial angels—
both in terms of their needs and their movement. What the host would
need, however, is not entirely clear. The original text may have stated that
whatever the angels might need God would provide, in order to ensure
the regularity of the motions of heavenly bodies. At issue may be observed
improprieties or imbalances in astral movement. The root חסר has this
sense in the Aramaic Astronomical Book (4Q209 26 3 [1 En. 79:5]).

4Q416 1 7–9

These lines assert the adherence of heavenly phenomena to the structure God provided for them. Line 7 stresses that God created "the host of
heaven," a reference to angels (see l. 4). This emphasizes their obedience to
him. The phrase "wonders and signs" (l. 8) typically refers in the Hebrew
Bible to the plagues of Egypt (e.g., Exod 7:3; Deut 6:22). Context suggests

---

11. Tigchelaar (2001, 178–79) has suggested that משורה is a variant spelling of
מסורה, which can denote "orbit" or the position of the stars (e.g., 4QEnᶜ 1 i 19 [1 En.
2:1]). See also Macaskill 2007, 96.

12. Tigchelaar 2001, 179.

13. Puech 2008b, 152.

that in this column the expression has an astronomical meaning.[14] The regular, predictable structure of the cosmos is presented as "wonders and signs," testimony to God's dominion over the natural world, not unlike the plagues in the Exodus story. The qualification added by the plausible reconstruction, "wonders and signs of [their] se[asons]," adds to the sense that these "wonders" are astronomical (or perhaps calendrical) in nature. Note the full expression "their wonders." The antecedent is probably "luminaries" of line 7, which would then convey a meaning similar to "their host," discussed above (ll. 4, 6). "Sign" (אות) has an astronomical meaning in other early Jewish texts (e.g., Sir 44:16, 18; 4Q216 6 7 [Jub. 2:9]; 4Q319 4 11–19). The term also has this sense in Gen 1:14, where it is used in conjunction with "luminaries" (and "seasons"), as in 4Q416 1 7–8. Since "stars" (l. 1) are mentioned in Gen 1:16 (כוכבים) and "their host" occurs in Gen 2:1, 4Q416 1 1–9 probably draws on the language of the seven-day creation account of Genesis to describe God's control over the cosmos.[15] The claim in line 9 that "they," presumably the host of heaven, complete and "make known" their assignments asserts that their celestial motions testify to the directives God gave them regarding their movement. While the word פקודה in line 9 refers to the appointment of the angels in their heavenly movement, this word elsewhere in 4QInstruction clearly has an eschatological sense (see the commentary to 4Q417 1 i 7–8).

4Q416 1 10

Lines 10–17 of 4Q416 1 provide an account of God's eschatological judgment. The other major judgment scene in 4QInstruction is in 4Q418 69 ii. By being preceded by the cosmological material in the column, divine judgment is construed as an inevitable and inherent aspect of the natural order. Whereas lines 11 and 12 emphasize the destruction of the wicked, line 10 proclaims that God will judge "the work of wickedness," suggesting that not only the wicked, but wickedness in a more abstract sense will be eliminated. This complements the claim in line 13 that all iniquity will come to an end (see below).

4Q416 1 proclaims an eschatological event that results in the destruction of the wicked and the favorable acceptance of "the sons of his truth" (l. 10). It has been suggested that the latter phrase denotes angels.[16] How-

---

14. Strugnell and Harrington 1999, 85.
15. Rey 2009a, 234; Wold 2005b, 89–91.
16. Tigchelaar 2001, 180. See also Garcia Martínez 2006, 32; Elgvin 1996, 151.

ever, the fact that "the sons of his truth" will be favorably accepted suggests that at issue are humans who will be deemed righteous. The expression likely refers to the group to which 4QInstruction is addressed. The ultimate fate of the righteous is not specified in 4Q416 1, but they were probably thought to join the angels after death (see section 6 of the introduction). The expression "sons of truth" denotes the elect several times in the Hodayot, but may also signify angels (15:32–33; 17:35; 18:29).[17]

"Truth" is a prominent term in 4Q416 1 and elsewhere in 4QInstruction that describes both God and the elect. 4Q416 1 14 refers to the "God of truth," stressing an affinity between him and the elect, "the sons of his truth" (cf. 4Q418 81 3; 4Q423 5 4). The moment of judgment is described as "the period of tru[th]" (4Q416 1 13). The judgment scene of 4Q418 69 ii is written to the "chosen ones of truth" (l. 10; cf. 4Q416 2 iii 7). 4Q416 4 3 urges the *mebin* to "rejoice in the inheritance of truth."[18]

4Q416 1 11

The term "period" (קץ) is significant for the eschatology of 4Q416 1 (ll. 11, 13, 14).[19] The word indicates that judgment will occur at a specific moment. קץ can mean not only a period of history but also "end" or final period (e.g., Dan 8:19; 4QEn^g 1 iv 23 [1 En. 91:15]). The full context of the word in line 11 has not survived but clearly involves judgment. The term קצה probably has a feminine suffix, but this is also a variant spelling of the word (e.g., Josh 18:19; Isa 62:11). The form קץ is in lines 13 and 14 of the column, suggesting that קצה has a suffix. The antecedent of the suffix of the word in line 11 cannot be identified with full certainty, but is probably the "work of wickedness" of line 10 (cf. 4Q418 121 2).[20] The term "period" would thus denote the time at which wickedness is to come to an end.

---

17. 1QH 14:32 is ambiguous and may describe the angels as "sons of his truth" who rouse themselves in judgment against the wicked (cf. 1QS 4:5–6; 1QM 17:8). The ambiguity on this point is precisely because the elect are often likened to the angels and some texts blur the distinction between the two groups (e.g., 1QS 11:7–8). Note also the expression "men of truth," which signifies the elect in the Hodayot (1QH 6:13; 10:16).

18. Also note 4Q418 88 ii 8: "In truth (באמת) your in[her]itance will be fulfilled" (cf. 4Q418 102 5).

19. Cf. 4Q416 4 1; 4Q418 123 ii 4; 4Q418 211 4. See Collins 2004, 53; Goff 2003b, 189–93.

20. Note that the word "judgment" in l. 13 also has a feminine singular suffix,

The judgment scene of 4Q416 1 is theophanic.[21] 4Q418 69 ii has theophanic elements as well (see commentary below). In 4Q416 1, dread in the face of God's judgment is palpable. The wicked will experience fear. They will shout (ויריעו)—a vivid expression of their reaction.[22] The screaming may denote that they realize that their doom is imminent and inescapable (cf. Wis 5:1–8). The second half of 4Q416 1 11, as expanded by Tigchelaar's reconstruction, emphasizes not only that the wicked shall shout in fear, but that the cosmos shall express dread as well (cf. Isa 13:13).[23] The sequence "heaven," "earth," and "seas" (l. 12) emphasizes that the entirety of the cosmos will react to God's judgment in this way (cf. 4Q418b 1 3–4). Cosmic upheaval is common in biblical theophanies to mark the disruption of the natural world caused by the advent of God the Divine Warrior (e.g., Judg 5:4–5; Hab 3:10; Mic 1:3–4; Sir 16:17–23).[24] 4Q416 1 never states that elements of the natural world melt or collapse into destruction in response to judgment. 1 Enoch, like 4QInstruction, begins with a theophanic judgment scene. In 1 Enoch 1 all the watchers, referring to all angels (not just those who sin), become afraid, and the mountains shake and melt (vv. 5–7; cf. 102:2; 1QH 11:27–37).[25] There is no indication in 4Q416 1 that the angels tremble or fear, although it is possible that this could have been claimed in the lost section of line 12 (see below).

In 4Q416 1 11, those who feel afraid and shout have defiled themselves with "it," referring presumably to the "wickedness" of line 10, as mentioned above. The verb התגללו, which is probably a *hithpoel*, refers in the Hebrew Bible to becoming physically dirty (2 Sam 20:12). In early Jewish literature the term describes those who are mired in sin, as in this line (also in *hithpoel*).[26]

---

which similarly refers to the judgment of wickedness (see below). Consult Strugnell and Harrington 1999, 85; Elgvin 1997a, 151.

21. Collins 2004, 52; Elgvin 1996, 150.

22. Using the same word, the foundations of the firmament cry out in 4Q418 69 ii 9.

23. Tigchelaar 2001, 180.

24. Goff 2003b, 179–81; Miller 1973.

25. Nickelsburg 2001, 146; VanderKam 1999, 342–43.

26. Sir 12:14; 1QS 4:19 (התגוללה); CD 3:17 (התגוללו); 1QH 14:25 (יתגוללו). See Rey 2009a, 233.

4Q416 1 12

After continuing the account of the natural world's quivering before God's judgment, line 12 provides another description of those who will perish in the final judgment. Whereas 4Q416 1 11 emphasizes that the wicked will be destroyed, line 12 affirms that "every fleshly spirit" will be eliminated. They will feel dread, as do those who defile themselves in wickedness in line 11 (both lines using the verb פחד). The expression "fleshly spirit" is prominent in the famous "vision of meditation" passage of 4Q417 1 i. The meaning of the expression in that pericope suggests that the phrase in 4QInstruction refers not merely to the wicked but to the non-elect in general. They do not possess the revealed knowledge necessary for eschatological salvation. 4Q416 1 12 conveys the expiration of the body that the non-elect will face in eschatological judgment. Not only will the wicked (l. 11) be destroyed at that moment, but the non-elect in general. Line 16 includes a fragmentary reference to a "fleshly inclination" (see below).

4Q416 1 12 asserts that every fleshly spirit will be "laid bare." The verb יתערערו should probably be read as a *hithpalpel* of ערר.[27] The word in this *binyan* refers to the destruction of Babylon's walls in Jer 51:58. The verb in 4QInstruction denotes the obliteration of the fleshly spirit. The variant of the term in 4Q418 2 4, יתר[, suggests that there was some confusion regarding this word among the scribes who copied 4QInstruction. The variant should probably be restored as יתר[ועעו], a *hithpolel* of רוע, "to shout."[28] This would produce parallelism between the fleshly spirit of line 12 and all those who pollute themselves in wickedness who "cry out" in line 11 (ויריעו), also employing the root רוע (probably in *hiphil*).

The last extant phrase of 4Q416 1 12 is "the sons of heav[en]" (בני [השמי]ם). This is reasonably understood as a reference to angels, as the editors of DJD 34 suggest, although it has been proposed that it denotes men who have been transformed into angels.[29] In early Jewish literature the phrase commonly signifies angels (e.g., 1QS 4:22; 1QapGen 2:16), and the expression, without a definite article, clearly refers to angels in 4Q418

---

27. Strugnell and Harrington 1999, 86; Rey 2009a, 233.

28. Tigchelaar 2001, 180.

29. See, for example, Fletcher-Louis 2002, 119–20 (discussing the expression in 4Q418 69 ii). Consult further García Martínez 2006, 33–37; Strugnell and Harrington 1999, 290 (also commenting on 4Q418 69 ii); Elgvin 1997a, 245; Puech 2005, 96; 2008b, 154.

69 ii 12–13 (see commentary below).[30] 4Q416 1 12 probably contains a contrast between the fleshly spirit, denoting humankind in general, and the angelic sons of heaven, marked with a disjunctive *waw*.[31] Unfortunately, the extant material in the line does not clarify the exact relationship between the fleshly spirit and the sons of heaven. It is also not clear what role the angels play in eschatological judgment. The editors of DJD 34 supplement the line so that the sons of heaven "sh[all rejoice]" on the day of judgment.[32] This is endorsed by other commentators.[33] This reconstruction is possible, but there is no evidence from 4QInstruction to support it. The line may have stated that the angels assist God in the implementation of judgment.[34] One could also suggest that, as part of the text's account of all the elements of the cosmos trembling before God's judgment, the angels are fearful as well, as in 1 Enoch 1 (see above on l. 11).[35]

4Q416 1 13

This line affirms that the destruction of iniquity will occur at a distinct eschatological moment. Lines 12–13 state that "its judgment," with its antecedent most likely being "wickedness" (l. 10), will happen on a particular day. The phrase "period of tru[th]" (l. 13) similarly conveys that judgment is to occur at a specific period in time. At that point "all iniquity" will be destroyed (cf. 4Q418 113 1; 4Q418 211 4). 4Q418 69 ii 8 likewise refers to the destruction of the "sons of iniquity" (see commentary below). The claim of 4Q416 1 13 that not only will human beings be destroyed, but iniquity itself as well, accords with the claim in line 10 that God will judge "the work of wickedness." Not simply wicked people but wickedness in general will be destroyed. 4Q416 1 may envision, without fully describing, a situation similar to that of 1 Enoch 10, the Treatise on the Two Spirits (1QS 4:18–21) and the book of Mysteries (1Q27 1 i 1–12).[36]

---

30. The phrase also does not have a definite article in the text that parallels 4Q416 1 12, 4Q418 2 4 (see textual notes above).

31. Frey 2002, 391–92.

32. Strugnell and Harrington 1999, 83.

33. Rey 2009a, 231; Puech 2005, 97.

34. Note the fragmentary reference to a heavenly council in 4Q418 69 ii 15, suggesting that angels play some sort of role in the judgment described in that column. Cf. 1 En. 1:4, 9; 1QS 4:12.

35. In this case the *waw* before "the sons of heaven" would be disjunctive, and would convey that "even the sons of heaven" would be afraid.

36. Elgvin 1996, 152.

These texts recount an eschatological transformation of the earth in which evil is utterly abolished. Mysteries, for example, states that wickedness will vanish, as will folly, at which point "knowledge will fill the world" (l. 7).[37] The verb in 1Q27 1 i 6 that describes the ultimate end of wickedness is a form of תמם. The same root is used in 4Q416 1 13. It is possible that the author of 4QInstruction understood the elect to enjoy a blissful existence on a restored, purified earth after the eschatological destruction of evil, as in Mysteries and the Book of the Watchers, but this trope is never explicit in the composition (see also the commentary on 4Q418 81 14). The variant for 4Q416 1 13 in 4Q418 2 5 states that all iniquity will come to an end "until he completes (עד ישלם instead of עוד ושלם) the period of truth." This likewise stresses that history culminates in judgment.

4Q416 1 14

The expression "all the periods of eternity" (כל קצי עד) does not have its full context available. It probably signifies the entire scope of time, from creation to judgment (cf. 1QS 4:16; 1QSb 5:18).[38] The phrase suggests some degree of periodization of history, as in the Apocalypse of Weeks (1 En. 91:12, 17).[39] 4Q416 1, however, provides no detailed schematization of history in the manner of this Enochic text. The declaration that the deity is a "God of truth" is in keeping with the prominence of the word "truth" in the judgment scene of 4Q416 1 (see above on l. 10).

4Q416 1 15

Little survives at the end of 4Q416 1. This portion appears to assert that God provides the righteous person with the knowledge of good and evil, but this cannot be stated with full certainty. This, however, would be appropriate after the text's account of the contrasting eschatological fates of the "sons of his truth" and the "fleshly spirit." The reference to good and evil in line 15 may not simply denote the addressee's capacity to act in an upright manner, but could also refer to the revelation given to him. The knowledge of good and evil is probably part of the revealed content of the vision of meditation. Elsewhere the addressee is entrusted with the garden of Eden, suggesting that the *mebin* has access to knowledge possessed by Adam, which would include good and evil (see the commentary on 4Q417

---

37. Goff 2007, 86–89.
38. Puech 2005, 155.
39. Elgvin 1997a, 103; 1996, 151.

1 i and 4Q423 1). I understand the key phrase of line 15 in light of the variant text of 4Q418 2 7, which reads צדיק, whereas 4Q416 1 15 itself reads צדק (see the textual notes section above). The former variant produces a better reading than the latter.[40] The "righteous person" is most likely the elect addressee, who is to follow dutifully the teachings he receives in 4QInstruction. God has given him knowledge, in the form of the mystery that is to be, which allows him to face the deity in judgment successfully and to receive eschatological rewards (see section 6 of the introduction).

4Q416 1 16

Line 16 contains an unfortunately fragmentary reference to a "fleshly [in]clination" (cf. 1QH 24:6).[41] The eschatological destruction of the fleshly spirit in 4Q416 1 suggests that, while 4QInstruction does not polemicize against the flesh as stridently as, for example, the letters of Paul, one should associate the "fleshly [in]clination" with conduct that is to be discouraged. This suggests that the term in 4Q416 1 is roughly similar to the well-known "wicked inclination" (יצר רע), which is also attested in 4QInstruction (4Q417 1 ii 12; see also the excursus in chapter 7).[42] So understood, the word "flesh" in 4QInstruction does not simply denote the finitude of the physical body, but can also signify forms of behavior that result in eschatological destruction. (See also the discussion of the "fleshly spirit" in the commentary on the vision of meditation passage, 4Q417 1 i 13–18.) The inclination of flesh may have been mentioned as part of a warning for the addressee to avoid deeds of wickedness. The "wicked inclination" functions in this way in 4Q417 1 ii 12. A similar interpretation of the fleshly inclination in 4Q416 1 16 would be in keeping with the stress in line 15 on knowing good and evil.

---

40. צדק may simply be a *defectiva* spelling of the variant in 4Q418.

41. Collins 2004, 52.

42. Frey 2002, 394–95.

3.
4Q416 2 I–II

Parallel texts: 4Q417 2 i–ii + 23 (underline); 4Q418 7b (dotted underline);
4Q418 8 (dashed underline); 4Q418a 19 (double underline)

TEXT[1]

COLUMN I (LINES 20–22)

חֿ[ס]כֿ̊ה	[בשפט] 20
	ואפס עוד וגם
ב]עֿברה	[אֿתֿהֿ מבין 21
	אם תאיץ ידכה
מ̇אל [שֿאל	[לבלתי שלֿוֿח 22
	טרפכה כי הוא

bottom margin

COLUMN II

top margin

למֿל]א כֿל מחֿ[סֿ]רֿי	פתח רחֿ[מיו לֿכֿל 1
	אוטו ולתת טרֿף]

---

1. See Strugnell and Harrington 1999, 88–110; Tigchelaar 2001, 44–47; Rey 2009a, 64–75; Elgvin 1997a, 209–21. The textual notes section, unless otherwise noted, refers to these works.

4Q416 2 i overlaps with 4Q417 2 i, which provides a better witness to the text they have in common. It is covered in the commentary on that column. 4Q416 2 i 20–22 is discussed here because it begins a topic that is continued in 4Q416 2 ii. The parallel texts from 4Q418 are difficult in their own right, and are supplemented with numerous other fragments from 4Q418. Fragments 26, 27, 64, 66, and 199 are joined to 4Q418 7b; 4Q418 8 is a composite text that includes 4Q418 8a, 8b, 8c (= 21), 8d (= 12), and 11. Tigchelaar (2001, 76–79) joins 4Q418 8a–b to the column mainly represented by frg. 7b, while putting 4Q418 8c–d and 11 in a separate column with material from frg. 9. See also Tigchelaar 1998, 589–93.

2	לְכֹל חי ואין מ֯[ת מפני הרעבה ואם] יְקְפֹּץ ידֹ[ו] ונאספ[ה] רֹוח כֹו[ל]
3	בשר אל תק֯[ל ערובת רעיכה פן תֵכֹשֹׁל בה ו]בֹחרפתֹ[ו] תֵכסה פניכֹה ובאולתו
4	מאסֹר כמה[ו] אם בהון הַנֹושה בו ישה ומהֹר]שֹלם ואתה תשוה בו כי כיס
5	צפוניֹכֹה פֹק[דתה לֵנושה בכה בעד רעיכה נֹתֹ]תֹה כל חֵייכה בֹז מהר תן אשר
6	לו זקח כֹיס[כה vac?] וּבֹדבריכה אל תמעט]רוחכה בכל הון אל תמר רוח קֹ֯ידֹשכה
7	כי אין מחיר שוֹה [בה כל אֹי֯[ש לא י֯טכה ברצון שחר פניו וכלשונו
8	דבֹר ואז תמצא חפצכֹה[מֵתֹרֹפֹתֹכה אל תֹמֹר]לֹו וחוקֹיכה אל תרף וברזיכה השמר
9	[לחֹי]כֹה אם עבודתו יפקֹיד לכֹהֹ [אל מֹנֹוֹח בֹנֹפֹשכה וא]ל תנומה לעיניכה עד עֹשותכה
10	[מֹצֹוֹתֹיו וא]ֹל תוסף ואם יש להַצֹ[ניֹע ר֯ מֹעֹ]ואל תותר לֹו אף הון בלֹז
11	[תֹגֹזֹ פֹן יומֹר בזֹנֹי֯ ונֹף֯]לֹ[ה א]וֹ[°°] וי֯[צֹוֹ]כה זֹראה כֹי רבה קֹנאת
12	[אנוש ועקוב הלֵב מכֹל]ֹ°[אֹם ברצוֹנו תחזֹיק עֹבודתו וחכמת אוטֹ
13	[ ]שֹוֹֹ֯° °°[תֹיעֹצֹנֹֹ֯ והיֹיתֹה]לֹוֹ לבן בכור וחמל עֹלֹיֹכֹה כאיש על יחידו
14	[כֹי אתֹה עבֹדֹו ובחֹי]רֹו ואֹתֹה א[ל] תֹבטֹח למה תשֹׂנֹא ואל תשקוד ממֹדהבכה
15	[דֹמה לו לעבד משכי]לֹ וגם אֹל תשפל נפשכה לאשר לא ישוה בכה ואֹז תֹהֹיֹה
16	[לֹו לאבֹ]° לאשר אֹין כוחכה אל תגע פן תכשל וֹחֹרֹפֹתֹכֹה תרבה מֹאֹדֹה
17	[אל תֹמ]כֹוֹ[ר נֹפֹשכה בהון טוב היותכה עֹבֹד בֹרֹוֹחֹ וחֹנֹם תעֹבֹוֹד נוֹגֹשיכֹה ובמחיר

אל תמכור כבודכה ואל תערבהו בנחלתכה פן יורי֯ש גוֹיתכה אל   18
תשבי֯עֹ לחֹם

ואין כסות אל תשת יין ואין אכל אל תדרוש תַעֲנוֹג ואתה   vacat   19

חסר לחם אל תתכבד במחסורכה ואתה רֹוֹש פֹּן   vacat   20

תבזז לחייכֶה וגם אל תקל כלי[ח]֯יֹקכה   vacat   21

bottom margin

TRANSLATION

COLUMN I

20 [with a staff …] and no more. And also
21 [you, *understanding one … in*] wrath. If you hasten your hand
22 [without send*ing … From God*] ask for your food, for he

COLUMN II

1 has released [his] compas[sion *to all … to fulfi*]ll all the ne[eds of his resources to provide food]
2 for every living thing and no one d[*ies from hunger … but if*] he closes his hand, then [will be gather]ed the spirit of al[*l*]
3 flesh. Do not disho[*nor the pledge of your neighbor lest you st*umble because of it and] with [his] shame you will cover your face. And with his folly (you will be covered)
4 by an obligation like h[im. If the creditor *loans* him money, *then quickly*] repay. And you, you are like him for the bag of
5 your treasures [yo*u*] have entr[usted to the one lending to you on behalf of your neighbor.] You have gi[ven] your entire life in exchange for it (the bag). Quickly give what
6 belongs to him and take back [your] bag. [*vacat*?   And with your words do not restrain] your spirit. For no wealth exchange your holy spirit,
7 because there is no price that is equal [*to it.* …] Do not let [*any* m]an deceive you. With pleasure seek his presence and according to his speech
8 speak. And then you will find your desire [instead of your shame. Do not op*pose*] him and do not abandon your obligations. Observe your mysteries

9   [*for the sake of*] your [*life*]. If he assigns his work to you [let there
      be no rest in *your soul and let there be n*]o slumber for your eyes
      until you carry out

10   [*his* directives. *But do n*]ot do more. And if it is possible to act
      hum[bly ...] And do not let (anything) remain for him, even tax-
      money

11   [... lest he say "he has despised me" and has fal]le[n ... *And* he]
      has commanded you. See that great is the zeal

12   [of man and the heart is more crooked than *anything else* ...] If
      in his favor you hold fast to his service and the wisdom of his
      resources,

13   [...] you will advise him [so that you may become] for him a first-
      born son and he will be compassionate towards you, like a man
      towards his only son,

14   [for you are *his* slave *and* his *chos*]en one. But you, do not be
      (overly) confident lest you become hated and do not lie awake
      over your distress.

15   [Become for him an intellige]nt [slave]. And also, do not lower
      yourself before one who is not your equal. And then you will
      become

16   [a father to him ...] For what is beyond your strength do not
      reach, lest you stumble and your shame will be very great.

17   [*Do not se*]ll yourself for wealth. It is good that you are a slave in
      spirit and without wages you serve your oppressors. For a price

18   do not sell your glory and do not pledge wealth for your inheri-
      tance lest he (God?) dispossess your body. Do not sate yourself
      with bread

19   *vacat*   when there is no clothing. Do not drink wine when there
      is no food. Do not seek fine food when you

20   *vacat*   lack bread. Do not glorify yourself with what you lack
      when you are poor, lest

21   *vacat*   you show contempt for your life. And also, do not dis-
      honor the vessel of your [*bo*]som.

TEXTUAL NOTES

    i 20. הכֺ֯◦[◦. Tigchelaar suggests transcribing תֺֿכֺֿנֺֿה or תֺֿכֺֿבֺֿה. The edi-
tors of DJD 34 propose כֺֿ[and Rey תֺֿכֺֿה[. The first visible trace of this
word appears to be on 4Q418 7b, as reconstructed by Tigchelaar (see pl.
III of Rey).

i 20. ‏ואפס; 4Q418 7b 11: ‏וֹאפץ.

i 22. ‏שֹׁאל. See PAM 42.556.

ii 1. ‏[כֹ]ול חסרי 14: 4Q418 7b ;‏כול מחסירֹיֹ :4Q417 2 ii 3 ;‏כל מחֹ[סירי].

ii 2. ‏מֹ]ת מפני הרעבה]. Rey uses this supplement, which the editors of DJD 34 suggest.

ii 2. ‏[ונאספ]הֹ רוח כוֹ[ל]. PAM 42.597 provides a good image of this text (see pl. IV of Rey).

ii 3. ‏תכֹשֹׁוֹל. Only the last two letters of this word are extant in 4Q417 2 ii 5. The editors of DJD 34 report that an earlier transcription records the *shin* and *kaf* (the first of which could also be a *mem*).

ii 4. ‏[כמה]וֹ אם בהון הֹנושה בו ישֹׁה ומהר. This reconstruction is based on the parallel text in 4Q417 2 ii 6. For criticism of conflicting transcriptions of this text in DJD 34, see Rey.

ii 5. ‏צפונֹיֹכֹה. The *yod* is not supralinear in 4Q418 8 4.

ii 5. ‏בכה; 4Q417 2 ii 7: ‏בדֹיֹה.

ii 5. ‏כל; 4Q417 2 ii 7: ‏כֹול.

ii 6. There is a scribal mark of uncertain significance in the margin at the beginning of this line (Tov 2004, 362 [fig. 5.9]).

ii 6. ‏לו זקח; 4Q418 8 5: ‏לוא יקח.

ii 6. ‏כיֹס[כה *vac?* ובדבריכה]. There is no gap between these words in 4Q417 2 ii 8 or 4Q418 8 5. In 4Q416 2 ii 6 there was either a *vacat* between these words, as Rey suggests, or a word that is now lost.

ii 6. ‏תמר; 4Q418 8 6: ‏תאמר.

ii 6. ‏קֹידשכה; 4Q418 8 6: ‏קדושה.

ii 7. ‏כֹי; 4Q417 2 ii 9 and 4Q418 8 6: ‏כיא.

ii 7. ‏שׁוה; 4Q417 2 ii 9: ‏שֹׁוֹוֹה.

ii 7. ‏ברצון; 4Q418 8 7: ‏ברצונו.

ii 8. ‏תֹ[מ]רֹ. This reading is suggested by Rey and Tigchelaar.

ii 8. ‏וחוקיכה; 4Q418 8 8: ‏[ה]חקיכֹה.

ii 9. ‏[לֹחיֹי]כֹה. This follows Rey. There is not enough space for the suggestion by Strugnell and Harrington, ‏[לנפשׁ]כֹה. Tigchelaar proposes ‏[מא]דֹה.

ii 11. ‏[יֹ]צֹ[ ][]כה. Strugnell and Harrington transcribe ‏[שׁ אֹ ע]יֹנֹ[יֹ]כה.

ii 11. ‏כֹי; 4Q417 2 ii 15: ‏כֹיֹא.

ii 12. ‏אוטֹ; 4Q418 8 13: ‏אטוֹ.

ii 13. ‏והיתה. Commentators reasonably supplement the *he* at the end of this word on the basis of the available space in the lacuna. The parallel text 4Q417 2 ii 17 reads ‏והיית.

ii 14. תשׁנֹאֿ. See PAM 42.597.

ii 15. תהיֿה. See PAM 42.597.

ii 18. תערבהו; 4Q417 2 ii 23: תערב הון.

ii 19. תענוג. I follow a join of 4Q418 11 proposed by Tigchelaar. The editors of DJD 34 (p. 237) transcribe the key word on that fragment as [ל]מֿענֹבֿ[ה], which Tigchelaar (2001, 81) justly critiques.

ii 20. במחסורכה; 4Q417 2 ii 25: במחסוריכה.

ii 21. כלי. The transcription of this word, which is debated, is discussed below.

COMMENTARY

4Q416 2 is the largest fragment of 4QInstruction. It contains a substantial portion of four columns. Much of the text has suffered damage and is difficult to read. According to Strugnell, some of this deterioration occurred when Kando, the famous middleman involved in the discovery of the Dead Sea Scrolls, hid the fragment under his shirt when going through a police checkpoint. The leather was damaged from perspiration.[2] 4Q417 2 i–ii and 4Q418 contain material that overlaps with 4Q416 2, allowing the plausible restoration of substantial portions of the text.

4Q416 2 i 20–ii 21 falls into five discrete units. 4Q416 2 i 20–ii 3 deals with charity, and presents God as a munificent provider of food. 4Q416 2 ii 3–7 discourages going surety, or guaranteeing a loan that someone else receives. Lines 7–17, probably written for someone who had become a debt slave, encourage an upright and responsible attitude towards one's work. 4Q416 2 ii 17–18, echoing lines 3–7, presents unsound financial arrangements as jeopardizing the addressee's elect status. Lines 18–21 stress the temperate use of resources.

4Q416 2 i 20–22

This section was preceded by text that corresponds to 4Q417 2 i, which, like much of 4Q416 2 ii, deals with borrowing and financial concerns. The end of line 20 begins an exhortation that deals with the topic of charity. The word תאיץ (l. 21) normally means "to hasten" but can also

---

2. Strugnell and Harrington 1999, 73. Fields is skeptical as to whether this actually occurred (personal correspondence). The incident is never mentioned in his richly detailed history of the discovery of the scrolls (2009). 4Q416 2 may have been damaged by the application of castor oil in the 1950s and 1960s. See Elgvin 1997a, 13.

denote becoming narrow or constrained.[3] The verb, used with "hand," is interpreted by the editors of DJD 34 in the latter way.[4] So understood, the expression signifies "shutting the hand." The verb would thus express an action that is similar in meaning to לקפוץ יד, literally "to close the hand," which in 4Q416 2 ii 2 conveys stinginess.[5] The editors of DJD 34 are probably correct that the term signifies stinginess in 4Q416 2 i 21, but not that it conveys "shutting the hand." The verb אוץ means "to hasten" or "to urge" more often than "to shut" or "to be narrow." The sense of haste conveyed by this word can express greed. This is the case, for example, in Prov 28:20: "The faithful will abound with blessings, but one who is in a hurry (אץ) to be rich will not go unpunished." Ben Sira utilizes the language of this proverb to make the same point (11:10). The language of "hastening your hand" in 4Q416 2 i 21 probably had a monetary sense as well. The addressee is warned not to rush his hand away without giving assistance. The אם-clause containing this image was probably followed by an apodosis that described a negative consequence of rushing one's hand away. Charity is encouraged in Proverbs and Ben Sira (e.g., Prov 14:20–21; 19:17; Sir 29:19; 34:25). 4Q416 2 i 21, though not complete, appears to be consistent with this tradition.

4Q416 2 i 22–ii 1

While the *mebin* may not offer a helping hand to a person in need, God shows compassion to all humankind. 4Q416 2 ii 2 stresses that he provides food "for every living thing."[6] Psalm 104 similarly asserts that he controls all life by making food available (ll. 27–30). 4Q416 2 ii 1 uses a verb in the perfect (פתח). That he has opened compassion probably indicates that he has created the world in a way in which sustenance is available and can be produced.[7] This is suggested by lines 1–2, which associate God's benevolence with his provision of food.

---

3. For the meaning "to hasten," see, e.g., Josh 10:13; Prov 21:5. The verb can also mean "to urge" (Exod 5:13). The sense of becoming narrow is in Josh 17:15.

4. Strugnell and Harrington 1999, 94.

5. The expression would have occurred in a lost section of 4Q416 2 i. The phrase is in 4Q417 2 i 24. From this one can infer that it was originally attested in 4Q416 2 i 17. See Strugnell and Harrington 1999, 88, 173–74.

6. Rey 2009a, 169.

7. The word רחמים ("compassion") in 4Q416 2 ii 1 attests the "plural of abstraction." See Joüon and Muraoka 2008, 471 (§136g).

4Q416 2 ii 1–2

God is exalted for making life possible by providing food. The phrase "the ne[eds of his resources]" (מח[סורי]סירי אוטו]) in line 1 utilizes two words that are characteristic of 4QInstruction. מחסור signifies lack, particularly in a financial sense (see commentary on 4Q417 2 i 17–18). אוט, while enigmatic, likely has a material sense as well, denoting assets or resources.[8] Both terms help assert that God fulfills one's basic needs, particularly with regard to food. 4Q416 2 ii 1 employs the term אוט with טרף ("nourishment"), as in 4Q418 81 16. 4Q417 2 similarly portrays God as reliable in a way that people are not. Lines 19–20 of that column read: "[And upon] his command everything comes into being. The nourishment that he provides for you, e[a]t. But do not take any m]or[e (than you need)." He is also told: "[And if] you lack, borrow, being without mo[ne]y, which you lack, for the treasury of [God] does not lack" (l. 19). These statements were intended for someone who is experiencing difficulty supporting himself (see commentary below). This may also be the case with 4Q416 2 i 22–ii 1, since one is told to ask God for food. 4QInstruction does not teach the *mebin* to expect some sort of miraculous event, by which God provides manna. Rather, the addressee is to sustain himself through the availability of food in the natural world, which can be grown or purchased. The envisioned *mebin* was probably intimately aware of this issue, since several texts of 4QInstruction understand that he is or likely could be a farmer (see the commentary on 4Q423 5).

---

8. This term occurs over fifteen times in 4QInstruction, but in all other early Jewish literature only once (4Q424 1 6): 4Q415 18 2; 4Q416 2 ii 12 (par. 4Q418 8 13); 4Q417 2 ii 3 (par. 4Q416 2 ii 1; 4Q418 8 1); 4Q418 79 2; 4Q418 81 16; 4Q418 101 i 3; 4Q418 103 ii 6; 4Q418 107 4; 4Q418 126 ii 2, 12, 13; 4Q418 127 5; 4Q418 177 8; 4Q423 2 i 5. Many of these instances are too fragmentary to interpret sufficiently. The word in the Hebrew Bible is generally an adverb that means "softly" or "gently" (e.g., 2 Sam 18:5; Isa 8:6) and is thus quite different from its meaning in 4QInstruction. Strugnell and Harrington (1999, 31–32), on the basis of 4Q424 1 6 (אט), translate the term as "secret." In 4Q424 the word has some sort of practical meaning, perhaps "business," referring to a job or assignment with which a lazy person should not be trusted. Most commentators understand the term in 4QInstruction as signifying a resource or asset from which the addressee benefits. This is clear from the usage of the word in 4Q418 126 ii, especially l. 13 (see commentary below). In 4Q418 103 ii 6 and 4Q418 107 4 the word is used with מסחור ("merchandise"). In 4Q418 81 16 and 4Q416 2 ii 1 the term is associated with food. See Goff 2003b, 152; Rey 2009a, 33; Elgvin 1997a, 154; Novick 2002, 77. For discussion of 4Q424 1 6, see Goff 2007, 189.

4Q416 2 ɪɪ 2–3

If God wishes, he could "close his hand" and extinguish the life of all creatures (cf. Job 12:10). This act is presented as a refusal to offer charity, expressed with the phrase לקפוץ יד. The phrase normally denotes being stingy. The expression occurs in biblical law in a teaching that encourages one to help his neighbor when in need (Deut 15:7).[9] Ben Sira uses this language to signify a refusal to give money charitably (4:31). According to 4Q416 2 ii 2, when God closes his hand all human life will come to an end (cf. 4Q418 88 ii 5). The continuation of human life reflects God giving his compassion to people by making food available (l. 1). This would end if his goodwill toward humanity were to cease. The phrase of 4Q416 2 ii 2–3 under discussion is found almost verbatim in 4Q419 8 ii 7.[10]

4Q416 2 ɪɪ 3–4

Lines 3–7 comprise a unit that warns the addressee about surety. The overall view in 4QInstruction is that this practice is dangerous and should be avoided. 4QInstruction also discourages going surety elsewhere (4Q416 2 ii 18; 4Q415 8 2; 4Q418 88 ii 3; cf. 4Q416 2 iii 4–7).[11]

Debt Security and Surety in the Ancient Near East and the Wisdom Tradition

As in the modern world, in antiquity the availability of loans required assurances to creditors that they would be repaid.[12] Some sort of pledge was needed to guarantee the loan. Pledges could take many forms, including land, labor, or an item of value.[13] Pledges are typically classified into two broad categories: possessory and hypothecary. Regarding the former, the pledge is held as a pawn by the creditor, who typically had right of

---

9. Compare Lev 25:25–28, which calls for similar action on behalf of a family member who has fallen upon hard times. See also Baker 2009.

10. This is one of the reasons that scholars have posited some sort of direct literary dependence between the two compositions. I have argued that there is not sufficient evidence to make this claim. See Goff 2007, 277–80.

11. 4Q418 87 7 reads "go surety for a stranger in …" This is the only visible portion of the line. Given the attitude toward surety in 4QInstruction, the sentence was probably qualified by a negation: "[Do not] go surety for a stranger in …" (cf. Prov 20:16; 27:13).

12. Baker 2009, 266–75; Westbrook and Jasnow 2001.

13. Westbrook 2001a, 3.

usufruct, or use of the pledge during the period of the loan.[14] A hypothecary pledge is assigned, but is not handed over to the creditor during
the assigned period of the loan. Possessory pledges were common in the
ancient Near East, and this kind appears to be at issue in 4QInstruction
(see 4Q416 2 ii 4–5).[15] A pledge would be forfeited or seized by the creditor if the loan defaulted. Standing or going surety was the practice of providing a pledge that guaranteed the loan for the borrower. The guarantor
would be responsible for the loan if the borrower defaulted.

There is a rich fund of loan and debt contracts from the ancient Near
East.[16] They provide a sense of the risks faced by the borrower. The interest
charged for the loan was, by modern standards, quite high. Exact figures
are not available for ancient Israel, but biblical prohibitions against charging interest suggest that usury (charging excessively high rates of interest)
was common (Exod 22:24 [Eng. v. 25]; Deut 23:19–20). The common rate
in Neo-Assyrian loan texts is 25 percent and can be as high as 33 percent.[17] Family members or property of the borrower who defaulted could
be seized to ensure payment. The Code of Hammurabi assumes the right
of the creditor to take such measures (§§114–116). Harsh and exploitative
practices carried out by creditors against debtors are attested in the Elephantine papyri and documents from the Judean desert.[18]

------

14. When productive assets are pledged, such as land, interest on the loan can
take the form of the income generated by the pledge. This is also known as an anti-
chretic pledge. The Code of Hammurabi includes a law regarding the use of crop land
offered in pledge to the creditor who provides the loan (§§ 49–50).

15. Baker 2009, 267.

16. Westbrook and Jasnow (2001) provide an overview of the relevant material.
See also Garfinkle 2004, 1–30.

17. Radner 2001, 276.

18. One text from Elephantine (456 B.C.E.), for example, referring to a loan of
silver, states: "And if a second year comes and I have not paid you your silver and its
interest, which is written in this document, you Meshullam or your children have
right to take for yourself any security which you will find (belonging) to me—house
of bricks, silver or gold, bronze or iron, slave or handmaiden, barley, emmer or any
food which you will find (belonging) to me—until you have full (payment) of your
silver and its interest" (TAD B3.1 ll. 7–11). The document then asserts that Meshullam will also have this broad right of seizure with regard to the writer's children, if he
were to die with the loan outstanding (cf. B3.13; 4.2). P. Yadin 11, part of the Babatha
archives, attests a loan contract from 124 C.E. in which a person puts up his father's
courtyard in En-gedi as a hypothecary pledge, of which the creditor will have full
rights of ownership if the loan and interest are not paid according to the stipulations

The guarantor exposes himself to the risk posed by non-payment of the loan.[19] The one standing surety for another person who borrows money could be regarded essentially as a co-debtor—except he would not receive the loan.[20] Such a guarantor faces all the risks of the loan while experiencing none of its benefits. Traditional wisdom harbors deep suspicion regarding surety and borrowing in general (Prov 22:7). Even though Proverbs urges one to help the needy and the poor, going surety for a "neighbor" (רע), a person who is known, is discouraged. Proverbs 17:18 claims that helping out a neighbor in this way is foolhardy (cf. 11:15; 22:26; 28:8). Proverbs 6:1–5 is directed to someone who has guaranteed a loan for his neighbor. The addressee is portrayed as trapped by, and under the power of, the person on whose behalf he has pledged.[21] One should implore with the neighbor, not the creditor, to release him from his obligation (6:3; cf. 4Q417 2 i 21–23). This would entail encouraging the neighbor to pay off the debt. Biblical law similarly shows sympathy for one who guarantees a loan with a pledge and the attendant risks of this practice.[22]

Ben Sira's advice with regard to surety is strikingly different from that of Proverbs. Though aware of the risks associated with the practice, the sage does not conclude that it should be avoided. Sirach 8:13 states: "Do

---

of the contract. The amount of the loan is forty denarii, but above that on the line (l. 3) the amount of sixty denarii is written, suggesting, as Napthali Lewis proposes, that the creditor lent forty denarii but unscrupulously compelled the borrower to sign a loan contract for sixty. See also the discussion of WDSP 10 in the excursus below on debt slavery. That section discusses other documents that acknowledge debts. Consult Rey 2009a, 80–81; Porten and Yardeni 1986–1999, 2.54–57; Porten et al. 2011, 204; Lewis 1989, 41; Porten and Greenfield 1969, 153–57. For scholarship on the economy of ancient Palestine, see Pastor 2010, 297–307; 1997; Sivertsev 2010, 229–45; Safrai 1994.

19. In one Old Babylonian document one who has gone surety seems to have not understood the risks entailed by this decision. He asks: "Why are they suing me for the silver (just) because I stood surety for X?" (AbB 7 75; cited in Westbrook 2001b, 79).

20. Porten and Greenfield 1996, 156.

21. "My son, if you have given your pledge to your neighbor … you are snared by the utterance of your lips, caught by the words of your mouth. So do this, my son, and save yourself, for you have come into your neighbor's power: go and grovel, and badger your neighbor" (6:1–3). See Fox 2000, 210–16; Sandoval 2006, 106–12.

22. Exod 22:26–27, for example, asserts that one should not retain full use of a garment taken in pledge but rather return it to the guarantor, so that he will not be cold at night. A similar attitude is espoused in Deut 24 (vv. 6, 10–13, 17). See Baker 2009, 269–75.

not give surety beyond your means; but if you give surety, be prepared to pay." The sage shows full awareness of the risks involved: "Going surety has ruined many prosperous people and tossed them about like the surging sea, has exiled the prominent and sent them wandering through foreign lands" (29:18; cf. v. 15). He recommends that his students engage in the practice with caution: "Go surety for your neighbor (πλησίον//ܫܒܝ) according to your means, but take care lest you fall thereby" (v. 20).[23] Proverbs 6 (and 4Q416 2 ii 4–5; see below) by contrast discourages standing surety for one's "neighbor" (רע).[24] Ben Sira's students were likely to be well off, unlike those of 4QInstruction and, consequently, the risks associated with surety were less likely to be catastrophic.

4Q416 2 ii 3–4 is very fragmentary. Line 3 begins with an incomplete vetitive, "Do not ... (אל תקן[)." Then there is a lacuna, after which the text tells the addressee that he will stumble because of it (a feminine suffix), and that his shame (a masculine suffix) will cover his face. There is also a reference to his folly (again a masculine suffix). Rey has suggested that the lacuna in line 3 be filled in the following manner: אל תקן[ח ערובת רעיכה פן תכשול בה].[25] So understood, the text warns the *mebin* not to take the surety of one's neighbor, or else he (the addressee) will stumble.[26] This supplement fits the lacuna physically and, given the rest of the pericope (esp. ll. 5–6), it is reasonable to posit that line 3 discusses surety. Furthermore, Rey's supplement provides a way to explain the suffixes in 4Q416 2 ii 3. The feminine suffix ("you will stumble because of it") would thus refer to the pledge, a feminine word (ערובה). The masculine suffixes ("his shame"; "his folly") would signify the neighbor. His "shame" and "folly" would denote the harsh consequences that would also affect the addressee if the

---

23. The translation of the imperative is based on the Syriac ܥܘܒ, which is cognate with the Hebrew verb for going surety (ערב). The Greek states that one should "assist" (ἀντιλαβοῦ) his neighbor. See Di Lella and Skehan 1987, 372; Rey 2009a, 78.

24. The Damascus Document, which stipulates a great deal of control over the financial decisions of members of the sect, recommends that on the Sabbath no one can lend to his "neighbor" (10:18; cf. 13:13–16). This may refer to other sectarians or other people whom members know.

25. He supplements the underlined portion in the lacuna. Rey (2009a, 64, 70, 77–79) translates: "Ne pre[nds] pas [la caution de ton prochain de peur que tu ne trébuches à cause d'elle]."

26. This other person may also be mentioned in 4Q417 2 i 26–27 (par. 4Q416 2 i 19–20). See the commentary below on this text.

neighbor-borrower were not to repay the loan.[27] The debt slavery instruction of lines 7–17 suggests that the author believes this is a likely outcome.

The reference to "his folly" is part of a text in lines 3–4 that is difficult to interpret. Strugnell and Harrington translate, "Nor at his folly (hide it) from you captive."[28] They transcribe מאסיר at the beginning of line 4. As the editors reasonably assume, the verb of the previous phrase ("with [his] shame you will cover [תכסה] your face") probably extends to the text in question. A better reading of the text is provided if one understands the verb in the sense not of "hide" but "cover." The folly of the neighbor who defaults on a loan for which the *mebin* has pledged would "cover" both of them, in that they would both be affected. Thus with Rey I read the first word of line 4 as מאסור, a preposition plus the word "obligation."[29]

Regarding Rey's reconstruction of line 3, my only misgiving regards the proposed supplement [ח]אל תקק ("Do not ta[ke]"). So understood, the line urges the *mebin* not to *take* the pledge of his neighbor (cf. 4Q416 2 iii 5). He would thus not be going surety for the neighbor, but rather receiving a pledge from him to secure his own loan. The neighbor would then be going surety for the *mebin*. 4Q416 2 ii 3–4, however, discusses the shame of the neighbor spreading to the addressee. The neighbor is the borrower, whose non-payment of the loan would affect the *mebin*. Moreover, when the verb לקחת is elsewhere connected with surety, it denotes not the pledging of an item to guarantee a loan, but rather the *seizure* of pledged assets.[30] I therefore reconstruct not [ח]אל תקק but rather [ל]אל תקל (the same verb used in l. 21), so that the line states that the addressee should not treat as insignificant the pledge that he has provided for the neighbor. Admittedly, there are no other examples of the verb קלל used in connection to surety or loans.

The phrase "you are like him" of line 4 probably means that the loan belongs in a sense to both individuals, the addressee and the neighbor, since they are both bound to its obligations. The *mebin* is also told to "com-

---

27. The idiom of shame covering one's face occurs in 4Q418 177 3 and 4Q418 178 4 (cf. Jer 51:51; Ps 69:8). See Wold 2005b, 109–11.

28. Strugnell and Harrington 1999, 93, 95. See also Kampen 2011, 66.

29. Rey 2009a, 64.

30. Neh 5:3; Prov 20:16 = 27:13; cf. Ezek 18:12; Amos 2:8. In 1 Sam 17:18 when the young David goes to the battle front to bring food to his brothers, he is to "bring tokens from them" (תקח ערבתם), so that Jesse may have some proof that they are still alive and well.

plete" (שלם) or pay back the obligation. This construes the addressee as if
he were the borrower, emphasizing that they both are under the burden
of the debt (l. 4).[31] Line 5 establishes that the *mebin* is the guarantor and
the person referred to in the third person is the recipient of the loan, the
neighbor. The call to "complete" the arrangement probably also encourages the addressee, not unlike Prov 6:3, to get out of this entanglement by
pestering the neighbor to pay off the loan (see also below on ll. 5–6).

4Q416 2 ii 4–5

The addressee has given the creditor an item of value ("the bag of your
treasures") to guarantee the loan, thus claiming that his very "life" is at
stake. The risks that the borrower-neighbor faces threaten the guarantor-
addressee. It is a possessory pledge, whereby an item of value is entrusted
to the creditor, as a pawn for the loan (l. 5). The *mebin* has gone surety for
the neighbor. The seriousness with which 4QInstruction regards the situation is patent. The text twice urges him to remove himself from this situation quickly (מהר; ll. 4, 5).[32] This is in full continuity with Prov 6:1–5 (discussed above), with its recommendation that one should insistently urge
the neighbor to pay off the debt. Some reliance upon Prov 6 on the part of
4QInstruction is likely.[33] 4Q416 2 ii 4–5 has in common with Prov 6 the
idea of not going surety to a "neighbor" (רע). Pledging a loan on behalf of
someone you know, and presumably trust, is more reasonable than doing
so for someone who is not known personally. Nevertheless the practice is
still considered dangerous. In notable contrast to 4QInstruction, Ben Sira
encourages one to stand surety while having a clear sense of its risks (see
excursus above).

4Q416 2 ii 5 describes the pledge that the *mebin* provides for the
neighbor as "the bag of your treasures" (כיס צפונ'כה). The word כיס probably refers to a pouch or bag that contains money or perhaps some other
items of value. This is the meaning of the term in Sir 18:33.[34] In 4Q416 2
ii 5 the "bag" is given to the creditor on behalf of the neighbor. The word

---

31. Wright 2004a, 114.

32. Murphy 2002, 181.

33. 4Q416 2 ii 9 uses language that is very similar to Prov 6:4 (see below).

34. "Become not a glutton and a winebibber with nothing in your purse (כיס)."
In the Hebrew Bible the word can signify the pouch in which one carries stones used
in scales (e.g., Deut 25:13; Prov 16:11). In Prov 23:31 the term כיס should probably be
read as כוס, "cup" (cf. Gen 40:21; Prov 23:5; Sir 32:5).

"your treasures" literally means "your hidden things." The *mebin* has some valuables stashed away, presumably for use when he comes upon financial straits. While he is not as well-off as the students of Ben Sira, he is not destitute either (see section 9 of the introduction). However, the addressee does not have an ample or sturdy safety net of resources to fall back on if he were to lose the bag and its contents. The vulnerability and exposure of the *mebin* caused by the creditor's possession of the pledge is evident from the seriousness with which 4QInstruction regards the situation.

4QInstruction never discusses why the addressee has gone surety for his neighbor. It is likely that the neighbor has fallen upon hard times and needs credit. Given that he is known to the *mebin*, who is poor, it is reasonable to imagine both individuals as living at roughly the same low financial level (see section 9 of the introduction). The addressee has assumed the risk of standing surety to help someone in need. This would be consistent with 4Q416 2 i 21–22, which probably encourages charity (see commentary above). Nevertheless, the author-teacher of 4QInstruction considers this move a grave mistake, as Prov 6 warns. In contrast to Ben Sira, the Qumran wisdom text reflects tension between charity and the addressee's precarious financial status. In 4QInstruction the latter concern is ultimately more dominant than helping a person in need.

4Q416 2 ii 5–6

Once he handed over his bag of treasures, the *mebin* has put his very life on the line.[35] This underscores the risk to which he is exposed if the neighbor defaults on the loan. Sirach 29:14–15 expresses the attendant dangers of standing surety in a similar way: "A good person goes surety for his neighbor, and only the shameless would play him false; forget not the kindness of your guarantor (χάριτας ἐγγύου), for he offers his very life (ψυχὴν αὐτοῦ) for you" (cf. Deut 24:6). 4Q416 2 ii 5–6 exhorts the addressee to "give what belongs to him (i.e., the creditor) and take back [your] bag," as if the *mebin* himself had borrowed the money.[36] As discussed above on

---

35. I read the *bet* preposition in the phrase נת]תה כל חייכה בו as the *bet* of price. Elsewhere in the column he is not to exchange his glory for a price (ll. 17–18). If l. 5 asserts that he had given his life *to* someone (i.e., the creditor or the neighbor), one would expect a *lamed* preposition, rather than a *bet*.

36. Rey (2009a, 79–80) proposes that the variant to this text in 4Q418 8 5 preserves a different debt arrangement than that of 4Q416 2 ii 5–6. See the textual notes section. The 4Q418 text can be read "Quickly give to him your bag that he will take."

line 4, this involves urging (and perhaps even helping), the neighbor to pay back the loan. By guaranteeing the loan, the *mebin* is under the same burden as the borrower-neighbor.

4Q416 2 ii 6–7

These lines elaborate upon 4QInstruction's negative attitude toward the *mebin's* going surety. He is to speak forthrightly, without restraining his spirit (cf. 4Q417 2 i 12). This expresses his resolve to put an end to the obligation to which he has pledged. The text does not specify to whom he should speak. It is likely that the speech is to be directed toward the borrower-neighbor, not the creditor, to express to him the importance of paying back the loan, since it places both him and the *mebin* in jeopardy (see above on ll. 3–5). Proverbs 6.3 states that when one has gone surety for one's neighbor he has fallen into his hands, not those of the creditor. Not unlike 4Q416 2 ii 6, the verse encourages one to speak honestly and directly to the neighbor. The guarantor's main problem, Prov 6 asserts, is with the borrower. This suggests that in 4Q416 2 ii 5–6 the *mebin* is to plead before the neighbor and appeal to him to repay the loan, allowing him to receive his bag of treasures back.

While Proverbs and 4QInstruction are in complete accord with regard to the mistrust of going surety, the Qumran wisdom text provides a rationale for this position that is alien to biblical wisdom. Lines 6–7 urge the *mebin* not to "exchange your holy spirit for any wealth." Lines 17–18 similarly state that he should not sell his glory for a price. 4Q416 2 iii 6–7 exhorts one not to "pledge your spirit." The basic thrust of 4Q416 2 ii 6–7 and these other texts is that unsound financial entanglements jeopardize not simply the material well-being of the *mebin*, but also his elect status.

A pillar of 4QInstruction's teaching is for the addressee to understand that he has a privileged place before God and a special affinity with the angels (see section 6 of the introduction). 4Q416 2 ii 6 conveys this by stating that he has a "holy spirit" (cf. 4Q418 76 3). In the Hebrew Bible the phrase refers to something that God possesses (Isa 63:10; Ps 51:11). This is

---

Thus, Rey suggests, 4Q418 preserves a hypothecary pledge, which is only assigned to the creditor, who would seize it in the event of non-payment of the loan. In 4Q416 the bag would, by contrast, function as a pawn to be held by the creditor until the loan is repaid. Rey may be correct, but it is difficult to understand why one manuscript of 4QInstruction would presuppose one loan arrangement and another would assume a different one.

also the case in early Jewish literature, as in the Hodayot. But the Qumran rulebooks describe the elect members of the Dead Sea sect as having a holy spirit.[37] The phrase in 4QInstruction similarly expresses the distinctive nature of the elect. 4Q416 2 ii 6 reminds the *mebin* of his holy spirit as an incentive not to go surety. His elect status is not guaranteed, but rather predicated on living according to the teachings espoused by the composition. This includes the avoidance of hazardous financial situations.

4Q416 2 ii 7–8

These lines begin a new section. 4Q416 2 ii 7–17 gives advice about relations with a superior regarding employment. The form of work is not fully evident. The consensus view, which is reasonable, is that this unit provides instruction for a debt slave.[38] The addressee is described as an עבד in lines 14 and 15. This word can, of course, be understood as "servant." The claim in line 17, however, that he is to serve his "oppressors" without wages suggests that the addressee is not paid for his labor. The entire section of lines 7–17 is framed by exhortations urging one not to go surety (ll. 6–7, 17–18), suggesting that the unpaid labor should be understood in the context of the risks associated with indebtedness. The pericope assumes that the *mebin* has stood surety for a neighbor, who defaulted on the loan. As a consequence, the creditor has forced the addressee to perform labor without compensation in order to pay off the loan.

Debt Slavery and Indebtedness in Early Judaism

Debt slavery was widespread in Israel and the ancient Near East.[39] People who could not pay back their loans could be forced to perform bonded labor and thus become a sort of indentured servant or temporary slave. The Code of Hammurabi, for example, states that outstanding debts can be paid if a person submits himself or a family member to labor for three years (§117).[40] Leviticus 25 advocates the just treatment of bonded

37. 1QS 3:7; 9:7; CD 7:3–4. For the expression in the Hodayot, see, for example, 1QH 4:38; 6:24; 8:20, 25.

38. Murphy 2002, 182; Goff 2003b, 161; Rey 2009a, 85.

39. Chirichigno 1993; Glass 2000, 27–39.

40. "If an obligation is outstanding against a man and he sells or gives into debt service his wife, his son, or his daughter, they shall perform service in the house of their buyer or of the one who holds them in debt service for three years; their release

laborers by their supervisors, suggesting that mistreatment of such workers was common (vv. 39–43, 47–55; cf. Exod 21:2–6; Deut 15:12–18).[41] In
2 Kgs 4 the prophet Elisha helps the wife of another prophet whose children are to be taken by creditors due to her outstanding debts.

Indebtedness was common in the Second Temple period.[42] Nehemiah
complains that creditors are charging too much interest and that people
are losing their land and homes because of usury (5:6–13). The ethnogra-
pher Hecataeus of Abdera (fourth century B.C.E.) claims that Moses pro-
mulgated a law designed to prevent individuals from selling their estates to
prevent the rich from acquiring more land (Diodorus Siculus 40.3.7); this
probably reflects a rise of land holdings by the elite in the early Hellenistic period.[43] The Ptolemaic period (third century B.C.E.) is characterized
by the concentration of land ownership by a small elite class. The Zeno
papyri provide evidence in this century both for the placing of people
into indebtedness by the wealthy and for resistance to debt collection.[44]
The Tobiad family provides an impression of the massive power that the
wealthy could accumulate during this period.[45] The Hefzibah inscription
gives the impression that extensive land ownership by elites continued

---

shall be secured in the fourth year." See Roth 2003, 2.343; Baker 2009, 159–60; Rey
2009a, 84.

41. Leviticus 25, reflecting the view that one Israelite should not enslave another,
envisages the debtor as a hireling rather than a debt slave. See Milgrom 2001, 2212–34.

42. Pastor 1997, 39, 40, 55; Goff 2004b, 145–48; Sivertsev 2010, 222–23. In this
volume consult also Safrai 2010, 246–63; Pastor 2010, 297–307; Hamel 1990, 308–24.
Note further Hezser 2005, 233–41.

43. Pastor 1997, 20; Tcherikover 1999, 122; Berthelot 2010, 718–19.

44. Zeno traveled throughout Coele-Syria between 260 and 258 B.C.E. on behalf
of Apollonius, a key financial advisor to Ptolemy II Philadelphus (285–246 B.C.E.).
Zeno dispatched officials to get a villager by the name of Jeddous to either repay a debt
or seize the pledge guaranteeing the loan (CPJ no. 6). The collectors were attacked and
chased out of Jeddous's village. See Hengel 1974, 1.39; Tcherikover and Fuks 1959,
1.129–30.

45. Josephus (Ant. 12.154–236) is an important source for understanding this
family, although its historicity is debated. The wealth of the Tobiads is confirmed
archaeologically by the remains of their Ammonite fortress, Airaq al-Amir. Also indicating their power, the Zeno papyri preserve two letters from Tobias (the father of the
Tobiads) to Apollonius (see note above), in which the former secures his standing in
the Ptolemaic court by giving the latter lavish gifts, including slaves and rare animals
(CPJ nos. 4–5). See Tcherikover 1999, 126–42; Tcherikover and Fuks 1959, 1.125–29;
Rosenberg 2006.

into the Seleucid period.[46] According to 1 Maccabees, the Seleucid king Demetrius I (162–150 B.C.E.) offered numerous incentives to the people of Judea to curry their favor, including the forgiveness of debts for those taking refuge in the Temple.[47] Demetrius, 1 Maccabees claims, realized that indebtedness was a problem and that there was substantial resentment among the people regarding this. Several debt contracts, most of which date to the first and second centuries C.E., have been found in the Judean desert: Sdeir 2, XḤev/Se 49 and 66, 4Q344, Mur 18, 114 and 174.[48] The New Testament parable of the unforgiving debtor (Matt 18:23–35) also suggests that indebtedness was a common feature of the social landscape in ancient Judea.

In the period in which 4QInstruction was written (second century B.C.E.), most Judeans were freeholders of small plots, subsistence farmers or tenant farmers who did not own their land.[49] People at this economic level would easily be in need of credit to survive during seasons of poor yield, such as the famine of 160 B.C.E. (1 Macc 9:23–24; Josephus, *Ant.* 13.3).[50] Usurious credit obligations would make it impossible for such people to repay the loans, resulting in their property being seized and/or their being forcibly required to perform labor without wages. Both Josephus and Philo show awareness of debt slavery and the harsh treatment slaves could endure from creditors.[51] The Wadi Daliyeh texts (fourth century B.C.E.) include a deed in which someone probably pledged a slave in

---

46. Pastor 1997, 28–29. This inscription contains correspondence between the Seleucid King Antiochus III (223–187 B.C.E.) and Ptolemy, strategos of Syria and Phoenicia. The king grants ample land holdings to Ptolemy in exchange for his services.

47. 1 Macc 10:43: "And all who take refuge at the temple in Jerusalem, or in any of its precincts, because they owe money to the king or are in debt, let them be released and receive back all their property in my kingdom." A similar promise is made by Antiochus VII (138–129 B.C.E.) in 1 Macc 15:8. See Bartlett 1998, 89–91.

48. XḤev/Se 49, for example, is a promissory note from 133 C.E., in which one Yehosef ben Ḥananyah acknowledges the reception of four silver *zuzin*, which he agrees to repay. For XḤev/Se 49 and 66, and 4Q344, see Cotton and Yardeni 1997, 121–22, 238–43, 289–91. Mur 18 and 144 are available in Benoit et al. 1961, 100–4, 240–41. For Mur 174, consult Eshel et al. 2008, 313–26. Sdeir 2 is available in Charlesworth et al. 2000, 125–29. See also Rey 2009a, 80–81.

49. Hamel 1990, 145–48.

50. Pastor 1997, 55–62.

51. Philo describes the biblical seventh year of remission as designed to alleviate the "cruel situation" debtors are in (*Virt.* 122–124). In his retelling of 2 Kgs 4, Josephus

exchange for a loan (WDSP 10), illustrating that slavery and indebtedness could be related in Palestine during the Second Temple period.[52] In his account of the Jewish revolt of 68–74 C.E., Josephus describes deep and pervasive class conflicts that came to a head during this crisis.[53] He claims, for example, that the Sicarii burned down the Record Office "to prevent the recovery of debts" (*J.W.* 2.427; cf. 4.508).

The intended audience of 4QInstruction would have been susceptible to the risks posed by indebtedness and debt slavery. The composition assumes that the *mebin* may need to borrow money. Being in debt is regarded as a serious problem (e.g., 4Q417 2 i 21–24; see also section 9 of the introduction). Several texts of 4QInstruction assume that he is likely a farmer (4Q423 5). Given the precariousness of this profession, the prospect of debt slavery was a legitimate possibility for some, if not most, members of the intended audience of 4QInstruction.

In contrast to 4QInstruction, Ben Sira discusses not how one should behave as a slave but rather how an owner should treat his slaves (33:25–33). Whereas biblical law stresses the ethical treatment of slaves (e.g., Lev 25:43), Ben Sira presses one to work his slaves and not be afraid to punish disobedient ones: "Fodder and whip and loads for an ass; food, correction, and work for a slave. Make your slave (עבדך) work and he will look for his rest; let his hands be idle and he will seek to be free. Yoke and harness are a cure for stubbornness; and for a refractory slave, punishment in the stocks" (33:25–26; cf. Prov 29:19; Ahiq. 88 [sg.]).[54] His endorsement of industriousness and intolerance of sloth are presumably informed by

---

emphasizes that the woman and her children are to become debt slaves (*Ant.* 9.47). See Hezser 2005, 236.

52. A slave by the name of Bagabarta appears to be given in pledge to one Yehose-lah who, the editors reasonably suspect, is the creditor who loans fifteen silver shekels to Bagabarta's owner. Bagabarta is not a debt slave but is himself the pledge to secure the loan. WDSP 13r is fragmentary but may also refer to a pledged slave. See Gropp 2001, 7, 97–101; Dušek 2007, 240–47, 281–89.

53. Goodman (1987, 57–58) has emphasized the predatory lending tactics of the wealthy during this period. He argues that immoral lenders gave loans to small land-owners and intentionally charged interest at a high rate such that they could not be repaid, in order to seize their land. See also Goodman 1982, 149.

54. In Ben Sira, as in early Jewish literature in general, the discussion of slavery is problematized by the fact that the term עבד can refer to either a slave or a servant. Sirach 33:25–33 is generally regarded as discussing slaves. Sirach 7:21 clearly refers to slavery (discussed below), since it mentions giving an עבד his freedom. See Collins 1997c, 73–74; Di Lella and Skehan 1987, 405–6.

traditional wisdom (e.g., Prov 6:6; 24:30–34; 26:13–16). Ben Sira endorses more positive treatment of an "intelligent slave" in 7:21, a phrase used in 4Q416 2 ii 15 (see below). The sage also recommends more humane treatment of slaves if the owner has only one (33:31; consult commentary on 4Q416 2 ii 13).

Ben Sira teaches his students to be ethical creditors. They should lend money because it provides help to people in need (29:2; cf. 20:15). One should do so even though the lender risks being unable to recoup the loaned funds.[55] Ben Sira and 4QInstruction promulgate similar debt ethics, teaching that one should handle the loan with honesty and forthright behavior. They do so, however, from very different perspectives. The Jerusalem sage instructs his well-off students to use money ethically, by making funds available to people in need of credit even though the loan may never be repaid. Ben Sira wants them to be ethical creditors. 4QInstruction, by contrast, teaches its students to be ethical borrowers, who repay their debts and honor their obligations (e.g., 4Q416 2 ii 9–10; 4Q416 2 iii 5–7; 4Q417 2 i 21–23). This difference reflects the fact that Ben Sira is produced in an upper-class milieu, whereas the intended audience of 4QInstruction endured genuine poverty.

The status of the *mebin* in relation to his master is probably at issue in lines 7–8, but this cannot be stated conclusively.[56] The assertion in line 7 that no man may deceive the addressee should be related to the previous advice about not going surety for his neighbor. This teaching would also work well regarding his relationship with his supervisor.

The *mebin* is to seek his presence and speak with "him" in lines 7–8. In lines 6–7 he is to speak forthrightly with the neighbor for whom he has gone surety. Here the emphasis is on approaching the person "with pleasure."[57] The Hebrew noun is רצון, which may convey that he should not speak with the person without his consent or permission. The addressee is encour-

---

55. "Till he gets it (i.e., the borrower receiving the loan), he kisses the lender's hand and speaks softly of his creditor's wealth. But when payment is due, he puts it off, makes excuses and asks for time. … With curses and revilement the borrower pays him back, with abuse instead of honor. Many refuse to lend, not out of meanness, but from fear of being cheated to no purpose" (29:5–7).

56. Hezser 2005, 149–78.

57. Note the variant "his pleasure" in 4Q418 8 7. See also the commentary to 4Q418 81 10.

aged to develop a good relationship with this person (l. 13) while maintaining his dignity (l. 15). The person with whom he is speaking has some
degree of power over him. The text at hand likely discusses the person for
whom the addressee is working as a debt slave. He should speak with him
"according to his speech" (כלשונו), probably referring to the *mebin* speaking to his superior in a way that is direct and, presumably, in response to
whatever he had said to the addressee previously.[58] Line 8 provides a clear
rationale for speaking—so that the *mebin* will find what he desires rather
than shame. He is taught to cultivate a good relationship with his superior.
This is to ensure that he will trust and respect the addressee and not treat
him harshly as a laborer.

The general posture endorsed is that the *mebin* should be responsible
in his duties as a debt slave and try to maintain his dignity in a difficult
situation. The legitimacy of the bonded labor is never questioned. 4Q416
2 ii 8 stresses that he should not be rebellious towards the person with
whom he is speaking, indicating that this individual has power over him.
He is urged not to abandon his obligations. Line 9 emphasizes that the
addressee be a diligent worker. He is similarly told in line 12 to hold fast
to his service. He should perform the work his supervisor asks him to do.

4Q416 2 ii 8–9

The *mebin* is told: "observe your mysteries" (ברזיכה השמר). The
term "mysteries" likely signifies the teachings he has received, in a general sense. The use of the term "mystery" to denote instruction reflects the
importance of the mystery that is to be for the education of the intended
audience of 4QInstruction.[59] He is urged to "understand your mysteries"
in 4Q417 1 i 25 (see commentary below). The fact that he has become a
debt slave does not mean he should abandon the instruction he has been
given. 4Q416 2 iii 12–13 similarly encourages the *mebin* to study despite
being poor. The term "mysteries" in 4Q416 2 ii 8 may also signify direc-

---

58. Similar terminology refers in the Hebrew Bible to speaking or writing in a
foreign language (e.g., Neh 13:24; Esth 1:22; 3:12; 8:9; cf. 1QH 12:17). There is, however, no other evidence in 4Q416 2 ii or the rest of 4QInstruction that would support
positing a bi-lingual relationship between the addressee and his master. See Strugnell
and Harrington 1999, 99.

59. Goff 2005b, 57–67.

tives or important matters that his superior discussed with him, which he is not to divulge (cf. Sir 8:18).[60]

4Q416 2 ii 9–10

The *mebin* is to be a loyal and trusted worker. He is told, with some hyperbole, that when given work assignments he should not sleep until they are completed. The language is similar to Prov 6:4.[61] This text emphasizes going without sleep in order to highlight the dangers of going surety (see above on 4Q416 2 ii 4–6). Line 9 uses this language to underscore the importance of completing the assignments that he is given.[62]

Line 10 teaches that, while the addressee is to carry out assigned tasks with zeal, he should not to do anything beyond what is he required. He is to fulfill his responsibilities but not tolerate exploitation as a debt slave. 4Q416 2 ii 10 discusses not leaving anything undone for "him" (ואל תותר לו), presumably referring to his work supervisor. This probably regards the completion of designated assignments, in keeping with lines 8–9.[63] If the addressee does his work well, he will be respected by his master, who would then be more likely to honor the assigned period of obligation and release the debt slave when he is supposed to (cf. the discussion of the "intelligent slave" in l. 15 below).

The full context of the statement has not survived, but 4Q416 2 ii 10 mentions being humble, as part of an if-clause. This probably refers to the attitude the *mebin* should adopt toward his work. Line 10 also contains a reference to "tax money" (בלו הון).[64] The term has some sort of financial

---

60. The imperative השמר in 4Q416 2 ii 8 could denote that the addressee should "guard" his mysteries in the sense that he should not disclose any of the group's teaching to the person for whom he is working. See Murphy 2002, 183.

61. Proverbs 6:4 states that one should not give "sleep for your eyes" (שנה לעיניכה) and, in parallelism, "slumber for your eyelids" (תמונה לעפעפיך). 4Q416 2 ii 9 affirms that one should not have "rest in [your soul]" (מנוח ב[נפשכה]) or "slumber for your eyes" (תמונה לעיניכה).

62. 4Q417 2 i 21–22 is also similar to Prov 6:1–5, affirming that one should go without sleep until outstanding debts are paid off (see commentary below).

63. Ben Sira 33:30 uses the phrase אל תותר in relation to not being excessive in the treatment of slaves (cf. 32:1). See also Strugnell and Harrington 1999, 101; Hezser 2005, 304.

64. The word בלו is in construct with הון ("wealth"), together understood here as "tax money." This suggests that one should read the word as בלו rather than בלי ("without"), as Strugnell and Harrington (1999, 101) propose. In the Dead Sea Scrolls בלו is

meaning. The precise meaning of the word remains obscure, however. The assertion in line 11 that one will say "he has despised me" most likely refers to what the supervisor might say about the *mebin* if he does something wrong.

4Q416 2 ii 11–12

These lines urge the addressee to understand the zeal of man and the crookedness of the heart. The full context of the statement has not survived. It may have functioned as a reminder to the *mebin* that, while he should maintain good relations with his supervisor, he should not trust him.

Line 12 urges the addressee to hold fast to his service (עבודתו) and "the wisdom of his resources" (חכמת אוטו). "His service" refers to the work of the supervisor, which the *mebin* is to complete. This is in keeping with the teaching that he should take a responsible attitude towards the work assigned to him (ll. 8–9). The phrase "the wisdom of his resources" is more obscure. The term אוט is enigmatic, but probably refers to resources of some sort (see commentary on 4Q416 2 ii 1). Combined with "wisdom," the expression may refer to the ability of the person to whom the *mebin* is bonded to earn assets. The claim that the addressee should hold on to these would help explain why he should treat his duties responsibly—his supervisor has resources, with which he can support the *mebin* during the time he is working for him.

4Q416 2 ii 13

The addressee may be able to develop a good relationship with his supervisor. Familial language describes the relationship that the *mebin* should seek to attain with him. The addressee can become his "first-born son" (בן בכור) and the supervisor may show compassion to him, as one would to his only son (יחידו). Lines 15–16 assert that the *mebin* can become like a father to someone (see below). As the use of the *kaf* preposition in the last clause of line 13 suggests, this appeal to family language

---

only found in this line (and its parallel in 4Q418 8 11). It occurs three times in the Aramaic of Ezra (4:13, 20; 7:24). Its exact sense there is unclear, although it has some sort of economic meaning. It refers to some sort of tax or tribute imposed by the Persians, and is combined with terms for taxes, מדה/מנדה and הלך. See Goff 2003b, 161–62.

should probably not be understood literally but rather as drawing upon a father-son relationship to describe the ideal worker-supervisor dynamic.[65]

The assertion that the *mebin* will become like an only son may indicate that he is the only slave possessed by his master. While 4QInstruction contains no explicit evidence for this view, it is suggested by Ben Sira. Normally the sage takes a rather harsh attitude towards slaves (see the second excursus of this chapter). However, if the owner has only one, the tone is much more positive: "If you have but one slave, treat him like yourself. … If you have but one slave, deal with him as a brother; your life's blood went into his purchase" (33:31).[66] One should treat his single slave like a brother. Ben Sira turns to familial metaphors in the context of slavery, as does 4Q416 2 ii 14, but from the standpoint of the owner, whereas 4Q416 2 ii is addressed to a debt slave.

4Q416 2 ii 14

This important line provides an explanation for the idealized father-son relationship described in line 13. The *mebin* is called his "slave" (עבד) in lines 14 and 15.[67] Line 14 also describes him as "[his chos]en one" ([בחי]רו), which would emphasize that the supervisor appreciates the labor of the *mebin*.

4Q416 2 ii 14 expresses moderation and caution, classic themes in wisdom literature. While he is urged to develop a good relationship with his master, at the same time he should not trust him too much, other-

---

65. While these claims of kinship should probably not be interpreted literally, the adoption of slaves by their owners is attested in the ancient Near East. The practice underlies some of the narratives of Genesis, as in chapter 15, when the childless Abram describes his slave Eliezar of Damascus as his heir to ensure continuation of the family line (cf. Exod 21:4). 1 Chronicles preserves an account of a master adopting his slave. This text mentions a man named Sheshan who has daughters but no sons. He marries one of his daughters to his slave Jarha, not unlike Sarah giving Hagar to Abraham (2:34–35). Jarha sires Attai, who is considered a legitimate member of the family. Also note an Elephantine text from 416 B.C.E., in which a person by the name of Uriah asserts that neither he nor anyone else in his family shall enslave a person named Jedaniah, who instead shall be regarded as Uriah's son (B3.9). See Knobloch 1992, 1.78; Hezser 2005, 138; Porten and Yardeni 1986–1999, 2.84–85; Japhet 1993, 84.

66. For the reconstruction of this verse, see Di Lella and Skehan 1987, 404.

67. As discussed in the commentary on ll. 7–8, the focus of 4Q416 2 ii on the risks of standing surety, and the claim that the addressee will have to work without wages (l. 17), suggests that עבד should be translated "slave" rather than "servant."

wise he may come to hate the *mebin*. Such an attitude may result in the addressee becoming too confident. This would jeopardize the good relationship he has forged with his owner (cf. Sir 13:10–11). He should have a balanced and cool-headed approach to his situation as a debt slave.

Line 14 also urges that the *mebin* should not be anxious about his "distress" (מדהבה). The term, though somewhat obscure, suggests that the oppression he endures has a financial basis. The word is rare in ancient Jewish literature, but occurs two other times in 4QInstruction, in fragmentary contexts (4Q418 176 3; 4Q418a 16 3). Strugnell and Harrington understand it as "oppressive tax gatherer"; Elgvin translates "creditor."[68] The word occurs in the Hodayot and is associated with the difficulties endured by the poor.[69] There is a relevant cognate term, מדהוב, in the Damascus Document. CD 13:9–10 reads: "He [the Inspector] shall have pity on them like a father to his sons, and will heal all their affliction (וישקה לכל מדהובם) like a shepherd his flock. He will undo all the chains which bind them, so that there will be neither harassed nor oppressed in his congregation."[70] The text is not fully available at Qumran (see 4Q267 9 iv 6–7) and the verb, often read as וישקה, is damaged on the Geniza copy. Baumgarten recommends instead that one should read וישקוד.[71] 4Q416 2 ii 14 supports this reading, since the line combines this verb with מדהבה (where, unlike CD 13:9, it is negated).[72] This passage in CD 13 deals with

---

68. The meaning of the term suggested by Strugnell and Harrington (1999, 104), is based on the term מדהבה in the Hebrew Bible (see also p. 400). There it is a *hapax*, occurring only in Isa 14:4. The word מדהבה was understood by its Septuagint translators as ἐπισπουδαστής ("taskmaster") and in Symmachus and Theodotion as φορολογία ("tribute"/"collection of taxes"). Blenkinsopp suggests that they understood the crux instead as מרהבה, since רהב can refer to causing distress (Isa 3:5; cf. Sir 13:5). Note the use of this root in Prov 6:3, in the context of pleading before a neighbor on whose behalf one has gone surety. See Blenkinsopp 2000, 284; Murphy 2002, 183–84; Elgvin 1997a, 212.

69. "The soul of the poor one dwells with tumults in abundance and disastrous calamities (הוות מדהבה) dog my steps" (11:26; cf. 20:21; 26:11). The phrase הוות מדהבה occurs in 4Q418 176 3.

70. Hempel (1998, 116) considers the word מדהוב in CD 13:9 a problem and, following other commentators, emends it. The present discussion suggests this move is not required.

71. Baumgarten et al. 1996, 108–9. See also Broshi 1992, 35.

72. This difference is probably due to the semantic range of the verb לשקוד, which can mean "to watch over," "to guard" or, relatedly, "to be wakeful." לשקוד when used with מדהוב in CD 13:9 (without a negation) probably means that the Inspector will

the alleviation of economic distress suffered by members of the Dead Sea sect.[73] The text alludes to Isa 58:6–7, which proclaims a loosening of the bonds of injustice suffered by the poor. The "chains" and the "distress" (מדהוב) are likely economic in nature and thus probably refer to indebtedness. CD 13:9–10 supports the interpretation that מדהבה in 4Q416 2 ii 14 refers to economic "distress," alluding to the indebtedness of the *mebin* and his difficult situation as a debt slave.

4Q416 2 ii 15–16

The *mebin* who can properly carry out the moderation espoused in line 14 is told in line 15 to become an "[intellige]nt [slave]" (עבד משכי[ל]). This expression occurs in Proverbs to signify that one's labor is valued and trusted (14:35; 17:2).[74] Ben Sira uses the phrase in exactly this way: "Let an intelligent slave (עבד משכיל) be dear to you as your own self; refuse him not his freedom" (7:21; cf. 10:25).[75] The labor of a competent slave has great value. While this would be an incentive to retain him as long as possible, Ben Sira teaches that such a slave should engender respect and the allotted term of his servitude should be honored.[76] 4Q416 2 ii 14–15 urges one to become a slave of this sort in order to receive fair treatment.

Line 15 also urges that the addressee not debase himself before one who is not his equal (cf. l. 4; Prov 16:19). The *mebin* is to maintain a sense of dignity and self-worth in a potentially very degrading situation of debt slavery. While he should understand the value of appeasing his master, he is under no obligation to lower himself to someone beneath himself.

"watch over" or protect them from distress. The two words together, with a negation in 4Q416 2 ii 14, likely denote that one should not be excessively worried about distress.

73. Murphy 2002, 40–44.

74. Proverbs describes the "intelligent slave" as just as good as, if not better than, family. Fox's translation of Prov 17:2 reads: "An astute slave will rule over a disappointing son and divide an inheritance among brothers." The proverb teaches that such a slave (or servant) is better than a bad son, imagining the good slave as sharing in the inheritance allotted to family members. See Fox 2009, 624–25.

75. Note the parallel in Pseudo-Phocylides: "Provide your slave with the tribute he owes to his stomach. Apportion to a slave what is appointed so that he will be as you wish. Insult not your slave by branding him. Do not hurt a slave by slandering him to his master. Accept advice also from a kindly disposed slave" (ll. 223–227; cf. Prov 30:10; Philo, *Spec. Laws* 2.122). See Hezser 2005, 152; Horst 1978, 255–57.

76. Biblical law states that slaves were manumitted after six years or in the jubilee year (Exod 21:2; Lev 25:39–43; Deut 15:12–15).

While he can become a sort of son to his supervisor (l. 13), he can become
a father to people who are not of his social status; presumably this means
they would be of a lower level than the *mebin*.

4Q416 2 ii 16

The *mebin* should not attempt to attain what is beyond his capability.
What he should not try to acquire is unstated. But if he does so he may
experience great shame. Strugnell and Harrington suggest that the line
teaches one to refrain from striking other men (particularly those who
are stronger).[77] For the sense of "to strike," however, the verb נגע normally
takes a *bet* (e.g., Gen 26:11; Josh 9:19). This verb normally does not take a
lamed preposition, as is the case in 4Q416 2 ii 16. The interpretation that
the *mebin* should not strain to reach something he cannot attain is consistent with the general emphasis of the debt slave instruction of lines 7–17
that he should accept his situation (e.g., ll. 9, 10). The caution of line 16
also accords with traditional wisdom.

4Q416 2 ii 17

Risky financial entanglements can jeopardize the elect status of the
addressee. This sentiment forms a sort of inclusio for the debt slavery pericope (ll. 7–17), since lines 6–7 assert that no price is equal to his holy
spirit (cf. l. 18). Line 17 urges that the *mebin* not exchange (מכר) his "soul"
(נפש) for wealth. Line 18 uses similar terms, such as the verb "exchange,"
and makes explicit that he should not jeopardize his elect status, described
with the terms "glory" and "inheritance," by poor financial decisions. The
word נפש in line 17, I suggest, should be understood in a somewhat parallel fashion, signifying the elect status of the addressee. This also echoes
lines 6–7, which assert that he should not exchange his "holy spirit" for
a price. This theme is invoked as an incentive to avoid unsound financial dealings. Since this passage is written to a debt slave, line 17 may also
mean that one should not exchange his soul *in addition to* having already
handed over his body (to a creditor) to work as a slave. The line seeks a way
for the *mebin* to find dignity in a potentially very demeaning situation.

It is good for the addressee to be a "slave in spirit" (עבד ברוח). This
phrase provides a theological understanding of his situation of servitude.
As a debt slave, he is working not for a salary but to pay off a debt. Since his

---

77. Strugnell and Harrington 1999, 105.

elect status includes affinity with the angels, worldly recompense is not his main priority (4Q418 81 4–5). Line 17 also affirms that the *mebin* should work for his oppressors (נוגשיכה) without wages. The Hebrew Bible uses this verb to describe oppression that is associated with debts (Deut 15:2; cf. Isa 58:3). This supports the view that the passage is addressed to a debt slave. The expression "slave in spirit" may also remind him that, during his time as a debt slave, he should remember that his ultimate master is God.[78] His "spirit," like his "glory" (l. 18), expresses his special connection to the heavenly world. He should remember his privileged status while working as a lowly debt slave.

4Q416 2 ii 17–18

Given the prominence of warnings against surety in this column, the claim that one should not exchange one's glory for a price is probably another assertion not to go surety.[79] The teaching also encourages one to avoid risky financial entanglements in general. "Glory," in parallelism with "inheritance," refers to the elect status of the addressee (cf. the phrase "inheritance of glory" in 4Q416 2 iii 11–12).[80] The text echoes 4Q416 2 ii 6, which instructs that one should not trade his "holy spirit" for wealth. When the addressee makes poor financial decisions, he jeopardizes not only his material well-being but also his elect status. 4Q416 2 ii 18 asserts that by giving up his glory for a price the *mebin* will lose his "body" (גויתכה). Caquot has suggested that instead of "your body" one read "your dignity" (גיותכה). The "body" reading (גיותכה) endorsed in DJD 34 should be preferred.[81] The word גויה occurs several times in 4QInstruction, normally as a reference to the human body.[82] So understood, the term helps establish that not only the elect status of the *mebin* is at risk

---

78. Compare Isa 42:1, which mentions an עבד upon whom God has placed his spirit. See Hezser 2005, 327–32.

79. The variant in 4Q417 2 ii 23 (אל תערב הון; "do not pledge wealth") provides a better reading of the text than 4Q416 2 ii 18, which reads אל תערבהו ("do not pledge it").

80. Note the fragmentary phrase "your glory in your inheritance" in 4Q416 2 iv 11. The word כבוד ("glory") is a prominent term throughout 4QInstruction, also occurring in 4Q416 2 iii 9, 12, 18; 4Q417 1 i 13; 4Q417 2 i 11; 4Q417 20 5; 4Q418 69 ii 14; 4Q418 81 5; 4Q418 126 ii 8, 9; 4Q418 159 ii 6; 4Q418 162 4; 4Q418 185a + b 4.

81. Strugnell and Harrington 1999, 107; Caquot 1996, 11. He understands the line in question as l. 23.

82. In 4Q415 11 6 (par. 4Q418 167a + b 6) the word is used to describe blemishes

but that his physical body is as well. The verb יוריש expresses that he risks dispossession of his own body by practicing surety.

4Q416 2 ii 18–21

The bulk of this section comprises a series of vetitives, or admonitions that are negated, which emphasize moderation. In terms of both form and content they are in strong continuity with the wisdom tradition.[83] They teach that one should live within his means.[84] Gluttony would surely have been frowned upon by the author of 4QInstruction but, strictly speaking, that is not the main thrust of this passage (cf. Prov 25:16; 27:7; 30:8; Sir 29:23). Rather, it is a question of priorities. One should not, for example, enjoy "fine food" (תענוג) when he does not have bread (4Q416 2 ii 19–20). While there is little reason to think that the intended audience had much access to luxury foods, items of this sort are not as such condemned. One should not buy them if he would then not have enough money for basic necessities. Ben Sira 18:33 offers a good parallel: "Become not a glutton and a winebibber with nothing in your money-bag."[85]

The moderate and balanced attitude endorsed in 4Q416 2 ii 18–21 is associated with a claim that the *mebin* is poor (רוש). The beginning of column iii continues discussion of this theme. 4Q416 2 iii 2 states "and remember that you are poor (ראש)." 4QInstruction does not simply provide instruction for people who are dealing with material hardship but also emphasizes that the envisioned addressee should remember that he is "poor" (see section 9 of the introduction). This reminder, mentioned repeatedly in 4QInstruction (especially in 4Q416 2 iii, in lines 2, 8, 12, 19), suggests that the poverty of the *mebin* does not simply signify material hardship.[86] 4QInstruction teaches him what it means to be poor. Poverty can represent ethical ideals espoused by the composition. This is also the case in the book of Proverbs (e.g., 15:16–17). In 4Q416 2 ii 20 being poor is connected to moderation. In 4Q416 2 iii 15–16 it is associated with filial piety.

---

on the body of a wife. See also 4Q416 2 ii 4 (par. 4Q418 9 + 9a–c 2). The term may denote a corpse in 4Q418 127 3.

83. Collections of vetitives are found, for example, in Prov 3:25–31; 22:22–28 and Sir 7:34–8:19.

84. Strugnell and Harrington 1999, 106; Kister 2003, 367; Murphy 2002, 189.

85. Rey 2009a, 87; Di Lella and Skehan 1987, 292.

86. Goff 2003b, 148–55; Wold 2007, 140–53.

4QInstruction can also link the poverty of the addressee to his elect status. It is construed as something more valuable than material wealth (e.g., ll. 6–7).[87] Understanding this explains the full statement of the reminder of poverty in 4Q416 2 ii 20, which tells him not to "glorify yourself (תתכבד) with what you lack (מחסורכה) for you are poor." This verb in the *hithpael* refers to boasting in other wisdom texts and this seems to be the meaning here.[88] The term מחסור is also prominent in 4QInstruction (see commentary on 4Q417 2 i 17–18). Rather than worry that the addressee will become morose or despondent because of his poverty, he must be cautioned not to boast about it (cf. 4Q417 2 i 9). This suggests that the *mebin* understood his poverty not simply in material terms but also as an aspect of, or indicative of, his elect status.

The last visible statement of 4Q416 2 ii has received much attention.[89] The end of line 21 states, according to the transcription in DJD 34, וגם אל תקל כלי [ח]יקכה ("And also, do not dishonor the vessel of your [bo]som"). One could read חיקכה or חוקכה. Strugnell suggests that כלי signifies one's wife, as a term for the vagina, which, *pars pro toto*, refers to the woman as a whole.[90] The phrase אשת חיקכה, which occurs twice in 4Q416 2 iv (ll. 5, 13), clearly refers to a man's wife (see the commentary on this text). This supports reading חיקכה rather than חוקכה in 4Q416 2 ii 21. The line, so understood, helps encourage a male addressee not to slight his wife but rather treat her with dignity and respect.

Elgvin argues that the word כלי is a euphemism not for the vagina but rather the phallus.[91] The line thus stresses self-control and restraint. The word has this meaning, he points outs, in 1 Sam 21:6 (Eng. v. 5).[92] For Elgvin, 4Q416 2 ii 21 is similar to 1QS 7:12–14, which stipulates punishment for members of the Dead Sea sect who uncover the penis, euphemis-

---

87. Murphy 2002, 167.

88. Kister (2003, 367) claims that this line is based on Prov 12:9. See also Strugnell and Harrington 1999, 108. Also note Sir 10:28: "Honor yourself with humility" (בענוה כבד נפשך). Cf. 3:10; Prov 10:26.

89. Strugnell and Harrington 1999, 108–10; Strugnell, 1996, 537–47; García Martínez 2006, 24–28; Wold 2005a, 205–11; Kister 2003, 365–70; Smith 2001, 499–504; Elgvin 1997b, 604–19.

90. Strugnell and Harrington 1999, 108.

91. Elgvin 1997b, 607.

92. This verse reads: "David answered the priest, 'Indeed women have been kept from us always when I go on an expedition; the vessels of the young men are holy even when it is a common journey.'"

tically described as the יד ("hand"). Elgvin's basic interpretation of the line has been endorsed by Smith.[93]

In 2003 Kister proposed a completely different understanding of the line.[94] He transcribes the key phrase as בלי חוקכה, which he translates: "And do not be disgraced by (living) not according to your prescribed portion."[95] Florentino García Martínez, in an issue of *Dead Sea Discoveries* fittingly devoted to John Strugnell, questions Kister's reading and defends Strugnell's transcription of כלי יקכה[ח].[96] García Martínez points out that the *kaf* is more easily recognizable in the earlier PAM photos, such as PAM 40.613 (taken in May 1953), as opposed to later ones.[97] García Martínez's analysis of the photos of the fragments, and his defense of Strugnell's transcription, are reasonable.[98] The validity of Strugnell's reading has been affirmed independently by both Rey and Tigchelaar.[99] In the parallel text 4Q417 2 ii 26 the disputed letter clearly has an upward flourish on the top stroke that can be easily read as a *bet*. The letter *kaf* in this fragment can also have a heightened upward tick, making it difficult to distinguish from the *bet*.[100] This suggests that one should resolve the issue not simply by orthographic analysis but by determining which materially possible transcription produces the best reading. Whereas Kister's proposal is somewhat awkward, reading כלי יקכה[ח] as a reference to the wife of the addressee, as Strugnell originally suggested, should be endorsed. The view that he

---

93. Smith 2001, 499–504.

94. Kister 2003, 366.

95. This interpretation in part depends on Kister's understanding of תקל as a *niphal* rather than a *hiphil* (Kister 2003, 367). As the present discussion suggests, the common understanding of the verb as a *hiphil* (meaning "to make light" or "to treat with contempt") makes sense.

96. García Martínez 2006, 28.

97. PAM 43.511, the standard photo used for 4Q416 2 ii, was taken in June 1960. By this point some deterioration had occurred in the relevant portion of the column. See García Martínez 2006, 27.

98. In 4Q416 2 ii 21 the relatively short top stroke and more rounded descending stroke of this letter are more consistent with the *kaf* than the *bet*.

99. Rey 2009a, 67; Tigchelaar 2001, 47. Wold (2005a, 211) argues that the transcriptions of both Strugnell and Kister are possible. See also Kampen 2011, 66.

100. García Martínez 2006, 28. Examine the word תתכבד in 4Q417 2 ii 25 (par. 4Q416 2 ii 20) in PAM 43.516. The *kaf* and *bet* of this word are very similar. Tigchelaar 2001, 57, and Strugnell and Harrington 1999, 193, transcribe כלי in l. 26 of this fragment. Comparison with the word כסות in l. 25 (par. 4Q416 2 ii 19) illustrates that the letter *kaf* can be written in different ways.

should respect his wife is in keeping with 4QInstruction's teaching on marriage. 4Q416 2 iii 20, for example, asserts that he should take a wife "in your poverty," which denotes in the composition not only material hardship but also values that are encouraged, such as humility (see commentary below).

Strugnell's reading of the crux, however, should be modified somewhat. The word כלי, which he interprets as "vagina" signifying the wife in general, means "instrument" or "vessel" and thus can denote a wide range of things. The phrase "your bosom" restricts the meaning of כלי. When the word חיק occurs as the second member of a construct chain, the term refers not to the person whose "bosom" is discussed but rather his or her spouse. In Deut 28:54, for example, a man's wife is called אשת חיקו and in v. 56 a woman's husband is a איש חיקה (see also the commentary on 4Q416 2 iv 5). This suggests that, *contra* Elgvin, the "vessel" does not refer to the phallus of the addressee but rather the wife.

One problem with Strugnell's interpretation, as he himself admits, is that כלי does not mean "wife" elsewhere in the Hebrew Bible or early Jewish literature.[101] The word כלי can, however, refer to the human body. This is the case, for example, in Sir 33:10: "So, too, all people are of [ves]sels of clay (כ[לי] חמר [E]), and from earth humankind was formed" (cf. 27:5; Gen 2:7). The speaker of the Hodayot metaphorically refers to himself as a "broken vessel" (כלי אובד; 12:10). כלי in 4Q416 2 ii 21, I would suggest, similarly denotes the human body. Given the full construct phrase "vessel of your bosom," the body in question would be that of his wife. As discussed in the commentary on 4Q416 2 iv, the composition emphasizes the man's possession of the wife's body. 4Q416 2 ii 21 is consistent with this perspective, describing the wife as if she were part of the man's "bosom." 4QInstruction stresses not only the man's control over the woman but also his obligation to treat her with dignity and respect. 4Q416 2 ii 21 makes this point by teaching that he should not "dishonor" her. The phrase "the vessel of your bosom" implies both ownership and intimacy, with regard to a man's relationship with his wife.

4Q416 2 ii 21 and 1 Thessalonians 4:4

Following a suggestion by Pierre Benoit, Strugnell claims that the phrase "vessel of your bosom" in 4Q416 2 ii 21 can assist in the inter-

---

101. Strugnell and Harrington 1999, 108; Smith 2001, 501.

pretation of a well-known crux in 1 Thess 4:4: "that each of you know how to control your own vessel (τὸ ἑαυτοῦ σκεῦος κτᾶσθαι), in holiness and honor."[102] New Testament scholars have debated the meaning of this verse. They are divided as to whether "vessel" (σκεῦος) denotes one's body in general, his penis, or his wife.[103] Strugnell suggests that 4Q416 2 ii 21 resolves this issue, arguing that σκεῦος in 1 Thess 4:4 should be understood along the lines of his interpretation of כלי in the 4QInstruction passage. Both terms, he suggests, refer to the wife and both passages encourage one not to slight his wife but rather treat her in a respectful manner. Elgvin agrees that the line is important for the interpretation of 1 Thess 4:4, but on the basis of כלי (and σκεῦος) as a euphemism for the phallus.[104] 1 Thess 4:4 is understood analogously as containing an exhortation for one to "guard his member," that is, to exert self-control over his sexual desires.

It does seem, as Benoit originally discerned, that 1 Thess 4:4 is in fact a good parallel to 4Q416 2 ii 21. The emphasis on "your *own* vessel" in the New Testament verse conveys a meaning that is similar to "bosom" in the line of 4QInstruction—that the "vessel" belongs to the addressee. The idea of treating one's "vessel" with honor is in both texts. The Thessalonians verse is ambiguous, but 4Q416 2 ii 21 provides new evidence that can be used to support the view that the "vessel" of 1 Thess 4:4 is one's wife.[105] In both passages, a reasonable interpretation is that one should not mistreat his "vessel," referring to his wife. It does not denote her vagina but her body as a whole, which is possessed by her husband (cf. 1 Pet 3:7).[106]

---

102. Strugnell and Harrington 1999, 109.

103. Fee 2009, 145–50; Furnish 2007, 89–91.

104. Elgvin 1997b, 617–19.

105. Fee 2009, 150, argues that the verse in 1 Thessalonians should be read in a manner similar to how Elgvin reads 4Q416 2 ii 21, as a call for a man "to master his vessel," that is, his penis. Fee (2009, 147) argues against understanding σκεῦος as "wife," apparently not aware of the parallel in 4QInstruction: "If Paul had meant 'wife,' why not say 'wife' rather than use this otherwise unknown metaphor?"

106. Wold 2005b, 196–97.

4.
4Q416 2 III

Parallel texts: 4Q417 2 ii (broken underline); 4Q418 9–11 (underline)

TEXT[1]

1   ל וא   [וֹכוֹ֗ל]
   [כֹ֯ה

2   וזכור כי ראש אתה]   ○[
ומחסורכה

3   ל[א תמצא ובמַעלכַה ת○○○]   אם   ○ים[
פֿ֗וקד לכה

4   אל תשלח ידכה בו פן תכוה [ו]באשו תבער גויתכה כא[שׁר לקח]ת֗וֹ
בן השיבהו

5   ושמֹ vacat חה לַכה אם תנקה ממנו וגם מכל איש ליֹא ידעֹתה אל
תקח הוַן

6   פֿן יוסיף על ר֯ישכה ואם שמו ברא'שֹ֗כֹה למות הפקידהו ורוחכה אל
תחבל

7   בו ואז תשכב עם האמת ובמותכה יפרֹ[ח ל]עו[ו]לֹ֗ם זכרכה ואחריתכה
תנחל

8   שמֹחֹה vacat אביון אתה אל תתאו זֹ֗וֹלֹת נחלתכה ואֹל תתבלע בה פן
תסיג

9   גבולכה וֹאֹ֗ם י֗שיבכה לכבוד בה התהלך וברז נהיה דרוש מולדיו וֹאֹ֯ז
תדע

10   נחלתו ובצדק תתהלך כֹ֯י יֹגֹיֹה אל ת֗[אר]הֹ֗וֹ בכל דרכיכה למכבדיכה
תֹן הֹדֹר

1. Strugnell and Harrington 1999, 110–23; Tigchelaar 2001, 47–48; Rey 2009a, 92–96, 183–84; Elgvin 1997a, 221–32. The textual notes section, unless otherwise noted, refers to these works.

11 ושמו הלל תמיד כי מראש הרים רא^ישכה ועם נדיבים הושיבכה
ובנחלת

12 כבוד המשילכה רצונו שחר תמיד *vacat* אביון אתה אל תאמר̊ רש אני
ול[וא]

13 אדרוש דעת בכל מוסר הבא שכמכה ובכל] °[צרוף לבכה וברוב
בי̊נ̊ה̊

14 מחשבותיכה רז נהיה דרוש והתבונן בכל דרכי אמת וכל שורשי עולה

15 תביט ואז תדע מה מר לאיש ומה̊ מתוק לגבר כבוד אביכה ברי̊שכה

16 ואמכה במצעדיכה כי כאב לאיש כן אבי̊הו̊ וכאדנים לגבר כן אמו כי

17 המה כו̊ר הוריכה וכאשר המשילמה בכה ז̊יצו̊ על הרוח כן עובדם
וכאשר

18 גלה אוזנכה ברז נהיה כבדם למען כבודכה וב̊] [ה̊ד̊ר̊ פניהמה

19 למען חייכה וארוך ימיכה *vacat* ואם רש אתה כשה°]

[

20 בלוא חוק *vacat* אשה לקחתה ברי̊שכה קח מולדי̊]ה̊

[

21 מרז נהיה בהתחברכה יחד התהלך עם עזר בשרכה] ככתוב על כן
יעזב איש[

bottom margin

Translation

1 [And all …] your …
2 And remember that you are poor … and what you need
3 you shall not find and in your disloyalty you will [… *if*] one
entrusts [*an item of value*] to you,
4 do not set your hand upon it, lest you will be burned [*and*] with its
fire your body will be ablaze. A[*s*] you [have tak]en it, so return it,
5 and you will have joy if you are free from it. And also, from any
man whom you do not know do not take money,
6 lest it increase your poverty. And if he sets it on your head to
death, take responsibility for it, but do not let your spirit be seized
7 by him. And then you will lie in repose with the truth and when
you die your memory will bloss[om *for ev*]er and in the end you
will inherit

8 joy. *vacat* You are poor, desire nothing except your inheritance. And do not be confused about it lest you move

9 your boundary. And if he restores you to glory, walk in it and through the mystery that is to be study its origins. And then you will know

10 its inheritance. With righteousness you will walk because God will make his cou[*nten*]ance shine upon all your ways. To the one who glorifies you, give honor.

11 Praise his name always, for from poverty he has lifted your head and with the nobles he has set you. Over an inheritance

12 of glory he has given you dominion. Seek his favor always. *vacat* You are poor—do not say, "I am poor, so I will n[*ot*]

13 seek knowledge." Bring your shoulder under all instruction and in all ... purify your heart and with much intelligence

14 your thoughts. Study the mystery that is to be and examine closely all the ways of truth and all the roots of injustice

15 discern. And then you will know what is bitter to a man and what is sweet for a person. Honor your father in your poverty

16 and your mother in your lowly state, for as God is to man so is his father, and as Lord to a person so is his mother, for

17 they are the crucible that conceived you. And as he gave them dominion over you and appointed (them) over the spirit, so serve them. And as

18 he revealed to your ear the mystery that is to be, glorify them, for the sake of your glory and ... honor them

19 for the sake of your life and length of your days *vacat* And if you are poor as ...

20 without a statute. *vacat* The woman you have taken in your poverty, seize [*her*] birth times ...

21 from the mystery that is to be. When you marry, walk together with the help of your flesh. [*As it is written, "therefore a man leaves*]

TEXTUAL NOTES

iii 1. וֹכֹוֹלֹ. This reading, adopted by Rey and Tigchelaar, is quite tentative. Consult PAM 42.581.

iii 1. ל וא. These letters are based on Tigchelaar's placement of 4Q418 11 in his reconstruction of 4Q418 8–9 (p. 78).

iii 3. פֹּקֹד; 4Q418 9 2: פקדו.

iii 6. בראׁיֹשֹׁכֹה; 4Q418 9 5: ברוׁשכה.

iii 9. יושיבוכה ;4Q418 9 8: יֹשיבכה.

iii 9. נהֹיה. Consult PAM 42.597.

iii 9. מולדיו ;4Q418 9 8: [מוֹ]לדו.

iii 10. בֹ. 4Q418 9 9 may read בֹז, as Tigchelaar, Rey and the editors of DJD 34 suggest. The scribe who copied 4Q418 9 9 erroneously wrote much of the same material in the following line 10, which was at some point erased. Rey and Tigchelaar suggest that 4Q418 9 10 reads בֹ, but there is not enough ink to make a conclusive reading.

iii 10. בכל. The editors of DJD 34 transcribe בכיֹל, but the word has no supralinear letter. Rey reads בכול. No *waw* appears to be present (so too Tigchelaar). The erased line of 4Q418 9 10 (see above) may read [בֹ]כֹוֹל.

iii 10. למכבדיכה ;4Q418 9 9, 10: למכבדכה.

iii 11. כי ;4Q418 9 11: כיא.

iii 11. ועם ;4Q418 9 11: עם.

iii 13. בכל ;4Q418 9 13: בכול.

iii 13. ובכל ;4Q418 9 14: וֹבֹכֹ[ו]ל.

iii 14. מחשבתיכה ;4Q418 9 14: מחשבותיכה.

iii 14. בכל ;4Q418 9 15: בכול.

iii 14. וכל ;4Q418 9 15: וכול.

iii 15. כבוד ;4Q418 9 17: כבד.

iii 16. במצעדיכה ;4Q418 9 17: במצעֹריכה. Tigchelaar and the editors of DJD 34 also give this transcription for 4Q416 2 iii. Rey transcribes במצעריכה in both texts. The reading of the disputed letter is difficult in both texts, particularly 4Q416 2 iii 16. Semantically, as discussed below, במצעריכה is to be preferred.

iii 16. כאב ;4Q418 9 17: כאל.

iii 17. המשילמֹה ;4Q418 9 18: המשילֹ{כה}ם. The letter *kaf* was erased and the *he* emended into a final *mem*.

iii 17. יֹצֹו. Following Rey. The editors of DJD 34 and Tigchelaar read יֹצֹר. If the last letter of the word were a *resh* one would expect its visible bottom tip to touch the base of the preceding *sade*.

iii 20. מולד[י]ֹה [. מולדֹי[כה] is also possible and one could transcribe מולדֹו.

Commentary

4Q416 2 iii is one of the most significant, and best preserved, texts of 4QInstruction. Several major themes of the composition are prominent in this column. These include caution in financial affairs (ll. 3–8) and the need for the addressee to study and learn, especially about the nature of his elect status (ll. 8–15). 4Q416 2 iii also provides instruction on parents (ll. 15–19) and marriage (ll. 20–21). The teaching on marriage is continued in 4Q416 2 iv.

4Q416 2 iii 1–3

Very little of lines 1–3 is extant. The addressee's poverty and material needs are topics in this section. The phrase "And remember that you are poor" is preserved in line 2. The term for "poor" (רש) is prominent, with several variant spellings, in this column (ll. 6, 11, 12, 15, 19, 20). 4Q416 2 iii 2 is one of several reminders that occur throughout 4QInstruction that urge the addressee to realize that he is poor. These reminders are particularly prominent in this column (ll. 2, 8, 12, 19; cf. 15).[2] The lost instruction of lines 1–3 was apparently in continuity with the end of 4Q416 2 ii, which also discusses the poverty of the *mebin* (l. 20). The "poverty" of the addressee in 4Q416 2 iii 2 denotes genuine hardship. Lines 2–3 assert that he will not find what he needs (מחסורכה) (cf. 4Q418 127 1). מחסור is frequent in 4QInstruction, signifying the addressee's lack of resources for his basic needs (see the commentary on 4Q417 2 i 17–18). His inability to fulfill his basic needs is discussed elsewhere in the composition (e.g., ll. 19–20).

4Q416 2 iii 3–5

These lines preserve a statement in which the *mebin* is warned not to touch an item that has been entrusted to him. Utilizing it would run the risk of physical injury. He would burn his "body" (גויה; l. 4; cf. Sir 8:10). His body is similarly placed in jeopardy by going surety (4Q416 2 ii 18). He will be rid of the anxiety produced by keeping the item when he returns it, which he should therefore do (ll. 4–5). At that point the *mebin* will experience "joy."[3]

The nature of the item possessed by the *mebin* and the one who owns it are unknown. He is told not to do anything with the item in question (l. 4). This suggests that the addressee can use it, but, in the opinion of the author, he should not. The *mebin* may have had the right of usufruct (the legal right of a person to benefit from property that is owned by another).

---

2. Consult section 9 of the introduction.

3. Joy is elsewhere associated with the eschatological rewards of the addressee. See below on ll. 7–8.

To identify the item commentators have turned to the traces of a word סי□ that precedes פוקד. Strugnell and Harrington have suggested reconstructing כסף ערבים (lit. "silver of pledges"), proposing that a deposit has been given in pledge to the addressee.[4] Murphy has suggested that the deposit should be understood as a dowry, which the man had the right to use as long as the marriage existed.[5] If this were the case, however, 4QInstruction's insistence that the item should be returned to its owner becomes difficult to explain. Elgvin has proposed reconstructing חפצים, in the sense of "assets."[6]

It is not clear, however, that one should understand סי□ as from the word that describes the item(s) that have been entrusted to the addressee. Not enough text survives to be confident that these letters are from what was originally the object of the verb. Line 4 refers to the item in question with a singular suffix ("do not set your hand upon it [בו]"), complicating the view that סי□ is the end of a plural word denoting "pledges" or "assets." The item in question remains unknown.

4Q416 2 iii 3–5 may discuss the deposit of a pledge, as Strugnell and Harrington argue.[7] But this is by no means obvious. If the addressee receives a pledge in these lines he would not be standing surety, as is the case in 4Q416 2 ii, since in that column he *gives* a pledge. Given his material hardship (e.g., ll. 2–3), the *mebin* should certainly not be understood as a creditor, who receives collateral from a third party to guarantee a loan. Also, surety terms, such as ערב or חבל, are not extant in these lines.[8]

A simpler explanation is that 4Q416 2 iii 3–5 discusses the issue of safekeeping an item of value. People today can keep valuables in a safe deposit box at a bank, but in the ancient world this option was in general not available.[9] The Code of Hammurabi provides substantial legisla-

---

4. Strugnell and Harrington 1999, 114.

5. Murphy 2002, 189–90. In Mur 115 (one of the texts from Murabbaʿat), for example, a person is required to return the dowry of a marriage after getting a divorce. Consult Rey 2009a, 98.

6. Elgvin 1997a, 221. This word is associated with material and financial concerns in 4QInstruction. See the commentary on 4Q418 126 ii 12.

7. I have previously endorsed their interpretation. See Goff 2003b, 142.

8. The word חבל is used in the financial teaching that follows the statement at hand (l. 6).

9. Baker 2009, 62–74; 2006, 27–42.

tion on safekeeping.[10] This composition makes clear the risks entailed by taking responsibility for items owned by another. If a person stores grain at another person's house and a loss of grain occurs, because the homeowner used it or for some other reason, he is to repay the owner of the grain twofold (§120; cf. 124). If the material is stolen from the person's house, he is to make restitution for the lost item to its owner (§125). Biblical law similarly states the person keeping the item may be liable if it is stolen from his house (Exod 22:6–7 [Eng. vv. 7–8]). The biblical laws on safekeeping establish that, even if the loss is not his fault, the homeowner would have to pay restitution for material under his care that became lost. Against this legal background, 4Q416 2 iii 3–5 becomes intelligible. 4QInstruction's attitude toward safekeeping is consistent with the work's general posture toward financial affairs—caution and awareness of the addressee's economic vulnerability are guiding concerns.

4Q416 2 iii 5–6

A new unit begins in 4Q416 2 iii 5, marked with וגם ("And also …"), that continues to the *vacat* in line 8. The *mebin* is warned not to accept money from a person whom he does not know. Here again 4QInstruction espouses a wary posture toward economic issues. The composition does not like risky financial dealings with people who are known to the addressee (4Q416 2 ii 3–7). It is not surprising that the text is leery with regard to borrowing from people who are unfamiliar.

The admonition not to take money in 4Q416 2 iii 5 likely refers to receiving a loan from a creditor who is not personally known by the addressee.[11] 4QInstruction gives teachings elsewhere regarding proper interaction with creditors. 4Q417 2 i 21–22, for example, urges the addressee not to lie to his creditor and to repay him diligently. The *mebin* could easily be in need of credit and thus would need creditors upon whom he could rely. They could charge excessive interest and in general treat their clients with impunity. Given this climate, it makes sense to know the creditor so that the *mebin* can assess how he would be treated by him.

---

10. The Mesopotamian law collection the Laws of Eshnunna also deals with the issue of safekeeping. See Baker 2009, 62–63. Also note Ahiqar 99 (sg.): "If your master will deposit (with) you water to watch, [do not] drink." The statement that follows probably urges the addressee not to touch gold owned by his master.

11. One could posit that the line is about receiving items for safekeeping, although it would not be clear why a stranger would entrust something with the addressee.

The beginning of line 6 provides a rationale for not taking money from an unknown person—the act may increase the poverty of the addressee. The emphasis on "increase" (יוסיף) suggests that the concern is not simply loan repayment but the extra or excessive interest that might be demanded. There is a pun on the word "poverty" (ריש) with "head" (ראוש) in line 6 (as in l. 11), with both terms emphasizing that the *mebin* is obliged to repay a creditor whom he does not know.

4Q416 2 iii 6–7

If the person whom the addressee does not know charges him with repayment, the *mebin* is to take responsibility for it.[12] Neither the subject nor the antecedent of the suffix of שמו (if "he sets it") is explicit, but they can be reasonably understood as the creditor and the loan, respectively.[13] The phrase למות is translated in DJD 34 as "until death." This meaning is better suited, however, to עד מות. The expression למות probably does not mean that the *mebin* has until he dies to pay off the loan.[14] Rather, being charged to repay the loan "to death" probably means that he is threatened with death to ensure repayment.[15] Creditors could easily intimidate or threaten the borrower. 4Q417 2 i 24–25 discusses the possibility that a lender may have the *mebin* beaten. Elsewhere מות with a *lamed* refers to people who are about to die. Note, for example, Prov 24:11: "Save those who are being taken away to death (למות), and those who are tottering on (the brink of) slaughter, do not stint (in helping)."

4Q416 2 iii 6 qualifies the assertion that the *mebin* should repay the loan with a phrase that probably begins with a disjunctive *waw*—but he should not let his spirit be "seized by him." The antecedent of "him" (or "it"; בו) is either the loan or the creditor. Semantically the latter option is to

---

12. I read with other commentators the word הפקידהו as an imperative with a suffix. Note the *plene* spelling. In terms of biblical Hebrew one would expect הפקד. See Strugnell and Harrington 1999, 112; Kampen 2011, 72; Rey 2009a, 94, 99; Qimron 2008, 19.

13. The suffix of the verb הפקידהו most likely has the same antecedent as שמו, namely, the money (הון) that the addressee received.

14. Debt contracts from the ancient world often stipulate that, if the lender dies without paying back the loan, his surviving family members become obliged to do so. See, for example, the Elephantine text classified as B3.1 (cited in the excursus on debt slavery in chapter 2). See also Rey 2009a, 99.

15. The phrase may also have this meaning in 4Q418 127 1 (cf. Ps 118:18; Jer 43:11; Sir 51:6). See Fox 2009, 747.

be preferred.[16] The addressee is to give the creditor what is owed him, but he should not give him anything beyond that (cf. 4Q416 2 ii 9–10). Otherwise he may "seize" the spirit of the *mebin*. The verb תחבל can be read as a *piel* (or a *pual*), meaning "to destroy" or "to ruin" (e.g., Isa 13:5; Qoh 5:5). The financial context, however, suggests its meaning in the *niphal*, signifying the seizure of pledged assets.[17] In light of the discussion of למות above, the seizure of the spirit of the *mebin* may refer to the possibility that he could be killed if he defaults on the loan. 4Q416 2 ii 6–7 exhorts the addressee not to exchange his "holy spirit" for wealth (cf. ll. 17–18). In the commentary above, I argued that this statement encourages the *mebin* to avoid unsound financial dealings by construing them as risking his elect status. 4Q416 2 iii 6–7 gives the same basic advice. He should repay the loan but never forget that he possesses a special "inheritance" that is superior to monetary wealth (cf. ll. 11–12). This helps him maintain his dignity and sense of self-worth while in a difficult situation of indebtedness. The assertion that the creditor may seize his spirit thus also functions as an incentive for the *mebin* to pay back the loan.

4Q416 2 III 7–8

These lines lay out the positive consequences of avoiding the financial entanglements described in the preceding lines. The addressee who does not lose his "spirit" will enjoy a good death, with his reputation intact as an upright person. This goal is also found in biblical wisdom and the Hebrew Bible in general (e.g., Prov 10:7). In 4Q416 2 iii 7 this classic trope is combined with the view that the addressee will receive a blessed afterlife (see section 6 of the introduction).[18] This is probably alluded to by the seemingly innocuous claim that he shall die "with the truth." "Truth" is a prominent term in the judgment scene of 4Q416 1 and throughout the

---

16. Strugnell and Harrington 1999, 115, prefer the other option. The preposition is probably the *bet* of manner.

17. Exod 22:25; Job 22:6; Sir 31:6. It has been argued that the root חבל refers to distraint, the confiscation of a debtor's property as punishment for violating the conditions of the loan. It has also been suggested that the verb refers to pledges that are hypothecary, meaning that it is agreed when the loan is made that the creditor will receive the pledge in the event of the loan's nonpayment. Since the *mebin* would not have agreed that the creditor could "seize" his spirit if the loan is not repaid, the former meaning of the word is more likely in 4Q416 2 iii 6. See Baker 2009, 270.

18. 4Q417 4 ii 3 stresses that one's name will "blossom" (יפרח) forever (cf. 4Q415 2 i + 1 ii 8).

composition helps express an affinity between God and the elect (see the commentary on 4Q416 1 10). The word "truth" in line 7 probably evokes the special inheritance of the *mebin*.

The anticipation of postmortem rewards is also evident in the claim that the addressee will "inherit joy" (תנחל שמחה). This phrase is prefaced by the word אחריתכה, which literally means "your end." The editors of DJD 34 understand this as the subject of the verb, translating "Your posterity will inherit joy."[19] So understood, if the *mebin* does not burden his surviving family members with outstanding debts when he dies, his children would inherit "joy."[20] This interpretation is intelligible, but the language of truth, inheritance, and joy elsewhere in 4QInstruction suggests that אחריתכה refers to the end of the addressee's life, at which point he will "inherit joy" (cf. Sir 7:36).[21] 4Q417 2 1 10–12 promises the addressee "eternal joy," a reference to eternal life (see commentary below). The use of the root נחל often refers in 4QInstruction to the special allotment in life given to the addressee by God, typically through the word "inheritance." Examples are discussed in the excursus below.

4Q416 2 iii 8–9

Lines 8–12 comprise a distinct unit, demarcated at its beginning and end with a *vacat*. This pericope begins with the phrase "You are poor" (אביון אתה) in line 8, as does the section that follows in line 12. Both are examples of the reminders of the poverty of the *mebin* that often occur in 4QInstruction (see section 9 of the introduction). 4Q416 2 iii 8–12 is important for understanding the envisioned addressee's "inheritance" and his "poverty."

4Q416 2 iii 8 teaches that, as a poor person, the *mebin* should focus on nothing but his inheritance. His poverty in this line does not simply denote material hardship but is also associated with broader teachings espoused by the composition. This includes knowledge that the addressee possesses an elect status which is superior to monetary wealth. This idea shapes the financial instruction of the composition (e.g., 4Q416 2 ii 6–7). His poverty

---

19. Strugnell and Harrington 1999, 116.

20. Rey 2009a, 101.

21. This interpretation is also consistent with the rest of l. 7, which does not stress the bequeathing of an estate to descendents but rather the death of the *mebin*. See also Kampen 2011, 72.

should not distract him from studying or understanding the nature of his elect status (ll. 12–13). What is truly important is his "inheritance."

The Inheritance of the *Mebin*

The term "inheritance" (נחלה) is paramount in 4QInstruction, occurring over thirty times. In the Hebrew Bible the word frequently has an economic meaning, denoting hereditary property—something to which a person is entitled but which that person does not yet fully possess (e.g., Ruth 4:5; Job 42:15). The word can also take on more theological meanings, describing a special allotment given to particular individuals by God. The Levites, for example, have no inheritance (נחלה) of land but Aaron has God as his "inheritance," signifying the dominion of the priests over the cultic apparatus (Num 18:20). 4QInstruction appropriates this meaning of the term and utilizes it to describe the elect status of the addressee. This is explicit in 4Q418 81 3, which claims that God himself is the special inheritance of the addressee: "He is your portion and your inheritance among the sons of Adam. [And over] his [in]heritance he has set you in authority." The line utilizes Num 18:20 to emphasize that his elect status makes him closer to God than other humans (see commentary on 4Q418 81 3 below).

4Q416 2 iii is important for understanding the inheritance of the *mebin*. Line 10 states that he will learn "its" inheritance (נחלתו) by studying the mystery that is to be. The antecedent is probably the word "glory" in line 9. This is suggested by lines 11–12, which claim that he has been given an "inheritance of glory" (נחלת כבוד; cf. Prov 3:35). In lines 7–8, discussed above, the addressee is to "inherit joy" when he dies (cf. 4Q416 4 3; 4Q418 185a + b 4). Rey understands 4Q416 2 iii 8–12 as revolving around two meanings of the term "inheritance," one referring to "l'héritage humain," denoting material wealth that is transferred from one generation to the next.[22] In the other the term signifies "l'héritage divine," the glory and holiness allocated to the addressee. While inheritance in the sense of transferring wealth to the next generation is not a major issue in 4QInstruction, Rey is correct that the addressee's inheritance has both worldly and heavenly aspects. 4QInstruction, reflecting a deterministic mindset, claims that everyone has an inheritance: "For God has distributed the

---

22. Rey 2009a, 56–57, 102.

inheritance of [eve]ry [living being]" (4Q418 81 20; cf. 4Q423 5 3). The composition also asserts that "from him [God] comes the inheritance of every living thing" (4Q416 3 2). The wicked are so because of the inheritance they have been given: "according to his inheritance (נחלתו) in it he (a wicked person) will be tr[eated as wicked]" (4Q417 1 i 24). The angels also have an inheritance: "the so[ns of] heaven, whose inheritance is eternal life" (4Q418 69 ii 12–13). All people have an inheritance or allotment from God that dictates their station in life. The mindset is similar to that of the Treatise on the Two Spirits, the dualistic scenario of which is an attempt to explain the "inheritance of man" (נחלת איש; 1QS 4:16).

The inheritance of the addressee, according to 4QInstruction, is much better than what most people have been given (cf. 1 En. 103:3). He is qualitatively different from other people. He has been separated from the "fleshly spirit," referring to humans that are unable to attain life after death (4Q418 81 1–2). He has an "inheritance of glory" (4Q416 2 iii 11–12). This includes affinity with the angels. His "inheritance" is connected to the claim that he has been placed in the "lot of the angels" in 4Q418 81 (ll. 4–5). This special inheritance is part of God's divine plan guiding reality and thus was established before the birth of the *mebin* (see below on l. 9). The vision of meditation passage teaches that he has a special connection to the angels (see commentary on 4Q417 1 i 17–18). The special inheritance given to the addressee includes eternal life after death. The angels possess this form of life and the trope that the addressee is to receive "eternal joy" should be understood as the prospect of life after death (consult the commentary on 4Q417 2 i 11–12). The claim in 4Q416 2 iii 7–8 that he will inherit joy alludes to this idea. This inheritance also includes access to supernatural revelation, in the form of the mystery that is to be.

4Q416 2 iii 8 continues with a vetitive that elaborates the teaching that the *mebin* should know his special inheritance. He should not be confused by "it," referring to his inheritance. The warning in lines 8–9 not to displace his boundary marker (פן תסיג גבולכה) derives from the Hebrew Bible, in which the phrase refers to people who move actual property markers. Proverbs 22:28, for example, exhorts: "Do not remove the ancient landmark (אל־תסג גבול עולם) that your ancestors set up" (cf. 23:10; Deut 19:14; 27:17; Hos 5:10). 4QInstruction reformulates this tradition. In 4Q416 2 iii 8–9 the phrase asserts that the inheritance of the *mebin* is his proper domain. Urging him not to move the boundary marker is a spatial metaphor that teaches him not to be confused about his inheritance, and to stay within his assigned allotment in his life. The metaphor asserts a deterministic understanding of his inheritance, in that it has been established as the proper station of the *mebin*. In 4Q416 2 iv 6 the expression describes another man who exerts authority over the addressee's wife.

4Q416 2 III 9

If God restores the addressee to glory, he should walk in "it." The feminine antecedent is probably the inheritance of the addressee.[23] "Glory" refers to the elect status of the addressee and denotes his reception of post-mortem rewards, his "inheritance of glory" (ll. 11–12). The imperative "walk," however, suggests that line 9 discusses his life in this world. In the *hithpael* the verb (התהלך) often refers to conduct in 4QInstruction (e.g., ll. 10, 21; 4Q416 2 iv 7; 4Q417 1 i 12).[24] It is implied that the *mebin* has gone astray from the teachings of 4QInstruction and that God might restore him. 4Q416 2 iii 9 never states what he has done wrong.[25] The return to glory signifies that the addressee has changed and is now living righteously and carrying out the ideals espoused by the composition.[26] The return to "glory" should not simply be associated with eternal life after death. This reward is predicated on ethical conduct during one's life.

4Q416 2 iii 9 also encourages the addressee to study the mystery that is to be. In 4QInstruction the *raz nihyeh* is the chief means by which the *mebin* can learn something (see section 5 of the introduction). Here he can learn "its origins" (מולדיו). The word מולד normally refers to birth (see commentary on l. 20). In 4Q416 2 iii 9 the term alludes, I suggest, to the special allotment in life that God had established for him. Like 4Q416 2 iii 8–12, 4Q417 2 i 10–12 asserts that through the mystery that is to be one can know who will inherit glory. This passage of 4Q417 2 i also claims that one can know "the birth times of salvation (מולדי ישע)." This reflects the view that a person's ultimate fate can be accessed through understanding one's time of birth (see commentary on 4Q417 2 i below). The most likely

---

23. The subject of the verb ישיב is most likely God. See Rey 2009a, 103.

24. This is the case in both the Hebrew Bible and early Jewish literature. Note, for example, Gen 3:8; Pss 35:14; 43:2; Sir 3:17; 1QS 3:18, 20, 21. See Rey 2009a, 173; Kampen 2011, 54.

25. The ambiguity surrounding the verb (ישיב) helps explain the variant in 4Q418 9 8 (יושיבו), which instead is a form of the verb "to sit" rather than "to restore" (cf. 4Q416 2 iii 11).

26. Strugnell and Harrington (1999, 117) suggest this may refer to a rise in the addressee's professional rank. Given his poverty, this is unlikely.

antecedent of "its origins" in 4Q416 2 iii 9 is "glory." This would fit with the connection between the "birth times of salvation" and inheriting glory in 4Q417 2 i 10–12. The phrase מולדיו, as part of a claim that the *mebin* can learn about the origins of his "glory," most likely expresses the idea that his "inheritance of glory" was established for him before his birth.[27]

4Q416 2 iii 9–10

These lines provide a rationale, marked with ואז ("And then …"), for the *mebin* to learn about "its origins." He will then know "its inheritance." The most likely antecedent is "glory," as with the term "origins" (see above). He will walk in righteousness. The verb "to walk" (in the *hithpael*, as in l. 9) refers to the addressee's conduct and his life in general. All his "ways" will receive divine favor, with God shining his countenance upon them (l. 10). The life of the *mebin* in this world will be somehow affected by this change, indicating, as in line 9, that "glory" does not refer exclusively to a blessed afterlife or other postmortem rewards for the elect.

4Q416 2 iii 10–11

The assertion that God will favor the *mebin* once he understands the nature of his inheritance is accompanied by an exhortation to praise God.[28] Lines 10–11 contain two parallel exhortations. Praising God is stressed elsewhere in the composition. 4Q417 1 ii 9 urges the addressee to bless him, even when beaten (see commentary below). 4Q418 81 exhorts the *mebin* to sing the praises of the holy ones, most likely a reference to the angels (ll. 1, 11–12; cf. 4Q418 126 ii 10; 4Q418 148 ii 8). Divine praise is an important part of 4QInstruction's education program. As the addressee comes to understand his "inheritance of glory," he learns more about God's dominion over the cosmos and his own privileged allotment in it (cf. 4Q417 1 i 6–12). Praising God is a natural result of, and thus a sign of, the addressee's comprehension of the natural world. Ben Sira provides a similar perspective. The wise person realizes the extent of God's grandeur: "But praise is offered by the tongue of the wise and its rightful master

---

27. Rey (2009a, 36) suggests that the line discusses the origins of the mystery that is to be.

28. The emphasis on praising God in this passage indicates that one should prefer reading the singular למכבדכה in 4Q418 9 9 over the plural variant למכבדיכה in 4Q416 2 iii 10. The plural form may reflect the view that he receives glory from the angels.

teaches it" (15:10; cf. 39:5). Ben Sira emphasizes this theme in connection to understanding God's creation of the cosmos (39:15; 43:30; cf. 11QPsᵃ 18:3–4). 4QInstruction evokes this theme in relation to the addressee's understanding of his own elect status.

4Q416 2 III 11–12

The composition provides an additional incentive for the addressee to praise God (cf. 4Q418 81 1, 11–12). The *mebin* has been lifted from poverty and placed with the "nobles" (נדיבים). He also has been given dominion over an "inheritance of glory" (נחלת כבוד). This refers to the elect status of the addressee (see excursus above; cf. 4Q416 2 ii 18). The verb המשיל, signifying the bequest of this status from God, is also employed in the claim that he is entrusted with the garden of Eden, a metaphor for his elect status (4Q423 1 2).[29] The assertion that he is being seated with the nobles is parallel to being lifted from poverty. Since this claim is explicitly connected to his reception of an "inheritance of glory," it is therefore reasonable to understand "nobles" as a reference to angels.[30] Admittedly the term נדיבים does not have this meaning elsewhere in ancient Jewish literature. The composition elsewhere associates the addressee's poverty and the "nobles" in unfortunately fragmentary texts (4Q418 177 5; cf. 4Q415 6 2). Given the superiority of his elect status to wealth, it makes sense to portray the angels as "nobles," as if the *mebin*, with limited access to material riches, is placed among an elite class—not worldly aristocrats but rather the angels in heaven (cf. 4Q418 126 ii 7–8).

The claim that the *mebin* is seated with "nobles," understood as angels, can appear extraordinary, along the lines of the apotheosis recounted in the Self-Glorification Hymn.[31] 4Q416 2 iii 11 does not, however, attest a "realized eschatology" in the full sense of the Self-Glorification Hymn. The addressee of 4QInstruction does not obtain in this life all the rewards allotted to him, which include eternal life with the angels after death (see section 6 of the introduction). He is a student who needs to learn more and live uprightly in order to attain such rewards.

---

29. The word describes the establishment of the addressee's elect status and its rewards in 4Q418 81 3, 9. The term is also attested in l. 15; 4Q415 9 8; 4Q416 2 iii 17; 4Q416 2 iv 2, 3, 6, 7; 4Q418 228 2; 4Q418 259 2; 4Q418a 18 4.

30. Wold 2005b, 156; Goff 2003b, 209.

31. Collins 1997b, 143–47.

Given the emphasis throughout the composition on the addressee's poverty and material hardship, it is rather unusual for line 11 to assert that God has removed him from his poverty.[32] This claim is literally surrounded by reminders to the *mebin* that he is poor (ll. 8, 12). This suggests that the assertion of line 11 that God has lifted him out of poverty should not be interpreted literally.[33] In an actual sense he is poor but, metaphorically speaking, he is wealthy since he has elect status. This latter idea is expressed by the claim that he has been removed from poverty. The assertion that he has been seated with the "nobles," understood as angels, fits with this interpretation very well (cf. 4Q427 7 ii 8–9). Both statements express the idea that the addressee has a special inheritance that is more valuable than material wealth. Like an inheritance in the conventional sense, his elect status is allotted to him but not fully realized until death has occurred, after which he will attain eternal life with the angels. Lines 11–12 inspire the addressee to continue in his education and understand the special inheritance allotted to him. In this way he will attain the full rewards of his elect status after death.

4Q416 2 iii 12–14

This unit, like the previous one (ll. 8–12), begins with a *vacat* and the phrase אביון אתה ("You are poor"). This is one of several instances in 4QInstruction that remind the addressee of his poverty (see section 9 of the introduction). 4Q416 2 iii 12–15 encourages him to study and learn. Line 12 states that he should not use his poverty as an excuse not to study. This suggests that poverty refers in this line to actual, material hardship. 'Avot de Rabbi Nathan makes a similar point: "In the future, at Judgment, Rabbi Akiba will put all the poor in a guilty light. For if they are asked, 'Why did you not study Torah?' and they say, 'Because we were poor,' they shall be told: 'Indeed, was not Rabbi Akiba even poorer and in more wretched circumstances!'" (ch. 6; cf. Pirqe 'Av. 4:9).[34] Ben Sira praises the sage who has the leisure time to study and become educated (38:24–34). It is considered a profession that is superior to physical, more

---

32. 4Q416 2 iii 11 contains a wordplay between "head" (ראש) and "poverty" (ריאש), as does l. 6.

33. Wold 2007, 140–53. See also Wright 2004a, 115–16.

34. Goldin 1983, 42.

strenuous kinds of employment.[35] 4QInstruction strives to ensure that the envisioned addressee does not share this point of view. His lowly economic station makes it more difficult for him to find the time to study. Nevertheless, he should do so.

In line 13, the *mebin* is told to bring his shoulder under all instruction (בכל מוסר הבא שכמכה). This is a call to study. This reading is supported by Sir 6:25: "Stoop your shoulders (הט שמכך) and carry her and be not irked at her bonds" (cf. 2Q18 2 6; Prov 23:12).[36] This occurs in a poem that is intended to instill in students the desire to seek wisdom (Sir 6:18–37).[37] Lowering the shoulders conveys the idea that the student submits to the discipline required to obtain wisdom (ll. 29–31). The metaphor relies on accepting "her yoke" (עולה; 6:30), referring to personified wisdom. The "yoke" also refers to the Torah (6:37; cf. Pirqe 'Av. 3:5; 4Q421 1a ii–b 10).[38] 4Q416 2 iii 13 also, I suggest, utilizes the image of submitting to a yoke to denote the discipline and rigor of study. From the use of the Torah in the composition one can infer that the addressee was urged to study this book, but, unlike Ben Sira, 4QInstruction never describes the Torah as a yoke.

4Q416 2 iii 13 urges the *mebin* to "purify" (צרוף) his heart and his thoughts. This verb literally refers to smelting and is used in the Hebrew Bible metaphorically to describe being tested by God (e.g., Pss 26:2; 66:10). Given the difficult conditions of poverty under which the *mebin* must study, this metaphor is not inappropriate. But he is to "purify" his thoughts not with hardship but rather "with intelligence."[39] This suggests the primary meaning of the statement, in keeping with the pedagogical rhetoric of the surrounding material, is that he should "purify" his mind, by focusing on understanding the special "inheritance" that God has given him (see excursus above).

4Q416 2 III 14–15

These lines offer further encouragement for the addressee to study. The mystery that is to be, used without a preposition, has an instrumental

---

35. Sir 38:24–25: "The scribe's profession increases wisdom; whoever is free from toil (ח[סר עסק]) can become wise. How can one become wise who guides the plow?"

36. Rey 2009a, 107–8.

37. Collins 1997c, 48–49.

38. Goff 2007, 165–67.

39. In the lacuna between ובכול and צרוף in l. 13 was probably a word with a parallel meaning such as "knowledge," as Strugnell and Harrington (1999, 119) suspect.

sense. He is to study this mystery, using the verb דרש, as in line 9. In this way he will come to understand "all the ways of truth" (כל דרכי אמת) and "all the roots of injustice" (כל שורשי עולה). The former phrase occurs several times in early Jewish literature but the latter is unique.[40] Like 4Q416 2 iii 14–15, 4Q417 1 i 6–8 combines the mystery that is to be with the imperative דרוש ("study"), and with attaining knowledge of truth and iniquity.[41]

In 4Q417 1 i 6–8, studying the mystery that is to be is connected to two additional pairs of opposites, wisdom/folly and good/evil (cf. l. 20). 4Q416 2 iii 14–15 similarly associates the study of the mystery with a contrasting pair, sweet/bitter. Pedagogically, learning about such oppositions conveys that there is a right path and a wrong one and that an educated person knows the difference between the two. The opposing pairs may also be understood as merisms—totalities expressed through polarities. That is, to learn about truth and iniquity involves not simply understanding these two extremes but appreciating the nature of creation in general. Other texts establish that studying the mystery that is to be helps the addressee comprehend how God has structured the flow of history and creation. 4Q417 1 i 10–12, for example, claims that the secrets of God's "plan" have been revealed to the addressee, which allows him to understand "every deed." Both of these options, that the pair expresses a "two ways" theology and that they are merisms, are probably at work in these lines. For the *mebin* to choose the path that God has allocated for him requires understanding the broader divine plan that guides creation and history.

The claim in 4Q416 2 iii 15 that the addressee can discover what people find sweet and bitter may be derived from Isa 5:20. This verse contains the same opposition of terms, placed with additional ones: "Ah, you who call evil good and good evil, who put darkness for light and light for darkness, who put bitter for sweet and sweet for bitter (מר למתוק ומתוק למר)" (cf. Prov 27:7). This verse relates the sweet/bitter opposition to the good/evil pair (cf. 4Q417 1 i 6–8). This suggests that in 4Q416 2 iii 15 the sweet/bitter pair, which corresponds to truth and iniquity (l. 14), may be an allusion to the knowledge of good and evil.

---

40. For the former, see CD 3:15; 1QSa 1:2; 1QH 5:20. For the latter, note the similar phrase שרש רע ("evil root") in the fragmentary 4Q418 243 3 (cf. 4Q418 55 9). See also Rey 2009a, 108.

41. The Treatise on the Two Spirits also opposes these two terms (1QS 4:17).

4Q416 2 iii 15–17

Lines 15–19 of the column constitute a distinct section that encourages filial piety.[42] The section begins with a long sentence that extends through lines 15–17. Honoring one's parents is a bedrock ethical principle in biblical law, constituting the fifth commandment of the Decalogue (Exod 20:12; Deut 5:16; cf. Lev 20:9).[43] The topic is also important in the wisdom tradition.[44]

4QInstruction combines language of the fifth commandment with themes that are not found in biblical law.[45] Exodus 20:12 and Deut 5:16 both begin with the exhortation: "Honor your father and your mother" (כבד את־אביך ואת־אמך). The Hebrew of the key phrase in 4Q416 2 iii 15–16 is strikingly similar: כבד אביכה ברישכה ואמכה במצעריכה.[46] This is identical to the fifth commandment, with two key additions, which are underlined. 4QInstruction provides an explanation regarding how one should honor father and mother—"in your poverty," and, respectively, "in your lowly state" (במצעריכה).[47] The *bet* preposition indicates a state or condition which the *mebin* is in (cf. Isa 29:13).[48] 4QInstruction thematizes the addressee's poverty as an ethical ideal (see section 9 of the introduction). The point is not that one shows respect for his parents by being destitute. Rather, being humble and ethical is a way of honoring one's parents. The claim that one should honor his parents through poverty is unique in ancient Jewish literature.

The imperative "honor" (כבד) is important in 4Q416 2 iii, occurring in both lines 15 and 18. The term clearly derives from the fifth commandment, as mentioned above. In the context of 4QInstruction, however, the term has a broader significance. The cognate word כבוד is a key *Leitwort* in this column, occurring in lines 9, 12, and 18 (cf. 10; see the commentary on 4Q416 2 ii 18). The elect status of the *mebin* is described as an "inheri-

---

42. Rey 2009a, 182–226; 2009b, 231–55; Wold 2008, 286–300; Reymond 2006, 177–93; Jungbauer 2002, 187–92.

43. Jungbauer 2002, 9–36.

44. See, for example, Prov 20:20; 23:22; 28:24; 29:15; Sir 7:27–28; Ahiqar 52 (sg.); Instruction of Any 7.17–18 (cf. Tob 4:3–4). Ben Sira 3 is discussed below.

45. Reymond 2006, 186; Rey 2009a, 213; Jungbauer 2002, 189.

46. The variant *piel* participle כבד in 4Q418 9 17 should be preferred to 4Q416 2 iii 15, which reads כבוד.

47. The parallelism between the two phrases argues against the variant reading במצעדיכה ("with your steps"). See the textual notes section above.

48. Reymond 2006, 180.

tance of glory" (ll. 11–12). 4Q418 81 uses the imperative כבד to encourage the *mebin* to honor both God and his angels (ll. 4, 11). 4Q416 2 iii 18, in an unfortunately fragmentary passage, directly connects honoring one's parents with the "glory" of the addressee: "Honor them (כבדם), for the sake of your glory (כבודכה) …" In an extension of the meaning of the root that goes beyond the fifth commandment, the term in lines 15–16 is related not only to respecting one's parents but also to the special inheritance God has allotted to the addressee. The author of 4Q416 2 iii 15–16, I suggest, understood the fifth commandment, on the basis of its imperative to "honor" (כבד) one's parents, as endorsing an overall theme of 4QInstruction: for the *mebin* to fulfill the ordained destiny God has given him, he must be upright, and carry out the moral and pedagogical ideals promoted in the composition. This includes filial piety. Ben Sira's treatment of filial piety similarly seizes upon the term כבד in the biblical commandment and makes it a refrain in his instruction on the topic.[49]

4QInstruction also provides a theological rationale for filial piety. Revering one's parents is similar to honoring God. One should regard his father in the way that God (כאל) is to a person, and, with regard to the mother, that the Lord (כאדנים) is to a person (4Q416 2 iii 16).[50] The parallelism of the line suggests that אדנים should be understood as "Lord," in the plural of majesty, rather than as plural "lords."[51] The compatibility of honoring God and parents is common in early Judaism.[52] This is the

---

49. "Whoever honors (מתכבד) his father will have a long life; he obeys the Lord who honors his mother … In word and deed honor (כבד) your father that his blessing may come upon you … His father's glory (כבוד) is a person's own glory (כבוד)" (Sir 3:6, 8, 11). See Rey 2009a, 192–212; Jungbauer 2002, 152–69, 191–92; Adams 2010, 566–67; Kister 2009b, 1.309.

50. Most commentators follow the variant in 4Q418 9 17 כאל over כאב in 4Q416 2 iii 16, on the grounds that the latter would produce a tautological reading ("as a father is to a man, so is his father"). Wold (2004, 151) has suggested that the כאב variant produces a valid reading, referring to God "as the father." Also note that the terms איש and גבר are used in parallelism in both ll. 15 and 16 of 4Q416 2 iii. See Rey 2009a, 185; Goff 2003b, 74; Strugnell and Harrington 1999, 120.

51. Prov 9:10; 30:3. *Contra* Wold (2004, 152) who understands the term as denoting angels. See also Wold 2008, 294. For the plural of majesty, see Joüon and Muraoka 2008, 469–70 (§136d).

52. See, for example, Philo, *Spec. Laws* 2.225; Josephus, *Ag. Ap.* 2.206; Sib. Or. 3.278–279, 3.591–596; Ps.-Phoc. 8. Consult further Rey 2009a 186; Rey 2009b, 236; Jungbauer 2002, 137–253; Reymond 2006, 191.

case, for example, in Ben Sira: "he obeys the Lord who honors his mother" (3:6b; cf. v. 16).[53]

4QInstruction explains the similarity of honoring parents and God through an appeal to creation. God created all humankind and the parents formed the addressee. They are called "the crucible that conceived you (כור הוריכה)." This is a reference to the womb. In the Hodayot the phrase כור הריה denotes "the crucible of the pregnant woman" (1QH 11:9, 11, 13).[54] The form of the phrase in 4QInstruction (כור הוריכה), however, is somewhat different from the relevant expression in the Hodayot (כור הריה).[55] The word הוריכה is probably a masculine *plural* participle (with a masculine singular suffix) of the verb הרה, "to conceive."[56] Strugnell and Harrington wonder how הוריכה could refer to the "womb" of both parents.[57] The next column of 4Q416 2, however, in its instruction on marriage relations, states that the man and the woman are "one flesh" (l. 4).

---

53. Kugel (2001, 166–68) has suggested that Sir 3 and 4Q416 2 iii attest the tradition that the Ten Commandments were written on two tablets of five each that were given to Moses. As the fifth commandment, honoring one's parents would be on the tablet with the first four, all of which deal with humanity's interaction with God. The remaining five commandments are on the second tablet and deal with relations among people. In his interpretation of the fifth commandment Philo explains that "parents by their nature stand on the borderline between the mortal and the immortal side of existence" (*Dec.* 106–107). It is possible that 4QInstruction's connection between honoring God and one's parents is based on an understanding of which stone tablet the fifth commandment is written upon, but there is no explicit evidence for this view in the composition. See also Wold 2008, 288–89.

54. Stegemann et al. 2009, 149, 155. See also Bergmann 2008; Goff 2004, 263–88.

55. Note also the phrase בכור הורתי ("in the crucible of she who conceived me") in 1QapGen 6:1.

56. It is possible that the participle is singular, as Reymond (2006, 181) suggests. One would have to grant that the final *he* (הורה) has dropped out. But this possibility is weakened by the fact that the "crucible" is equated with "they." This also problematizes the view that הוריכה represents the alternative form of the *qal* feminine singular participle of III–*he* verbs, קוֹטִיָה (e.g., Lam 1:16; Isa 22:2). See *GKC* §75v. The phrase literally reads "the crucible of the ones who conceived you." Rey (2009a, 189) suggests that the word could be a perfect of the root ירה in the *hiphil*, "to instruct." The combination of the word in question with כור suggests that birth is at issue and that that the key term should be understood as a form of הרה. However, the "instruct" meaning can reasonably be understood as a double meaning, to which the word hints. As the book of Proverbs exhorts (e.g., 1:8), the teaching parents give their children is worthy of respect.

57. Strugnell and Harrington 1999, 121.

The husband has authority over the wife and in that sense her body is his
(see commentary on 4Q416 2 iv). 4Q415 9 2 expresses this idea in relation
to childbirth, referring to the wife's womb modified by a masculine suffix
("your womb"), as if it were the husband's. The "crucible" image in 4Q416
2 iii 17 similarly conveys the view that the womb is part of the woman's
body and as such belongs to the husband. The line is not trying to assert
male control, but rather to provide a basis for filial piety. Since the father
and the mother together comprise the "womb" that bore the *mebin*, they
both deserve to be honored.

4Q416 2 iii 17–19

The parents not only give birth to the addressee. Line 17 asserts that
they have been given divinely endowed authority over him. The unnamed
subject of the verb המשיל ("to give dominion") is most likely God. Their
dominion over the *mebin* is presented as a reason that he should serve his
parents (עובדם). The word המשיל is crucial elsewhere in 4QInstruction,
describing the addressee's authority over his wife and his elect status (see
above on ll. 11–12 and below on 4Q416 2 iv).

The second half of line 17 also asserts that God has bestowed upon
parents authority over their children. According to Strugnell and Harrington, the key passage reads: "And just as he has set them in authority
over you and fashioned you according to the spirit (ויצר על הרוח), so serve
them." [58] This text, so transcribed, states that the addressee has been fashioned in such a way as to serve his parents. But, as mentioned above in the
textual notes, the reading ויצו should be preferred over ויצר. This would
produce the reading that "he appointed (them) over the spirit," referring to
the "holy spirit" or soul of the addressee (cf. 4Q416 2 ii 6).[59] This would be
in parallelism with the preceding claim that God gave the parents dominion over the addressee.

4Q416 2 iii 17–18 connects an exhortation to practice filial piety with
the mystery that is to be. The *mebin* is reminded that this mystery has
been revealed to him. He should therefore "honor them, for the sake of
your glory." The root כבד is prominent in this statement, as it is throughout 4Q416 2 iii (see above on ll. 15–17). Lines 17–18 combine heavenly
revelation with practical instruction on filial piety. In line 21 the mystery

---

58. Strugnell and Harrington 1999, 122.
59. Reymond 2006, 181–82. See also Rey 2009a, 190.

that is to be is connected to taking a wife. García Martínez, after discussing 4Q416 2 iii 18, concludes that all the instruction of 4QInstruction,
whether on "worldly" topics like filial piety or "heavenly" concerns such
as life after death, should be understood as "heavenly" wisdom, since the
composition's teachings as a whole are grounded in the mystery that is to
be.[60] Lines 17–18, however, do not describe filial piety or knowledge of
this moral value, as disclosed by the mystery that is to be. He is not told to
study this mystery to learn about honoring parents. Rather in lines 17–18
the *mebin* is reminded that God has already revealed the *raz nihyeh* to him.
This is a rationale to practice filial piety (cf. 4Q418 123 ii 4; 4Q418 184 2).
Studying the mystery that is to be provides him with knowledge about
the created order, the dominion of God, and his own elect status. Attaining these insights has ethical ramifications. The revelation of the mystery
that is to be does not disclose worldly wisdom, but rather fosters practical
ethics that are consistent with the traditional wisdom of Proverbs.

The *mebin* is to practice filial piety "for the sake of your life and length
of days" (למען חייכה וארוך ימיכה; l. 19). The fifth commandment itself
presents long life as a consequence of honoring one's parents: "Honor your
father and mother, so that your days may be long (למען יארכון ימיך) in
the land that the Lord your God is giving you" (Exod 20:12). The version of this commandment in Deut 5:16 also connects filial piety with long
life, using the same terminology as in Exod 20:12. 4Q416 2 iii 19 employs
much of the same vocabulary (למען, the root ארך, ימיכה). This is another
indication that the author of 4Q416 2 iii 15–19 relied upon the language of
the fifth commandment.[61] Ben Sira likewise presents long life as an incentive to practice filial piety.[62] In his instruction the prospect of living a long
life has a this-worldly meaning—by having a good relationship with one's
parents, it is more likely that one will lead a long and fulfilling life. While
this is likely the case in 4QInstruction as well, attaining long life probably

---

60. He writes that 4QInstruction "is not worldly and heavenly wisdom, it is
revealed wisdom, and thus thoroughly heavenly." See García Martínez 2003, 13–14.
Consult also Goff 2005b, 57–67.

61. 4QInstruction follows the exhortation to honor parents with two למען clauses
(ll. 18, 19), as does Deut 5:16. The idiom ארוך ימיכה occurs elsewhere in Deuteronomy (30:20) and in biblical wisdom (e.g., Prov 3:1–2). See also 4Q418 137 4.

62. Sir 3:1: "Children, pay heed to a father's right; do so that you may live"; 3:6a:
"Whoever honors his father will live a long life." Note also Eph 6:2–3: "'Honor your
father and mother'—this is the first commandment with a promise: 'so that it may be
well with you and you may live long on the earth.'" Consult Rey 2009b, 238–41.

also alludes to the reward of eternal life after death. This is supported by
the Treatise on the Two Spirits. There "length of days" (אורך ימים) is listed
among the eschatological rewards the elect can obtain; it is associated with
eternal life and a "crown of glory" (1QS 4:7).[63] Given the prospect of eternal life for the addressee, it is reasonable to think that "length of days" has
a similar meaning in 4Q416 2 iii 19.[64]

4Q416 2 iii 20–21

These lines introduce the topic of marriage, which is continued in
column iv of 4Q416 2. Line 20 associates poverty with marriage. This is
in keeping with lines 15–16, which connect filial piety to poverty. As discussed in the commentary on those lines, in 4QInstruction poverty does
not simply refer to material hardship, but can also signify a posture of
humility and righteousness that one should adopt in family relations. This
is also the case in line 20.

4Q416 2 iii 20 contains a fragmentary statement that can be translated
"seize [her] birth times (מולדי[ה])." The term מולד denotes birth and in
4Q416 2 iii 9, as argued above, should be understood as "origin," a reference to the origins of the addressee's elect status. Line 20 is ambiguous but
מולדי[ה] likely signifies the assessment of the wife by her *mebin* husband,
to determine if she is among the elect. This is not evident from 4Q416 2
iii 20 itself but is rather suggested by the use of the relevant terms elsewhere in the composition. In line 20 itself it is evident that the addressee
has married and that he is to "seize" (קח) her מולדים. This imperative is
coupled with this object three other times in 4QInstruction: 4Q415 11 11,
4Q418 202 1 and 4Q417 2 i 11. Of these the latter is best preserved. In that
text one is to "seize" (קח) the "birth times of salvation" (מולדי ישע). There
the phrase refers to understanding the birth times of the elect; people's
potential for salvation can be understood through their times of birth.[65]
The time a person is born is part of the deterministic divine plan guiding

---

63. The phrase also denotes the eternal life of the elect in the War Scroll (1QM 1:9;
cf. 1QH 5:35). The Syriac version of Sir 3:1 (unlike the Greek) states that the person
who practices filial piety will live a life "that is forever and ever (ܕܠܥܠܡ ܠܥܠܡ)." See Rey
2009a, 198; Di Lella and Skehan 1987, 155.

64. In 1QS 4:7 "length of days" is linked to a "crown of glory"; in 4Q416 2 iii the
addressee can acquire both "length of days" and an "inheritance of glory" (ll. 11–12).

65. This text and other relevant attestations of the word מולד are discussed in the
commentary on 4Q417 2 i 11.

the cosmos and from this birth one can assess whether the person was given elect status. The wife of the addressee is understood to have a status similar to that of her husband (consult the first excursus in chapter 1). How the *mebin* would have made this assessment is not described, but presumably reflection upon the mystery that is to be made such knowledge possible to attain.

It is also possible that [מולדי[ה refers to "[her] offspring," in which case 4Q416 2 iii 20 discusses the production of children by the addressee and his wife.[66] This has some support elsewhere in the text, although not as much as the first interpretation of the phrase given above. 4Q415 11 11 reads, according to DJD 34: "And if she separates when pregnant for you, take [her] birth [times]" (קח מו[לדיה]).[67] The instruction of this column regards the wife of the addressee, but is fragmentary.[68] It may refer to seizing her birth times, in the sense of determining the status of the wife on the basis of her birth. Since childbirth is discussed it is perhaps better to reconstruct מו[לדיהם], "[their] birt[h times]" in 4Q415 11 11, referring to assessing the elect status of the children born to the addressee and his wife.

4Q416 2 iii 21 connects the theme of marriage to supernatural revelation. The line begins a reference to the mystery that is to be, coupled with the preposition *mem*. The *raz nihyeh* is normally allied with the *bet* preposition (e.g., 4Q417 1 i 8; 4Q418 77 4). Its usage with *mem* is found only here. It is reasonable to suggest, as the editors of DJD 34 do, that the full phrase was originally something like "[Take care lest you be distracted away] from the mystery that is to be."[69] Since the addressee is reminded of the revelation of this mystery in line 18 in order to encourage him to practice filial piety, it is likely that here he is to recall this revelation to ensure that he will adopt an ethical and upright approach toward marriage. The verb that denotes getting married in line 21 (להתחבר) means to "make an

---

66. Wold (2005b, 187) suggests that the term refers to her origins in this line. Rey (2009a, 169) argues that the expression refers to determining that the children are legitimate.

67. 4Q418 202 1 is too fragmentary to interpret. For the transcription of 4Q415 11 11 given above, see Strugnell and Harrington 1999, 58; Rey 2009a, 147. See also Tigchelaar 2001, 36. I agree with Rey (2009a, 151) that the verb "to separate" refers to birth (the separation of the child from the mother; cf. Gen 25:23).

68. 4Q415 2 ii 9 uses the phrase בית מולדים, which describes the house in which the wife of the addressee is born. See the commentary on this text.

69. Strugnell and Harrington 1999, 113.

alliance" or "to associate with someone" (Dan 11:6; Sir 13:2). The root חבר describes getting married in Ben Sira.[70]

4QInstruction's instruction on marriage, in 4Q416 2 iii 21 and column iv, relies heavily on Gen 1–3.[71] The phrase "walk together with the help of your flesh (עזר בשרכה)" reformulates terminology from Gen 2.[72] In Gen 2:18 God realizes that Adam should not be alone, so he creates animals (v. 19) in order to make him "a help as his partner" (עזר כנגדו).[73] None of the animals are sufficient for this role, so God creates Eve (vv. 20–21). 4QInstruction draws on this language to describe the wife of the addressee. 4Q423 1 likens the addressee to Adam, metaphorically describing his elect status as being given responsibility over the garden of Eden (see commentary below). Adam takes a wife in Genesis. 4QInstruction uses this tradition to encourage the *mebin* to marry.

4QInstruction modifies the description of Eve in Gen 2, adding the word "flesh." The wife is "the help of your flesh" (עזר בשרכה), whereas Gen 2:18 and 20 read עזר כנגדו. This probably draws from the assertion in v. 23 that the woman is the "flesh of my flesh."[74] The claim that she is the "flesh" of the *mebin* should be taken seriously.[75] 4Q416 2 iv utilizes Gen 2:24 to state that the man and woman are "one flesh" (l. 4; cf. 1). The rest of the column stresses that the man has control over his wife (e.g., ll. 2, 6, 7). The assertion that she is a help of "your flesh" puts forward the view that the wife is the possession of the husband and that her body is essentially an extension of his own.[76] The use of the word יחד ("together") in 4Q416 2 iii 21 probably helps express this point (see also the commentary on 4Q416 2 iv 5).

---

70. Sir 7:25: "Giving your daughter in marriage is an end to anxiety; but give her (חברה) to a sensible man" (ms A; cf. Mal 2:14). Ms C reads זבדה instead of חברה. See Rey 2009a, 170.

71. Wold 2005b, 185–91; 2008, 297–99; Lichtenberger 2008, 283–85.

72. Strugnell and Harrington (1999, 490) suggest that the phrase is also in 4Q418a 16b + 17 3. Tigchelaar (2001, 135–36) is critical of the join of fragments 16b and 17 of 4Q418a, favoring instead connecting fragments 16 and 16b.

73. Cf. Tob 8:6. See also the excursus on Gen 1–3 and marriage in the following chapter.

74. Wold 2005b, 187.

75. Rey 2009b, 244–45.

76. The patent allusions to Genesis allow one to speculate that the addition of the term "flesh" to term "helper" in 4Q416 2 iii 21 may allude to the creation of Eve from Adam's rib in Gen 2:21. This motif is compatible with the idea that Eve's body belongs to Adam (see above on l. 17). This verse uses the word בשר: "Then he took

Understanding the proper relationship with his wife helps the addressee to "walk" (התהלך) with her (l. 21). This root in the *hithpael* can denote not only motion but also conduct and behavior (see commentary on l. 9). This is the case in 4Q416 2 iii 21. The exhortation "walk together with the help of your flesh" is about control. The *mebin* should understand that he possesses the wife's body. 4Q416 2 iv 6–7 similarly employs the verb להתהלך, in reference to the woman's obeying the will of the husband. In this context, referring to the wife as a "help" of the husband in 4Q416 2 iii 21 denotes that she is to be with him in a subservient role.[77]

One should supplement to the end of line 21 a quotation from Gen 2:24: "As it is written, 'therefore a man leaves.' "[78] This is supported by the next line, 4Q416 2 iv 1, which begins with language from this verse: "his father [and] his mother, so you will [cling to your wife and she will become one flesh]." This is discussed in the commentary on 4Q416 2 iv below.

---

one of his ribs and closed up its place with flesh (בשר)." Jubilees 3:4–7 connects the idea that husband and wife are "one flesh" to the tradition that Eve is created from a rib of Adam.

77. Note 4Q418 178 2, which reads: "[in] your house she will help (תעזור)."
78. So also Rey 2009a, 168; Strugnell and Harrington 1999, 113.

Parallel text: 4Q418 10 (underline); 4Q418a 18 (dotted underline)

Text[1]

את אביו [ו]א̇ת אמו ז̇ת[דבק באשתכה ותהיה לבשר <u>**אחד**</u>]   1

<u>אותכה המשיל</u> בה ותש[מע בקולכה   אביה]   2

לא המשיל בה מאמה הפרידה ואליכה [לְבְבְ̇הָ̇ הִי̇א ותהיה]   3

לך לבָ̇שׂ̇ר אחד בתכה לאחרֹ יפריד ובניכה] לְבְ̇גֹ̇וֹ̇ת רֹעִיכֹהֹ]   4

ואתה לֹוחד עם אשת חֹיקכה כי הִי̇א שאר ערֹ[וֹתְכֹהֹ]   5

וַאֲשֶׁר ימשֹׁל בֹ̇ה זולתכה הסיג גבול חייהו בֹ[רוחה   ]   6

<u>המשֹׁילך</u> להתהלך ברצונכה ולא להוסיף נדר ונדב[ה]   7

השב רוחכה <u>לרצונכה</u> וכל שבועת אסרה לנדר נדֹ[ר   ]   8

חפר על מוצא פיכה וברצֹונכה הנֹיֹאֹ[ה   [לֹ]   [9

שפתיכה סלה לה למענכה אל תֹ̇רֹב]   [10

כבודכה בנחלֹתֹכה]   [11

בנחלתכה פן] vacat   [12

אשת חֹיקכה וחרפ]   [13

[   ]לֹ̇oooooȯֹה]   [14

Translation

1   his father [and] his mother," and thus you will [cling to your wife
    and become one flesh (with her).]

---

1. Strugnell and Harrington 1999, 123–31; Tigchelaar 2001, 48–49; Rey 2009a,
167–69; Elgvin 1997a, 232–37. The textual notes section, unless otherwise noted,
refers to these works.

2   He has given you dominion over her and she will ob[*ey your voice
    ... To her father*]

3   he has not given dominion over her and from her mother he
    has separated her. Rather towards you [*is* her heart *and she will
    become*]

4   for you one flesh. Your daughter he will separate to another and
    your sons [*to* the daughters of your neighbors.]

5   And you are to become one with the woman of your bosom
    because she is the flesh of [your] na[kedness].

6   And whoever rules over her aside from you has moved the bound-
    ary of his life. Over [her spirit]

7   he has given you dominion so that it (her spirit) may walk in
    accordance with your will. So as not to increase either vow or free-
    will offe[*ring,*]

8   turn her spirit to your will. And every binding oath to confirm a
    vo[*w,*]

9   annul (it) by an utterance of your mouth and at your pleasure nul-
    lify [it ...]

10 of your lips. Forgive her for your own sake. Let her not increase ...

11 your glory in your inheritance ...

12 in your inheritance lest *vacat* ...

13 The wife of your bosom and shame ...

TEXTUAL NOTES

iv 1. [דבק]תֹֹוֹ. Tigchelaar opts not to reconstruct this word but grants
that [דבק]תֹוֹ fits the traces well. Rey reads [ק]דֹבֹוֹ. The editors of DJD 34
prefer [ק]בֹºדֹוֹ while granting the readings suggested by Rey and Tigchelaar as possibilities. This line is generally understood as a quotation of
Gen 2:24. In this case one would expect ודבק. The traces, however, suggest [דבק]תֹוֹ. The second visible stroke is too close to the third to be
from a *dalet* and is better read as the first downward stroke of a *tav*. This
reading suggests that 4QInstruction reworks Gen 2:24 (see commentary
below).

iv 2. אותכה; 4Q418 10 5: ואותכה.

iv 3. לֹבֹבֹהֹ. Tigchelaar reads לֹבֹבֹוֹ in 4Q418a 18 1 (p. 133). The editors
of DJD 34 transcribe לֹבֹבֹהֹ (p. 490). Tigchelaar corrects the reading of
4Q418a 18 1 in DJD 34 by pointing out that there is a slightly incorrect
placement of the top right part of this fragment on the photo. But his
reading לֹבֹבֹוֹ, while materially possible, is problematized by the fact that

the context demands a feminine, not a masculine, suffix (as the editors of DJD 34 and Rey discern). The fact that part of the fragment must be shifted allows for the possibility that what Tigchelaar discerns as a *waw* is perhaps a poorly preserved descender of a *he*. Another possibility is to read לבבו with Tigchelaar but to consider the masculine suffix an error and emend it to a *he*. Commentators regularly make a similar move in line 8 (see below). The editors of DJD 34 (p. 491) and Rey do not endorse the join between 4Q418a 18 and 4Q416 2 iv, but there seems to be enough correspondences between the two fragments to agree with Tigchelaar that they overlap.

iv 5. כי; 4Q418 10 7: כיא.

iv 7. המשילך להתהלך; 4Q418a 18 4: [למ]שׁילכה להתה[לך]. My transcriptions of 4Q418a 18 follow Tigchelaar (p. 133).

iv 7. ברצונכה. So also Rey. The editors of DJD 34 and Tigchelaar transcribe ברצׄונֹכה. The reading is certain. See PAM 43.512.

iv 8. רוחכה. I follow the suggestion by the editors of DJD 34 that one should emend רוחכה ("your spirit") to רוחה ("her spirit"). This emendation makes sense on semantic grounds (see commentary below), but is not supported by conclusive textual evidence. Of the phrase in question only a trace of the final *he* survives in 4Q418 10 8. The physical evidence does not exclude either option.

iv 9. חפר. As the editors of DJD 34 and Tigchelaar explain, this is a scribal error. The intended word is likely הפר.

iv 10. סלה. This, too, is reasonably considered a scribal error. Read סלח.

iv 13. וחרפ. One would expect וחרפה or perhaps וחרף. There is a clear blank space on the manuscript after the *pe*. This may be a case of a medial letter written in final position. This does occur elsewhere with *pe* in the Dead Sea Scrolls (4Q365a 2 ii 6).[2]

COMMENTARY

Column iv is the last surviving column of 4Q416 2. Marriage is the overriding theme of the text (see also the excursus in the chapter on 4Q415 2 ii). 4Q416 2 iv stresses the authority of the husband over the wife. The column continues instruction on marriage from 4Q416 2 iii (l. 20). 4Q416

---

2. Tov 2004, 232.

2 iv can be divided into three sections. Lines 1–7 discuss the husband's dominion over his wife, relying extensively on Gen 1–3. Lines 7–10 take up the vows and oaths of the wife and the husband's power to annul them. This section reflects familiarity with Num 30. Very little survives of the remainder of the column, the rest of line 10 to line 14. This section presumably also dealt with marriage (e.g., l. 13).

4Q416 2 iv 1

Lines 1–7 repeatedly assert that the husband has authority over his wife (ll. 2, 3, 6, 7). Line 1 contains a quotation of Gen 2:24 that begins in the last line of column iii (l. 21).[3] Several factors support this assertion. 4Q416 2 iii 20 introduces the topic of marriage and adapts language from Gen 2 ("help of your flesh"; see commentary above). The extant portion of 4Q416 2 iv 1 accords with the language of Gen 2:24—"his father [and] his mother." This suggests that the end of 4Q416 2 iii 21 originally contained the beginning portion of this verse ("Therefore a man leaves …").[4] The parallel text 4Q418 10 5 indicates that the final word of 4Q416 2 iv is "one." This is the last word of Gen 2:24, in the phrase "one flesh" (cf. l. 4). This expression is thus safely reconstructed in 4Q416 2 iv 1.

Genesis 1–3 and Marriage in 4QInstruction and Ancient Jewish and Christian Texts

4Q416 2 iv establishes that 4QInstruction is an important witness for the use of Gen 1–3 for discussions of marriage in ancient Jewish and Christian literature. In the synoptic tradition Jesus cites Gen 2:24 in relation to marriage, along with Gen 1:27, using them as prooftexts against divorce (Matt 19:4–5; Mark 10:7–8).[5] Ephesians cites Gen 2:24 for similar reasons, arguing that wives should be subservient to their husbands (5:31;

---

3. Rey 2009a, 170–74; Strugnell and Harrington 1999, 126; Wold 2005b, 188; Barzilai 2007, 20–24.

4. Notice the switch in person from 4Q416 2 iii 21, which describes the wife as the "help of *your* flesh," to the third person ("his father," "his mother"), with the antecedent being the word "man" from Gen 2:24.

5. Kister 2009a, 195–229.

cf. 1 Cor 11:12).[6] Gen 2:24 is also a foundational text for discussions of marriage in rabbinic Judaism.[7]

Early Jewish texts aside from 4QInstruction turn to Gen 1–3 to understand marriage. The postexilic book of Malachi may allude to Gen 2:24 when arguing against divorce, but the key passage, Mal 2:14–15, is a disputed crux (see the commentary on 4Q415 2 ii 4).[8] The Damascus Document appeals to Gen 1:27 to argue against divorce and/or polygyny (CD 4:20–21).[9] The Book of Jubilees connects the origin of marriage to Gen 2:18–24, utilizing the trope that Eve was created from Adam's rib, asserting that husband and wife become "one flesh" (3:7; cf. Philo, *QG* 1.29).[10] 4Q416 2 iv uses the same biblical phrase to assert that the body of the wife belongs to the husband-addressee (see below on l. 4). Ben Sira presupposes a similar perspective. In Sir 25:24 the sage makes the infamous statement that "in a woman was sin's beginning" and that because of her we all die, attesting the view that Eve should be blamed for the primal couple's expulsion from Eden (cf. 1 Tim 2:11–14).[11] Ben Sira goes on to urge that a man "be not indulgent to an erring wife": "If she walks not by your side, cut her away *from your flesh* with a bill of divorce" (25:25–26, emphasis added).[12] The recommendation to divorce a disobedient wife presupposes that the husband and wife are "one flesh," as if the man cuts the woman away from his own body.[13] Sirach 36:29 originally described a man's wife as "a help like himself" (עזר כעצמו), an allusion to Adam calling Eve "bone of my

6. Paul turns to Gen 2:24 when arguing against fornication (1 Cor 6:16). For further parallels between 4QInstruction and Ephesians, Rey 2009b, 242–53; Wold 2008, 298–99.

7. See, for example, Gen. Rab. 8:12–13; 18:1; b. Sanh. 58a. Consult further Satlow 2001, 57–67.

8. Collins 1997d, 127.

9. Doering 2009, 150.

10. Ruiten 2000, 40–48.

11. Di Lella and Skehan 1987, 348; Collins 1997c, 67. Ellis (2011, 723–42) has recently disputed the reasonable view that the Hebrew of Sir 25:24 alludes to Eve.

12. Cf. 7:26; 28:15; b. Sanh. 100b. In the secondary textual tradition Greek II, not the earlier Greek I, the text refers to divorce. The Syriac accords with GII since the verse ends "and release her from your house" (ܘܫܪܝܗ ܡܢ ܒܝܬܟ). Note the parallel in Eph 5:28: "husbands should love their wives as they do their own bodies." See Di Lella and Skehan 1987, 55, 346; Vattioni 1968, 136; Trenchard 1982, 83–85; Rey 2009b, 25; Calduch-Belanges 2008, 90–91.

13. No Hebrew for Sir 25:26 is available, but the verb "to cut" (ἀπότεμε// ܦܣܘܩ) is presumably based upon the Hebrew לכרות. This root is used to signify a bill of divorce

bones" (Gen 2:23), but the Hebrew of the verse has become corrupted.[14] Some later rabbinic texts also attest the view that the wife is the "flesh" of the husband.[15]

The book of Tobit appeals to Gen 2 in the context of marriage.[16] After Tobias takes Sarah as a wife, he says a prayer: "You made Adam, and for him you made his wife Eve as a help and support ... You said 'It is not good that the man should be alone; let us make a help for him like himself.' I now am taking this kinswoman of mine, not because of lust, but with sincerity. Grant that she and I may find mercy and that we may grow old together" (8:6–7; cf. 7:13). This verse quotes a version of Gen 2:18, overlooking that this verse refers to the creation of animals, not Eve. The prayer of Tobias stresses not the husband's dominion over the wife but rather the authenticity of a man's love for his wife.

4QInstruction accords with other early Jewish interpretations of Gen 1–3, but also utilizes this material in a distinctive way. The description of the wife as the "help of your flesh" in 4Q416 2 iii 21 has a parallel in the claim of Tob 8:6 that God made Eve "as a help and support" for Adam.[17] Other relevant texts, discussed above, appeal to Gen 2:24 in the context of divorce (e.g., Sir 25:26; Mark 10:7). Divorce, by contrast, never unambiguously comes up in 4QInstruction, although 4Q415 2 ii 3–5 may allude to this issue (see commentary above). 4QInstruction turns to Gen 1–3 to assert that the husband's authority over his wife is granted to him by God (cf. Eph 5:28–31).[18] The composition's interest in these chapters is motivated by the view that the addressee should understand himself as being like Adam (4Q423 1). 4Q416 2 iv applies this idea to his daily life. As Adam

---

in Deut 24:1 (סֵפֶר כְּרִיתֻת). See Kister 2009a, 208–9; Collins 1997d, 115–19; Collins 1997c, 65.

14. The word עֵזֶר is retained. The corresponding passage in the Greek (36:24) preserves the phrase βοηθὸν κατ' αὐτὸν ("a help like himself"). 4QMMT makes a brief reference to becoming "one bone," presumably in reference to marriage (B 40). See Collins 1997c, 120; Di Lella and Skehan 1987, 427.

15. For example, y. Ketub. 11:3 [34b] interprets the phrase "your flesh" in Isa 58:7 as referring to one's former wife. See Kister 2009b, 209; Satlow 2001, 63.

16. Ruiten 2000, 36–39.

17. The Greek word for "help" in this verse is βοηθὸν, as in LXX Gen 2:18 (cf. v. 20).

18. Kister (2009b, 207) understands 4QInstruction as reading Gen 2:24 nomistically, as a divine commandment, rather than etiologically, as an explanation of the origin of marriage.

took a wife, so should the *mebin*. The frequent repetition in 4Q416 2 iv
of the husband's dominion is not simply a reflection of patriarchal norms
from the time. This topic is also shaped by the view that the wife, as part of
the body of her husband, was considered to have a form of elect status (see
the excursus on marriage and women in the commentary on 4Q415 2 ii).
The author of 4Q416 2 iv reminds the husband incessantly that his wife is
subservient to him probably because she possesses an exalted status before
God that most men do not have.

While it is reasonable to understand 4Q416 2 iii 21–iv 1 as attesting
a quotation of Gen 2:24, 4QInstruction appears to rework language from
this verse. The verse in the MT, after mentioning father and mother, uses
the word ודבק. The man is to "cling" to his wife rather than his parents.
The corresponding term in 4Q416 2 iv 1 is difficult to read (see textual
notes section) but the letter traces appear to attest ותד[בק] rather than
ודב[ק]. So transcribed, the line may preserve a different textual version of
Gen 2:24, but it is reasonable to interpret תדבק as a conscious alteration of
the biblical verse. The word ודבק in Gen 2:24 is in the third person and its
subject is "a man," alluding to Adam but also oriented towards men more
broadly, who are to "cling" to their wives and leave their parents. Reading
תדבק, 4QInstruction applies this general principle to the *mebin*, addressing him in the second person. This would be consistent with 4QInstruc-
tion's preference for the second person singular. See below, for example,
the adaptation of Gen 3:16 in 4Q416 2 iv 3.

The verb לדבוק conveys sticking to or being close to something (e.g.,
Ezek 29:4; Ps 44:26). Its use in Gen 2:24 conveys intimacy between husband and wife. Rashi, for example, read this verse as referring to the sexual
congress of a married couple and their production of children (cf. y. Qidd.
1:1 [58c]).[19] The verb "to cling" may similarly denote martial intimacy in
4Q416 2 iv, but the author probably understood a sense of closeness signi-
fied by the word as denoting that the man assumes control over the wife.
This is suggested not only by the prominence of the husband's dominion in
the column, but also by the understanding of the phrase "one flesh" from
Gen 2:24 evident in 4Q416 2 iv 4. This line uses this expression to affirm
that the body of the wife belongs to the husband (see below). The phrase
probably has a similar meaning in line 1.

---

19. Diamond 2009, 204; Kister 2009b, 206.

4Q416 2 iv 2

Line 2 stresses that the male addressee has been given dominion over his wife. The verb is המשיל. The column employs this word several times to signify the bestowal of authority to the husband over the wife (ll. 3, 6, 7; cf. 4Q415 9 8). The word המשיל occurs frequently in 4QInstruction, often to convey that God has given the *mebin* elect status.[20] 4Q416 2 iii 11–12 asserts, for example, "over an inheritance of glory he has given you dominion (המשילכה)" (cf. 4Q423 1 2). The unnamed subject in 4Q416 2 iv 2 is thus likely God, underscoring that the husband has divinely given authority over the wife.[21] The preference for this verb in 4Q416 2 iv conveys that the man's control over his wife is an important part of the special "inheritance" that God has allotted for him (see the excursus in chapter 4). Fulfilling the lot in life which God has apportioned for him includes taking a wife.

Genesis 3:16 uses the verb משל in the *qal* to assert that Eve is to be subservient to Adam: "yet your desire shall be for your husband, and he shall rule over you (הוא ימשל־בך)." Given the allusions to Genesis in the passage, the use of this verb in 4Q416 2 iv 2 is reasonably understood as alluding to Gen 3:16. In this verse the statement is uttered by God to Eve. The language is reconfigured in 4QInstruction, so that it is directed towards the male *mebin*.[22] The switch to the *hiphil* is consistent with 4QInstruction's preference for this *binyan* when using this verb (see above). The emphasis on the husband's dominion allows for the reasonable reconstruction in line 2 of the phrase "and she will ob[ey your voice]."[23] As the male addressee is similar to Adam, it is implicit that his wife is like Eve.

4Q416 2 iv 3

The wife is no longer under the authority of her own parents but rather of the husband-addressee.[24] Line 6 similarly asserts that no one else aside from the husband controls his wife. 4Q415 2 ii analogously stresses that

---

20. Barzilai 2007, 21–22; Rey 2009a, 175.

21. 4Q416 2 iii 17 uses this verb in the *hiphil* to assert that God has given to the parents of the *mebin* authority over him.

22. Note the unusual reference to Eve in 4Q418 126 ii 9: "all the children of Eve (כול בני חוה)."

23. Strugnell and Harrington 1999, 124; Rey 2009a, 167.

24. The phrase "her father" is reasonably reconstructed at the end of l. 2 on the basis of parallelism with "her mother."

control over the woman shifts from her parents to her husband upon marriage (ll. 7–9). Line 3 of 4Q416 2 iv extends the basic logic of Gen 3:16. It
is implicit in this verse's assertion of the husband's control that the wife's
parents relinquish power over her. This view becomes explicit in 4Q416 2
iv 3. Line 4 applies a similar reasoning to sons and daughters (see below).
As in line 2, the unnamed subject of המשיל is probably God.

The last extant phrase of 4Q416 2 iv 3 is ואליכה. This accords with Gen
3:16, which reads: ואל־אישך תשוקתך ("yet your desire shall be for your
husband"). The editors of DJD 34 reasonably understand this language
as reliant upon Gen 3:16, reconfigured to fit the second person format of
the instruction. They thus append to the line "her desire" (תשוקתה; cf.
Gen 4:7; 4Q418 168 3).[25] Their suspicion that the line echoes Gen 3:16 is
probably correct, but the overlap with 4Q418a 18, which Tigchelaar discerns, suggests that the lacuna should not be filled in with "her desire"
but the roughly equivalent phrase "her heart" (see textual notes section).
The parents do not have authority over their daughter but rather (reading the *waw* of ואליכה as disjunctive) she will be devoted to her husband,
the addressee. 4Q416 2 iv 3 draws upon Gen 2:24 and 3:16 to emphasize
that the man, not the wife's parents, has control over her. Genesis 2:24 is
interested in the husband leaving *his* parents to "cling" to his wife. 4Q416
2 iv 3, by contrast, shows no interest in the parents of the male addressee.[26]
Attention turns rather to the parents of the wife, emphasizing that they no
longer control her.

4Q416 2 iv 4

The first three words of this line are important for understanding how
4QInstruction conceptualizes the wife of the *mebin*. The line contains the
phrase "one flesh" (בשר אחד), a patent reliance upon Gen 2:24 (cf. l. 1).
There we read "and they become one flesh" (והיו לבשר אחד), referring
to man and wife. 4Q416 2 iv 4 reworks this biblical language. Before the
words "one flesh" is the prepositional phrase לך, which is not in Gen 2:24.
This is a small but significant addition. The wife will become "one flesh"
for the male addressee. This allows for the reasonable supplement of ותהיה
(rather than והיו) at the end of line 3. The author presumably interprets
the biblical expression "one flesh" as denoting the man's ownership of his

---

25. Strugnell and Harrington 1999, 127.

26. 4QInstruction has no qualms about asserting that the parents of the male
addressee have authority over him (4Q416 2 iii 17).

wife's body. Genesis 2:24 itself emphasizes that the man is to have proximity with his wife rather than his parents. The verse says nothing about his dominion over her. A widely attested variant of Gen 2:24, available in the Septuagint, the Samaritan Pentateuch, and other witnesses, reads "*the two will become one flesh*" (ἔσονται οἱ δύο εἰς σάρκα μίαν; italics mine).[27] This variant supports the view that the man and woman come together as two distinct selves to form a united pair in marriage. This is not the opinion endorsed in 4QInstruction. The body of the woman not only belongs to her husband but is regarded as an extension of his own body. 4Q416 2 iii 21 reworked the language of Genesis to express this idea, adapting עזר כנגדו ("a help as his partner"; Gen 2:18, 20) into עזר בשרכה ("the help of your flesh"), as discussed above. Line 5 of 4Q416 2 iv also attests the view that the wife is the "flesh" of the male addressee (see below). 4Q415 9 2, when addressing the male addressee, states "your womb will conceive for you." The term for womb (בטן) has a second person *masculine* suffix.[28] 4QInstruction's perspective is similar to that of Sir 25:26 which, as discussed above, describes the man who divorces his wife as one who cuts off flesh from his body.[29] In both Ben Sira and 4QInstruction husband and wife are "one flesh"—the husband's.

The rest of 4Q416 2 iv 4 extends the mindset of Gen 2:24 to family relationships not addressed in that verse. Line 4 asserts that the male addressee's daughter will be "separated" to another man, using the same verb in line 3 that denotes the removal of his wife from her parents. Treatment of daughters is also the topic of 4Q415 11.[30] 4Q416 2 iv 4 also extends the principle of separation to sons, who will be separated to the daughters of other men.

---

27. Variations on this reading are found in the Peshitta, the Vulgate, and the Pseudo-Jonathan and Neofiti Targums. The variant is also attested in the citations of Gen 2:24 in Matt 19:5; Mark 10:8; 1 Cor 6:16; and Eph 5:31. See Doering 2009, 140; Kister 2009b, 206; Tosato 1990, 389–409.

28. This is also the case in the fragmentary text 4Q423 3 4, which reads "the fruit of your womb" (פרי בטנכה).

29. Note the parallel in Eph 5:28–29: "husbands should love their wives as they do their own bodies … For no one ever hates his own body, but he nourishes and tenderly cares for it." See Rey 2009b, 252–53.

30. Ilan 1996a, 44–56.

4Q416 2 iv 5

This line stresses the unity of man and wife, who is construed as the "flesh" of the male addressee. The expression ואתה לוחד is grammatically difficult but expresses that the *mebin* is to become one with his wife.[31] Similar language of "unity" occurs in the context of marriage in 4Q416 2 iii 21: "When you marry, walk together (יחד) with the help of your flesh." This suggests that the "unity" language in 4Q416 2 iv 5 refers to marriage. The line does not construe the man and the woman coming together as equal partners. Rather, the man unifies *with* the woman, an act initiated by the male and accepted by the female. Sexual intercourse and the production of children may be at issue here, but they are not mentioned explicitly.

The rest of the line provides a rationale for the male to unify in marriage with his wife—she is part of his flesh. This interpretation relies upon the understanding of the biblical phrase "one flesh" evident in line 4 (see above). Line 5 calls the woman "the wife of your bosom" (אשת חיקכה), a phrase also attested in line 13.[32] The expression could be rendered אשת חוקכה, "your lawful wife." The stress on the woman being part of the husband's flesh favors the former reading. The phrase "the wife of your bosom" also occurs in Deuteronomy, emphasizing that the man is close to his wife.[33] In 4QInstruction the expression is similar to the phrase "help of your flesh" (4Q416 2 iii 21). Both expressions describe the wife as if she were an extension of the man's body. The extant portion of line 5 ends with another assertion that the wife is the flesh of her husband, although

---

31. I read לוחד as a *niphal* infinitive of the root יחד with the expected *he* dropped out. The omission of this letter in verb forms does occur in Qumranic Hebrew (e.g., 1Q14 8 7). The phrase could be read adverbially, לְיַחַד. As an infinitive it may denote a command, as suggested by Strugnell and Harrington 1999, 128. The phrase could be translated, "And you, become one with ..." See Qimron 2008, 48, 71; Rey 2009a, 173–74; 2009b, 244–45.

32. Wold 2005b, 189–90.

33. Deuteronomy 13:7 teaches that one should not agree with the "wife of your bosom" or other people with whom one is close if they advocate the worship of other gods. Deuteronomy 28:54 is part of a curse that describes people who are starving and not sharing scarce food with close family members (cf. v. 56; 11Q19 54:20; 11Q20 16:2). Also note Sir 9:1–2: "Be not jealous of the wife of your bosom, lest you teach her to do evil against you. Give no woman power over you to trample upon your dignity." See too the commentary on 4Q416 2 ii 21.

it must be reconstructed: she is the "flesh of [your] na[kedness]" (שאר
[ער]ותכה).[34]

4Q416 2 iv 5 provides an important insight into the conceptualiza-
tion of marriage in 4QInstruction. The woman does not become the flesh
of the husband when they marry. Rather the addressee should marry a
woman because she is a natural part of his body. There is room for speculation that the woman is the flesh of the man *before* marriage. This probably reflects a conception of woman as subservient wife that is not based
on Eve's disobedience in the garden, but rather on her having been created from the body of Adam (contrast 1 Tim 2:14). This would provide a
sort of "natural law" for marriage as a male-dominated institution—the
wife is an extension of her husband's body because Eve was created from
Adam. He is, in a sense, not only her husband but also her father. Philo
preserves a similar understanding of Gen 2, interpreting the trope that
Eve was formed from Adam's side as meaning that a woman should honor
her husband as a father (*QG* 1.27).

4Q416 2 iv 6

No one aside from the husband has control over the wife. This is consistent with line 3, which asserts that her parents do not have authority
over her. This principle is expanded to make clear that no one, neither her
parents nor anybody else, may exert dominion over her aside from her
husband. The preferred root משל again expresses dominion (see above on
l. 2). The phrase להסיג גבול ("to move a boundary") is a biblical expression
used in sapiential and covenantal literature to signify the moving of actual
property stones, which is prohibited. The phrase also occurs in 4Q416 2 iii
8–9.[35] The expression conveys in line 6 that the wife is the exclusive property of the husband.

---

34. Strugnell and Harrington 1999, 128; Tigchelaar 2001, 48; Rey 2009a, 167.
Wold 2005b, 190–91, suggests one should reconstruct instead [שאר ער]ומכה. This is
an interesting proposal since the word ערום describes the nakedness of the first couple
(cf. 3:1). The overlap, however, with 4Q418a 18 3 confirms the reading used by most
scholars, as presented in the edition of the text at the beginning of this chapter.

35. The background for the expression and relevant texts are discussed in the
commentary on those lines.

4Q416 2 ɪᴠ 6–7

At the end of line 6 begins yet another affirmation that the male addressee exerts authority over his wife. The root משל (in the *hiphil*) is once more employed (ll. 2, 3, 6). In 4QInstruction the root הלך in the *hithpael* refers to one's conduct (see the commentary on 4Q416 2 iii 9). This infinitive most likely refers to the phrase "her spirit" of line 6, emphasizing that it will behave in accordance with the "will" of the *mebin* (רצונכה; cf. l. 8).[36] 4Q415 9 8 may also urge him to rule over the "spirit" of his wife: "… her spirit. Rule over it (רוחה המשל בה)" (cf. 4Q415 11 9). Elsewhere the addressee is said to have a "holy spirit," which denotes his elect status (4Q416 2 ii 6–7, 17). The word "spirit" may likewise signify in 4Q416 2 iv 6 that the wife has some sort of privileged station before God. The *mebin* would have been encouraged to marry a woman considered to be among the elect (see the excursus on women and marriage in the commentary on 4Q415 2 ii). In any case, the spirit of the wife is inferior to that of her husband. 4Q416 2 ii 6–7 shows concern that the male addressee may lose control of his "holy spirit" by exchanging it for a price. The author shows much less concern about the wife losing control over her spirit.

4Q416 2 ɪᴠ 7–8

Lines 7–10 apply the principle of the husband's authority to a specific topic: the vows and oaths made by the wife. The husband has the right to annul them. Vows and oaths are important topics of biblical law (e.g., Lev 22:17–23; 27:1–13; Num 15:1–10; 30:1–16).[37] There are two types of oaths.[38] An assertory oath is when one invokes the name of God to clear a charge (Exod 22:7 [Eng. v. 8]; Lev 5:20–26 [Eng. 6:1–7]). A promissory oath, which is the more common type, places an obligation upon the oath taker. Jacob and Laban, for example, make this type of oath in Gen 31:53 when they agree to honor a boundary that demarcates their respective regions (cf. 1 Kgs 1:13, 17, 29–30). Vows are also promissory but conditional as well. They are to be fulfilled if an agreed upon event transpires.[39]

---

36. The word רוח is normally considered a feminine word, but it can be masculine (e.g., Ezek 20:32; Mal 2:15–16).

37. Cartledge 1992.

38. Milgrom 2001, 2409–12.

39. Jephthah, for example, vows that if God grants him victory over the Ammonites, he will offer up to God the first person of his house to greet him upon his return—who, unfortunately, turns out to be his daughter and only child (Judg 11:30–

Vows were often fulfilled by a sacrifice (e.g., Lev 7:16; 22:18; Num 15:3, 8–10). This helps explain the rationale behind the husband's control over the wife's vows in 4Q416 2 iv. The fulfillment of vows and oaths could be expensive.[40] Given the poverty of the male addressee, it is in his financial interest to restrict them.[41] The column's emphasis on controlling oaths in 4Q416 2 iv suggests that they are promissory, since this type of oath places an obligation upon the oath taker.

4Q416 2 iv 7–8 exhorts the *mebin* to turn the "spirit" of his wife towards "his will" in order to restrict the number of vows and freewill offerings that she makes. This understanding of the text is based on the emendation of רוחכה ("your spirit") to רוחה ("her spirit").[42] The word השב is likely an imperative, given the sequence of imperatives in this text (ll. 9, 10). So understood, combining this imperative with the phrase "your spirit" produces an awkward reading. One could read "turn your spirit towards your will." "Your spirit" and "your will," so understood, would tautologically both stress that the turning of the addressee's spirit be done in accordance with his own wishes. Emending the text to "her spirit" gives the imperative an explicit object. This would also be consistent with lines 6–7, which assert that the *mebin* has been given dominion over "her spirit." Ensuring that the wife's vows are in accord with the "will" (רצון) of the *mebin* is an important theme of the pericope (ll. 7, 8, 9).

The Vows and Oaths of Wives in Numbers 30 and Early Jewish Texts: 4QInstruction, the Damascus Document and the Temple Scroll

4Q416 2 iv draws upon Num 30, which deals with the vows of women.[43]

---

31). Other examples are in Num 21:2 and 2 Sam 15:8. Cf. Deut 23:22–23; Prov 20:25; Sir 18:22; 41:19. Consult Cartledge 1992, 162–99; Hyman 2009, 31–38; Levine 2000, 434–37.

40. One example is the famous case of Hannah, who vows that if God gives her a son she will give him to the sanctuary as a nazirite (1 Sam 1:11). Her husband Elkanah does not disapprove, but one can imagine that not all husbands would have been pleased with this agreement (vv. 21, 23; cf. Lev 27:1–8). See Cartledge 1992, 185–93; Fidler 2006, 374–88.

41. Levine 2000, 436, 440. Cartledge (1992, 34–35) suggests that one reason behind the man's right of annulment is that a wife might vow to abstain from sex.

42. Strugnell and Harrington 1999, 129. See also the textual notes section above.

43. Jefferies 2008, 87–98; Rey 2009a, 176–77; Strugnell and Harrington 1999, 129. For scholarship on Num 30, see Levine 2000, 425–41.

The biblical chapter has not been rigidly incorporated, but rather has been reformulated.[44] Line 7, for example, mentions both a vow and a freewill offering. The latter is not mentioned in Num 30. 4QInstruction's inclusion of the freewill offering effectively expands the power of the husband over the wife beyond Num 30. 4Q416 2 iv harmonizes this chapter with the rest of biblical law, since the vow and the freewill offering are often mentioned together in this corpus (Lev 7:16; 23:38; Num 29:39; Deut 12:6; 23:24). Numbers 30 restricts the husband's right of annulment to the time when he hears the vow or oath (ביום שמעו; vv. 6, 8, 13; cf. 9, 15).[45] He may nullify them at some time after this, but then he would be responsible for them (v. 16 [Eng. v. 15]). 4QInstruction, by contrast, gives no impression that the husband is supposed to restrict the vow or freewill offering only when he learns that they have been made. Such a qualification could have been attested in a part of the column that has not survived, but the omission of this restriction is consistent with the column's emphasis on the authority of the husband. The constant reference to the "will" of the husband (רצונכה; ll. 7, 8, 9) suggests that he could annul the wife's vows whenever he wishes. Also, Num 30 shows an interest in the oaths of women in general, including not only wives, but also women who are not yet married (vv. 4–6), widows and divorced women (v. 10). 4Q416 2 iv, by contrast, discusses wives alone. The column never discusses the power of the wife's father over her vows or the transfer of this right to the husband, whereas Num 30:4–6 stipulates that her father can annul her oaths while she remains unmarried and living at his house (cf. 11QT 53:16–21). In 4Q416 2 iv the man is told, through a string of imperatives, to control the oaths and vows of his wife. In the biblical chapter the husband is not spoken to directly, but rather discussed in the third person. Additional differences between Num 30 and 4Q416 2 iv are discussed below with regard to specific lines of the column.

The opinion that 4QInstruction increases the power of the husband over the vows of the wife stipulated in Num 30 is supported by comparison to the Damascus Document and the Temple Scroll. CD 16:10–12

---

44. Jefferies 2008, 95–96; Rey 2009a, 178.

45. Num 30:15 [Eng. v. 14]: "But if her husband says nothing to her from day to day, then he validates all her vows, or all her pledges, by which she is obligated; he has validated them, because he said nothing to her at the time that he heard of them."

(4Q271 4 ii 10–12) and 11QT 53:16–54:5 utilize this biblical chapter.[46]
CD 16:10–12, in striking contrast to 4QInstruction, restricts the authority of a husband over the oaths of his wife.[47] His right of annulment is
more limited than in Num 30. He may only nullify oaths that would result
in a transgression of the covenant. The father of the wife exerts the same
right of annulment as the husband, whereas in 4QInstruction the husband is the sole bearer of authority over the woman.[48] 11QT 53–54 contains no substantial reconfiguration of a husband's control over the vows
of his wife as presented in Num 30. 11QT 54:2–3 deals with a vow or
binding oath "of self-affliction," as does Num 30:14.[49] Neither the Temple
Scroll nor the Damascus Document accords with 4QInstruction's expan-
sive interpretation of the husband's authority in Num 30.[50] Indeed, the
Damascus Document, like m. Nedarim, moves in the opposite direction
by restricting the husband's rights of annulment. The stringent exegesis
of 4QInstruction is consistent with the emphasis of 4Q416 2 iv on the
husband's control over the wife.

4Q416 2 iv 8–9

Line 8 mentions a "binding oath" (שבועת אסר) and line 9 continues by asserting, in parallelism, that the male addressee can annul with
an utterance from his mouth and nullify in accordance with his "will"
(רצונכה).[51] The acts of annulling and nullification refer to the "binding

---

46. Schiffman 1991, 199–214; 2004, 90–94; Rey 2009a, 177–78; Bernstein 2004,
206–7; Jefferies 2008, 92.

47. CD 16:10–12: "[Concern]ing the oath of a woman: As to what he sa[id] that
her husband may annul her oath: No one should annul an oath if he does not know
whether it should be carried out or annulled. If it would violate the covenant, he
should annul it and should not carry it out. And the regulation applies also to her
father." See Schiffman 2004, 91–92.

48. In the mishnaic tractate on vows, the vows of a betrothed woman are annulled
by her father and husband together (m. Ned. 10:1).

49. 11QT 54:2–3: "(As to) [any vow] or any binding o[ath to afflict oneself], her
husband may con[firm it], or her husband may annul it on the day when he hears it,
in which case I will forgive [he]r." See Schiffman 2004, 93.

50. Also note that Ben Sira expresses concern about excessive oaths in general,
without bringing up the topic of a wife's vows. Sirach 23:9–11 reads in part: "Just as
a slave that is constantly under scrutiny will not be without welts, so one who swears
continually by the holy Name will not remain free from sin" (v. 10). Consult further
Wright 2004b , 252.

51. In the end portion of l. 9 it is evident that the lost text contained a lamed.

oath." This compliments the claim in lines 7–8 that he can bring her vows and freewill offerings in accordance with his "will." In the Hebrew Bible the phrase "binding oath" is only found in Num 30:14 and signifies "a binding obligation assumed under oath."[52] The verbs that denote the act of annulment in 4Q416 2 iv 9, להפר and להניא, are found in Num 30.[53] The phrase "annul (הפר) (it) by an utterance of your mouth" of 4Q416 2 iv 9 echoes Num 30:13, which uses this same verb in the imperfect form (יפר). The phrase that follows in line 9, על מוצא פיכה, clearly referring to the man's utterance by which he annuls the oath, is similar to the description of the speech of the wife in Num 30:13 [Eng. v. 12]. In this verse "whatever proceeds out of her lips" (כל־מוצא שפתיה) regards a vow or oath that the husband has nullified (cf. Deut 23:24). Note also the phrase "your lips" in 4Q416 2 iv 10 (see below). The application of this language to the husband constitutes a significant departure from Num 30, which never discusses *how* the man nullifies a vow or oath.[54] 4QInstruction, by contrast, explains that he annuls them with an utterance of his mouth. In 4Q416 2 iv the voice of the wife, when compared to Num 30, is effectively silenced.[55]

4Q416 2 iv 10

This line begins with the phrase "your lips." The editors of DJD 34, observing that Num 30 discusses the lips of the wife rather than those

---

Strugnell and Harrington (1999, 125) include here in their translation "fr[om performing the rash utterance] of her lips" (see below regarding his emendation in l. 10 of "your lips" to "her lips"). Tigchelaar (2001, 48) transcribes [מב]לו[י עשות מוצא שפתיכה.

52. Levine 2000, 433. He also argues (p. 430) that in Num 30 אסר denotes "a binding agreement sanctioned by oath," with the oath not required but rather volunteered, indicating a person's commitment to fulfill the obligation. See also Cartledge 1992, 23.

53. Numbers 30:9 [Eng. v. 8] reads, for example: "But if, at the time that her husband hears of it, he expresses disapproval (יניא) to her, then he shall nullify (הפר) the vow by which she was obligated, or the thoughtless utterance of her lips, by which she bound herself." The verb להפר takes the direct object marker את in Num 30 (e.g., vv. 9, 13), whereas 4Q416 2 iv 9 combines the verb with the preposition על.

54. It is implicit in Num 30 that the man by speech annuls the oath (e.g., v. 11); this is explicit in 4Q416 2 iv.

55. Numbers 30 mentions not only her speech regarding a vow that the husband has already nullified (v. 13; Eng. v. 12), but also the "thoughtless utterance of her lips" (מבטא שפתיה; v. 9 [Eng. v. 8]). Neither of these speech-acts by the wife are reproduced in 4Q416 2 iv 7–10.

of the husband, emend the phrase to "her lips."[56] The discussion regarding line 9 provides a coherent understanding of the text as it stands. The phrase "your lips," although its full context has not survived, is consistent with an emphasis in 4Q416 2 iv on the husband's, not the wife's, speech.

Line 10 also urges the addressee to forgive the wife. This comprises a rather unusual reconfiguration of Num 30. This biblical chapter repeatedly asserts that, once the husband nullifies his wife's vows, "the Lord will forgive her" (יהוה יסלח־לה; vv. 6, 9, 13; cf. 11QT 54:3). God does not expect the annulled vow to be fulfilled and thus does not hold it against the wife as an obligation. 4Q416 2 iv 10 reconfigures this language using an imperative, "Forgive her for your sake." The husband, not God, forgives the wife. The verb in line 10 can, of course, be read as a perfect, with God understood as the subject ("[God] has forgiven her for your sake").[57] However, the sequence of imperatives in this passage (ll. 8, 9) suggests that this word is an imperative as well.[58] The husband annuls the woman's obligations and declares that she is no longer bound to fulfill them. He should forgive them for his own sake (למענכה), without mention of his wife's, an addition which has no parallel in Num 30.

4Q416 2 iv 11–14

Only a few words are extant in these lines. This is unfortunate. They apparently discuss the "inheritance" of the addressee, a term that often denotes his elect status in 4QInstruction. This term occurs in both lines 11 and 12. In line 11 it is coupled with the phrase "your glory." 4Q416 2 iii 11–12 asserts that the *mebin* has an "inheritance of glory." His wife was also a topic in 4Q416 2 iv 11–14. She is mentioned in line 13 as "the wife of your bosom," a phrase that also occurs in line 5.

---

56. Strugnell and Harrington 1999, 130.

57. So Jefferies (2008, 91).

58. Since God's forgiveness of the obligation can only come after the vow has been annulled, it does not make sense to read the annulling verbs as imperatives and סלח as a completed action, a verb in the perfect.

6.
4Q417 1 I

Parallel texts: 4Q418 43–45 i (underline); 4Q418a 11 (dotted underline)

Tᴇxᴛ[1]

[ ]ו̇[י̇]אתה מב[י̇]ן[ו̇] 1

<u>ראש תשכיל הנוראים אל א̇י̇[פל ברו̇ז̇ו̇]</u>] oo[זה̇oo] ob[2

o] [

<u>נהיה ומה למה קדם</u> ומעשי נהיה ברז והבט̇[ה oooכה] oooo[ב̇פ̇ oo[ ] 3
[ומה נהיה]

<u>למה</u> ולם לתש̇[ע̇ו̇] oo[ל]יהיה במ̇ה נהיה] 4
[הויא]

מ̇עשה[כ̇ו̇ל̇ oש̇ [יהיה במה נהיה ולמ̇ה] 5
[ומ̇עשה]

ועול אמת תדע ואז תמיד ודורש נ]היה ברז הגה ולילה יומם[ ] 6
חכמה

קצי לכ̇ול פ̇ק̇ו̇ד̇ת̇ם̇ ע̇ם̇ דרכיהם בכול[מ̇ע̇ש̇[יהם oo [ת̇ ת̇[ו̇אל̇ו̇] 7
ופקודת עולם

אמת סו̇ד̇ הדעות אל א[י̇]כ̇ [הם]ע̇ש̇[י כמ]ב ל[ו̇ט̇]ב̇י̇ן̇ תדע ואז עד 8
נהיה וברז

<u>מ̇מ̇שלת</u> מה יצרה [בער] ולכל[מ̇ה בח̇כ]ע̇[שה ו̇ע̇ש̇ה̇ א̇ו̇ש̇ה את פ̇ר̇ש̇ 9
מעשיה

לכול ינ̇[תם]ב̇[ל̇מ̇ לם פרש פ̇ בא̇oo ל[ו̇]כ̇ ת̇[א]וכ̇ול ל̇מ̇o[לל̇מ̇ȯ[ל̇]ו̇[ל̇]ב̇ל̇ 10
להתהלך ה̇[עש]מ̇

1. Strugnell and Harrington 1999, 151–69; Tigchelaar 2001, 52–54; Tigchelaar 2009, 103–18; Rey 2009a, 278–82; Wold 2005b, 138–41; Goff 2003b, 83–88; Puech 2003a, 137–39; Lange 1995, 49–51; Elgvin 1997a, 256–58 (Lange and Elgvin classify 4Q417 1 as 4Q417 2). The textual notes section refers to these works.

ב[יצר] מבינתו ̇זפרש לא̇[נוש] [̇ ̇ ̇ ̇ ̇כ̇י̇] [   ] ̊סריה ובכושר מבינות נוד̊[עו 11
נ̊ס[תרי

מחשבתו עם התהלכו] כי ת[̇ ̇מ̊י̊]ם בכול מ[עשיו אלה שחר תמיד 12
והתבונן [בכו]ל

תוצאותמה ואז תדע בכבוד ע̊[וז] ̊ס רז̊י פלא̊ו וגבורות מעשיו ואת̊ה 13

מבין רוש פעלתכה בזכרון הע[ת כי]בא חר̊ו̊ת {חוק}כה וחקוק כול 14
הפקוד̊ה̊

כי חרות מחוקק לאל על כול ע[ו]נ̊[ו]ת̊ בני שית וספר זכרון כתוב 15
לפניו

לשמרי דברו והוֿאה חזון ההגות ספר זכרון וינחילה לאנוש עם עם רוח 16
בֿ[י]א̊

כתבנית קדושים יצרו ועו̊ד לוא נתן הגוֿי לרוח בשר כי לא̊ ידע בין 17

[ט]ב̊ לרע כמשפט ר[וחו vac]ואתה בן מבין הבֿט vac ברז נהיה ודע 18

[נתיבו]ת̊ כול חי והתהלכו ̇הפקוד על מ̊ע̊ש̊[י]ו [ל] [̇ס]ועו̊[ל 19
ל [

[הב]י̊ן בין רוב למעט ובסוד̊כמה] 20   [

[צ̊י̊כה ברז נהיה̊] ל 21   [   ]

י̊ כול חזון דע̊ וב̊כ̊ו̊ל] ל 22   [   ]

ו̊ת[ת]חֿז̊ק תמיד אל תגע בעולה̊] 23   כיא כול הנוגע[

בה לא̊ ינקה כפי נ̊חלתו בה יר[שע 24   ואתה[

בן משכיל התבונן ברזיכה ובא̊וֿש̊י עולם דע 25   [

י]ו̊סד̊ז בכה כ̊[ול מע]שיהן עם פ̊עולת̊ אחרי 26   [

ל̊וֿא תתרו אחרי̊ לבֿבכ̊מה[ו̊{ו̊}עי̊[נ]יכמה̊] אשר אתם זנים אחריהם [27
bottom margin

Translation

1 [… *and*] you, under[*stan*]ding one …
2 … and … [*and*] the wond[*ro*]us mysteries [*of the God of awesome deeds you shall understand. The origin of* …]
3 … your … and gaze [*upon the mystery that is to be and the deeds of*] old, at what exists and what
4 [has existed, upon wh*at will be*] … [*for*]ever to … [at what exists]

5   [and at wh*at* has existed, upon what *will be*] … all … deed upon
     d[*eed*]

6   [… *day and* night meditate upon the mystery that] is to be and
     study (it) constantly. And then you will know truth and iniquity,
     wisdom

7   [*and foll*]y. You … [*their*] deed[*s*] in all their ways together with
     their punishment in all the everlasting ages and the punishment

8   of eternity. And then you will know the difference between [*go*]od
     and [*evil according to their*] deeds, [*f*]or the God of Knowledge is
     a foundation of truth. With the mystery that is to be

9   he spread out its foundation and indeed m[*ade* (it) *with wis*]dom
     and, regarding everything, [*with cleve*]rness he fashioned it. The
     dominion of its deeds

10   for a[*l*]l … and all [*wi*]th a[*l*]l … He [*has l*]aid out for their un[*de*]r-
     standing every d[*ee*]d so that one may walk

11   in [the inclination of] his intelligence, and he spread out for
     A[*dam*] … ᶠᵒʳ … and with precision of intelligence were made
     kn[*own the sec*]rets

12   of his plan, together with his walking [*for* (he is) *pe*]rfe[*ct in all*]
     his [*d*]eeds. These things seek constantly and understand [*al*]l

13   their consequences. And then you will know the glory of [*his*]
     st[*rength together*] with his wondrous mysteries and the mighty
     acts of his deeds. And you,

14   understanding one, inherit your reward in remembrance of the
     per[*iod for*] it comes. Engraved is ᵗʰᵉ statute and ordained is all the
     punishment

15   because engraved is that which is ordained by God against all the
     in[*iq*]uit[*ie*]s of the sons of Sheth. And the book of remembrance
     is written before him

16   for the ones who keep his word—that is, the vision of meditation
     of the book of remembrance. He bequeathed it to Adam (אנוש)
     together with a spiritual ᵖᵉᵒᵖˡᵉ be[*cau*]se

17   according to the likeness of the holy ones he fashioned him. But
     no more did he give what is meditated upon to the fleshly spirit,
     for it did not distinguish between

18   [*go*]od and evil according to the judgment of its [*sp*]irit. *vacat*
     And you, understanding son, gaze *vacat* upon the mystery that is
     to be and know

19 [*the path*]s of all life and the manner of one's walking that is
    appointed over [*his*] deed[*s*] … and iniqui[*ty*] …

20 [*under*]stand the difference between great and small. In your
    counsel …

21 … your … in the mystery that is to be …

22 … every vision know. And in all …

23 B[*e s*]trong constantly. Do not be touched by iniquity [… *for all
    who touch*]

24 it will not be considered innocent. According to his inheritance in
    it he will be co[*nsidered wicked … And you,*]

25 intelligent son, understand your mysteries and the [*eternal*]
    foundation[*s know …*]

26 founded by you are a[*ll*] their [*dee*]ds, together with the reward of
    …

27 Never follow afte[*r*] you[*r*] heart and ^{after} your e[*y*]es [*after which
    you lust …*]

TEXTUAL NOTES

i 5. וְלֹמָֿה. The *lamed* may have a cancellation dot over it (4Q418 43 3).

i 6. ודרש. Read ודרוש, as the editors of DJD 34 suggest (so too Rey).
They understand the *waw* as erased intentionally by a scribe. This is possible but problematized by the fact that this section of the manuscript suffers from extensive ink abrasion.

i 7. דֹרכיהם; 4Q418 43 5: דרכיהמה.

i 7. פְּקֹוֹדֹתֿםֿ; 4Q418 43 5: פקודות[ם].

i 9. אֿתֿ. Rey reads כֹֿלֿ. The traces are very difficult to discern, but אֿתֿ
is to be preferred. This is read by most commentators (the editors of DJD
34, Tigchelaar, Lange). One must grant, however, that some of the ink of
the *aleph* has eroded.

i 9. וֹמֹמֹשׁלת; 4Q418 43 7: וממשל.

i 11. מבִֿינתֿוֹ. This follows Tigchelaar. The editors of DJD 34 grant this
reading as possible, but prefer מבֿינתֿםֿ.

i 12. התהלכו. There is a brief hole after this word, leaving room for a
couple letters. I supplement כי.

i 14. [ת]הֹעֿ. The Preliminary Concordance transcribes [ת]הֹעֿ, as do
Tigchelaar (2009) and Lange. Strugnell and Harrington read in DJD 34
הֹשֿ[לֹוֹם], which contains too many letters for the lacuna. Rey and Puech

propose [ץ]קֹהַ.[2] Elgvin opts for [ט]עֹהָ ("the stylus"). I have previously suggested [ןו]עֹהָ (cf. [וְן]עֹ in l. 13). Reading *ayin* best fits the traces. The reconstruction [ת]עֹהָ also accords with the eschatological context of the passage.

i 14. החוק. The suffix -כה has been erased from this word, presumably when the supralinear definite article was added. The corresponding term in 4Q418 43 11 is החוק and has no suffix.

i 15. תֹ[ו]נֹ[ו]עָ. This reading is also favored by Tigchelaar (2009) and Rey. Commentators have also read עַ[ולוֹת] (the editors of DJD 34, Lange). Context (the judgment of the sons of Sheth) demands an "iniquity" term of some sort.

i 16. ההגוֹתֹ. Only a slight trace of the letter transcribed as a *tav* survives. The word has often been transcribed as ההגוֹי (Tigchelaar 2001; DJD 34; Goff). This option remains materially possible. Transcribing ההגוֹתֹ, endorsed by Tigchelaar (2009), Puech, and Rey, has the support of the feminine suffix in the word later in the line (see below). Lange reads ההֹגֹהֹ; Elgvin transcribes ההגי, discerning traces of an erased final *mem* at the word.

i 16. סֹפר. The editors of DJD 34 read לֹספר, and I previously adopted this reading. A dark area before the *samek* resembles the top-stroke of a *lamed* (PAM 42.578). But the black streak follows a wrinkle in the fragment and is better interpreted as shading rather than ink. This is confirmed by PAM 41.978, in which no dark shading before the *samek* is visible. Lange does not read the *lamed*. So also Tigchelaar (2001). He later includes it but calls it "doubtful" (2009). Elgvin reads וספר.

i 16. וינחילה. I previously favored וינחלֹוֹ (so too Tigchelaar 2001). The editors of DJD 34 argue that וינחילה was the original reading but that a scribe changed it to וינחילוֹוֹ. This complicates the issue unnecessarily. The end of the word can easily be read as *he* (so also Tigchelaar 2009; Lange, Puech, Elgvin). The need to posit a second hand derives from the problem of identifying the antecedent of the feminine suffix. This is resolved by reading ההגוֹתֹ (see above).

i 17. הגוֹי. Rey, following Puech, reads החֹזֹו[ן] ("the vision"). The הגוֹי reading is certain.

i 17. לֹא; 4Q418 45 i 1 (joined to 4Q418 43 13): לֹוֹאֹ.

---

2. Puech 2008a, 98.

i 20. הֹֿ[הב]. 4Q418 43 15 may read הֿ[נביה], but the key letter traces in both texts are too fragmentary to be conclusive.

i 20. רוב; 4Q418 43 15: רב.

i 27. אחר[י]. There is not enough space after the *resh* for an additional letter. This line is a quotation of Num 15:39 (see below). As Rey discusses, since the verse reads אחרי, it is reasonable to posit that a scribe added a supralinear *yod*.

COMMENTARY

4Q417 1 and 2 both have two columns and preserve a substantial amount of text. The conventional classification assumes that 4Q417 1 preceded fragment 2 in the original structure of the composition. In earlier (pre-DJD 34) scholarship, the order of the two fragments was reversed. Much of 4Q417 1 i, particularly its top half, suffers from extensive ink abrasion, making it difficult to read. Nevertheless, the column can be divided into several units. Lines 1–5, the worst preserved section, describe the vast knowledge that can be acquired through the mystery that is to be—the past, the present, and the future, using a tripartite division of time. Lines 6–13 also provide an impression of what one can learn by means of the *raz nihyeh*. This section describes God's creation of the world, asserting that he fashioned the world with a deterministic plan that guides the cosmos. 4Q417 1 i 13–18 comprises the famous vision of meditation passage. This text makes a distinction between the fleshly spirit and the spiritual people, who have access to supernatural revelation. Lines 18–27, which are quite fragmentary, urge the addressee to avoid iniquity. The end of line 24 probably begins a new section of the exhortation.

4Q417 1 i 1

A single phrase is preserved in line 1: "[and] you, under[stan]ding one." This expression, and variations on it, often introduces exhortations in 4QInstruction.[3]

4Q417 1 i 2

The addressee can learn about "wond[ro]us mysteries" ([א]רזי פל), a

---

3. See, for example, ll. 13–14, 18; 4Q416 2 ii 4; 4Q416 4; 4Q418 81 15; 4Q418 168 4; 4Q418 176 3.

phrase that signifies God's power. This is suggested by line 13, which associates these mysteries with his strength and glory (see below; cf. 4Q418 219 2). The term *raz* denotes that this knowledge has the status of supernatural revelation. In 1QH 12:28–29 the poet declares to God, "Through me you have illumined the faces of many … For you have made me understand your wondrous mysteries (רזי פלאכה)."[4] According to the Community Rule, one of the responsibilities of the *Maskil* is to teach the sectarian community "the wondrous mysteries and truth," so that its members shall behave in accordance with what has been revealed to them (1QS 9:18–19; cf. 11:5; CD 3:18). In 4QInstruction the phrase signifies God's grandeur that the elect community comprehends through supernatural revelation.[5]

The expression "wondrous mysteries" is somewhat different in meaning from the mystery that is to be. The *raz nihyeh* is not simply revealed knowledge, but the means by which knowledge is acquired, through regular contemplation and study (e.g., 4Q417 1 i 6). 4QInstruction never urges the *mebin* to study the "wondrous mysteries." This suggests that line 2 does not state that through the wondrous mysteries the addressee can attain knowledge.[6] Rather, he comprehends them. The *mebin* is to learn what the wondrous mysteries are. So understood, "origin" (ראש) is likely the beginning of a new sentence, the rest of which has not survived.[7] The column's focus on the beginnings of creation (e.g., ll. 9–10) suggests that ראש refers to the "origin" of creation or the world and does not mean "poverty" or "head."

The "mysteries of wonder" is combined with the phrase "the God of awesome deeds" (אל הנוראים). The word נורא conveys that God is transcendent and awe-inspiring.[8] This is also the case, for example, in Jacob's night vision at Bethel and Ezekiel's throne-chariot vision (Gen 28:12; Ezek 1:22). There are other examples of נורא together with פלא.[9] One could translate "the God of the Awesome Ones" in 4Q417 1 i 2, as do the editors

---

4. See also 1QH 5:19; 9:23; 10:15; 15:30; 19:13, 19 (cf. 1Q27 1 i 7). Note also the phrase רזי נפלאות (e.g., 1QM 14:14; 4Q401 14 ii 2). The word פלא in the Hebrew Bible denotes God's power, often expressed by great acts of judgment or deliverance. See, for example, Exod 3:20; Josh 3:5; Ps 77:12. See Thomas 2009, 136–50.

5. Goff 2003b, 36–37; Thomas 2009, 147; Elgvin 1998, 132.

6. *Contra* Rey 2009a, 280: "dans les mystères des merveil[les redoubtable de Dieu, tu comprendras l'origine …"

7. So also Kampen 2011, 94.

8. This usage of נורא with the masculine plural and the definite article is somewhat unusual.

9. Ben Sira 43:29, for example, reads: "Awesome ([אר]ונ//φοβερός) indeed is the

of DJD 34, who understand הנוראים as a reference to angels.[10] The word is used this way in the Songs of the Sabbath Sacrifice (4Q400 2 2 [par. 4Q401 14 i 8]; cf. 4Q440 3 i 23). This section of the column, however, has little to say about angels, while stressing over and over again the power of God. הנוראים is better understood as a reference to his mighty deeds (cf. l. 13). In the Psalms, the term, in the feminine plural (cf. l. 26), often refers to God's "awesome deeds," denoting his majesty and dominion.[11] It is not impossible that the word in 4Q417 1 i 2 alludes to a mighty divine act such as the Exodus, but God's great deeds in the history of Israel are never a prominent theme in 4QInstruction. It is more likely that his power is evoked in a general sense, without appeal to a specific "awesome deed."

4Q417 1 i 3-5

These lines give an impression of the immense range of knowledge that is available to the addressee through the *raz nihyeh*. The supplement of the phrase "the mystery that is to be" in line 3 makes sense given the imperative "gaze" (הבט), which has ברז נהיה as its object elsewhere in the composition (4Q416 2 i 5 [par. 4Q417 2 i 10–11]; 4Q417 1 i 18). The *niphal* participle נהיה conveys that the revealed "mystery" contains knowledge about God's orchestration of the cosmos, from creation to judgment (see section 5 of the introduction). 4Q417 1 i 3–4 constitutes important evidence for this view. Line 3 advocates the study of the mystery that is to be *and* the deeds of old (מעשי] קדם]). The book of Mysteries provides a useful parallel. 1Q27 1 i 3 states that those who will perish in the final judgment know neither the mystery that is to be nor the "former things" (קדמוניות; cf. 4Q418 148 ii 6). These expressions refer, respectively, to the eschatological future and the beginnings of creation. Together they signify the entirety of history, from beginning to end.[12] The pairing of the mystery that is to be and "the deeds of old," I suggest, has a similar function in 4Q417 1 i 3. The parallelism of the phrases suggests that the mystery that is to be signifies the eschatological future, as part of a description of the

Lord and wonderful (נפלאות) is his power" (Bm). See also Exod 15:11; Pss 96:4–6; 106:23; 4Q372 1 29; 4Q504 8 3.

10. Strugnell and Harrington 1999, 156.

11. E.g., Pss 65:6; 139:14; 145:6 (cf. 4Q286 1 ii 5).

12. Goff 2007, 75–76. For a different interpretation of קדמוניות in the book of Mysteries, see Kister 2004, 32–33.

divine deterministic plan that guides all of history (see also below on ll. 8–12, 18–19).

The theme of learning about the entire breadth of history is conveyed in lines 3–4 by a tripartite division of time. This threefold sequence signifies the entire scope of the chronological order, fittingly in parallelism with the mystery that is to be and "the deeds of old." Together the two expressions function as a merism, by which totalities are expressed through polarities, in this case the end and beginning of history. Lines 4–5 contain another tripartite division of time, although its immediate context has not survived ("at what exists and at what has existed, upon what will be"). There is another in 4Q418 123 ii 3–4: "Everything that exists in it, from what has been to what will be in it (כול הנהיה בה למה היה ומה יהיה בו)."[13] This text, like 4Q417 1 i 3–5, links its references to time with the mystery that is to be. The *niphal* participle נהיה in early Jewish literature can refer to future events, but also to the past or present, often in the context of describing all of the chronological order. The Treatise on the Two Spirits states, for example: "From the God of Knowledge stems all that is and what will be (נהייה)" (1QS 3:15).[14] 4QInstruction's three tripartite divisions of time likewise use *niphal* participles of היה to help express the entire scope of history. In each instance the *niphal* participle denotes specifically either the past, present or future as part of a longer formula that signifies the entirety of time. If one posits that all three texts express the same sequence of time (which, admittedly, is not necessarily the case), it is reasonable to suggest that they refer, in order, to the present, the past, and the future.[15] This schematic is illustrated by the following table:

---

13. It is possible that this passage would have been attested in column 3 of 4Q417 1, which is lost. See the discussion of the text of 4Q417 1 ii in the following chapter.

14. Cf. 10:4–5; 11:11; CD 2:9–10; 4Q180 1 2; Sir 42:19; 1QM 17:5. The participle normally refers to a past action in the Hebrew Bible (e.g., Prov 13:19). For this participle with an exclusively future orientation, see 1QM 1:11–12. Note the use of the *niphal* participle to denote all things that exist. The Songs of the Sabbath Sacrifice asserts: "For from the God of Knowledge came into being everything [which exists forever] (נהיו כול [הוי עד]; 4Q402 4 12; cf. 1QH 5:28–29; 4Q418 69 ii 7; 4Q369 3 2). For a fuller discussion of the temporal range of נהיה, see Goff 2003b, 54–61; Thomas 2009, 150–51. See also section 5 of the introduction.

15. Elgvin (1997a, 258) translates the key texts of 4Q417 1 i as attesting, in sequence, the past, present and future. Rey (2009a, 278–80) places a heavy emphasis on the past, supplementing נהיה in 4Q417 1 i 3–4 and 4–5, whereas I supply יהיה.

Tripartite Divisions of Time in 4QInstruction[16]

Textual Sequence	4Q417 1 i 3–4 (par. 4Q418 43 2)	4Q417 1 i 4–5 (par. 4Q418 43 3)	4Q418 123 ii 3–4	Temporal Aspect
first	למה נהיה	למה הויא	כול הנהיה בה	present
second	ומ[ה] נהיה	ולמ[ה] נהיה	למה היה	past
third	במ[ה] יהיה	במה [יהיה]	ומה יהיה	future

The sequence present, past, and future is supported by the היה verbs in this chart that are not *niphal* participles. The first foot of the second example (4Q417 1 i 4–5) is a *qal* participle of היה and denotes the present. The second part of the third text (4Q418 123 ii 3–4) is a perfect and easily understood as signifying the past. The third foot of this passage is an imperfect and likely expresses the future. Fronting the present in this sequence suggests that the first part of the formula refers not only to the present moment but also the eternal nature of God's creation, which is then further elaborated by appeals to the past and future in the second and third feet of the sequence.[17]

The proposed sequence of present, past, and future in 4QInstruction has support from other, admittedly later, texts. The book of Revelation attests a tripartite division of time that follows the same order: "Grace to you and peace from him who is and who was and who is to come (ὁ

---

16. Note that the two key texts of 4Q417 1 i (not 4Q418 123 ii) attest a common structure. In both cases, the first foot is preceded by a *lamed*, the second a *waw*, and the third a *bet*. I read the *lamed* as giving greater specification to the object of study, the mystery that is to be and the deeds of old. The *mebin* is told to gaze "upon" the *raz nihyeh* (using a *bet*) and "at" what exists (present). The *waw* continues this sequence (past) and the *bet* in the third foot performs a function that is similar to the beginning of the sentence, to gaze "upon" the future.

17. Assuming that the three texts attest the same sequence means that the *niphal* participles do not always have the same meaning in these texts. For example, in 4Q417 1 i 3–4, according to this schema, the first *niphal* participle refers to the present and the second to the past. As discussed above, the semantic range of this participle allows for such variety.

ὢν καὶ ὁ ἦν καὶ ὁ ἐρχόμενος)" (1:4).[18] The chronological formula in this text, not unlike those in 4QInstruction, signifies the full scope of history to describe God's eternal nature. The present-past-future sequence also occurs in Rev 1:8; the schema past-present-future occurs in 4:8 (cf. 1:17–18). The Pseudo-Jonathan Targum to Deut 32:39 also associates God with a tripartite division of time that has a present, past and future sequence: "When the Memra of the Lord will be revealed to redeem his people he will say to all the nations: 'See now that I am He who is and who was and I am He who will be (אנא הוא דהווי והוית ואנא הוא דעתיד למהוי).'"

4Q417 1 i 6–7

Lines 6–13 contain exhortations to study the *raz nihyeh* and acquire knowledge about God's mastery over the created order. Line 6 emphasizes that the addressee should study incessantly, employing the parallel phrases "day and night" and "constantly."[19] The imperatives in this line, הגה and דרוש, are also in parallelism (see textual notes). In 4QInstruction the former term ("to meditate") only occurs in 4Q417 1 i 6 (par. 4Q418 43 4), but evokes the vision of meditation (l. 16; see below). The latter word ("to study") is often used to encourage the *mebin* to study the mystery that is to be.[20]

The word pairs of lines 6–7 indicate what the *mebin* can learn—truth and iniquity, and wisdom and folly. The technique of using polar opposites is continued in line 8, which asserts (repeating the expression ואז תדע; also in l. 6), that the addressee can learn good and evil (cf. l. 13). In lines 6–7 (and l. 8) these opposed pairs signify merisms. One can, through the study of the mystery that is to be, understand not just wisdom and folly,

18. The verse alludes to the famous text of LXX Exod 3:14, "I am the one who is." Note Exod. Rab. 3:6: "R. Isaac said: God said to Moses: 'Tell them that I am the one who was (הייתי) and that I exist now (עכשו) and in the future to come'; for this reason is the word אהיה written three times [in Exod 3:14]." See Elgvin 1997a, 259; Aune 1997, 30–33.

19. Elsewhere the phrase "day and night" helps express the assertion that one should study the Torah continually (1QS 6:6–7), whereas 4QInstruction stresses one should contemplate always the mystery that is to be. This by itself is not sufficient evidence that the Torah should be equated with the mystery that is to be. 4Q417 1 i 6 probably, however, utilizes language from the Bible to describe its call to study. Psalm 1:2, for example, urges one "day and night" to "meditate" upon the Torah. See Lange 1995, 62.

20. 4Q416 2 iii 9, 14. Cf., e.g., 4Q417 1 ii 13; 4Q418 81 7; 4Q418 96 2.

but attain a more profound insight into the nature of reality, in the form
of God's deterministic plan that guides history and creation. This broad
perspective accords with the two tripartite divisions of time in lines 3–5.
Note also that the ואז clause of lines 6–7 is similar in meaning and structure to 4Q416 2 iii 14–15. Line 14 urges one to examine the mystery that is
to be, using the verb "to study" (לדרוש), as in 4Q417 1 i 6. Like 4Q417 1 i
6–7, 4Q416 2 iii 14–15 uses ואז תדע and lists two polar oppositions, truth/
iniquity and bitter/sweet, to explain what one can learn from studying the
raz nihyeh.

4Q417 1 i 7–8

In these fragmentary lines the term פדודה is prominent.[21] The term is
common in 4QInstruction, occurring fifteen times.[22] It is normally translated "visitation" or "punishment," and in the composition it generally
refers to eschatological judgment. The word denotes the final judgment
in 4Q417 1 i 14, and this may also be the case in 4Q418 68 2 (cf. l. 3) and
4Q418 113 2. The term פדודה conveys the regularity of the created order
in 4Q416 1 9, which helps express that the final judgment (ll. 10–14) is a
regular and established feature of God's plan for the world. The word helps
connect the theme of eschatological judgment to God's control over all of
creation. This is probably also the case in 4Q417 1 i. Line 7 associates "all
their punishment" (plural in 4Q418 43 5) with "all their ways," followed by
a joint reference in lines 7–8 to all the everlasting periods and "punishment
of eternity" (פדודת עד). The first use of פדודה is associated with conduct
("ways") but the fragmentary state of the text hinders interpretation. It
is not clear whose ways or punishment is discussed (that of the wicked?
humanity as a whole?). The next attestation of the word פדודה relies on
a sort of parallelism between the entirety of history and its concluding
period of eschatological judgment. This combination highlights the inevitability of eschatological judgment by understanding it as part of history,
understood in a deterministic sense, as in 4Q416 1.[23] The Hodayot use the
same expressions to assert a deterministic mindset and praise God as the

---

21. Collins 2004, 51–52; Tigchelaar 2001, 240–42; Strugnell and Harrington
1999, 28.

22. See, *inter alia*, 4Q416 3 2; 4Q416 7 2; 4Q417 2 i 8; 4Q418 17 1; 4Q418 126 ii 6;
4Q418 169 + 170 2; 4Q418a 21 1.

23. Lange (1995, 61) argues against an eschatological interpretation of the word,
seeing the key language as instead denoting human conduct. The terminology is

creator of the world.[24] פדודה also occurs repeatedly in the deterministic Treatise on the Two Spirits (e.g., 1QS 3:14, 18; 4:6, 11, 19, 26).

4Q417 1 i 8

The addressee can learn two opposed things: good and evil. As in lines 6–7, this pair should be understood as a merism, expressing that one can understand the nature of reality as a whole, rather than simply the moral opposites good and evil (see above). Attaining the knowledge of good and evil has additional significance since the addressee is likened to Adam elsewhere in 4QInstruction. 4Q423 1 claims that he has been given authority over the garden of Eden. Learning good and evil is an important aspect of fulfilling the elect status allotted to him. The knowledge of good and evil should probably also be understood as a divinely revealed disclosure about God's deterministic plan that orchestrates creation and history (see below on ll. 16–17).

4Q417 1 i 8 describes the deity with the epithet "the God of Knowledge" (אל הדעות), who is also called a "foundation of truth" (סוד אמת; cf. 4Q418a 12 2). The expression "the God of Knowledge" is used in deterministic descriptions of the natural order elsewhere in early Jewish literature.[25] The Treatise on the Two Spirits associates its highly deterministic worldview with the phrase: "From the God of Knowledge stems all that is and what will be. Before they existed he established their entire design" (1QS 3:15). The equivalent אלוהי דעת has a deterministic resonance in the Songs of the Sabbath Sacrifice: "because from the God of Knowledge comes all [which exists forever. And from his knowledge and his purposes have come into existence all the things which were eternal]ly [appointed]" (4Q402 4 12–13 [par. Mas1k 1 2–3]).[26] The Hodayot similarly reads: "For the God of Knowledge has established it (creation) and there is none other with him" (1QH 20:13–14).[27] The Thanksgiving hymns also, like 4Q417 1

---

clearly eschatological, but Lange is right insofar as a deterministic conception of the world and the final judgment affects how one understands the human world.

24. 1QH 5:24–27: "And these are what [you] es[tablished from]ages [of old] … [according to] all the plans for them for all the everlasting ages (לכול קצי עולם) and the punishment of eternity (פקודת עד)." Cf. 4Q419 8 ii 4–6.

25. Lange 1995, 129, 150; Tigchelaar 2001, 197; Hengel 1974, 1.219.

26. 4Q400 2 8; 4Q401 11 2; 4Q405 20 ii–22 7; 4Q405 23 ii 12; 11Q17 7 10. Cf. 4Q510 1 2; 4Q511 1 7–8.

27. Cf. 4Q299 35 1; 4Q299 73 3; 4Q504 4 4.

i 8, connect the phrase "the God of Knowledge" to a "foundation of truth" in a deterministic context.[28] This is similar to 4Q418 55 5–6, which, like 4Q417 1 i 8, associates the epithet with the nature of creation and "truth": "Is not [the] God of Knowledge … upon truth, to establish all [their ways upon un]derstanding." In the context of eschatological judgment, 4Q416 1 14 calls the deity a "God of truth," and uses the term "truth" to emphasize a connection between God and the elect (see the commentary on 4Q416 1 10). 4Q417 1 i 8 praises God for having created the world according to a divine plan. 4QInstruction's deterministic theology is elaborated further in the column (see below on ll. 11–13 and 18–19).

4Q417 1 I 8–9

These lines proclaim that God created the world by means of the mystery that is to be.[29] The object of the verb is אושה ("its foundation"; l. 9), a relatively rare term, with a feminine suffix, denoting that God fashioned the world (cf. 1QH 11:36; 15:12). The Hebrew of the phrase in question can be transcribed as אישה ("woman"), in which case the statement refers not to the creation of the world but of woman. Wold has promoted this interpretation.[30] Materially either reading is possible. The context of the statement, with its focus on determinism and the nature of the created order, strongly favors אושה ("its foundation"). The phrase of line 8, "foundation of truth" (סוד אמת), supports reading a "foundation" term at the beginning of line 9. The verb of creation יצר in line 9 has a feminine suffix ("he fashioned it"), another argument for reading "its foundation."[31] The term "foundation" is also associated with "mystery" in a fragmentary context in 4Q417 i 25 (cf. 4Q418 95 1). The feminine suffix of אוש presumably refers to "truth" (l. 8).[32] The claim of 4Q417 1 i 8–9 that God created by means of the mystery that is to be, with the preposition *bet* used in an instrumental sense (ברז נהיה), has justly intrigued commentators. The

---

28. 1QH 9:25–26 reads: "Everything is engraved before you (God)." Lines 28–29 assert "To you, yourself, the God of Knowledge, belong all righteous deeds and a foundation of truth."

29. Goff 2003a, 163–86.

30. Wold 2005b, 99, 208. This transcription has also been suggested in Caquot 1996, 17; and Lange 1995, 50.

31. The feminine suffix in the phrase "the dominion of its deeds" (ממשלת מעשיה) in l. 9 also supports the view that אושה has a feminine suffix.

32. Strugnell and Harrington 1999, 158.

assertion recalls the statement in Prov 3:19 that God created the world "with wisdom" (בחכמה).[33]

Use of the term *raz* in 4Q417 1 i 8–9 implies that full understanding of creation is only available through supernatural revelation. These lines indicate that the mystery that is to be also signifies God's act of creating the world. This mystery signifies God's power and dominion over the world. In line 13 the word רז is parallel to גבורה (literally, "strength"; see below). The mystery that is to be normally denotes supernatural revelation by which the *mebin* acquires knowledge. 4Q417 1 i 8–9 indicates that the *raz nihyeh* can also refer to the *content* of what is revealed—the nature of creation and God's dominion over it. To adapt a famous phrase, the mystery that is to be is the medium and the message. The *mebin* can attain deep insights into reality through the study of the mystery that is to be because God used this mystery to create the world.

The verb that denotes the act of creation in 4Q417 1 i 8–9 is פרש, which is parallel to the verb יצרה ("he fashioned it"). Given the theme of creation, one might expect instead the pairing of יצר with ברא, as in Genesis 1–2. The root פרש, however, is a preferred term in texts of 4QInstruction that discuss the nature of the cosmos. This verb is used in the discussion of divine creation in 4Q418 126 ii 4–5 (see commentary below). פרש is a *Leitwort* in 4Q417 1 i itself, occurring again in lines 10 and 11. The verb is consistent with the double meaning of the mystery that is to be. As mentioned above, the *raz nihyeh* denotes both God's act of creation and the means by which the addressee can attain knowledge of this deed. The root פרש can mean both "spread out" (פרש) and "expound/explain" (פרש).[34] 4QInstruction draws upon both meanings of the root. God spread out the foundations of the world *and* made them intelligible for the addressee. Both acts are associated with the *raz nihyeh* and the verb פרש. The first topic is evident in lines 8–9 and the second in line 10 (see below).

4Q417 1 ɪ 10–11

Little survives of the first half of line 10. The term "all" occurs there repeatedly (three times). In the second half of line 10 the verb פרש emphasizes that God has made the nature of the world intelligible to the addressee.

---

33. See the discussion of 4QInstruction vis-à-vis the sapiential and apocalyptic traditions in sections 4 and 8 of the introduction.

34. For the former meaning, see 1 Kgs 8:38; Ezra 9:29–33; Sir 48:20; for variations of the latter, see Exod 25:20; Num 4:6–8; Deut 22:17.

He spread out "every deed" for "their un[de]rstanding" (למ[ב]ינתם).[35] The word "understanding" occurs twice in line 11. Line 10 connects epistemology to ethics. The *mebin* is to learn about God's mastery over the world, so that he can behave in an upright and ethical manner that is consistent with this knowledge. The verb "to walk" in the *hithpael* (התהלך) is associated with conduct elsewhere in 4QInstruction (see the commentary to 4Q416 2 iii 9). He has made knowledge of the world available so that "their" understanding (the elect, probably) of it may be in harmony with his (מבינתו; cf. l. 19).[36] One is to act ethically and live in harmony with God's plan, which orchestrates the unfolding of creation.

4Q417 1 i 11 connects the topic of "intelligence" to the term יצר ("inclination"; cf. 1QH 23:12). The word denotes a person's innate capacity for either good or evil (see the commentary on 4Q417 1 ii 12). The term "inclination" helps express the idea that one can act in a way that is in accordance with God's plan that governs the world (4Q417 1 i 10–11). The vision of meditation passage uses the root יצר to describe the "spiritual people" as similar to the angels (l. 17).

A third instance of the verb פרש is, unfortunately, highly fragmentary (l. 11). The key phrase is ויפרש לא[. The editors of DJD 34 reconstruct ויפרש לא[נוש].[37] I tentatively endorse this proposal, but conclusive interpretations of the phrase are not attainable. Strugnell and Harrington translate "And he laid out for m[an]." In 4Q417 1 i 16 the term אנוש, I argue below, refers to Adam, to whom the vision of meditation has been made available. Line 11 may contain a similar idea. The relevant phrase can be translated, "And he laid out for A[dam]." What is being laid out is not clear, but context suggests that knowledge of the created order and God's dominion over it are disclosed to this figure. 4Q417 1 i emphasizes that knowledge of the natural order is attainable through the mystery that is to be (e.g., ll. 3, 6; cf. the phrase "[the sec]rets of his plan" in ll. 11–12). This suggests that the knowledge in question is available not to humanity

---

35. The key issue of *whose* understanding is not clear because of the fragmentary condition of the text. God has presumably made this knowledge available to the elect. See Strugnell and Harrington 1999, 159.

36. The masculine singular suffix on "understanding" may denote that each person may walk in accordance with "his" own understanding. This would not produce a substantively different meaning, since the passage emphasizes that a person's understanding comes from God.

37. Strugnell and Harrington 1999, 154.

in general, but rather to the elect addressee. This argues against the "man" reading. As discussed below, the "Adam" interpretation of אנוש in line 16 is supported by 4QInstruction's effort to liken the addressee's elect status to Adam's stewardship over the garden of Eden (4Q423 1). 4Q417 1 i may anticipate this theme earlier in the column, stating first that knowledge of the created order was spread out (פרש) for the elect (l. 10) and then that it was previously spread out (פרש) for Adam (l. 11).

4Q417 1 i 11–12

These lines engage key themes that are important throughout 4Q417 1 i: revelation, creation, determinism, and ethics. Lines 11–12 assert that hidden truths of God's "plan" (נס[תרי מחשתבו]) have been disclosed so that one may act in a way that is in keeping with this knowledge. The word "secrets" (נסתרים) conveys that this knowledge has the status of super-natural revelation (cf. 1QS 5:11; 11:6; CD 3:14). The phrase "with precision of understanding" (בכושר מבינות) indicates that these "secrets" are fully appropriate for the addressee to acquire, perhaps suggesting that there is some debate on this point.[38] Contrast Ben Sira, who declares that one should not occupy himself with revealed "secrets" (3:22). The term "understanding" is also prominent in line 10 (see above).[39]

The phrase "[the sec]rets of his plan" signifies the deterministic schema established by God according to which reality unfolds. This is clear from the focus on creation and determinism in 4Q417 1 i and from the term מחשבה ("plan") elsewhere in early Jewish literature. The word is often associated with a deterministic mindset. The Treatise on the Two Spirits declares: "From the God of Knowledge stems all that is and what will be. Before they existed he established their entire plan (מחשבתם) ... they will execute all their works according to his glorious plan (כמחשבת כבודו), without altering anything" (1QS 3:15–16; cf. 4:4; 11:11). The Hodayot describe God as having fashioned the elements of creation "[according to] all the plans (מחשבותם) for them for all the everlasting epochs and the eternal punishment" (5:26–27; see above on 4Q417 1 i 7). The determin-

---

38. The term כשר is relatively rare in early Jewish literature (see the commentary to 4Q417 2 i 2).

39. The word מבינות here is a plural, but has a singular meaning ("understand-ing"). As Strugnell and Harrington (1999, 159) note, use of the plural is somewhat common in the Hebrew Bible with regard to abstract nouns (e.g., 1 Sam 2:3; Isa 40:26). Consult Joüon and Muraoka 2008, 471 (§136g).

ism of 4QInstruction is not exactly the same as that of the Treatise. The former composition never explicitly states that God's "plan" predates his actual creation of the world, unlike the Treatise or the Hodayot (9:21–22), although 4Q417 1 i 11–12 suggests that such a view is implicit in 4QInstruction. The wisdom text nevertheless puts forward a deterministic mindset that is compatible with those of the Treatise and Hodayot. One who understands God's "plan" is to "walk" in a way that reflects comprehension of this knowledge. The word התהלך denotes conduct (see above on l. 10; cf. 4Q417 1 ii 5; 4Q416 2 iii 9).

4Q417 1 i 12–13

The addressee is to study. This is a prominent motif in the column (ll. 3, 6, 18 and 22) and 4QInstruction in general. He is to "these things seek" (שחר אלה), referring to the teachings about the created order that the column provides. The most immediate antecedent is "his deeds," referring to those of God, presumably his actions that created the world.[40] The *mebin* is to comprehend "[al]l their consequences" (תוצאותמה)—the consequences of "his deeds." The key word, a nominal form of the root יצא, literally means "out-goings." The term often has a geographical sense in the Hebrew Bible, referring to outlying areas and the limits of borders (e.g., Num 34:4–5; Josh 19:22). More rarely, the word can have a more abstract meaning, as in Prov 4:23: "Above all else, guard your heart, for it is the source of life (ממנו תוצאות חיים)."[41] How one's life turns out is determined by one's heart, the seat of intelligence (cf. 2:10). The term has the sense of "results" or, perhaps better, "outcomes." In 4QInstruction the addressee is to understand "outcomes"—what happens in a person's life (4Q420 1a ii–b 3–4 [par. 4Q421 1a ii–b 14–15]; cf. 4Q299 1 7). In 4Q417 1 i 13, unlike Proverbs, these outcomes have a strong deterministic sense. They do not issue simply from one's decisions but, more broadly, from God's "deeds," his creation of the world according to a deterministic plan.

Line 13 describes the results of studying the "consequences" of God's works. One can know his glory, his wondrous mysteries and powerful acts (lit. "strength," גבורה, in the plural) of his deeds. These terms signify profound insights into the nature of God and his dominion over the world. The statement begins "and then you will know" (ואז), as in lines 6

---

40. The addressee is also urged to "seek" (שחר) in 4Q416 2 ii 7; 4Q416 2 iii 12 (cf. 4Q418 35 3; 4Q418 69 ii 10). See Lange 1995, 67; Rey 2009a, 285.

41. Fox 2000, 184.

and 8. "Glory" (כבוד), probably here in construct with "[his] st[rength]"
(ע[וז]), often refers in 4QInstruction to the elect status of the addressee
rather than God, as is the case here.[42] The phrase "mysteries of wonder"
denotes God's grandeur and majesty that are obtainable through supernatural revelation (see also l. 2 above). The expression "mighty acts" may
allude to God's salvific acts in the history of Israel, such as the Exodus.
The phrase, however, probably expresses his power in general, rather than
solely specific instances in the past when he displayed his supremacy, none
of which are mentioned in 4Q417 1 i. The terms פלא and גבורה are often
combined in early Jewish literature, particularly in hymnic praises of God.
The War Scroll, for example, uses these terms together (along with "glory"
and "plan"), as in 4Q417 1 i 12–13. Column 15 states that "The people of
Israel are to praise his name: for your mighty deeds (גבורותיכה) ... for
great is the p[lan of] your [glo]ry and your wondrous mysteries in [your]
height[s]" (ll. 13–14).[43]

4Q417 1 i 13–14

Lines 13–18 are demarcated as a new unit by the phrase ואתה ("And
you ..."), which also begins the subsequent section in line 18. 4Q417 1
i 13–18 constitute the famous vision of meditation passage (sometimes
called the vision of Hagu or Haguy; see the textual notes section). The
scholarship on this pericope has been extensive.[44] The unit as a whole
resonates with key themes of 4QInstruction, such as supernatural revelation and the elect status of the addressee, but is unique in several ways.
Nowhere else in the document is there an opposition between the "spiritual people" and the "fleshly spirit." 4QInstruction mentions the vision of
meditation only in this passage. The pericope is an intentionally enigmatic
teaching upon which the *mebin* is to contemplate and reflect. In that sense
the unit is like a parable. A key lesson that he is to derive from studying

---

42. 4Q416 2 ii 18; 4Q416 2 iii 9, 18; 4Q418 81 5; 4Q418 159 ii 6. Cf. 4Q418 126 ii
8; Exod 24:17; Ps 26:8; Ezek 3:12.

43. The usage of פלא with גבורה is common in the War Scroll (1QM 11:9; 13:9;
16:14). See also 1QH 14:14; 4Q403 1 i 22; CD 13:8; 4Q299 5 2; Sir 42:21.

44. Studies of the passage include Rey 2009a, 292–303; Tigchelaar 2009, 103–
18; Macaskill 2007, 76–85; Barzilai 2007, 9–19; Wold 2005b, 124–49; Werman 2004,
125–40; Goff 2003b, 80–126; Collins 1999, 609–18; Lange 1995, 67–90; Elgvin 1998,
139–47. See also Goff 2009b, 383–86.

4Q417 1 i 13–18 is that he should strive to be like the spiritual people and not like the fleshly spirit (see below on ll. 17–18).

The initial exhortation of the passage urges the *mebin*, who is addressed directly, to "inherit your reward," while keeping in mind that "the per[iod]" will come (l. 14). The word רוש, here understood as an imperative ("inherit") can be read as ריש and thus equivalent to ראש, "poverty" or "origin."[45] The introductory phrase "And you, understanding one," has a vocative sense, suggesting that an imperative follows.[46] Reading "inherit" accords with the deterministic view that the elect status of the *mebin* has been established by God.[47] The phrase "your reward" (פעלתכה) evokes the elect's blessed recompense that has been established for him.[48] He should understand that the moment of judgment will arrive (it "comes"; בא), and behave in a way during his life that will allow him to survive this ordeal (cf. 4Q417 2 i 15–16).[49]

4Q417 1 ı 14–15

These lines emphasize the inevitability of eschatological judgment. The theme of determinism is paramount, as in the rest of the column, and is expressed here with writing terminology. The word "engraved" (חרות) and variations of the root חקק ("to inscribe, decree") both occur twice in lines 14–15. Line 15 mentions a heavenly "book of remembrance" in which God's plan that guides reality is written (see below). Judgment, evoked by the term "the punishment" (הפקודה; l. 14; cf. ll. 7–8), is presented as a key part of the divine plan established by God that guides the world.

The meaning of the expression "engraved is the statute" has been debated. The word החוק ("the statute") easily brings to mind the Torah. The tablets of Moses are "engraved" (חרות) in Exod 32:16, as is the stat-

---

45. For the former, Lange 1995, 51; for the latter, Elgvin 1997a, 256.

46. Rey 2009a, 292; Tigchelaar 2009, 106.

47. Following a suggestion by Strugnell and Harrington (1999, 162), Tigchelaar (2009, 115) favors understanding רוש as an error for דרוש (an imperative, "search").

48. The phrase "your reward" also occurs in 4Q418 107 4 and 4Q418 137 5 (cf. 4Q417 1 i 26; 4Q418 108 2).

49. Werman (2004, 135–36) emends בא to בו, producing the translation "since in it ([the book of] predestined history) the law is engraved." This is plausible, but the Hebrew in its present form is readily intelligible. Given the reliance of this passage upon Mal 3 (see below on ll. 15–16), accepting this text as it stands is supported by Mal 3:19 [Eng. 4:1]. This verse describes the judgment as imminent by proclaiming "the day is coming (בא)." See also Elgvin 2000b, 25.

ute of 4Q417 1 i 14. Lange concludes that the line refers to the Torah.[50] The parallelism of "engraved is the statute" and "ordained is all the punishment" suggests that their meanings are roughly similar. The ordained "punishment" clearly refers to the final judgment. The engraved "statute" thus likely underscores the inevitability of judgment by describing it as a law that is "engraved." Other examples of the key terms (חרות, חוק) describe the regulated and orderly nature of the created order. The Community Rule praises God for the harmonious structure of the cosmos: "With the offering of lips I shall bless him, in accordance with the decree recorded (כחוק חרות) forever. At the commencement of the years and in the turning of their seasons, when the decree (חוק) of their disposition is carried out …" (1QS 10:6–7; cf. ll. 8, 11). The Hodayot assert: "Everything is engraved (חקוק) before you in an inscription of record (בחרת זכרון) for all the everlasting seasons and the numbered cycles of the eternal years with all their appointed times" (9:25–26). In the Songs of the Sabbath Sacrifice, the relevant terms describe God's establishment of a law that guides the established and regular movements of the angels in the heavenly sanctuary.[51] These texts emphasize not the Torah, but the divine structure of creation. If 4Q417 1 i 14 contains an allusion to the Torah, it is secondary to the theme of judgment. By repeating both the word חרות and the root חקק, lines 14–15 emphasize the ordained nature of the decree of judgment as an inherent element of the created order.[52]

Judgment will occur "against all the in[iq]uit[ie]s of the sons of Sheth" (בני שית; l. 15). The phrase has been understood as invoking the patriarch Seth or the "Shethites" (or sons of Sheth), a Transjordanian tribe that is mentioned in Num 24:17 (cf. Jer 48:45). In the Hebrew Bible both names are spelled שֵׁת. There is also a *hapax legomenon*, שאת ("perdition"; Lam 3:47); the phrase in 4Q417 1 i 15 could thus be understood as "sons of

---

50. Lange 1995, 83.

51. "He has engraved his ordinances (חרת חוקיו) for all spiritual creatures," according to which "the holy ones sanctify themselves perpetually" (4Q400 1 i 5, 15; cf. 4Q402 4 3). Note also 4Q180 1 2–3: "Before creating them (the periods of history), he determined [their] operations [according to the precise sequence of the ages,] one age after another age. And this is engraved (חרות) on the [heavenly] tablets [for the sons of men]" (cf. T. Mos. 12:4). See Rey 2009a, 293–94.

52. Morphologically, the word מחוקק of 4Q417 1 i 15 can either be a *pual* (מְחֻוקָּק) or a *poel* (מְחוֹקֵק) participle. Context indicates that the participle is passive, favoring the former option, as Strugnell and Harrington 1999, 162, suggest (cf. Prov 31:5).

perdition."[53] Lange has argued that the line refers to the biblical Seth.[54] This can be supported by understanding the term אנוש of line 16 as Enosh, the son of Seth (see below). However, the בני שית will be judged by God for their iniquities. In the Second Temple period Seth is an overwhelmingly positive figure. Josephus, for example, says the patriarch "strove after virtue" (*Ant.* 1.68). In the Animal Apocalypse he corresponds to a white bull, like Adam and the righteous vindicated at the eschaton (1 En. 85:9; cf. Philo, *Post.* 173). This venerable view of Seth derives from Gen 5:1, which states that he was made in the likeness of God, reformulating the "image of God" trope of Gen 1:27.[55] The view that the expression "sons of Sheth" adapts the language of Num 24:17 has much more support (hence the spelling "Sheth" over "Seth"). The tribe mentioned in that verse is obscure, but the proclamation of their destruction is explicit.[56] In early Jewish literature the verse is utilized as a prooftext for the assertion that God will destroy the wicked.[57] This is the case, for example, in the Damascus Document and the War Scroll (CD 7:18–8:1; 1QM 11:6–7; cf. 4Q175 13). The "sons of Sheth" of 4QInstruction accord with this tradition, since they are to be punished when the final judgment occurs.[58] 4Q417 1 i 15 is reasonably read as alluding to Num 24:17.[59] There is not enough evidence to conclude that the expression denotes a specific group, such as the Gentiles or a sect that rivals the group behind 4QInstruction. The phrase "sons of Sheth" functions as a general designation for the wicked.[60]

4Q417 1 i 15–16

Line 15 mentions a "book of remembrance" (ספר זכרון) that is written before God. Line 16 associates this book with the vision of meditation. The statute of judgment and inscribed punishment of line 14 are reason-

---

53. Note also the phrase "son of perdition (or destruction)" in 2 Thess 2:3.

54. Lange 1995, 87. See also Turner 1998, 37; Brooke 2002, 213.

55. In rabbinic literature Seth is also viewed favorably (cf. Pirqe d. R. El. 22–23; 'Abot R. Nat. 2). Consult Turner 1998, 35.

56. Num 24:17: "A star shall come out of Jacob, and a scepter shall rise out of Israel; it shall crush the borderlands of Moab and the territory of the Shethites."

57. Collins 2010, 71–73; Beyerle 2008, 163–88.

58. The obscure term שאת ("perdition") of Lam 3:47 may also be evidence of the "Shethites" becoming a byword for a destroyed people.

59. Rey 2009a, 297; Kampen 2011, 99; Wold 2005b, 139.

60. Note, however, that the wicked are not called "sons of Sheth" in the judgment scenes of 4Q416 1 and 4Q418 69 ii.

ably understood as written in this book. Eschatological judgment comprises an important aspect of the content of the tome. Since it is written before God, it is in heaven. The "book of remembrance" can be reasonably compared to the "tablets of heaven" prominent in 1 Enoch and Jubilees, as well as the "tablets of destiny" of Mesopotamian tradition, especially the Enuma Elish, upon which the fate of humanity is recorded.[61] 1QH 9:25–26 (cited above) attests a similar motif, in which God's deterministic plan for creation is inscribed in heaven. The prominence throughout 4Q417 1 i of the deterministic nature of creation suggests that the divine plan according to which history unfolds is written in the book of remembrance. Werman has persuasively argued that the book contains "the predestined plan" of history.[62] The writtenness of this divine plan gives it legitimacy and authority.

The phrase "book of remembrance" is derived from the book of Malachi: "The Lord took note and listened, and a book of remembrance (ספר זכרון) was written before him of those who fear the Lord and think of his name" (3:16; cf. Esth 6:1; Ezra 4:15).[63] This group will be spared when the eschatological day of the Lord arrives (3:17–20). The book of 4Q417 1 i 15 is likewise connected to the theme of judgment, as mentioned above. The term "remembrance" in Mal 3:16 has been reasonably understood to mean that the volume in question is a sort of "divine ledger" in which the words and the deeds of the pious are recorded.[64] The book in 4Q417 1 i 15 is written "for those who keep his word," presumably a reference to the elect (cf. 4Q418 81 8). The tome of 4Q417 1 i 15, like that of Mal 3:16, can be understood as containing a heavenly record of who will be spared in the eschatological judgment and who will not.

In Mal 3:16 the relationship between the "book of remembrance" and the righteous is conveyed by the preposition *lamed* (ליראי יהוה). According to the NRSV, the book is written *of* the pious. The author of 4Q417 1

---

61. See, for example, 1 En. 93:2: "I will speak these things ... according to that which appeared to me in the heavenly vision, and (which) I know from the words of the holy angels, and understand from the tablets of heaven" (cf. 90:20; 103:1; Dan 7:10; 12:1; Jub. 4:32; 6:30; 16:3). See Baynes 2011; Elgvin 1997a, 88; Lange 1995, 69–79; Paul 1973, 345–53.

62. Werman 2004, 136.

63. Note the similarity of ויכתב ספר זכרון לפניו ("a book of remembrance was written before him") to ספר זכרון כתוב לפניו in 4Q417 1 i 15. Consult Rey 2009a, 295; Lange 1995, 53, 71; Collins 1997c, 126.

64. Hill 1998, 340.

i 15–16 apparently understood the *lamed* as meaning that this heavenly book is available *for* the elect on earth. The identification of the book of remembrance as the vision of meditation (see also below) can be understood as answering an exegetical question—if the book of remembrance is in heaven and available for the elect on earth, how do they get access to it? Line 16 explains that it is (והואה) a "vision of meditation" *of* "the book of remembrance."[65] They receive on earth a vision of a book in heaven.

The heavenly "book of remembrance" can be interpreted as a heavenly prototype of the Torah. The vision of meditation (ההגות) relies upon the verb הגה ("to meditate"), which is explicitly associated with the Torah in the Hebrew Bible and early Jewish literature (e.g., Josh 1:8; Ps 1:2; Sir 14:20; see also below). But identification of this book with the Torah is not the main point of the passage at hand. One should not, as Lange does, understand 4Q417 1 i 15 as an early attestation of the rabbinic trope, classically expressed in Genesis Rabbah 1, that the order of creation is inscribed in the heavenly Torah.[66] This is a later, fuller elaboration of the tradition attested in 4QInstruction that God's deterministic plan which guides the structure of the world is written in a heavenly book. 1 Enoch is a closer parallel to 4QInstruction, since the composition presents God's plan for humankind as written down in heaven, with minimal evidence that this divine writing should be equated with the Torah.[67] Similarly, the corresponding book in Mal 3:16 is not the Torah, but rather heavenly written proof that the pious will be spared when judgment occurs. 4QInstruction appeals to the "book of remembrance" to assert the inevitability of divine judgment, not that the nature of creation is inscribed in a heavenly Torah.[68] While 4QInstruction uses verses from the Torah, the composition never thematizes

---

65. See Tigchelaar 2009, 113. For a different understanding of והואה, see Werman 2004, 137. Consult also Strugnell and Harrington 1999, 164; Macaskill 2007, 80.

66. Lange 1995, 85. Genesis Rabbah begins with an explication of the crux אמון of Prov 8:30, which refers to personified Wisdom, understood by the rabbis as the Torah. Genesis Rabbah 1:1 continues: "The Torah declares: 'I was the working tool of the Holy One, blessed be He.' In human practice, when a mortal king builds a palace, he builds it not with his own skill but with the skill of an architect. The architect moreover does not build it out of his head, but employs plans and diagrams to know how to arrange the chambers and the wicket doors. Thus God consulted the Torah and created the world." See also Rey 2009a, 295; Hengel 1974, 1.174.

67. Nickelsburg 2001, 50.

68. The book of remembrance invites comparison to Exod 17:14, in which God says to Moses: "Write this as a reminder (זכרון) in a book. ... I will utterly blot out the

or praises it in the manner of Ben Sira, who associates the Torah with the heavenly figure of personified wisdom (24:23).

The word "remembrance" has a double meaning. As a "book of remembrance," it is a memorial in which the fate of humankind is inscribed. In line 14 the term זכרון also encourages the addressee to remember that this judgment will occur. The engraved statute of judgment written in a heavenly book can be compared to Dan 7:10, in which books are opened when the wicked fourth beast is judged.[69] 4QInstruction's "book of remembrance," by contrast, is never opened. In Daniel the books are unsealed to provide an image of what happens when God's judgment takes place. 4Q417 1 i 15 wants the *mebin* to remember that it will occur.

"The book of remembrance" is associated with an enigmatic "vision of meditation" (חזון ההגות). The Damascus Document and the Rule of the Congregation repeatedly mention ספר ההגו which has been understood as "the book of Hagu (or Hagi)" or "the book of meditation" (CD 10:6; 13:2–3; 14:7–8; 1QSa 1:6–7).[70] The verb הגה means "to think" or "meditate" (also "to mutter" or "groan") and is connected to the study of the Torah, as mentioned above. The "book of meditation" has thus been understood as a reference to the Torah.[71] The "book" mentioned in the Qumran rulebooks is described as an actual volume of which leaders of the sect had to be knowledgeable, although nothing is stated about its contents.[72] The "vision of meditation" in 4QInstruction, by contrast, is never treated as a physical book, but rather is associated with a volume that is in heaven ("the book of remembrance"). Since the "book of meditation" remains somewhat enigmatic, its value for assessing the "vision of meditation" in 4QInstruction is limited. The fact that the composition equates the "vision of meditation" with a book allows for the possibility that this vision was a formative influence in the Dead Sea sect's "book of meditation," or at least inspired its title (see section 10 of the introduction).

---

remembrance of (זכר) Amalek from under heaven." This verse, like 4Q417 1 i 15, uses the word זכרון to assert the arrival of future judgment.

69. 1 En. 90:20; 4Q530 2 ii 18–19; cf. Rev 6:1–17; 10:2, 8.

70. Werman (2004, 140) understands it as containing "meditations on creation and history." See also Hempel 2002, 285–86; Steinmetz 2001, 40–58.

71. For this view, see Rabinowitz 1961, 109–14. The book of meditation has also been understood as some sort of sectarian work. Consult, for example, Goshen-Gottstein 1958, 286–88. Note also Ginzberg 1976, 50–51.

72. CD 13:2–3, for example, asserts that for a priest to be a leader in the camps he must be trained in this book.

The term חזון denotes divine revelation. The word is used this way both in early Jewish literature and in the Hebrew Bible, particularly in the prophets.[73] The word "vision" is not common in 4QInstruction, elsewhere occurring only later in 4Q417 1 i (l. 22). The word ההגות clarifies that the vision is to be studied and contemplated. In language unique to this pericope, the phrase "the vision of meditation" evokes a theme that is pervasive throughout 4QInstruction—the value of studying supernatural revelation.[74] Using the same root (הגה), line 6 of 4Q417 1 i urges the addressee to "meditate" upon the mystery that is to be. The "vision of meditation" is a vision of the "book of remembrance" that one is to contemplate. The book is in heaven, written before God. The trope of a seer being lifted up to heaven and shown secrets à la 1 Enoch plays no role whatsoever in 4QInstruction. A human learns about the "book of remembrance" through a revelation of it. As one can understand God's plan that guides history through the study of the mystery that is to be, so the content of the heavenly "book of remembrance" is acquired through contemplation of a vision of it. The "vision of meditation" in 4Q417 1 i 16 should not be thought of as a distinct revelation in addition to the mystery that is to be but rather a veiled reference to it. This is in keeping with the conceit that lines 13–18 constitute an intentionally enigmatic lesson which the addressee is to understand only after much study (see also below on ll. 17–18).

4Q417 1 i 16–17

The rest of the "vision of meditation" pericope focuses on who is and who is not given access to the vision. Lines 16–17 affirm that God has bequeathed "it" (וינחילה) to אנוש and the "spiritual people" who were created in the likeness of the angels. The antecedent of the feminine suffix is most likely "meditation." God created אנוש and the "spiritual people" with the intellectual capacity to study and understand the revelation given to them. This is not the case with the "fleshly spirit" (see further below).

Two major interpretative options for אנוש have been proposed—that the word signifies the patriarch Enosh or is a general term for humankind. Lange opts for the former, arguing that the fall of the angels (and the rise of iniquity that led to the flood) is to be correlated with the offspring of the

---

73. See, for example, Isa 1:1; Nah 1:1; Dan 9:24; Hab 2:2–3; Sir 36:20; 1QH 12:19; 4Q300 1a ii–b 2–3.

74. Werman 2004, 137.

patriarch Seth (recall the "sons of Sheth" in line 15 above).[75] Enosh, however, is never proclaimed as a recipient of revelation in the Second Temple period.[76] The view that אנוש denotes humankind has been defended by Wold. For him, all of humanity was given access to the "vision of meditation," but it was later taken away from some of them, who are referred to as the "fleshly spirit" (see below for discussion of this phrase).[77] Given that the "spiritual people" are reasonably understood as a category of people (see below), it is not clear why line 16 would state that the vision is given to them *and* to humanity in general.[78]

John Collins has put forward a more persuasive understanding of the term אנוש: it is a reference to Adam.[79] In this understanding, the knowledge acquired through the study of the "vision of meditation" was previously possessed by Adam in the garden of Eden. The word אנוש alludes to Gen 1:27 in the Community Rule (1QS 3:17–18).[80] The focus on good and evil in the passage (4Q417 1 i 18) supports an allusion to Adam, as does the word יצר in line 17, which also evokes Genesis 1–3.[81] Furthermore, the construal of Adam as a recipient of heavenly knowledge is consistent with his depiction elsewhere in early Jewish literature. He is often associated with angels and heavenly knowledge. The Book of Jubilees, for example, claims that angels taught Adam in the garden (3:15). The Treatise on the Two Spirits associates "the wisdom of the sons of heaven" with "the glory of Adam," generally understood as a reference to eternal life (1QS 4:22–23; cf. CD 3:20; 1QH 4:27).[82] According to the Septuagint version of Gen 3:5, once Adam and Eve eat the fruit they will possess knowledge of good

---

75. Lange 1995, 88. See also Wold 2005b, 125–28.

76. Elgvin 1997a, 88. Consult further Fraade 1984; 1998, 59–86.

77. Wold 2005b, 148–49. Rey (2009a, 281) translates the key term as "*homme*." See also Fletcher-Louis 2002, 114.

78. Strugnell and Harrington 1999, 164–65. The editors do not favor one of these options in their translation ("Man/Enosh") of 4Q417 1 i 16, but in their discussion of the passage they prefer the former.

79. Collins 1999, 612; 1997c, 121–25. See also Macaskill 2007, 83; Wold 2005b, 131–35.

80. "He created man (אנוש) to rule the world."

81. Note, however, that nowhere else in 4QInstruction does the word אנוש refer to Adam (4Q416 2 ii 12 [par. 4Q418 8 12]; 4Q418 55 11; 4Q418 77 3).

82. For discussion of the phrase, consult Bunta 2006, 55–84; Golitzin 2003, 275–308. Note also Niskanen 2009, 417–36.

and evil and be "like divine beings" (ὡς θεοί)—understanding the Hebrew
כאלהים as a plural rather than as a reference to God.[83]

"The vision of meditation" is also given to "the spiritual people" (עם
רוח). They are mentioned nowhere else in 4QInstruction. Since they were
fashioned "according to the likeness of the holy ones" (כתבנית קדושים),
they themselves are not "holy ones"—a common early Jewish term for
angels—but rather people who were created in a way that made them similar to the angels.[84] This would explain why they have access to a heavenly
book. The creation of the "spiritual people" is expressed with the root יצר,
which recalls the formation of humankind in Gen 2:7.[85] The expression
כתבנית קדושים probably contains another allusion to Genesis. Collins has
plausibly suggested that the phrase reworks the expression בצלם אלהים
("in the image of God") from Gen 1:27, with אלהים understood not as
God but a regular plural, signifying angels.[86] This also supports reading
אנוש as a reference to Adam.

Since the "fleshly spirit" does not have the knowledge of good and evil
(l. 17), one can infer that the "spiritual people" do. It can be deduced further that this knowledge is inscribed in the heavenly book of remembrance.
This suggests that the knowledge of good and evil does not merely denote
the ability to choose right from wrong but also signifies broad insights into
the nature of reality and God's deterministic plan that shapes it, which is
inscribed in this book (see above on ll. 15–16).[87] Elsewhere 4QInstruction
claims that the angels have eternal life (4Q418 69 ii 13). Since the spiritual
people are created like the angels and distinguished from "fleshly" beings

---

83. Sir 49:16; Apoc. Mos. 28:4; 3 Bar. 4:7–15; 2 En. 30:11; Luke 3:38.

84. Lange 1995, 86; Collins 1999, 613.

85. The word יצרו can be understood as either a verb with a suffix, as in the above
translation (and Gen 2:7), or as a noun with a suffix ("his inclination") without a major
difference in meaning.

86. Collins 1999, 615. The word תבנית has a well-attested range of meanings in
the Hebrew Bible and early Judaism, such as "form," or a "blueprint" of something to
be built. This term is used for the plan for the construction of the tabernacle in Exod
25:9, 40. In the Songs of the Sabbath Sacrifice the angels bless the תבנית of the divine
throne (4Q405 20 ii–22 8; cf. 11Q17 7 11; 11Q17 8 3). See also Barzilai 2007, 11–12;
Strugnell and Harrington 1999, 165.

87. Recall the discussion above regarding the use of opposing pairs (including
good/evil) as merisms in 4Q417 1 i 6–8. The Treatise on the Two Spirits associates
its deterministic conception of the world with the knowledge of good and evil (1QS
4:25–26).

(see further below), they can be linked to eternal life as well. It is reasonable to suggest that they have the prospect of life after death.[88]

4Q417 1 ɪ 17–18

The people of the "fleshly spirit" (רוח בשר), in contrast to the "spiritual people," do not have access to the vision of meditation. This is because they do not possess the knowledge of good and evil. They are not given הגוי, a passive participle, denoting "what is meditated upon," in reference to the meditation (ההגות) of the vision in line 16. Unlike the spiritual people, the fleshly spirit has no affinity with the angels. 4QInstruction shows no interest in the creation of the fleshly spirit. By contrast, it stresses that the spiritual people were fashioned like the angels. In the eschatological judgment scene of 4Q416 1, those who are to perish are referred to as the fleshly spirit: "Every fleshly spirit will be laid bare" (l. 12). The "vision of meditation," by providing access to the heavenly book of remembrance, conveys knowledge of the final judgment (see above on 4Q417 1 i 15). The fleshly spirit does not have this knowledge. In 4Q418 81 the addressee is told that he, like the spiritual people, has been separated from the fleshly spirit (l. 2). The fleshly spirit denotes people who are not among the elect. They do not possess the revealed knowledge required to receive positive recompense during the final judgment. The term "flesh" denotes their mortality and lack of access to supernatural revelation.[89] The Hodayot, the only other ancient Jewish text that uses the expression "fleshly spirit," supports this interpretation. The speaker, in his humility before God, refers to himself as a "fleshly spirit." In keeping with the composition's *Niedrigskeitsdoxologie*, its "low" anthropology, the poet is pained by the tension between his reception of heavenly knowledge and his base, creaturely existence: "In the mysteries of your understanding [you] apportioned all these in order to make known your glory. [But how i]s a fleshly spirit to understand all these things?" (5:30–31; cf. l. 15; 4:37). In 4QInstruction the "fleshly spirit" is emphatically denied revelation. The composition avoids the theo-

---

88. Wold (2005b, 134) asserts that those of the fleshly spirit are "just as immortal" as the spiritual people because "they survive for punishment in the hereafter." The fleshly spirit is destroyed in the final judgment. If one grants that the people of this spirit suffer eternal punishment after death—a position never explicit in the text—this would be manifestly different from the immortality possessed by the spiritual people.

89. Rey (2009a, 301) emphasizes that the fleshly spirit should be associated with iniquity, and the spiritual people with virtue.

logical conundrum of the "flesh of the elect" that plagues the author of the Hodayot by asserting that those who have access to the vision of meditation are like the angels. The "spirit" of the spiritual people denotes their affinity with the heavenly world, whereas the "flesh" of the fleshly spirit signifies its separation from this realm.

Genesis 1–3, Dualistic Conceptions of Humankind, and Two Adams

4QInstruction posits two opposed types of humankind, one associated with spirit and the other with flesh, and grounds this dichotomy in the language of Gen 1–3. Collins has observed that this schema is similar to the well-known "double creation of man" in Philo.[90] The Alexandrian sage observes tensions in the account of Adam in the book of Genesis, such as his association with heavenly beings in Gen 1:27 and the dust in 2:7 (*Opif.* 134–135; *Alleg.* 1.31). Philo explains this by positing that Genesis recounts the creation of two different kinds of man—one heavenly, and one earthly. The apostle Paul makes a similar but not equivalent distinction between spiritual and fleshly kinds of people (1 Cor 3:1). 4QInstruction may attest to early Jewish exegetical traditions that shape reflection on the nature of humankind in both Philo and Paul.[91] The Qumran wisdom text establishes that in Palestine in the second century B.C.E. a flesh/spirit dichotomy could be supported with language from Gen 1–3.

4QInstruction, however, does not explicitly posit two opposed Adams, as do Philo and Paul. In "the vision of meditation" passage Adam is associated prominently with the spiritual people, not with the fleshly spirit. The connection between the fleshly spirit and Adam is more indirect. The Hebrew רוח בשר ("fleshly spirit") may paraphrase the expression נפש חיה ("living being") of Gen 2:7. The claim that God gave Hagu "but no more" (ועוד לוא) to the fleshly spirit in line 17 suggests that the fleshly spirit once possessed the vision of meditation, but that it was later taken away from it.[92] The line thus contains a veiled reference to Adam's expulsion from Eden. This explains the fleshly spirit's lack of access to the knowledge of good and evil. The association between Adam and the spiritual people establishes that 4QInstruction reflects a positive conception of Adam (4Q423 1). It is thus not surprising that the text never directly

---

90. Collins 1999, 615–17. See also Tobin 1983; Wold 2005b, 141–46.
91. See further Goff 2009a, 114–25; 2011, 41–59; Frey 2002, 367–404.
92. Wold 2005b, 119; Goff 2009b, 384–85.

mentions his disobedience in the garden and expulsion. The composition shows little interest in explaining how the vision of meditation was taken away from the fleshly spirit. An allusion to Adam is explicit in the case of the spiritual people and is at best implicit with regard to the fleshly spirit.

Despite the dichotomy of the "spiritual people" (עם רוח) and the "fleshly spirit" (רוח בשר), they have an unusual factor in common—the word "spirit" (רוח). The "fleshly spirit" does not know good and evil "according to the judgment of its [sp]irit" (כמשפט ר[ו]חו; l. 18). The fleshly spirit's lack of knowing good and evil is consistent with the nature of its spirit.[93] The term "spirit" has an epistemological or intellectual connotation. The word often signifies one's temper or mental attitude. The lowly or downtrodden, for example, can be described as having a "broken spirit" (רוח נכאה) or being "smitten in spirit" (נכה־רוח).[94] Proverbs 29:11, for example, states "A fool gives full vent to anger," asserting literally that the fool's "entire spirit brings forth" (כל־רוחו יוציא). His mental state (anger) is expressed by the word "spirit."[95] In the Community Rule the term is in parallelism with יצר, which denotes one's mental inclination for either good or evil behavior.[96]

It is beyond the scope of the present task to examine comprehensively the term רוח in ancient Jewish literature. Suffice it to say that the term can refer not only to God's spirit (e.g., Gen 41:38), but also to a person's mental comportment, without a firm delineation of the modern conceptions of "mind" or "emotion" as distinct psychological categories. The word "spirit" signifies in 4QInstruction an important, non-physical attribute of the addressee.[97] He jeopardizes his "holy spirit" through unsound financial arrangements (4Q416 2 ii 6; cf. 4Q416 2 iii 6).[98] The "spirit" of the *mebin* was presumably given to him by God. The term, 4Q417 1 i 18 suggests, can also express one's mental posture.[99] The key difference

---

93. See, e.g., Judg 13:12; 1 Kgs 18:28; 2 Kgs 11:14. Consult Tigchelaar 2009, 110.

94. Isa 66:2; Prov 15:13; 17:22; 1QM 11:10; 1QH 23:16.

95. Deut 2:30; Prov 14:29; Qoh 7:11; Sir 7:11.

96. The establishment of the community council of twelve men and three priests is, among other things, to "preserve faithfulness in the land with firm purpose and repentant spirit (ביצר סמוך ורוח נשברה)" (1QS 8:3). In the *yaḥad* one's "spirit" is judged, along with one's "insight" and "deeds" (e.g., 5:23–24).

97. I suggest in the commentary below that the phrase "spirit of life" in 4Q418 126 ii 8 refers to the vitality of a living person. Note also the unfortunately fragmentary phrase "spirit of understanding" (רוח בינה) in 4Q418 58 2 and 4Q418 73 1.

98. He dominates the "spirit" of his wife (4Q416 2 iv 8; 4Q415 9 8).

99. Recall the debate regarding the term "spirit" in the Treatise on the Two Spir-

between the "fleshly spirit" and the "spiritual people" is the *kind* of spirit they possess. As was discussed above, there is a prominent association between the revealed vision of meditation and the study of it. The "spirit" of the "spiritual people" denotes not only their affinity with heaven but also their mental acumen and psychological bearing to meditate properly upon heavenly knowledge; the "spirit" of the "fleshly spirit" does not include this capability.

The spiritual people signify the elect, who are like the angels and possess access to revelation. The fleshly spirit represents the non-elect. They are denied revelation. Whereas the spiritual people can reasonably be understood as attaining eternal life, like the angels, the fleshly spirit denotes human mortality and the finitude of creaturely existence. A key lesson for the *mebin* to derive from the pericope is that he is like the spiritual people. They represent an ideal for him to emulate. The addressee is distinguished from the fleshly spirit, as are the "spiritual people" (4Q418 81 1–2). He has access to the mystery that is to be; the spiritual people have the vision of meditation. They are fashioned "according to the likeness of the holy ones." The *mebin* is in "the lot of the angels" (4Q418 81 4–5). The "spiritual people" are associated with Adam (אנוש), and the addressee has authority over the garden of Eden (4Q423 1). The "vision of meditation" passage as a whole constitutes a lesson from which, after much reflection, the *mebin* could attain understanding about key aspects of his elect status. This includes his inherent affinity with the angels and access to supernatural revelation. He is to understand that he is like the spiritual people.

4Q417 1 i 18–19

A poorly preserved section (ll. 18–27) begins in line 18 with a *vacat* followed by an exhortation (cf. ll. 6, 13; cf. Sir 47:12). Lines 18–19 urge the *mebin* to study the mystery that is to be. In this way he can know "[the path]s of all life" and "the manner of one's walking that is appointed over [his] deed[s]." He can learn how a person's conduct is a result of how God has established his deeds. Lines 18–19 are similar to lines 11–13, which claim that one can learn the "[sec]rets of his plan" guiding the world and all of the "consequences" of this divine scheme. The term "walking" (התהלכו) in line 19 describes a person's actions that are established by God, as in

---

its. Wernberg-Møller (1961, 413–41), e.g., argued that it mainly has a psychological meaning in the Treatise. It has also been asserted that the term has both psychological and cosmological meanings in this work. Consult, e.g., Popović 2007, 183.

line 12 (cf. l. 10). "Deeds" (מעשים) occurs in line 19 and is common in the column (ll. 7, 9, 10, 13). Line 26 associates a deterministic mindset with the term "deeds" (see below).

4Q417 1 i 20

The addressee is to distinguish "between great and small." This is similar to lines 6–8, which assert that the addressee can understand several opposing concepts, including truth and iniquity, wisdom and folly, and good and evil. The contrasting terms convey the broad scope of knowledge that is available through the study of the mystery that is to be. This may also be the case in line 20, but one cannot be sure, since most of the line has not survived. Also note the second person plural suffix on "counsel" (cf. l. 27). This is not in keeping with the composition's preference for the singular.

4Q417 1 i 22

This line preserves the phrase "every vision" and the imperative "know." Line 22 likely discusses the addressee's comprehension of supernatural revelation. The focus on multiple visions is striking, given the earlier focus of the column on the vision of meditation. Unfortunately, not enough survives of the line to interpret it sufficiently.

4Q417 1 i 23

This line and line 24 contain a plea to be ethical. The *mebin* is to remain strong and untouched by iniquity. Line 24 suggests that this moral instruction should be understood in the context of eschatological judgment.

4Q417 1 i 24

All who are touched by iniquity will not be considered innocent, but rather will be regarded as wicked. This combination of terms suggests that the line describes the eschatological punishment of the wicked (cf. 4Q416 1 12; 4Q418 69 ii 7–9). This is supported by the rest of the column, which stresses the inevitability of judgment (ll. 7–8, 12, 14–15).[100] The *mebin* is to remain ethically vigilant to avoid harsh recompense when he is judged. The claim that he will be considered wicked "according to his inheritance

---

100. Note the use of the verb נקה in the context of eschatological judgment in 4Q418 102a + b 5 (cf. CD 5:15).

(נחלתו)" underscores the composition's deterministic perspective. 4QIn-
struction teaches that each person is given a particular allotment by God
(see the excursus in chapter 4). One is urged not to be wicked in lines
23–24. This implies free choice, but the text also understands a person's
conduct as divinely established.

4Q417 1 i 24–25

A new section presumably begins in lines 24–25. Line 25 calls the
addressee an "intelligent son," and offers the imperative "understand." This
reads like the beginning of an exhortation. On this basis, the phrase ואתה
("And you") is supplemented at the end of line 24 (cf. ll. 1, 18). The instruction discusses supernatural revelation and knowledge of the created order.
The *mebin* is urged, in the second person singular, to understand his
"mysteries" (רזיכה) and the "[eternal] foundation[s]" ([אוש]י עולם])." A
call to learn mysteries is also found in 4Q418 177 7a. Recall the assertion in 4Q417 1 i 8–9 that God created the "foundation" (אוש) by means
of the mystery that is to be. Line 25 probably stated something similar.
4QInstruction repeatedly refers to the disclosure of a single revelation, the
mystery that is to be (e.g., 4Q416 2 iii 18; 4Q418 123 ii 4). This suggests
that "your mysteries" in line 25 does not refer to multiple revelations. The
phrase is better understood as equivalent to "your teachings"—the lessons
of 4QInstruction in a general sense (see also the commentary on 4Q416
2 ii 8–9). A call to study the mystery that is to be is not found in every
exhortation of the document. The contemplation of this mystery, however,
provides insight into how the natural order functions, and is thus crucial
to the pedagogy of 4QInstruction. In that they provide ways to understand the world and succeed in it, all of the composition's teachings are
grounded in the study of the mystery that is to be. It thus makes sense to
refer to the composition's teachings in general as "mysteries."

4Q417 1 i 26

This line contains a fragmentary reference to the establishment of
"their deeds." The suffix of the noun is in the feminine plural; the antecedent, now lost, was perhaps "ways" (דרכים) or "spirits" (רוחות; cf. 1QS
3:25).[101] The claim that they are founded "by you" (בכה) suggests that the
line refers not to the *mebin* but to God. The line likely contains remnants

---

101. Strugnell and Harrington 1999, 168.

of an exaltation of God who is praised, as in the Hodayot, for his establishment of the elements of the created order (e.g., 1QH 9:10–22).

4Q417 1 i 27

This line corresponds to language from Num 15:39. The biblical verse reads: "You have the fringe so that, when you see it, you will remember all the commandments of the Lord and do them and *not follow after your own heart and your own eyes*, after which you lust." (The language corresponding to l. 27 is italicized.)[102] A second hand corrected ועיניכמה to ואחרי עיניכמה. The change brings the text closer to the version of the verse that stands in the MT (and the Septuagint and Samaritan Pentateuch). The reading ועיניכמה may have been considered less authoritative than the ואחרי reading.[103]

Elsewhere, 4QInstruction encourages the *mebin* to observe patterns and structures in the natural world (4Q418 69 ii 3–4; 4Q423 5 6). 4Q417 1 i 27 asserts that what one can deduce from his own senses is less valuable than knowledge learned from the study of heavenly revelation. This constitutes a genuine epistemological shift from traditional sapiential literature, in which the observation of the world is paramount.

Numbers 15:39 is part of an assertion that Israelites are to wear "fringes" on their garments (vv. 37–41; cf. Deut 22:12). This is to ensure that the people of Israel remember the covenant, despite human fallible senses. 4QInstruction shows no interest in the requirement of wearing the fringes and never stresses keeping the commandments. Rather, the composition appropriates language from the verse to emphasize that relying upon supernatural revelation is more important than one's own eyes and ears.

4QInstruction keeps Num 15:39 in the second person plural. Contrast its reformulation of Numbers 30 and Genesis 2 in 4Q416 2 iv (see com-

---

102. One could posit that the quotation of Num 15:39 began at the end of l. 26 and continued into l. 27. This position, however, is problematized by the fact that l. 27 begins with לוא and the corresponding phrase in the biblical verse is ולא. The absence of the initial *waw* argues against the view that the text in question continues a statement that began in l. 26.

103. The change was considered necessary by a scribe, even though semantically there is no major difference between the two options. The *waw* variant is preceded by a phrase that begins with אחרי. The *waw* in ועיניכמה would have simply continued the sense of the preceding preposition (אחרי).

mentary above). Normally the composition prefers the second person singular, but occasionally it indicates that it addresses more than one person (e.g., 4Q418 123 ii 4; 4Q418 221 3). 4Q417 1 i 18–27 is inconsistent in this regard, switching back and forth from the singular to the plural. Line 20 uses a plural suffix, for example, in "your counsel" (סודכמה), whereas "your mysteries" in line 25 has a singular one (רזיכה).

7.
4Q417 1 II

Parallel text: 4Q418 123 i (underline)

TEXT[1]

[הבט]	]○[ ]	2
[	ברז נֿהֿ]יֿ[הֿ]	3
[	נחומים לפֿ]	4
[	התהלך תמֿ]ים	5
[	ברך שמו]	6
[	מֿשמחתבֿה חֿ]	7
[	גדולים רחמי אֿ]לֿ	8
[	הלל אל ועל כול נגע בר̇]ך שמו	9
[	בֿרֿצונֿו היו יֿהזאה מבין]○	10
[	יֿפקֿוד כול דרכיכה ע]○[ ]○[ ]	11
[	אל תפתכה מחשבת יצֿר רע]	12
[	לאמת תדרוש אל תפתכה מֿ]	13
[אל]	בלוא נבונות בשר אל תשגכ]ה ^{צוה}	14
[	תחשוב] [אל תאמֿרֿ]	15
[	כֿן] כֿול הוֿן○	16
[	] ○ וכֿחזקכה	17
[	] לֿ	18

---

1. Strugnell and Harrington 1999, 169–72; Tigchelaar 2001, 54; Elgvin 1997a, 265–66. The textual notes section refers to these works.

TRANSLATION

2   ... [... *gaze*]
3   upon the mystery that is to [*b*]e ...
4   comfort to ...
5   walk per[*fectly* ...]
6   bless his name ...
7   from your joy ...
8   great is the compassion of G[*od* ...]
9   praise God and upon every strike ble[*ss his name* ...]
10   by his will they came into being ᵃⁿᵈ he causes understanding ...
11   he will punish all of your deeds ...
12   Do not let the thought of an evil inclination mislead you ...
13   for truth you shall search. Let not ... mislead you ...
14   without ʰⁱˢ ᵃᵖᵖᵒⁱⁿᵗⁱⁿᵍ understandings of flesh. Let not ... lead you
      astray ... [*do not*]
15   think ... do not say ...
16   thus ... [all wealth ...]
17   [... and according to your statute ...]

TEXTUAL NOTES

    ii 10: בְּרֹצוֹנוֹ. So also Tigchelaar. The editors of DJD 34 read וּבְרֹצוֹנוֹ,
but there is not enough space for this transcription.
    ii 15: תֹאמֹר; 4Q418 123 i 2: תֹאומֹר.

COMMENTARY

    Only the upper right-hand side of 4Q417 1 ii survives. The column
does not preserve a single sentence in full. Lines 4–10 appear to be remnants of a hymnic text that praises God, and lines 11–15 urge the addressee
to be ethical and to avoid the evil inclination (l. 12). There is a minor overlap between 4Q417 1 ii 14–15 and 4Q418 123 i 1–2. In this case, 4Q418
123 ii was originally part of a now lost column 3 of 4Q417 1.

4Q417 1 ɪɪ 2–3

    The beginning of the column presumably contained a call to study the
mystery that is to be. The combination of the *raz nihyeh* with the preposition *bet* in line 3 is common in exhortations in 4QInstruction (e.g., 4Q416
2 iii 9; 4Q417 1 i 18). This explains the supplement of the word "gaze" in

line 2, which is often used with the mystery that is to be (see the commentary to 4Q417 1 i 3–5).

4Q417 1 ii 5

The prominence of imperatives in the column (ll. 6, 9, cf. ll. 12–13) suggests that the word התהלך in line 5 is likely an imperative as well. "Walking perfectly" is a common phrase in the Dead Sea Scrolls, typically denoting behavior that is encouraged.[2] 4Q417 1 ii 5 probably made a similar point (see also the commentary to 4Q416 2 iii 9; cf. 4Q417 1 i 12; 4Q415 2 i + 1 ii 3).

4Q417 1 ii 6

Line 6 urges one to "bless his name." The same phrase is reasonably reconstructed in line 9. Cultivating a pious attitude in the *mebin* is an important part of the education program of 4QInstruction, as in Ben Sira (15:10). In both texts the student is to understand the power of God and how he created the world. A natural result of this realization is to praise God. 4Q416 2 iii 11 exhorts the addressee to do this constantly (cf. 4Q418 81 1, 11–12).

4Q417 1 ii 7

This line contains a fragmentary reference to "your joy." "Eternal joy" is an eschatological reward the addressee can receive according to 4Q417 2 i 11–12. Line 7 may have discussed this trope. Since this section of the column includes praise of God, the second person suffix may refer to the deity instead of the *mebin*. Not enough of the text survives to decide which option is preferable.

4Q417 1 ii 8

The surviving phrase of this line, "great is the compassion of G[od]," is likely a remnant of a hymnic description of God. There is limited evidence that the column extols the deity as the creator of the world (see l. 10).

---

2. See, for example, 1QS 2:2; 9:19; CD 2:15; 1QSb 1:2; 4Q525 5 11 (cf. Ps 15:2; Prov 28:18).

4Q417 1 ii 9

Like line 6, this line exhorts the addressee to praise God. Line 9 employs the imperative "praise" (הלל). A call to "bless his name" is reasonably reconstructed on the basis of parallelism. The language and intent of 4Q417 1 ii 9 are similar to 4Q416 2 iii 11, which encourages the *mebin* to "praise (הלל) his name constantly." Line 9 affirms that one should bless God "upon every strike" (על כול נגע). The term נגע can mean "affliction" (e.g., 1QS 3:23). It can also denote plague, sickness, or a physical blow. The limited evidence available suggests the last option. 4Q417 2 i 25 mentions a beating from a creditor. In this line, as in 4Q417 1 ii 9, there is never any sense of resisting the beating. One should bless God, even while being beaten.[3] 4Q418 81 urges the elect addressee to bless the angels to emphasize the parity between them, since the angels praise God constantly (ll. 1, 11). If he becomes a debt slave, he is to accept this degrading position and work hard (4Q416 2 ii 7–16). Blessing God even when being beaten illustrates that the *mebin*, who is poor, possesses a form of divine favor that is not expressed in worldly terms, but rather through his connection to and affinity with the heavenly world.

4Q417 1 ii 10

This line praises God as a creator. The subject of the verb (היו) is not extant, but refers to things that were brought into being by his will (רצונו). 4Q418 126 ii 5 uses the term when asserting that elements of the created order came into being according to God's wishes. 4Q417 1 ii 9 probably made a similar point.

The second part of 4Q417 1 ii 10 may simply mean "he understands (מבין)."[4] The *hiphil* participle could also denote that God creates understanding. The focus on creation suggests the latter, but there is not enough text to decide the issue. 4Q417 1 ii 10 may have stated not only that all things came into existence because of God's will but also that he made the elements of the natural order intelligible. These two tropes are combined in 4Q417 1 i 8–12 (see above).

---

3. *Contra* Strugnell and Harrington (1999, 171), who translate "despite every strike."

4. Syntax suggests the word is not here the common term for the addressee.

4Q417 1 ɪɪ 11

God, this line asserts, will judge the deeds of the addressee. In 4QIn-struction the verb פקד often denotes eschatological judgment (see the commentary to 4Q417 1 i 7–8). Line 11 provides context for lines 12–15, which encourage the *mebin* to live ethically. The addressee is to learn that judgment is inevitable and that he should behave in a way that will allow him to survive this event. A call for ethics is placed against an eschatologi-cal horizon (cf. 4Q417 1 i 11–15).[5]

4Q417 1 ɪɪ 12

Line 12 contains an intriguing exhortation: "Do not let the thought of an evil inclination (מחשבת יצר רע) mislead you ..." In 4QInstruction the phrase "evil inclination" only occurs here. The "evil inclination" of 4Q417 1 ii 12 (no definite article) denotes a tendency toward behavior that should be avoided. The addressee is to resist this impulse. The exhortation shows concern that the *mebin* may not heed the teachings given in 4QInstruc-tion. The possibility that he may go astray is likely an issue in 4Q417 1 ii 13–14.

The term "inclination" in 4QInstruction signifies a person's inherent proclivity toward good or bad behavior.[6] In an unfortunately fragmentary context, 4Q416 1 mentions a "fleshly inclination" (l. 16). The reference occurs in the context of the destruction of the "fleshly spirit" during escha-tological judgment, suggesting that the expression denotes a predilection to sinful behavior. In 4Q417 1 i 17 the "spiritual people" are "fashioned" (יצרו) like the angels, using the same root. This presumably emphasizes a tendency to be upright rather than wicked.[7] Lines 10–11 of 4Q417 1 i declare that God has made all deeds understandable, so that one can "walk in [the inclination of] his intelligence." This signifies that one should act in harmony with the divine plan that guides human conduct (cf. 4Q418 217 1; 4Q418 301 1). The internal evidence for understanding the evil *yetzer* in 4QInstruction, which is limited, suggests that it was understood as a proclivity toward wicked behavior that should be resisted.

---

5. Macaskill 2007.

6. Collins 1997e, 378.

7. The line can be understood as stating that their *yetzer* makes them like the angels. See the commentary to 4Q417 1 i 17.

4Q417 1 ii 12 and the Evil Inclination in Ancient Judaism

4Q417 1 ii 12 contains important evidence for assessing the development of the tradition of the evil *yetzer* (יצר הרע).[8] In rabbinic literature the phrase has a wide range of meanings, but is used to explain human conduct. The rabbis trace the tradition to biblical discussions of an "inclination" toward good or bad behavior. As is well known, Genesis Rabbah (14:4) states that the etiology of the two *yetzarim* is the two *yods* of the phrase וייצר in Gen 2:7, the verb for God's creation of Adam.[9] The inclination can be understood as a propensity toward sin that is an inherent element of the human being. For example, 'Avot de Rabbi Nathan presents the evil *yetzer* as growing within the womb as part of the individual, a sort of rabbinic id.[10] Rabbis also describe the *yetzer* as a demonic or supernatural entity that enters a human being, combating his desire to be good. A saying attributed to the Amora Resh Laqish, for example, equates יצר הרע with Satan and the angel of death.[11] In rabbinic literature, the "evil inclination" is more prominent than the good one.[12]

---

8. The scholarship on this topic is vast. Key studies include Rosen-Zvi 2008, 1–27; 2011; Cook 2007, 81–92; Schofer 2005, 84–115; Collins 1997e, 369–83; Cohen Stuart 1984; Urbach 1979, 471–83.

9. See also the discussion of Gen 6:5 and 8:21 below. Isaiah 26:3 mentions a positive "steadfast inclination" (יצר סמוך; cf. 1QS 8:3). In 1 Chr 29:18 David urges God to preserve forever the (presumably good) "inclination of the thoughts (יצר מחשבות) of your people's heart" (cf. 28:9; Ps 103:14). The two *yetzarim* have been exegetically derived from the two *bets* in the phrase "your heart" of Deut 6:5 ("You shall love the Lord your God with all your heart [לבבך]") (Sifre Deut. §32). See Collins 1997e, 373; Cook 2007, 84; Schofer 2005, 86.

10. Chapter 16 (Recension A) reads: "In the mother's womb the evil inclination begins to develop and is born with a person. If he begins to profane the Sabbath, it does not prevent him; if he commits murder, it does not prevent him; if he goes off to another heinous transgression, it does not prevent him" (cf. m. 'Avot 2:11). Later in the chapter another rabbi (R. Reuben ben Aṣṭroboli) places the origin of the *yetzer* even earlier in the formation of a human being, in the semen that develops into a fetus. Schofer (2005, 29, 87–88) dates the composition of 'Avot de R. Nathan to the second century, with additional material slowly accumulating until it took its final form between the sixth and ninth centuries. See Goldin 1983, 83, 85.

11. B. B. Bat. 16a: "Satan, the evil inclination and the angel of death are all one." See Cohen Stuart 1984, 214.

12. Rosen-Zvi (2008, 21, 24) argues that rabbinic literature by and large does not

4QInstruction and other early Jewish texts suggest that the "evil incli-nation" should be attributed not simply to two *yods* in Gen 2:7, but to Second Temple traditions about the nature of evil, which rabbis later elab-orated and developed.[13] Early Jewish literature attests the evil inclination tradition and its link to the book of Genesis. This is clear in the phrase מחשבת יצר רע of 4Q417 1 ii 12.[14] This is similar to Gen 6:5, which reads "every inclination of the thoughts of their hearts was only evil (כל־יצר מחשבת לבו רק רע) continually."[15] The phrase מחשבת יצר and variants of it occur elsewhere in the Dead Sea Scrolls, signifying a propensity to immoral behavior.[16]

Other early Jewish texts refer to an "inclination" to explain human conduct. Perhaps the best known example is Ben Sira. Ben Sira 15:14 states that when God created humankind (אדם), he "placed him in the power of his inclination" (ויתנהו ביד יצרו; cf. 4 Ezra 3:21–22).[17] This evokes Genesis in its use of the term Adam; the word *yetzer* recalls Gen 2:7. The term "inclination" by itself does not necessarily denote a compulsion toward wickedness. The context of this verse emphasizes free choice.[18] One's "inclination" can be toward good or evil, as mentioned above. Ben Sira also stresses, using the root יצר, that God is a "potter" who forms humans according to his wishes.[19] The sage employs the term *yetzer* to assert that God fashioned humankind not with complete free will but rather with divinely given proclivities toward kinds of behavior.

---

envision two opposed *yetzarim* as contesting with one another within each human being. The two *yetzarim* are contrasted in m. Ber. 9:5 (cf. b. Ber. 61b).

13. This problematizes the view of Cohen Stuart (1984, 263) that the יצר הרע does not signify the evil inclination before the Bar Kochba Revolt. See also Cook 2007, 92; Rosen-Zvi 2011, 61.

14. Strugnell and Harrington 1999, 171.

15. Genesis 8:21 reads "the inclination of the human heart is evil (יצר לב האדם רע) from youth."

16. 1QS 5:5; CD 2:16; 4Q280 2 2; 4Q286 7 ii 7. Cf. 4Q525 7 4.

17. Ben Sira 15:14 also declares, in parallelism with the quoted material, that God "set him (man) in the power of his spoiler (חותפו)." This may equate the inclination with some sort of demonic power. It is apparently a secondary addition in the Hebrew, as neither the Greek nor the Syriac contains this material. See Collins 1997c, 84; Di Lella and Skehan 1987, 269; Cook 2007, 85.

18. Sir 15:15: "If you choose, you can keep his commandments; fidelity is the doing of his will" (cf. v. 17).

19. "Like clay in the hands of a potter (יוצר), to be molded according to his plea-sure, so are people in the hands of their maker" (33:13; cf. 11:14).

The "inclination" is attested in the Dead Sea Scrolls. 4Q422 1 12 (4QParaphrase of Genesis and Exodus) attributes Adam's disobedience in the garden to a יצר רע (cf. 4Q370 1 i 3). The speaker in 4QBarki Napshi praises God for having given him a pure heart and having removed an "evil inclination" from him (4Q436 1a–b i 10). The related phrase "guilty inclination" (יצר אשמה) appears in the Damascus Document as a force to which wickedness throughout history is attributed (CD 2:16). Some early Jewish texts understand the "evil inclination" as a form of supernatural evil that exerts malevolent influence upon humankind.[20] 1QH 15:6–7 states: "For Belial (is present) when their destructive inclination (יצר הוותם) manifests itself." One of the non-canonical psalms, the "Plea for Deliverance," contains a speaker asking God to forgive him: "Let not Satan rule over me, nor an evil spirit, let neither pain nor evil inclination (יצר רע) take possession of my bones" (11Q5 19:15–16 [par. 11Q6 4–5 15–16]).[21]

There is room for speculation that the evil inclination in 4QInstruction is an external entity that enters the human being, or is even a manifestation of an evil entity such as Belial. Nothing of this sort, however, is ever explicit in the composition. It is interesting, however, that the verb connected to the "evil inclination" in line 12 is פתה in the *piel* (cf. l. 13). The word in this *binyan* often means "to persuade," with a connotation of deceit (e.g., Ps 78:36; Ezek 14:9). The verb can have the meaning of "entice."[22] The Temple Scroll uses this verb (in the *piel*), to describe a man seducing a virgin.[23] In the Hebrew Bible the spirit that deceives King Ahab "entices" him, also using this verb in the *piel* (1 Kgs 22:19, 22). There is no evidence, however, in 4QInstruction that an evil inclination "seduces" or is a personified entity that somehow deceives or entices the *mebin*. The verb "to lead astray" (*hiphil* שגה), used in 4Q417 1 ii 14, does not denote being enticed, but rather leaving the right path in a general sense (Ps 119:10;

---

20. Collins 1997e, 379–80. See also Rosen-Zvi 2011, 45–53.

21. Note the connection between a compulsion to do evil and Beliar in T. Ash. 1:8–9: "But if the mind is disposed toward evil, all of its deeds are wicked; driving out the good, it accepts the evil and is overmastered by Beliar, who, even when good is undertaken, presses the struggle so as to make the aim of his action into evil, since the devil's storehouse is filled with the venom of the evil spirit."

22. Rosen-Zvi (2009, 264–81) argues that the association between the evil inclination and sexual passion is a development restricted to the Babylonian Talmud.

23. 11QT 66:8–9: "If a man seduces (יפתה) a young virgin who is not betrothed, and she is permitted to him by the law and he lies with her …" (utilizing Exod 22:15 [Eng. v. 16] and Deut 22:28; cf. 4Q184 1 7).

Deut 27:18). A more probable parallel is Prov 1:10: "My son, if sinners entice you (יפתוך), do not consent" (cf. 16:29).[24] The passage recommends that one refuse the offer of the wicked to plunder the innocent and acquire riches malevolently (vv. 11–19). 4Q417 1 ii 12 likewise shows concern that the *mebin* could find wicked thoughts produced by an evil inclination tempting.

4Q417 1 ii moves from the praise of God (ll. 4–10) to urging the addressee not to be deluded by evil (ll. 11–15). The column is too fragmentary to allow solid conclusions, but 4Q417 1 ii may have operated originally with a dualistic opposition not between the good and evil inclinations, but between an evil inclination and God.[25] The evidence within 4QInstruction (discussed above) establishes only that this inclination denotes an impulse to act wickedly. It is never stated whether it is an inherent part of a human being (as in Sir 15:14) or whether it approaches and inhabits a person like a demonic force (à la 1QH 15:6–7). 4Q417 1 ii 14 (in a second hand) suggests that 4QInstruction may have stated that the origins of "fleshly understandings," a phrase that probably signifies wicked ways of thinking, should *not* be attributed to God (see below). This allows for speculation that God did not create the wicked *yetzer* (contrast Sifre Deut. §45, which claims he did).

4Q417 1 ii 13

One should, the line asserts, search for truth. The preposition in לאמת suggests the phrase means "for truth" rather than "truthfully," as in DJD 34 (cf. 4Q418 103 ii 5; Ps 142:5).[26] Elsewhere in 4QInstruction, "truth" is associated with both the elect and God (see the commentary on 4Q416 1 10). Line 13 urges, in a fragmentary warning, not to let something mis-

---

24. The Hodayot use the word to describe the waywardness of teachers with whom the author disagrees. 1QH 12:17 reads: "they come to inquire of you by means of the mouth of lying prophets, who are themselves seduced by error (מפותי תעות)" (cf. Sir 30:23). See also the discussion of the verb פתה in Holloway 2008, 230–33.

25. The מחשבה ("thought") of the evil inclination may have been understood as opposing God's מחשבה, a term that signifies in 4Q417 1 i 11–12 the divine plan that guides reality (see commentary above). CD 2:15–16 opposes walking perfectly with God and following the "guilty inclination." Later rabbinic tradition opposes the influence of the evil *yetzer* with Torah study (e.g., Sifre Deut. §45). See Rosen-Zvi 2008, 8; Urbach 1979, 472.

26. So also Kampen 2011, 102. For the adverbial sense one would expect באמת. See also Strugnell and Harrington 1999, 172.

lead him, using the same word employed in line 12 (אל תפתכה; see the excursus above), but the object of the verb is not extant. On the basis of a fragmentary *mem* that follows the verb, one can posit that the expression "the thought (מחשבת) of the evil inclination" appears not only in line 12 but in line 13 as well.[27] Line 13 may have contained a contrast between seeking truth and avoiding an evil inclination.

4Q417 1 ii 14

Line 14 contains another vetitive, also broken off, recommending that one not let something lead him astray (אל תשגכ]ה; see the excursus above). Here again the object is not preserved. This line probably exhorted the addressee not to turn away from upright behavior and the teachings advocated by 4QInstruction. 4Q417 1 ii 14 contains the intriguing but fragmentary expression "without understandings of flesh" (בלוא נבונות בשר). The phrase echoes the "fleshly inclination" of 4Q416 1 16. The "understandings of flesh" of 4Q417 1 ii 14 may be similar to the "evil inclination" of line 12, denoting ways of thinking that lead to wrong behavior which should be resisted. A second hand added the word צוה, changing the phrase to "without his appointing understandings of flesh." As the editors of DJD 34 discern, this obscure phrase apparently means that the "fleshly" modes of thought mentioned in the line are not established by God (see also the excursus above).[28]

4Q417 1 ii 14–15

Very little of this material survives, but the text presumably discourages the addressee from mistaken ways of thinking. The phrase "do not say" is preserved. 4Q416 2 iii 12–14 teaches that the *mebin* should not say that he is poor, as an excuse not to study. The "do not say" form is a common disputation technique in Ben Sira (cf. 4Q418 69 ii 11, 13).[29] 4Q417 1 ii 14–15 probably employed the same structure. What one should not say, however, is not preserved. One can infer from lines 11–14 that lines 14–15 were originally part of an exhortation that encouraged the *mebin* to be ethical and not deviate from the teachings of the composition.

---

27. Strugnell and Harrington 1999, 170.

28. Strugnell and Harrington 1999, 172. For the construction בלא plus a perfect verb meaning "without," see Qimron 2008, 77 (§400.10).

29. Ben Sira 5:1, 3–4; 11:23–24; 15:11; 16:17; 31:12.

8.
4Q417 2 I + 26

Parallel texts: 4Q416 2 i (underline); 4Q418 7a (dashed underline); 4Q418 7b (+ 64, 199, 66, 26, 27) (double underline); 4Q418a 22 (dotted underline)

TEXT[1]

[	בֹּכֹיל עת פן ישבעכה וכרֹוֹחֹז דבר בו פן ישֹנֹאכה וגמֹ]	1
[	בלוא הוכח הכשר עבור לו והנק שר מֹעֹזֹן בעֹתֹ]	2
[	וגם את רוחֹז לא תבלע כיא בדממה דברתֹ]הֹ	3
[	ותוכחתו ספר מהר ואל תעֹבֹור על פשעיכה]	4
[עֹריכה ובגבוה רוח]	יֹצדק כמוכה הזאה כיא הזאה {כיא הזאה} שר בשֹ	5
[	יֹעשה כיא מה הזאה יחֹד בכול מעשה לבלֹתֹיֹ ○○	6
[לכה לבֹלֹתֹיֹ הרֹיֹעכה]	ואיש עול אל תחשוב עזר וגם אין שֹזֹנֹא vacat	7
צֹדֹקֹהֹ[	רֹשע מעשיו עם פקדתו ודע במה תתֹהֹלך עמו]	8
[נֹפֹשכֹהֹ בראשכֹהֹ]	אל vacat תמֹזֹש מלבכה ואל לכה לבדכה תרֹחֹב	9
[הבֹטֹ ברז]	כיא מה צעיר מרש ואל תשמֹ[יח באבלכה פֹן תעֹמֹל בֹחֹזֹכֹה	10
[שים לנכאי רוֹח]	נֹהֹיה וֹקח מֹזֹלדי ישע ודע מי נוֹחֹל כבֹוֹד ועֹל הֹלוֹא	11
[	ולֹאבֹלֹיֹהֹמֹה שמחת עולם היֹהֹ בֹעֹל ריב לֹחֹפֹצֹכֹה ואיֹזֹ]	12
הֹ[	לֹכֹוֹל נֹעֹוֹזֹתֹ]הֹ דֹבֹֹרֹ [מֹשפטיכה כמושֹל צֹדֹיֹק אֹל תֹקֹ]חֹ	13
[	ואל תעֹבֹוֹר עֹלֹ] פֹשֹ[עֹיכה היה כֹאֹיֹש עֹנֹיֹ בֹרֹיֹֹבֹֹך מֹשפֹטֹ	14
vac פֹ[נֹוֹ אֹ]לֹפֹ[יֹ]	קח ואז יראה אֹל זֹשֹב אֹפֹו וֹעֹבֹר על חטאתֹכֹֹה [כֹיֹ]אֹ לֹפֹ[יֹ אֹ]פֹ[וֹ	15

---

1. 4Q417 2 ii overlaps with 4Q416 2 i 21–iii 1 and thus is not given separate treatment in this commentary. Rather it is incorporated into the discussion of the relevant material from 4Q416 2. For 4Q417 2 i, see Strugnell and Harrington 1999, 172–77; Tigchelaar 2001, 55–56; Rey 2009a, 42–47 (covering ll. 7–28); Elgvin 1997a, 195–98. For 4Q417 2 i 17–19, note also Tigchelaar 1998, 589–93. The textual notes section refers to these works.

16 [לֵוא יעמוד כול ומי יצדק בְּמִשְׁפָּטוֹ וּבלי סֵלִיחַתה] אֹ[יֹכה [יצדק כול]

17 אביון ואתה אם תחסֹר טרף מחסֹורכה ומותריכה [ה]בֹּא בֹּ[יֹחד אֹ[ם

18 תותיר הובל למחזֹ חפצו ונחלתכה קח מֹמנו ואל תוסף עוֹ[ד ואם

19 {וֹאם} תחסר לוא מבלֹי ה[וֹ]ן מחסורכה כיא לוא יחסר אוצרֹ[אל ועל]

20 פיהו יֹהיה כול ואת אשר יטריפכה אֹכֹוֹל ואל תוסף עֹ[וֹ]דֹ פֹ[ן תקציר]

21 vacat חייכה vacat אם הון אנשֹ[י]ֹם תלוה למחסורֹכה אל [דומי לבֹ]הֹ

22 יומם ולילה ואל מנוח לנפשכֹה עֹד [השיבכה לנֹוֹשֹ[ה כֹ]וֹ[ל אל תכזב

23 לו למה תשה עון וגם מחרפה לֹ[ס] ולא תאמין עֹ[וֹ]ד לרעהו

24 ובמחסורכה יקפץ ידו כמוֹ כֹ כֹחכֹה] וכמוֹהוֹ לוה ודע מאֹגֹ[רֹ]

25 ואם נגע יפגשכה ואֹ[ין] כי תשלם נשיכֹה והֹזֹוֹב אל תסתר מנֹשֹׁ[הֹ]בֹכֹה]

26 פֹן יגלה חרֹ[פֹ]תֹכֹה ה[נֹושה] מֹושֹל בו ואֹז

27 לֹא יכנו בשבֹטֹ] חֹ ○○כֹה ואפֹס]

28 עֹ[וֹד]וֹגם אֹתֹהֹ] מבֹין בֹעֹבֹרֹה]

bottom margin

TRANSLATION

1 at every time lest he have enough of you. And according to his spirit speak with him lest he hate you. And also …

2 without reproaching the prosperous person, forgive him and keep a person of note free from punishment in the time of …

3 And also do not engulf his spirit because calmly yo[u] have spoken …

4 And his reproach recount quickly and do not overlook your own transgressions …

5 He is innocent like you, even though he is a person of note in [your] ar[ea and with a haughty attitude]

6 he may act. For how unique is he in every deed, without …

7 *vacat* And do not consider a man of iniquity a helper. And also let there be no one who hates [you, so that no *harm may come upon you.*]

8 The wickedness of his actions (goes together) with his punishment. And know how you shall walk with him …

9 do not *vacat* let [*alm*]sgiving be absent from your heart and do not for yourself alone widen [*your throat in your poverty*,]

10 for what is more lowly than a poor man? Do not rejoice in your mourning lest you toil in your life. [Gaze upon the mystery]

11 that is to be and seize the birth times of salvation. Know who is to inherit glory and (who) iniquity. Has he not [*established for the contrite of spirit*]

12 and for those who mourn eternal joy? Be an advocate on behalf of your own interests and let there not be …

13 by all your perversions. Utt[er] your judgments like a righteous ruler. Do not ta[ke …]

14 And do not overlook your [*trans*]gressions. Be like a humble man when you dispute a case …

15 take. And then God will appear, turn away his wrath and forgive your sins, [beca]use before [his] wr[ath *vacat*]

16 no one can stand. Who will be righteous in his judgment? Without forgiveness [*h*]ow [*can any*] poor man [*be righteous?*]

17 And you, if you lack the food that you need, then [br]ing your surpluses to[gether, if]

18 you have a surplus. Bring (it) to its trading place and take your inheritance from it. Do not take any mo[re. And if]

19 you lack, borrow, being without mo[*ne*]y which you lack, for the treasury of [God] does not lack. [And upon]

20 his command everything comes into being. The nourishment that he provides for you, eat. But do not take any m]*or*[e] (than you need), le[*st you sho*rten]

21 *vacat* your life. *vacat* If you borrow money of m[*e*]n for what you need, let there be no [*sleep for yo*]u

22 day and night, and let there be no comfort for yourself [*vacat until*] you have returned to the credit[*or everyt*]hing. Do not deceive

23 him, lest you carry guilt. And also a reproach for [… and you will no lo]nger [trust] his neighbor.

24 And when you lack he will be tight-fisted. Your strength [… and like him borrow and know the one who gathe*rs*.]

25 And if a beating befalls you, and he urges [*that you repay your debts, then* do not hide *the de*bt from the person who len*t* (it) *to* you,]

26 lest the [*creditor*] reveal your sh[*a*]me [… who rules over him. And then]

27 he will not strike him with a rod [… and no]

28 mo[re.] And also you, [*understanding son … in* wrath]

Textual Notes

i 1. יִשׂוֹנׄאכה וגׄםׄ. The last letters of 4Q417 2 i 1 are ׄיׄ. The reading above follows a proposal of Tigchelaar that 4Q417 26 should be placed here as a distant join, adding נׄאכה וגׄםׄ. The letter trace after the *yod* is understood as a *shin*.

i 2. מׄעׄוֹן בעתׄ. From 4Q417 26 2. Tigchelaar reads בׄעׄוֹן. Both *bet* and *mem* are possible but the latter is to be preferred (cf. Num 5:31; Job 10:14; 4Q418 102a + b 5). One must assume that the first *ayin* of 4Q417 26 2 is partially abraded.

i 8. צׄדׄקה. The editors of DJD 34 and Tigchelaar do not reconstruct these traces. The letter before the *qof* cannot be identified with certainty. I tentatively follow Rey's reading, which is materially possible, because it produces a semantically attractive parallel statement in lines 8–9 (see below).

i 9. תרׄחׄב. Most commentators endorse this reading (the editors of DJD 34, Tigchelaar, Rey). Elgvin transcribes תרׄהׄב. I have previously as well.[2] Materially either option is possible. Transcribing תרׄחׄב is supported by the parallelism of lines 8–9 (see below).

i 10. בחייכה; 4Q416 2 i 5: בחייכה.

i 11. ועׄל. The editors of DJD 34 read וׄעׄמׄל, which is impossible, but they grant that one could read ועׄול. Tigchelaar transcribes ועׄ[ו]לׄ. Rey and Puech suggest ועׄל, translating "élévation."[3] The latter transcription is to be preferred materially but is better understood as an unusual spelling or misspelling of ועׄול (see below).

i 13. לכול; 4Q416 2 i 7: לׄכׄל.

i 13. צדיק; 4Q418a 22 2: צדׄ'ק.

i 14. מׄשפט. The editors of DJD 34 read מׄשׄפׄטׄוׄ. This is not supported by PAM 42.602, which attests a space after the *tet*. The parallel text, 4Q418a 22 3, is highly fragmentary but appears to attest a variant. There one should with Rey read either מׄשׄפׄטׄךׄ or מׄשׄפׄטׄ[ה].

i 15. חטאׄתׄכׄה. Other commentators read חטאותׄכׄה (Rey, Tigchelaar, the editors of DJD 34). Strugnell and Harrington grant that the reading I adopt is possible. If one reads the stroke after the *aleph* as a *waw*, the fol-

---

2. Goff 2003b, 151–52.

3. Puech 2004b, 649. See also 2006, 88.

lowing base stroke becomes difficult to explain. חטאתכֿה is probably a plural written defectively (cf. [פֿשֿ]עיכה in l. 14).

    i 15. The lost end of the line contained a *vacat*. 4Q418a 22 4 reads אפו [ולא]ל.

    i 16. יצדק; 4Q418 7a 2: ק[צֿ]דֿיק.

    i 16. ובלי סליחה; 4Q416 2 i 10: א[ולבלו] סליחה.[4]

    i 16. במשפטו; 4Q418 7a 2: במשפטיו.

    i 19. {וֿאֿם}. I agree with Tigchelaar that ואם originally occurred at the end of line 18 (see the parallel text 4Q418 7b as expanded through joins), and that the same expression was then accidentally written at the beginning of line 19, and later scratched out. It is also possible that the abrasion of ואם in line 19 is natural (so Rey). In this case there was a *vacat* at the end of line 18.

    i 23. תשה; 4Q418 7b 4 (l. 6 of the expanded text): שא[ה].

    i 23. עון; 4Q418 7b 4 (l. 6 of the expanded text): עוון.

    i 23. ל॰[. The editors of DJD 34 reconstruct לֿ[ון]לֿ[ושי], but the trace after the *lamed* is unlikely to be a *nun*. It is not clear that a conclusive reading can be established (so also Tigchelaar). Rey opts for *kaf*.

    i 24. יקפץ; 4Q418 7b 5 (l. 7 of the expanded text): יקפֿוֿץ.

    i 25. חֿוֿבֿ. Most commentators (the editors of DJD 34, Rey, Tigchelaar) read אֿבֿ. The surviving top stroke before the *bet*, however, fits well with *waw*, as the editors of DJD 34 grant. The *Dead Sea Scrolls Study Edition* reads חוב.[5]

    i 27. לא; 4Q418 7b 8 (l. 10 of the expanded text): לוא.

    i 27. ואפס. 4Q416 2 i 20 reads ואפס; 4Q418 7b 9 (l. 11 of the expanded text): וֿאפץ.

COMMENTARY

4Q417 2 i is important for understanding several major themes of 4QInstruction. These include the borrowing of money, indebtedness, and eschatological judgment. Chief among the texts that overlap with 4Q417 2 i are 4Q416 2 i and 4Q418 7b. The latter text has been expanded by Tigchelaar with several small fragments, including 4Q418 64, 66 and 199.[6] Since the overlap between 4Q416 2 and 4Q417 2 starts at 4Q417 2 i 6 (par.

---

4. For this variant, see Tigchelaar 2011, 321.

5. García Martínez and Tigchelaar, 1997–1998, 2.856.

6. Tigchelaar 1998, 589–93; 2001, 77. Strugnell and Harrington (1999, 420)

4Q416 2 i 1), one can infer that 4Q416 2 i was preceded by material that corresponds to the beginning of 4Q417 2 i.

4Q417 2 i can be broken down into three sections. 4Q417 2 i 1–6 contains instruction regarding the resolution of a conflict between the addressee and a person of higher social standing. Lines 7–17 urge the *mebin* to be ethical, in part to ensure mercy from God during eschatological judgment. 4Q417 2 i 17–28 offers financial instruction and is important for understanding the poverty of the addressee. Like 4Q416 2 ii, the column stresses the prompt payment of debts.

4Q417 2 i 1

Lines 1–6 discuss speech in the context of a dispute between the *mebin* and a person who has some type of authority. The passage is too fragmentary to discern the nature of the conflict fully. There is probably additional teaching on proper speech in lines 12–14. 4Q417 2 i 1 shows concern that the other person (whose identity cannot be recovered, but see l. 2) may grow weary of the *mebin* and come to hate him. The first verb of the line is probably a *qal* of the root שבע, "to have enough of someone."[7] The word has this meaning in Prov 25:17, where it is in parallelism with the verb "to hate," as in 4Q417 2 i 1.[8] The act of speaking "according to his spirit" probably teaches that the *mebin* should talk to the person in a manner that is consistent with the mood or disposition of this individual (cf. ll. 3, 13).[9] The addressee should speak with the other person honestly and explain his concerns. This is consistent with 4Q416 2 ii 7–8. These lines recommend that the *mebin*, in the context of speaking with his supervisor when working as a debt slave, "according to his speech speak" (כלשונו דבר). 4Q416 2 ii also states that he should not restrain himself with his words (l. 6), while urging that he remain loyal to his master and dutifully carry out his obligations (ll. 9–10). He is to accept his lowly position, but should also voice his concerns to his supervisor and try to maintain his dignity. 4Q417

---

express reservations regarding Tigchelaar's joins to 4Q418 7b, but his suggestions are plausible. See how the fragments fit together in Rey 2009a, pl. 3.

7. Strugnell and Harrington (1999, 177) suggest that the verb ישבעכה is a *piel* ("to sate") or, less likely, that it is a *hiphil* ("to conjure, cause to swear").

8. Prov 25:17: "Let your foot be seldom in your neighbor's house, otherwise the neighbor will become weary of you and hate you (פן־ישבעך ושנאך)."

9. See the commentary to 4Q417 1 i 17–18, where I discuss psychological usages of the term "spirit."

2 i 1–6 similarly involves speech with a person with social power and recommends that he should speak honestly with this person when conflicts
arise, but without rebuking him or pressing charges (see l. 2). On the basis
of 4Q416 2 ii, one can speculate that the dispute envisaged in 4Q417 2 i
1–6 is between the *mebin* and his supervisor in the context of employment, perhaps in a debt slave relationship. Unfortunately, the nature of
the relationship between the two individuals cannot be recovered. This
section of the column was probably designed to help the addressee resolve
conflicts that might arise between him and people who are more powerful
and prosperous.

4Q417 2 i 2

The *mebin* is to forgive a powerful person without reproaching him. It
is not clear what has taken place between them, but 4QInstruction urges
the addressee not to be vindictive. That he is instructed not to rebuke the
other person suggests he has done something to the addressee that merits
reproach. Line 3 warns him not to speak angrily to this person, also implying that he has somehow wronged the *mebin*. Line 4 states that he should
recount the reproach of the other person quickly (see below).

The other individual is called הכשר. The editors of DJD 34 translate
"the noble." The word probably denotes someone who is proper and/or
successful, but not necessarily noble or of royal (Hasmonean) lineage.[10] In
4Q417 1 i 11 the word signifies proper understanding and this may also be
the case in the fragmentary text 4Q418 77 2. The related word כשרון signifies skill in Qoheleth (2:21; 4:4; cf. 5:10; Ps 68:7). The root signifies being
useful in Sir 13:4.[11] It also occurs in Tobit, meaning "right."[12] The person
in 4Q417 2 i is reasonably considered wealthy and of a higher social standing than the addressee. One does not get the impression that the *mebin* is
in training to give counsel to a "prince" as a royal advisor or sage, in the
manner of Ben Sira.

---

10. Strugnell and Harrington (1999, 178) admittedly express doubt that the word
means "noble." See also Murphy 2002, 175.

11. "If you are useful (תכשר//χρησιμεύσῃς) to him (a rich person) he will enslave
you, but when you are exhausted he will have nothing to do with you."

12. "For me it is not right (כשר) to h[ang myself]" (4Q200 1 ii 3; cf. Tob 3:10).
Here כשר corresponds in the Greek (in the S text), as in Sir 13:4, to χρησιμεύω. The
rabbinic usage of the term to denote foods that are ritually permitted derives from
older meanings of the word such as "right" or "appropriate." See Moore 1996, 149–50.

The second half of 4Q417 2 i 2 probably argues that the *mebin* should not seek punishment against the other person. This would parallel the first half of the line. The editors of DJD 34 understand שר הנק as a single word, with the word space being accidental, translating "he who is bound up."[13] However, the word שר occurs in line 5, suggesting it should be read in the same way here. This would also read well in parallelism with הכשר.[14] שר is a common term for "prince," but it can also denote a chief or some other type of important person, not always a member of royalty.[15] The word הנק is probably a form of נקה, "to be innocent."[16] The root often refers to being blameless or going without punishment (e.g., 1 Sam 26:5; Prov 6:29; 16:5). This meaning is apt, since the term in question is followed by עון, a common term for guilt or punishment. The *mebin* is to avoid seeking retribution against "a person of note."

4Q417 2 i 3

The addressee is not to speak angrily to the other person. The *mebin* is not to "engulf his spirit" (את רוחו לא תבלע). The antecedent of "his spirit" is the powerful individual, whose "spirit" is also mentioned in line 1. The verb לבלע can mean "to confuse/confound" or "swallow," and also "to destroy" (cf. 4Q416 2 iii 8).[17] The rest of 4Q417 2 i 3, and the use of "spirit" in line 1, suggests the phrase has to do with speech. The *mebin* should not keep his mouth wide open and speak with anger. The second half of line 3 indicates that the *mebin* previously discussed the matter with the prosperous person and did so calmly. The admonition not to confront him with a loud outburst suggests that the addressee has been maligned somehow by this other person and that previous discussion about the matter with him accomplished little.

---

13. Strugnell and Harrington 1999, 178. This is accepted by Murphy (2002, 175) and Kampen (2011, 105).

14. Note, however, that the first term has a definite article and the second does not.

15. The "taskmasters" overseeing the work of the Israelite slaves in Egypt, for example, are שרי מסים (Exod 1:11; cf. Gen 39:21; 1 Kgs 9:22; 1QSa 1:14–15; 4Q418 140 4).

16. It is probably a *niphal* imperative, although one would expect the final *he* of the root.

17. The verb is used for the land's swallowing up of Korah and his rebellious party (Num 16:32) and the great fish's swallowing of Jonah (Jon 1:2). This word is generally not combined with רוח (but see 1QH 15:8). Cf. Isa 28:4; Hos 8:7; Prov 1:12; 1QpHab 11:5, 7.

4Q417 2 I 4

The *mebin* should recount quickly "his reproach" and not overlook
his own sins. He is to rebuke the prosperous person while showing awareness of his own shortcomings. The suffix "his" again most likely signifies
the prosperous person. The line is in tension with line 2, which asserts
that the *mebin* should *not* reproach the prosperous person. There may
have been a lost "if"-clause at the end of line 3 that explained the circumstances regarding the reproach mentioned here. 4Q417 2 i 4 may mean
that the addressee should forgive the prosperous person, but also give his
criticism quickly and calmly, without undue speech. Also, it is not clear to
whom the addressee should recount this reproach. He could be speaking
to the other person or someone else, perhaps a judge who is adjudicating
the dispute.

4Q417 2 I 5–6

Strugnell and Harrington understand this line as being about God,
translating "He indeed will declare righteous like you, for he is a prince
among prin[ces]," reconstructing the end of the sentence as שר בש[רים.[18]
Above I argued that שר refers, in parallelism, to the prosperous person
with whom the *mebin* has a conflict (l. 3). A good reading is produced in
line 5 by understanding the word in the same way. The first part of the line
is profitably interpreted as stating, "And he is innocent like you," referring,
respectively, to the prosperous person and to the *mebin*.[19] This accords
with line 2, which stresses that no penalty should go toward the successful
person. Line 5 teaches that, while there is some sort of dispute between
them, both parties can be considered innocent of wrongdoing, making it
difficult for one side to blame the other. This realization helps minimize
the conflict between them.

I suggest that the כיא clause of 4Q417 2 i 5 is concessive, with the
lacuna filled as follows: "And he is innocent like you, even though he is
a person of note in [your] ar[ea and with a haughty attitude] he may act"
(ll. 5–6). Rather than reconstruct [שר בש[רים ("prince among prin[ces]")
with the editors of DJD 34, I tentatively supplement בש[עריכה ובגבוה
רוח] יעשה. This fits the available space and produces a coherent reading. The addressee is not to act angrily or loudly toward the prosperous

---

18. Strugnell and Harrington 1999, 176.

19. Strugnell and Harrington (1999, 176) understand the verb יצדק as a *piel*, but
for this one would expect an object; it is better understood as a *qal*.

person (ll. 2–3), even though he may act that way toward the *mebin*. He should remember that they are both equally innocent, even though the prosperous person may consider himself superior. The word שערים, literally "gates," can have a more general meaning of "location(s)" or "town(s)," perhaps denoting the public square or market, where the successful person's reputation would have been known.[20] The phrase גבוה לב is used in Prov 16:18 (cf. 10:4; 2 Chr 32:26).

4Q417 2 i 6

Strugnell and Harrington, with trepidation, read this line as stating that God is "unique among every creature."[21] A better reading is produced if one understands line 6 as not about God, but rather the prosperous person, in keeping with line 5 (see above). The text rhetorically asks if the person in question is unique in every deed (not "creature"; מעשה).[22] The clear answer is "no." The "person of note" may think that his actions are more important than those of the *mebin* but, 4QInstruction teaches, this view is mistaken.

4Q417 2 i 7

Line 7 begins a new unit, demarcated with a *vacat*. Lines 7–17 stress ethical behavior in the context of eschatological judgment. Line 7 itself provides teachings on social relations. The addressee should be able to recognize negative types of people with whom he should not associate. This kind of teaching, and its terminology, resonates with traditional wisdom. The *mebin* should not rely upon a "man of iniquity" (איש עול). Proverbs 29:27 also warns against this type, affirming that the righteous consider such a person an abomination. Sapiential texts often mention types of people whom one should avoid.[23] 4QInstruction is no exception.

4Q417 2 i 8

Line 8 continues the instruction on how to interact with the wicked individual. His deeds, referring to the negative type of person mentioned

---

20. E.g., Deut 12:12; Jer 14:2; 15:7; Prov 14:19. The term can signify urban settings in the Dead Sea Scrolls (4Q184 1 12).

21. Strugnell and Harrington 1999, 179.

22. Kampen 2011, 103.

23. See, for example, Prov 16:27–29; Sir 8:15–17; 11:33; 4Q424 1 10, 12; Amenemope 11.13–14. Consult also Rey 2009a, 54.

in line 7, go together with "his punishment" and the *mebin* should know how to "walk" with him.[24] The term "walk" in the *hithpael* refers to conduct (see the commentary to 4Q416 2 iii 9). 4QInstruction recommends caution. The addressee should stay away from such an individual, or at least be very careful around him. This wary attitude regarding the wicked is fully consistent with the book of Proverbs (e.g., 12:6). However, the rationale 4QInstruction provides for this posture diverges from traditional wisdom. The term for "punishment" in 4Q417 2 i 8 is פקודה. Elsewhere in 4QInstruction this word refers to eschatological judgment (see the commentary to 4Q417 1 i 7–8). Divine judgment is prominent in 4Q417 2 i (ll. 10–12, 15–16). One should not associate with wicked people, because they are condemned to be destroyed in the final judgment.[25] 4QInstruction provides an early Jewish justification for a traditional sapiential teaching.

4Q417 2 I 8–9

Line 9 and the end of line 8 contain two parallel statements that recommend that, despite his poverty, the *mebin* be generous and avoid selfishness. The second one (which is more intact than the first) asserts that he should not have a wide נפש in his poverty, with נפש denoting not "soul" but rather "throat" or "appetite."[26] At issue could be overeating (cf. 4Q416 2 ii 18–20). The key terms (רחב, נפש), however, signify a greedy person. Proverbs 28:25 reads, for example: "The greedy person (רחב־נפש) stirs up strife, but whoever trusts in the Lord will be enriched."[27] The *mebin* of 4QInstruction is not necessarily destitute, but is economically vulnerable and could easily fall into material hardship.[28] He should be generous with his scant resources.

---

24. The antecedent of "his actions" in l. 8 appears to be not just the one who hates in l. 7 but also the man of iniquity. The two phrases in l. 7 do not denote two distinct kinds of people, but rather with different terminology describe the same type of person.

25. 4QInstruction does not deny that the wicked receive this-worldly recompense; rather the composition's emphasis is on eschatological retribution. See further Adams 2008.

26. See the textual notes section above. The word נפש is reasonably supplemented. For this term signifying "appetite," see Prov 27:7 (cf. 10:3; Qoh 6:2). For the meaning "throat," note Jon 2:6; Ps 69:2. Both Kampen (2011, 105) and Rey (2009a, 46) translate נפש as "appetite," as do Strugnell and Harrington (1999, 181).

27. Cf. Isa 5:14; Hab 2:5; 1QS 4:9. See Rey 2009a, 48; Fox 2009, 831.

28. See below on ll. 18–19. Consult also section 9 of the introduction.

The statement in lines 8–9 can be understood as parallel to that of line 9. The extant part of the text reads "not let … be absent from your heart" (cf. 4Q415 2 ii 2; 1QS 6:3; 11Q19 3:11). The object of the verb has not survived in full, but is likely attested by the visible קה° at the end of line 8. Rey has offered a semantically attractive reconstruction: [צ]דקה, "[alm]sgiving."[29] Giving alms should not be absent from the addressee's heart. The second statement elaborates the preceding one that he, despite his poverty, should not be selfish. He should be charitable. The mindset is similar to Tob 4:8: "If you have many possessions, make your gift from them in proportion; if few, do not be afraid to give according to the little you have."

4Q417 2 i 10

Lines 10–12 place the column's teachings on ethics and poverty in an eschatological context. After urging the *mebin* to be charitable despite his poverty (ll. 8–9), line 10 asks what is more "lowly" (צעיר) than a poor person. The term צעיר has a positive connotation, associating poverty with humility (Jer 30:19; Zech 13:7; CD 19:9). In the version of Psalm 151 from the great Cave 11 Psalms Scroll the word describes David, expressing that he is younger than his brothers, and denoting the low status which makes his selection for the throne unlikely (11QPsᵃ 28:3; cf. 4Q175 23). The word may also convey the difficulty a poor person faces in life. In Ben Sira the related term צער is paired with "turmoil," and in Qumran Aramaic texts this word can denote suffering or grief.[30] The *mebin* is to identify with the lowly poor man of 4Q417 2 i 10. The addressee's poverty does not simply signify his material hardship, but also conveys an ethical comport-

---

29. The term צדקה is used in this way in Ben Sira and Tobit, as opposed to "righteousness" in a more general sense. Ben Sira 3:30–31, for example, reads: "As water quenches flaming fire, so alms (צדקה) atone for sins. The kindness a person has done crosses his path as he goes; when he falls, he finds a support" (cf. 7:10; 29:8; 40:24). This statement also provides a rationale for charity that would explain its endorsement in 4QInstruction—it is not only ethical but practical to do so, since, by being charitable to others, they would be likely to help when you are in need. The word צדקה refers to almsgiving in 4Q198 1 1, which corresponds to Tob 14:2 (cf. 12:8; 14:8–11; Luke 21:1–4; 2 Cor 8:12; b. Giṭ. 7a). The term also denotes almsgiving in 4Q200 2 6, 8 and 9 (cf. Tob 4:6–9). 4Q416 2 i 21–ii 2 may endorse charity, but the key texts are fragmentary (see commentary above). See Di Lella and Skehan 1987, 165; Moore 1996, 167; Murphy 2002, 178; Rey 2009a, 43–44.

30. Sir 31:20; 4Q530 1 i 2; 4Q580 4 5.

ment that he should adopt (see section 9 of the introduction). He should
be humble (l. 10) and generous (ll. 8–9).

The difficulty of the life of the *mebin* is elaborated further in line 10,
which urges that he not rejoice (תשמח) in his mourning. This should be
read in tandem with the claim in line 12 that God has established "eternal joy" (שמחת עולם) for those who mourn. The passage hinges upon
an opposition between "mourning" (אבל) and "joy" (שמחה), as do the
Hodayot (1QH 23:14–16; see the excursus below).[31] "Mourning" is identified in line 10 as a state that the *mebin* is in, or at least could enter, during
his life. "Joy," by contrast, is allocated for mourners, but they are not to
experience it in the present. This suggests they are to attain this joy, which
is "eternal," at some future date (l. 12). "Joy," attested in lines 10 and 12,
should be understood in an eschatological sense, denoting the postmortem rewards of the elect. The passage portrays the addressee's present life
as "mourning," and the blessed afterlife allocated to him after death as
"eternal joy." The content of line 11 is clearly eschatological, proclaiming
that the *mebin* can know who will inherit glory and who toil (see below).
Lines 15–17 of 4Q417 2 i also discuss eschatological judgment. Elsewhere
the promised postmortem rewards of the *mebin* are described with "joy"
terminology. In 4Q416 2 iii 7–8, for example, he is told that he will "inherit
joy."[32] 4Q418 69 ii 13 asserts that the "inheritance" of the angels is eternal
life. Since the addressee is in the lot of the angels (4Q418 81 4–5), one can
infer that upon death he can attain eternal life, presumably with the angels
(see section 6 of the introduction). If the *mebin* is promised eternal life
after death, "eternal joy" can be understood as a reference to the blessed
life intended for the elect. Mourning signifies the life of the addressee in
this world and eternal joy in his afterlife.

The linking of eternal life to "joy" is attested elsewhere in early Judaism.[33] The Epistle of Enoch envisages a form of astral immortality for the
righteous, in which they shine like the stars of heaven, promising that they
are to "have great joy like the angels of heaven" (1 En. 104:2, 4; cf. v. 13).[34]
Using terminology that resonates with 4Q417 2 i, the Treatise on the Two
Spirits declares that the elect shall receive several eschatological rewards,

---

31. Biblical texts that contrast these terms include Lam 5:15 and Esth 9:22 (Isa
61:1–3 is discussed below). See Rey 2009a, 55–56.
32. 4Q416 4 3; 4Q418 102a + b 5; 4Q417 1 ii 7.
33. Goff 2003b, 165–66; Elgvin 1997a, 110.
34. Dan 12:3; 1 En. 5:9; 10:16.

including "eternal joy with endless life" (שמחת עולמים בחיי נצח) (1QS
4:7; cf. Jub. 23:30–31; T. Jud. 25:4).

There is some tension between 4Q417 2 i 10–12 and 4Q416 2 iii 11.
The latter text asserts that the *mebin* has been lifted from his poverty and
is seated with the "nobles," a term that likely denotes angels (see commentary above). This statement probably attests a type of "realized eschatology" that is available in the present, whereas the passage at hand affirms
that one cannot receive "eternal joy" during one's life. 4Q416 2 iii 11 suggests that 4Q417 2 i 10–12 should not be taken too literally, as if the *mebin*
should never experience joy in his daily life. Lines 10–12 acknowledge that
his present life can be difficult, and affirm that a blessed afterlife awaits
him. This is compatible with the composition's frequent reminders that
the addressee is poor. To fulfill the postmortem awards allotted to him, he
must adopt a lowly and humble posture during his life. His reception of
"joy" is ultimately not in this world but in the next.

Third Isaiah, Mourning, and Eschatological Joy

The trope of mourning to signify those who are lowly and downtrodden is famously expressed in Third Isaiah, in which a prophet declares that
God has sent him "to bring good news to the oppressed (ענוים), to bind
up the broken-hearted ... to proclaim the year of the Lord's favor and the
day of vengeance of our God; to comfort all who mourn (לנחם כל־אבלים);
to provide for those who mourn in Zion (אבלי ציון)—to give them a gar-
land instead of ashes, the oil of gladness instead of mourning (אבל) ..."
(Isa 61:1–3; cf. 60:20; 66:10). The mourners of Zion shall receive "eternal
joy" (61:7), the same phrase as in 4Q417 2 i 12 (cf. Isa 35:10; 51:11). Third
Isaiah takes contemporary mourning practices and reconfigures them
to signify not exclusively those who are in ritual mourning, but rather a
broad range of people who are poor and browbeaten.[35] They are comforted
by the prospect of an eschatological moment in which their status will be
dramatically reversed.

Third Isaiah's powerful idea of eschatological hope for the poor was
taken up in early Jewish literature.[36] In the Hodayot the poet declares to
God: You "open the f[oun]tain of your truth ... to proclaim good news to
the poor (ענוים) according to the abundance of your mercy, [and to s]atisfy

---

35. Blenkinsopp 2003, 223.
36. Collins 1997a, 225–40.

from the fountain of kn[owledge all the contr]ite in spirit and those who mourn (that they may have) eternal joy (ואבלים לשמחת עולם)" (1QH 23:14–16; cf. 10:7, 26:23). This text does not emphasize an eschatological day of the Lord to the extent of Isa 61:1–3, but rather takes the language from the Isaianic passage to highlight the divine revelation the elect have received. Like 4QInstruction (4Q417 2 i 10, 12; see above), the passage relies on a distinction between mourning and eternal joy. Ben Sira praises Isaiah for providing comfort to those who mourn, a comfort he associates with the eschatological future.[37] The eschatological proclamations of 11QMelchizedek include comforting those who mourn (11Q13 2 20). The New Testament Sermon on the Mount also appropriates Isaiah 61, promising comfort for those who mourn.[38]

The promise of eternal joy for those who mourn in 4Q417 2 i 10–12 is likely another early Jewish utilization of the eschatological proclamation of Isa 61:1–3.[39] This realization explains the supplement "contrite of spirit" (נכאי רוח) at the end of 4Q417 2 i 11, in parallelism with "those who mourn," who are promised eternal joy (cf. Isa 66:2).[40] 4QInstruction's reliance upon this biblical text is not extensive or direct. The theme of Zion, a major element of Isa 61:1–3, plays no role in 4QInstruction. However, understanding 4Q417 2 i 10–12 as alluding to Isaiah 61 helps explain why those who are in mourning do not rejoice now but have "eternal joy" allocated to them, in the context of God's judgment (4Q417 2 i 16–17).[41] Those who mourn are comforted by the prospect of "eternal joy."[42] The "mourners" in 4Q417 2 i 10, 12 are not lamenting departed loved ones, but

---

37. Sir 48:24–25: "By his dauntless spirit he looked into the future and consoled the mourners of Zion (וינחם אבלי ציון). He foretold what should be till the end of time, hidden things that were yet to be fulfilled" (cf. 22:12; 38:16–17).

38. Matt 5:4: "Blessed are those who mourn, for they will be comforted." The context of this statement associates those who mourn with the lowly and downtrodden, as in Isa 61 (cf. Matt 11:5–6; Luke 7:22).

39. Elgvin 1995b, 446; Elgvin 1997a, 203; Rey 2009a, 49.

40. Strugnell and Harrington 1999, 176.

41. The description of the elect as an "eternal planting" in 4Q418 81 13 may also reflect familiarity with Third Isaiah (see commentary there). Note also the intriguing but fragmentary phrase אבלי צדק in 4Q418 172 2. The meaning of the expression, which could be translated "righteous mourners" or perhaps "those who mourn for righteousness," is unfortunately not clear.

42. However, the verb לנתם, which is crucial in the Isa 61 passage, does not occur in 4Q417 2 i 10–12 (or in 4QInstruction as a whole).

rather are the members of the intended audience of 4QInstruction. Many of them suffer poverty and hardship. This is consistent with the focus in Third Isaiah on the dejected and downtrodden.

4Q417 2 i 10 explains that one should not rejoice in mourning "lest you toil (תעמל) in your life." The basic meaning of the verb in the Bible (as a *qal*) is "to exert oneself" (e.g., Prov 16:26; Ps 127:1; Jon 4:10). The root has a positive meaning in 4Q418 55 3, referring to studying that allows the addressee to acquire knowledge and intelligence (see below).[43] In other wisdom texts the root signifies labor in a more negative sense, and that appears to be the case in 4Q417 2 i 10 as well. In Qoheleth the root denotes "the tiresome effort expended over an enterprise of dubious result."[44] "Toil" is identified by the sage as הבל (literally, "vapor"), his characteristic term for the fleeting and ephemeral character of life (e.g., 1:3; 2:21; 4:4; cf. 5:14; 6:7). Ben Sira similarly associates "toil" with weary labor.[45] In 4Q417 2 i 10 the word probably denotes labor that is ultimately unsuccessful. In context the term has an eschatological meaning in 4QInstruction, in contrast to its usage in Qoheleth and Ben Sira (cf. ll. 11, 15–16). The verb לעמול in line 10 probably refers to toiling in this world without a firm expectation of the reception of "eternal joy" after death. The envisioned addressee endures material poverty and excessive labor in his life. Ultimately such labor is not wasted if he comports himself with humility and lowliness in his regular life. With the right ethical posture he can receive a blessed afterlife.

4Q417 2 i 10–11

These lines provide an impression of the eschatological knowledge that is available to the *mebin* through the study of the mystery that is to be. He is to "seize the birth times of salvation" (קח מולדי ישע). Elgvin has argued that the "birth times" signify tribulation and upheaval that are to accompany an eschatological scenario, "the pangs of salvation."[46] How-

---

43. The root also occurs in 4Q418 78 3; 4Q418 122 i 6; 4Q418a 16 3. עמל is rare as a verb in early Jewish literature (1Q21 3 2; Sir 33:18). See Rey 2009a, 48.

44. Seow 1997, 113.

45. "The sign of a good heart is a radiant look; withdrawn and perplexed is the toiling schemer (מחשבת עמל)" (13:26). Note also Sir 11:11: "One may toil (עמל) and struggle and drive, and fall short all the same" (cf. 31:3–4). See Di Lella and Skehan 1987, 255.

46. Elgvin 2000a, 233; 1997a, 79.

ever, there is no sense in 4QInstruction that the final judgment is to be preceded by eschatological travails.

The word מולד denotes birth, as is suggested by its root. There has been some speculation that the term reflects an astrological conception of human birth. Schmidt, turning to the term מולד, has proposed that the mystery that is to be provides a way to attain knowledge of "la science de l'horoscope ou généthlialogie," genethialogy being astronomical knowledge that focuses on the birth of individuals.[47] The term מולד explicitly signifies one's astrological sign in 4QHoroscope: "this is the sign (המולד) in which he was born (ילוד)" (4Q186 1 ii 8; cf. 4Q186 2 i 8). The term may have a similar meaning in the book of Mysteries, a composition with a strong deterministic impulse. 4Q299 3a ii–b 13 uses the term in a claim of supernatural revelation: "the [p]lan of the time of birth (מ]חשבת בית) מולדים) he opened before them" (cf. 4Q299 1 4; 4Q299 5 5).[48] In this text מולד signifies a deterministic understanding of human birth—the birth of a particular individual is part of a greater divine plan according to which history unfolds. This perspective is fully compatible with astrology, but there is no explicit attestation of astrological lore in Mysteries. The same can be said for the "birth times of salvation" of 4QInstruction. Schmidt may be correct that the mystery that is to be conveys astronomical knowledge. But this cannot be stated conclusively. A deterministic conception of the natural order is a major theme of the composition (e.g., 4Q417 1 i 6–13). It follows that every human birth occurs according to God's schema, which guides history.[49] Such assertions, however, are never accompanied in 4QInstruction by any references to astronomy.

From the understanding of מולד argued above, it follows that "the birth times of salvation" signify the times of birth of the elect.[50] The elect,

---

47. Schmidt 2006, 53, 59. Consult also Morgenstern 2000, 141–44; Rey 2009a, 35–36; Puech 2006, 88; Tigchelaar 2001, 238.

48. The phrase בית מולדים occurs in 4Q415 2 ii 9 (see commentary above). In this line the phrase denotes birth, but without any apparent astronomical meaning, referring to the actual house in which the wife of the addressee is born. "House" (בית) has an astrological sense in 4QHoroscope (e.g., 4Q186 1 ii 7–8), and this may also be the case in 4Q299 3a ii–b 13. Consult Popović 2007, 132–35; Hengel 1974, 1.237.

49. The Hodayot also associate the word מולד with a deterministic understanding of time: "All the births of time (מולדי עת), the foundation of the season, and the cycle of the festivals in the order fixed by their signs, for all their dominion in proper order, reliably, at the command of God" (1QH 20:10–12; cf. 11:12).

50. In 4QInstruction the word ישע ("salvation") occurs only in 4Q417 2 i 11.

who are in the lot of angels and have access to the mystery that is to be, have the potential to achieve salvation. An interest in their birth times may be evident in 4Q416 2 iii 9, which urges one to study מולדיו ("its origins") through the mystery that is to be. The antecedent of the suffix is probably the word "glory," a term the passage explicitly associates with the elect status of the addressee, who has an "inheritance of glory" (נחלת כבוד) (ll. 11–12). This exact topic is at issue in 4Q417 2 i 11, which claims that one can know who will "inherit glory" (נוחל כבוד; see also below). Through the study of the mystery that is to be one can know whom God established "in the lot of the angels"—humans who have the potential, through proper training and study, to fulfill the destiny allotted to them and join the angels after death. Unfortunately, 4QInstruction provides no detail in terms of *how* one could determine, based on a person's time of birth, that he or she is among the elect. Presumably such knowledge was available through the mystery that is to be.

The *mebin* is to "seize" (קח) the birth times in 4Q417 2 i 11. This signifies assessing whether a person's time of birth indicates that they are among the elect or not (cf. 4Q418 77 2, 4). In three other texts one is to "seize" the birth times—4Q415 11 11, 4Q416 2 iii 20 and 4Q418 202 1. None of these three fragments preserves enough context to interpret them conclusively. 4Q415 11 11 exhorts one to take birth times when his wife gives birth. This suggests that at issue is the determination of whether the children of the *mebin* and his wife are among the elect or not. 4Q416 2 iii 20 urges that one "seize" the birth times of his wife. This text probably recommends that one examine the time of birth of the woman to determine if she has elect status (see commentary above). 4Q416 2 iii 20 and 4Q415 11 11 likely discuss the determination of the elect status of family members of the male addressee. He was encouraged to marry someone who had such status, and it was therefore critical to determine whether a potential wife was in fact among the elect (see the commentary to 4Q415 2 ii and 4Q416 2 iv). It was also important to know whether any children born to them should be so considered as well. Establishing a person's elect status played an important role in the family life of the *mebin*. The "birth times" in 4Q417 2 i 11 are not associated with particular family members but rather the elect in a general sense.

4Q417 2 i 11 teaches that there are two opposed eschatological fates: glory and iniquity. The *mebin* can learn which of these a person will receive. Those who are to "inherit glory" (נוחל כבוד) include the audience to which 4QInstruction is directed, as mentioned above (cf. 4Q416 2 iii

11–12). The Hebrew reads כבוד ועל, which could be understood as "glory and elevation," as Rey and Puech suggest (see the textual notes section). על is better understood as an error for or an unusual *defectiva* spelling of עול, "iniquity." Two factors support this position. One, there are to the best of my knowledge no examples of על as a nominal form of the root עלה ("to go up") in the Hebrew Bible or early Jewish literature. Two, 4QInstruction elsewhere connects a call to study the mystery that is to be with two opposing terms to elaborate upon the knowledge that can be thus attained. In several instances one member of the word pair is from the root עול. In 4Q417 1 i 6–7 the *mebin* is to meditate upon the *raz nihyeh* to learn truth and iniquity (עול). In 4Q416 2 iii 14–15 he is to understand the ways of truth and the roots of "injustice" (עולה; cf. 4Q417 1 i 20). The word pair כבוד ועל in 4Q417 2 i 11 also represents knowledge that can be acquired through the mystery that is to be. The terms should be understood not as complementary terms, but rather as polar opposites.

4Q417 2 i 12

For the tropes of "eternal joy" and "mourning" in this line, see above on line 10 and the excursus earlier in this chapter. After this statement on these topics begins a new section (ll. 12–17) that provides instruction on speech and discusses eschatological judgment. Line 12 urges the *mebin* to advocate for his own interests, but the Hebrew is ambiguous. He is told to be a בעל ריב, literally a "master of dispute." The expression elsewhere occurs only in 1QH 15:25–26, where it refers to the enemies of the speaker, "those who have a cause against me" (בעלי רבי). In 4QInstruction, by contrast, the phrase has a positive meaning, denoting a type of person whom the addressee should emulate. Strugnell and Harrington suggest that the expression is equivalent to the biblical איש ריב (Judg 12:2; Jer 15:10) or perhaps יריב, meaning "adversary" or "advocate" (e.g., Jer 18:19; cf. 4Q418 81 7).[51] The editors are probably right that the *mebin* is to be an advocate of some sort. He is to promote his own חפץ, a term that often means "desire." The word can refer in 4QInstruction to one's needs or interests in a financial sense (see the commentary on 4Q418 126 ii 12). 4Q417 2 i 12 may urge the *mebin* to struggle to be economically self-sufficient. Lines

---

51. Strugnell and Harrington 1999, 183. In the Bible the phrase איש ריב describes people who are in engaged in a struggle. Jeremiah 15:10 reads, for example, "Woe is me, my mother, that you ever bore me, a man of strife (איש ריב) and contention to the whole land!"

12–14 are better understood, however, as continuing the theme of proper speech in the context of a dispute that is introduced in lines 1–6.[52] The word "dispute" (ריב) is in lines 12 and 14. Lines 13–14 teach one to speak forthrightly while not overlooking one's transgressions, as in line 4. To be a "master of dispute" probably means that one should be direct and engaged when involved in a conflict with someone else. As in lines 1–6, the exact nature of the conflict is not stated.[53] Given the economic resonance of the word "desire," the author of line 12 may have had in mind disputes that affect the *mebin* financially.

4Q417 2 i 13

The addressee is to speak his "judgments" (משפטיכה; cf. l. 1). The line presents him as a powerful, regal figure, who utters his pronouncements "like a righteous ruler." The editors understand the person addressed as a judge.[54] There is no evidence in 4QInstruction, however, that the *mebin* speaks from the standpoint of authority. Viewing him as a judge does not accord with the emphasis on his poverty (see below on ll. 19–20). He is supposed to act like a humble or poor person during a dispute (l. 14). This suggests that he does not speak with judicial *gravitas*. Rather, the reference to a ruler is metaphorical. He should speak during a dispute directly, but not with excessive anger or desire for revenge, as would a just king.[55]

4Q417 2 i 14

The *mebin* is to remember that he has transgressions of his own. This echoes line 4, in which he is not to overlook his faults when recounting the misdeeds of another person. Line 14 similarly recommends that he be like a "humble man" (עני) in the context of a dispute. This forms a nice contrast with the claim in line 13 that he should speak like a "ruler." Lines 13–14 advocate balance and moderation in the context of speech during a dis-

---

52. *Contra* Rey (2009a, 57–58), who tentatively suggests that 4Q417 2 i 12–14 advocates asceticism.

53. Lines 12–14 do not emphasize not seeking punishment against the other person, in contrast to ll. 1–6 (esp. l. 2).

54. Strugnell and Harrington 1999, 10. See also Kampen 2011, 111; Rey 2009a, 58. For משפט in the sense of legal decisions see, e.g., Exod 21:9; Ezek 23:24.

55. Rey (2009a, 46) reconstructs the missing portion of l. 13 as urging that one not take revenge against his enemies.

pute. He should be direct and forthright, like a just king, but also humble and lowly, like a poor person.

4Q417 2 i 15–17

Lines 15–16 and the beginning of line 17 discuss eschatological judgment. No one can survive God's wrath. Humanity requires his forgiveness to withstand this ordeal. There is a theophanic element to this soteriological claim, since line 15 states God will be seen. This is too much for a human being to endure (see, e.g., Gen 16:13). Ideally, divine wrath will be turned away and not visible at the moment of judgment.[56] Line 16 asserts that people do not have enough righteousness on their own to merit a good outcome. There is a similar rhetorical question in the Hodayot: "Who can be righteous before you when he is judged," asserting that "none is able to stand before your wrath" (1QH 15:31–32).[57] 4QInstruction, like the Hodayot, emphasizes that the addressee's upright conduct does not automatically merit a positive recompense when God judges. Rather, one's ethical behavior functions as an incentive for God to forgive his sins. Clemency is also endorsed in the context of a dispute with a powerful person (l. 2). Lines 10–12 remind the *mebin* that a poor person (רש) is "lowly" (צעיר), stressing that such a person can receive "eternal joy," which signifies eternal life (see above). Lines 16–17 are reasonably reconstructed as discussing the reception of eschatological rewards—a "poor man" (אביון) can survive judgment but only with forgiveness. Poverty terms such as אביון denote in 4QInstruction not simply material hardship, but also values such as humility and ethics (see section 9 of the introduction). The reminder of divine judgment in 4Q417 2 i 15–17 encourages the addressee to be ethical and to follow the teachings advocated by the composition. This rationale for appealing to judgment is found elsewhere in 4QInstruction (e.g., 4Q417 1 i 13–18).

4Q417 2 i 17–18

A new section is demarcated in line 17 with ואתה. Lines 17–28 are important for understanding the financial teachings of 4QInstruction and the poverty of the addressee. The pericope centers around five if-clauses (ll. 17 [2x], 18, 21, 25).[58] The first three describe ways the *mebin* can meet

---

56. Kampen 2011, 111.
57. Rey 2009a, 59.
58. Rey 2009a, 60–61.

his material needs, including the borrowing of money. The last two focus on the consequences of borrowing. Lines 17–18 state that if the *mebin* needs food, he should assemble his surpluses and sell them.[59] The word מחסור denotes what the addressee lacks with regard to his basic material needs. The term is common in 4QInstruction, occurring over twenty-five times, though only three times in the rest of the Dead Sea Scrolls.[60] The word is prominent in this section, also occurring in lines 19, 21 and 24.

The editors of DJD 34 understand 4Q417 2 i 17–18 as being about "the moderate use of resources."[61] The focus of the lines is rather on the addressee using his resources to meet his basic needs. The surpluses (מותריכה) in question are to ensure that he will have enough food (cf. 4Q418 126 ii 15).[62] Several texts of 4QInstruction assume that the addressee has goods to trade and possesses a degree of financial stability.[63] 4Q417 2 i 17–18 is consistent with this material. The second if-statement in these lines grants that he may not have a surplus. The author recognizes that his current economic self-sufficiency could change for the worse (see further on ll. 18–19).

The expression הבא ביחד of line 17 denotes the addressee's assembling of his surpluses together (see textual notes above). Some commen-

---

59. I read טרף ("food") as a substantive. The word can be understood as an imperative (*defectiva*), as Rey (2009a, 34, 50) and Caquot (1996, 8) suggest, but this would not substantially change the meaning of the line. The term is normally used in 4QInstruction as the noun "food" in a general sense (4Q417 2 ii 3 [par. 4Q416 2 ii 1]; 4Q418 81 16). As a verb it denotes nourishment that God provides in 4Q417 2 i 20. Tigchelaar (2011, 321) has endorsed Rey's reading of the statement on stylistic grounds, since it would produce a chiastic structure: protasis (ואתה אם תחסר)—apodosis (טרף מחסורכה); apodosis (ומותריכה הבא ביחד)—protasis (אם תותיר).

60. Note, for example, 4Q416 1 6; 4Q416 2 ii 1, 20; 4Q416 2 iii 2; 4Q417 2 i 17, 19, 21, 24; 4Q418 81 18; 4Q418 87 6; 4Q418 88 ii 5; 4Q418 97 2; 4Q418 107 3; 4Q418 126 ii 13; 4Q418 159 ii 5 (cf. 1QH 7:29; 4Q299 65 5; 4Q424 1 8; Sir 40:26). The word is rare in the Hebrew Bible as a whole, but common in Proverbs (e.g., Judg 19:20; Prov 6:11; 11:24; 22:16; 28:27). See Rey 2009a, 36; Fabry 2003, 148–50, 156–57.

61. Strugnell and Harrington 1999, 186.

62. The exact nature of the surpluses is not clear, but the logic of the passage suggests that they are not agricultural produce. If he had a surplus yield from his crops to sell, he would not be in need of food.

63. 4Q418 107 4, for example, reads "the resources, your merchandise, and the recompense in the business dealings of (בחפצי) …" 4Q418 81 18 urges: "Bring forth what you need to all those who seek business (חפץ)." See also the discussion of חפץ below.

tators read the word יחד in a sectarian sense. On the basis of this word, Murphy has suggested that lines 17–18 describe the "sectarian pooling of resources."[64] However, there is insufficient evidence to understand the term as implying that the provenance of 4QInstruction is from the sectarian movement that produced the Qumran rulebooks (see section 10 of the introduction). Rey translates "Et ton surplus [p]orte-le [à la communauté]."[65] He stresses that reading יחד as "la communauté" is not necessarily a reference to the sect that produced the rulebooks, but more likely in his view an Essene, pre-Qumran community. However, there is no sense in 4QInstruction that his business dealings are coordinated with any sort of leader of the group, or with other members of his community, as one finds in the literature of the *yahad* (e.g., CD 13:14–15). The phrase ביחד is better understood adverbially, denoting that the *mebin* brings his surplus items "together" to trade.[66]

Having assembled his surplus, the *mebin* is to bring it to מחוז חפצו, literally "its desired haven." The term חפץ is common in 4QInstruction, referring to desires, often in a financial sense, as is the case here (see commentary to 4Q418 126 ii 12). The expression מחוז חפצו is from Ps 107:30, where it refers to a port to which God brings sailors who weathered a storm.[67] The word מחוז refers to a "harbor," and in rabbinic usage comes to mean "market" or "trading place."[68] 4Q417 2 i 18, with its focus on selling, appears to be an early attestation of the latter sense of the term. "Inheritance" (נחלה) in line 18 does not refer to the elect status of the addressee, as is often the case in 4QInstruction (e.g., 4Q416 2 iii 11–12). Rather the term has a material sense, denoting what he receives in exchange for the sale of his surpluses.

4Q417 2 I 18–19

Line 19, and the end of line 18, address the same basic situation as lines 17–18: the *mebin* has difficulty meeting his material needs. The statement in lines 18–19 shares several textual elements with that of lines 17–18. Each sentence begins with "if you lack" (אם תחסר) and describe the addressee's lack with the word מחסורכה. There is, however, one crucial

64. Murphy 2002, 117.
65. Rey 2009a, 47, 51.
66. Strugnell and Harrington 1999, 186; Tigchelaar 1998, 592.
67. 4Q418b 1 3–4 contains a quotation from Ps 107:26–27.
68. See, for example, Tg. Ps.-J. to Ezek 27:3. Note also 4Q552 1 ii 10.

difference between the two texts: in lines 18–19 he does not have surplus to trade and in lines 17–18 he does. Not only is there no surplus in lines 18–19—the *mebin* is "without mo[ne]y" for his basic needs (ה[ו]מבלי; l. 19). He is supposed to "borrow" from God.[69] His abundance is stressed, in contrast to the *mebin* who is experiencing lack (cf. 4Q418 237 3). 4Q416 2 i 22–ii 1 similarly urges him to ask the deity for his food (טרף), stressing his abundance and compassion, but without mentioning the addressee's economic distress in the manner of 4Q417 2 i 18–19. Lines 21–25 discuss borrowing from creditors and the problems that arise. The act of borrowing from God in lines 18–19 is distinguished from borrowing money. This suggests a total reliance upon the deity for one's basic needs. 4Q417 2 i advocates a form of asceticism. Whether through foraging, begging, reliance on charity, or other means of support, any sustenance obtained by the *mebin* not through his borrowing or his own generation of income is considered testimony to God's bounty.[70] This extreme material dependence upon the deity can be compared to that of John the Baptist and Bannus, both of whom eschewed food cultivated by people and relied instead on God for all their needs (Josephus, *Vita* 11; Matt 3:3–6). The Sermon on the Mount advocates a similar posture.[71] The asceticism endorsed by 4Q417 2 i 18–19, however, is not nearly as radical as that of John the Baptist or Bannus. Ideally the *mebin* is industrious and has the ability to support himself. Lines 18–19 envisage a situation in which that is no longer possible. Normally 4QInstruction encourages the addressee to borrow money in a time of need, as in the following text (l. 21), not to rely utterly upon God. Lines 18–19 provide a theological framework for understanding a situation of genuine hardship. Lacking sufficient resources, the *mebin* is to adopt a radical dependence on God.

4Q417 2 i 17–18 is directed to someone who can be in need of food but has the wherewithal to solve the problem. Lines 18–19 are for someone who no longer has that ability. The poverty of the intended addressee does

---

69. I understand the word לוא in l. 19 not as "no" but rather as a *qal* imperative of the root לוה, "to borrow" (cf. l. 24). See Strugnell and Harrington 1999, 187; Rey 2009a, 51; Murphy 2002, 179; Fabry 2003, 157.

70. Contrast Sir 40:28–29: "My son, live not the life of a beggar; better to die than to beg. When one has to look to a stranger's table, one's life is not to be considered a life."

71. Matthew 6:26 reads, for example: "Look at the birds of the air; they neither sow nor reap nor gather into barns, and yet your heavenly father feeds them."

not necessarily denote someone who is destitute.[72] The intended audience of 4QInstruction attests a range of levels of economic self-sufficiency. The composition focuses on people who range from being self-sufficient to being destitute. This accords with what can be inferred about the professions of the people for whom 4QInstruction was written. These include farmers, artisans and debt slaves (see the commentary on 4Q418 103 ii and 4Q423 5). The poverty of the *mebin*, while often having a metaphorical usage, clearly denotes material suffering.

4QInstruction's socio-economic portrait of the envisioned addressee is consistent with what can be known about the economy of Palestine in the Second Temple period (see the excursus on indebtedness in this era in chapter 3). In the second century B.C.E. there was no middle class in Judea in the modern sense of the term. As in most traditional agricultural economies, most people were farmers or small-scale tradesmen, and they were susceptible to drastic changes in fortune. Their ability to support themselves and their families could easily vanish. People in such situations were forced to borrow, and were exposed to exploitation from unscrupulous creditors. The stress on borrowing in 4QInstruction suggests that the *mebin* needed credit with some regularity (see also below on ll. 22–26).

4Q417 2 i 19–21

God is an abundant creator who provides food. All things come into being at his command. Line 20 uses טרף as a verb to assert that God makes food available (cf. 4Q416 2 ii 1).[73] Line 17 uses the same root (see above). The *mebin* is not to eat anything beyond what God provides. Similar advice is given in line 18 with regard to food he acquires through his own labor. 4QInstruction stresses moderation. The addressee is to receive enough food to meet his needs and nothing else.

4Q417 2 i 21–22

If the *mebin* borrows money, he should work ceaselessly to repay the loan. 4QInstruction shows acute awareness of the problems associated with indebtedness. 4Q416 2 iii 5–7 urges the repayment of debts. 4Q416 2 ii, discussing surety, addresses problems that can accrue from non-payment

---

72. Tigchelaar 2000, 62–75; Goff 2003b, 155–62.

73. 4Q417 2 i 20 literally states that things come into being "on account of his mouth," referring presumably to creation via divine speech. It is an interesting choice of words to express God's desire to create food for humanity.

of debts, including becoming a debt slave (ll. 7–17). Significantly, the composition never complains about interest, even though rates could be usurious. The addressee is to accept his indebtedness, regardless of the fairness of the arrangement, and work hard to pay it off. To emphasize the intensity with which one should be devoted to eliminating the debt, 4Q417 2 i 22 employs the image of going without "comfort" day and night.[74] 4Q416 2 ii 9–10 uses similar language, probably derived from Prov 6, in connection with work that is assigned to the *mebin* as a debt slave (see commentary above; cf. Ahiq. 45–46 [sgs.]). In 4Q417 2 i 21 the word מחסור describes the difficult economic situation of the *mebin* that necessitates borrowing. Line 19 employs the term in the same way, prompting him to "borrow" from God (see also ll. 17, 24). Since advice on borrowing money follows just after 4QInstruction's call to rely wholly on God (ll. 19–20), the author probably recognized that some of his students would find this unpalatable and choose instead the more conventional route of borrowing from a creditor.

4Q417 2 i 22–24

The addressee is not to deceive his creditor. Line 25 similarly insists that he should not hide any obligation from him. 4QInstruction encourages the *mebin* to be an ethical borrower. This is in stark contrast to the creditor, who could have him flogged (l. 25). The rationale for this ethical posture is eminently practical—if the addressee deceives a person from whom he has borrowed money, he might be unwilling to lend him money in the future. The composition assumes that the *mebin* will need credit beyond the present problem that necessitated borrowing money (מחסור; l. 24).

The end of line 23, though fragmentary, states that if the addressee were dishonest with his creditor he would no longer trust "his neighbor" (רעהו). The neighbor in 4Q416 2 ii (which corresponds to 4Q417 2 ii) is an acquaintance of the *mebin*, who guarantees a loan for his acquaintance through a pledge (e.g., 4Q416 2 ii 5). This is probably not the meaning of the term in 4Q417 2 i 23. Here the "neighbor" is someone known to the person who loaned money to the *mebin*—that is, another creditor. The person in question is the most likely subject of the beginning of line 24,

---

74. Strugnell and Harrington (1999, 188) reconstruct "let there be no [sleep for yo]u" (אל [דומי לכ]ה) on the basis of Ps 83:2 [Eng. v. 1]: "do not hold your peace or be still (אל־דמי־לך), O God!" See Wright 2004a, 117.

which states that he will close his hand when the addressee is in need.[75] If he gets a reputation for being dishonest among creditors, they might refuse to lend him money. Not being able to "trust" the neighbor refers to being unable to rely on him to provide a loan. Line 26 probably discusses the undesirable prospect of the creditor's revealing the "shame" of the *mebin*.[76] Note the contrast between borrowing from creditors and God (l. 19). A human can easily refuse to offer assistance by closing his hand, whereas God has opened his compassion (4Q416 2 i 22).[77]

4Q417 2 I 24–26

Line 25 is not well preserved but describes the addressee being flogged. The line probably teaches that the *mebin* should not be deceitful with regard to his outstanding loan, even if he is beaten. There is no indication whatsoever that he should resist the beating or seek revenge. 4Q418 87 may also refer to beatings in the context of advice on borrowing.[78] The discussion in 4Q417 2 i continues on the topic of potentially violent relations with a creditor, but the key texts are not well preserved. Line 27 mentions *not* being struck by a rod (see below). After discussing the beating, line 25 uses the verb אוץ (cf. 4Q416 2 i 21). The editors of DJD 34 translate "hasten," but the verb can also mean "to urge" or "insist upon."[79] The latter meaning is to be preferred in 4Q417 2 i 25. Its lacuna can be supplemented so that the line states that the beating was carried out by someone who urged the *mebin* to pay his debts.[80] 4QInstruction stresses the importance of the addressee's honesty with regard to his obligations, even when the

---

75. For the idiom "to close the hand," see the commentary to 4Q416 2 ii 2.

76. Line 23 contains a fragmentary reference to "shame," which the *mebin* would feel if he were dishonest to his creditor.

77. The content of 4Q417 2 i 22–24 would have preceded the beginning of 4Q416 2 ii. The image of the creditor shutting his hand in 4Q417 2 i 24 would have occurred in 4Q416 2 i 17. God closes his hand in 4Q416 2 ii 2.

78. In 4Q418 87 8 the phrase "your blow" is in parallelism with מכה, "wound" (cf. 4Q418 303 4). That l. 8 discusses being struck physically by lenders is suggested by l. 7, which mentions surety. See Burns 2004, 30–35.

79. In Exod 5:13, for example, the word describes the taskmasters of Egypt, who urge the Hebrew slaves to work (cf. Jer 17:16; Sir 7:17; 11:10).

80. "If a beating befalls you, and he urges [that you repay your debts, then do not hide the debt from the person who lent (it) to you], lest the [creditor] reveal your sh[a]me" (ll. 25–26). Kampen (2011, 104) reads the key term (נגע) as "affliction" rather than "beating."

creditor engages in unsavory practices. The addressee's "sh[a]me" (or: "rep[ro]ach"; חרפ[ה]תכה) being revealed most likely refers to the creditor making known that the *mebin* is an unreliable borrower (see above on ll. 22–24).[81] This would make it difficult for him to secure a loan later on when in need of credit.

Who strikes the addressee is not clear. Just before the reference to the beating in line 25, line 24 advises: "know the one who gathe[rs] (מאג[ר])." This is obscure. I tentatively suggest that this refers to someone sent by the creditor to intimidate the *mebin* and/or to extract the debt. The root in the Hebrew Bible refers to gathering or piling up grain collected in harvest (e.g., Deut 28:39; Prov 6:8). In Qumran Aramaic it can mean "wages" (e.g., 1Q20 7:5; 4Q196 16 1). Admittedly, there is no instance of the word denoting collecting a debt. Given that the envisioned addressee grew crops, perhaps the person has been sent to take forcibly some of the yield. Understanding the "gatherer" in this way helps explain why the *mebin* is to know him—he is to be wary of him. The wealthy creditor probably did not carry out such tasks himself but rather hired others to so so.

4Q417 2 i 26–27

These lines are highly fragmentary. Line 27 asserts, "he will not strike him with a rod." Someone avoids a beating, presumably from the striker mentioned in line 24 ("the one who gathe[rs]"), but the person's identity is not clear.[82] Not enough material survives to say why he would not be struck. The text of 4Q417 2 i 25–28 overlaps with the end of 4Q416 2 i. 4Q416 2 ii, as covered in the commentary above, provides financial instruction regarding surety that involves three people—the creditor, the *mebin*, and his neighbor (רע), for whom the addressee has gone surety (e.g., 4Q416 2 ii 5). One can therefore speculate that the person of 4Q417 2 i 27 (par. 4Q416 2 i 19–20) who is not beaten is the addressee's neighbor. Perhaps he guaranteed the loan about which the *mebin* is being struck in line 25.

4Q417 2 i 28

This overlaps with 4Q416 2 i 20–21 and is treated in the commentary on that text.

---

81. Wold 2005b, 222–24.

82. Line 26 refers to someone in the third person in a fragmentary context: "who rules over him."

Text[1]

[הׄ זֹנֹפֹשֹׁוֹן] 1

[vacat] 2

בעמל נכרה דרכיה vacat נרגיע]ׄם[3

vacat ושקד יהיה בלבבנו [בכול קצים]וׄבטׄוׄח בכול דרכינו 4

דעׄ]ת{ דעה ולא שחרו בינ]ה וברצון אל ל]אׄ בחרו vac הלוא אל 5
ה]דׄעות 6

על אמת להכין כול] דרכיהם על ב]ינה הוא פלג לנוחלי אמת 6

שקד בא]]עׄשׄ[ ]הלוא שלום והשקט 7

הלוא ידׄ]עׄתם אם לא שמעתמה כיא מלאכי קודש ל]וׄ[בשמים 8

אמת וירדפו אחר כול שורשי בינה וישקדו על]דׄעהׄ[9

ולפׄ]י דעתם יׄכבדו איש מרעהו ולפי שכלו ירבה הדרׄז 10

]הׄכאׄנׄוׄש הם כי יעצל ובן אדם כי ידמה הלוא 11

]ׄזׄ°ׄ והם אחזת עולם ינחלו הלוא ראיתם 12

bottom margin

Translation

1   ... and his soul ...
2   ... *vacat* ...
3   ... with toil we explore its ways. *vacat* We will be at rest ...
4   ... Then vigilance will be in our heart [*at all times*] and security in all our ways. *vacat*

---

1. Strugnell and Harrington 1999, 265–67; Tigchelaar 2001, 89–90, 208–9; Rey 2009a, 304–5; Elgvin 1997a, 274–75. The textual notes section refers to these works.

5   ... knowledge. And they have not sought understand[*ing and the
      will of God*] they have [*no*]t chosen. *vacat* Is not [*the*] God of
      Knowledge ...

6   ... upon truth, to establish all [*their ways upon un*]derstanding.
      He has apportioned to those who inherit truth ...

7   ... vigilance in ... Are not peace and tranquility ...

8   [... *Do*] you [*not kn*]ow or have you not heard that the angels of
      holiness belong to h[*im*] in heaven ...

9   ... truth. They pursue after all the roots of understanding and are
      vigilant over [*knowledge*] ...

10   [... *And according*] to their knowledge they are glorified, each one
      more than his neighbor, and according to one's intelligence his
      splendor will be increased.

11   ... Are they like a man? For he is slothful. Or a human? For he is
      still. Is not ...

12   ... As for them, they will inherit an eternal possession. Have you
      not seen ...

Textual Notes

55 1. וֹנִפֹּשׁוֹ. Following Tigchelaar and Elgvin. The editors of DJD 34
and Rey read וֹנִפֹּ[ו]לֹהֹ. There is not enough space to add a letter after the
pe. Abrasion of some ink makes reading the last letters difficult.

55 10. ֹי[ולֹפֹ]. So also Elgvin. Tigchelaar transcribes ֹ[ֹי, as Strugnell
did in the Preliminary Concordance. In DJD 34 the editors read וֹל[ֹפֹי.
While it is not clear that there are traces of two letters, reconstructing ולפי
is a reasonable suggestion (so also Rey). Not enough of the downward
stroke of the visible trace is evident to read a final *nun*. The verbatim
match of this text with 1QH 18:29–30 also argues against the *nun* (see
below).

Commentary

4Q418 55 urges its addressees to strive to achieve wisdom. To encourage this pursuit the column invokes the angels, who eagerly pursue the
truth. The use of angels as models of conduct in a pedagogical sense is
unusual in early Jewish literature, but it is also found in 4Q418 69 ii (see
the next chapter). 4Q418 55 is distinguished among the fragments of
4QInstruction by its use of the second person plural (ll. 8–12), whereas
the composition typically prefers the second person singular. 4Q418 69 ii

also relies on the plural form, and the two texts have several other features in common. They contain, for example, rhetorical questions (e.g., 4Q418 55 5; 4Q418 69 ii 3), with both texts using the interrogative *he* attached to nouns and in the form הלוא ("Is it not ..."). They employ the first person plural, as in 4Q418 55 3 and 4Q418 69 ii 11.[2] The two texts share several distinctive terms, such as שקד ("to watch over," "to be vigilant"; 4Q418 55 4, 7, 9; 4Q418 69 ii 10, 11). Drawing upon a suggestion in DJD 34 that 4Q418 69 ii contains an originally separate text that was incorporated into 4QInstruction, Tigchelaar speculates that 4Q418 55 and 69 ii should be distinguished from the rest of 4QInstruction.[3] The points in common between fragments 55 and 69 ii are indeed striking, but they do not necessarily provide enough evidence to understand them as having been added later to the work. The terminology and major themes of both fragments, as discussed below, are fully compatible with the rest of the composition (see especially on 4Q418 55 5–6).

4Q418 55 can be divided into two sections: lines 1–5 and 6–12. The first portion, though fragmentary, distinguishes between a "we" group, which strives for learning, and a "they" group, which does not. Using the second person plural, the second portion encourages the addressees to be like the angels, seeking the truth.

4Q418 55 3

Line 3 affirms, in the first person plural, that the intended addressees are studying and that they will receive rewards for their efforts. The first person usage continues into line 4. The *mebinim* are depicted as the speakers in lines 3–4. This is one of the few instances in 4QInstruction that reflects grammatically that the composition is addressed to a group of students (cf. 4Q418 221 3). The studying under discussion probably refers to contemplation of the mystery that is to be, a practice advocated throughout the composition (e.g., 4Q417 1 i 7–8).[4] In lines 3–4 the author probably conveys what the ideal student-addressees *should* say. A similar rhetorical approach is found in 4Q418 69 ii 11–12, which depicts, in the first person plural, what the student-addressees should not say.

---

2. Tigchelaar 2001, 208–24 (esp. 218); Kampen 2011, 126.

3. Strugnell and Harrington 1999, 14; Tigchelaar 2001, 211–12.

4. Note, however, that the *raz nihyeh* is not mentioned in the surviving text of 4Q418 55.

The addressees are to exert "toil" (עמל) in their acquisition of knowledge. In 4Q417 2 i 10 the term signifies labor expended that may not result
in the achievement of rewards (see commentary above). In 4Q418 55 3,
by contrast, the word clearly denotes effort that produces benefits (see l.
4). The word נכרה is probably from the root כרה, literally meaning "to
dig," but here signifying the intellectual act of investigation or exploration (cf. CD 6:3, 9).[5] Other Qumran wisdom texts use the verb כרה in a
similar way. In 4QBeatitudes this root is combined with "her ways," as in
4Q418 55 3, to assert that the intelligent strive to acquire wisdom: "the
clever explore [lit. dig] her ways" (4Q525 5 12).[6] "Her ways" in this text of
4QBeatitudes probably refers to Torah and wisdom, which are combined
in the document.[7] The identity of the feminine antecedent of "her ways" in
4Q418 55 3 is probably a term such as בינה ("intelligence"; which occurs in
ll. 5, 6) or חכמה ("wisdom"), signifying the path of education and knowledge upon which the "we" group has embarked (cf. the word "our ways"
in l. 4). The emphasis on studying in 4Q418 55 is fully consistent with the
pedagogical emphasis of 4QInstruction as a whole.

4Q418 55 4

This line, in good parallel fashion, asserts that the addressees are to
have vigilance in their hearts and security in their "ways," using the same
word as in line 3. The term "vigilance" (שקד) most likely refers to possessing ("keeping watch over") the intelligence and learning that the group
attains through study. The term also occurs in a fragmentary context in
line 7.[8] 4Q418 69 ii 10–11 uses the root to describe the "chosen ones" keeping vigil "over all knowledge," signifying that they possess it (see commentary below). The meaning of the root is presumably similar in 4Q418 55 4.
The verb can mean "to protect" or "to guard" (e.g., Job 21:32; Prov 8:34).
This meaning would help explain the parallel use of בטוח ("security") in
4Q418 55 4, conveying that the "we" group will be confident or secure
in its possession of knowledge.[9] The imperfect יהיה presumably denotes

---

5. The image of "digging" denotes effort and labor, which fits well with the line's
stress on "toil."
6. The phrase לכרות מחשבות signifies "to devise plots" in 4Q424 3 6. See Brin
1996, 286–88.
7. Goff 2007, 207.
8. Cf. l. 9; 4Q418 169 + 170 5; 4Q418 118 2; 4Q418 225 2.
9. The two roots are employed in parallelism in 4Q416 2 ii 14.

the future, as translators have observed.[10] The tense conveys that the "we" group will attain the knowledge for which its members are toiling. Line 4 conveys the reward that will be achieved by the "toil" of line 3. A long *vacat* at the end of line 4 helps demarcate the distinction between the group in lines 3–4 and that in line 5.

4Q418 55 5

The "we" group that acquires knowledge (ll. 3–4) is contrasted with another group that is unwilling to do so. They have sought neither understanding nor the will of God. They represent a path of life that the intended audience should not adopt. The line uses verbs in the perfect tense to describe their refusal to seek knowledge, whereas imperfects denote the studying of the "we" group (l. 4; cf. 4Q418 69 ii 11). Employing the perfect does not necessarily imply that the "they" group's refusal to study is a completed action in the past. It is more likely that its members are being lazy in the present and that this is consistent with their previous behavior. They have not "sought" (שחרו) understanding. The *mebin* throughout the composition is urged, using the same verb, to "seek" knowledge (e.g., 4Q416 2 ii 17; 4Q416 2 iii 12; 4Q417 1 i 12). The group of bad students mentioned in line 5 is not identified directly. Its members may be the "foolish of heart"—a prominent expression in 4Q418 69 ii (ll. 4, 8)—who will perish in the eschatological judgment (see the next chapter). This option is assumed by the editors of DJD 34, who supplement this phrase in 4Q418 55 5.[11] In 4Q418 69 ii the phrase "foolish of heart" does not refer to a specific social group from the time of the text's composition, but rather represents the wicked in a general sense (see commentary below). There is not enough evidence of factionalism or sectarian tensions in 4QInstruction to suggest that the "they" group of 4Q418 55 4 represents a community that splintered off from the group to which 4QInstruction is addressed. It is more likely that the "they" group and their refusal to seek knowledge represents an attitude that the student-addressees should not adopt.

---

10. Rey 2009a, 305; Tigchelaar 2001, 208; Kampen 2011, 125; Strugnell and Harrington 1999, 267.

11. Strugnell and Harrington (1999, 269) suggest that the beginning of the line reads: ואוילי לב לוא דרשו [דעה] ("[And the foolish of heart did not search for] knowledge"). Note that the fate of the group in question is never mentioned in 4Q418 55, whereas the recompense of the "foolish of heart" is a major feature of 4Q418 69 ii. See also Rey 2009a, 305.

The material that follows places the distinction between the two opposed camps of lines 3–5 in a broader theological context. At the end of line 5, marked with a *vacat* indicating a new topic, is a rhetorical question, the beginning of which has not survived, that mentions "[the] God of Knowledge." Elsewhere in 4QInstruction the expression occurs when asserting a deterministic conception of the natural order, as do other early Jewish texts, such as the Treatise on the Two Spirits and the Hodayot (see the commentary on 4Q417 1 i 8). The phrase is likewise combined with deterministic claims in 4Q418 55 (see below on l. 6). Lines 5–6 associate the epithet "the God of Knowledge" with the term "truth," as does 4Q417 1 i 8 (cf. 4Q418 55 9).

4Q418 55 6

The beginning of this line affirms that God has established all "their ways"—a supplement that is reasonably added to the text. Line 6 makes a deterministic statement about God, who ordained beforehand how events shall unfold. This is a major theme of 4QInstruction (see commentary on the preceding line). The focus on the elect in line 6 and elsewhere in the column (e.g., ll. 3–4) suggests that this line affirms that God established the "ways" of the elect "upon truth." Line 6 describes the elect with language of "truth" ("those who inherit truth"; נוחלי אמת). Elsewhere the composition uses this term to emphasize a link between God and the elect (see the commentary on 4Q416 1 10). God, 4Q418 55 6 asserts, allotted to them their privileged status. In terms of both theme and terminology, this resonates with the rest of 4QInstruction, as does the use of the phrase "[the] God of Knowledge" in line 5. In addition to the term "truth," the root נחל ("to inherit") commonly describes in 4QInstruction the apportionment of elect status given to the addressee. Note, for example, the "inheritance of glory" in 4Q416 2 iii 11–12. The composition elsewhere teaches that the elect status of the *mebin* was established by God. 4Q418 81 states that God has separated him from the rest of humankind and that he is in the lot of the angels (see commentary below). 4Q417 1 i 13–18 associates the elect status of the addressee with the angels. In this regard it is significant that 4Q418 55, after mentioning the elect in line 6, discusses angels extensively (ll. 8–12).

4Q418 55 6 describes the elect in the third person. In lines 3–4 the first person is used for them. Presumably line 6 intends the addressees to understand that they are like, or should identify themselves with, "those who inherit truth." So understood, they are equivalent to the "we" group that toils for understanding in line 3. After lines 3–5 mention two oppos-ing groups, one choosing knowledge and the other failing to seek it, line 6 asserts that, whichever of these two paths one decides to take, God has determined the outcome. The student must choose a life of study and con-templation to achieve postmortem rewards such as life after death, but his elect status has been established by God (see section 6 of the introduction).

4Q418 55 7

Very little survives of this line. It attests the word "vigilance," an important term in line 4 that refers to the elect's possession of knowledge. The end of line 7 preserves the beginning of a rhetorical question, the rest of which has not survived. The question mentions "peace and tranquility." The column is too fragmentary to be certain, but it probably employed a wordplay between "vigilance" (שקד) and "tranquility" (שקט). "Tran-quility" is also mentioned in 4Q418 69 ii 5 (cf. 4Q416 3 3; 4Q418 116 2).[12] Since the material that follows in 4Q418 55 deals with angels, one can speculate that "peace and tranquility" describes aspects of the lives of angels. The term שקט is prominent in descriptions of angels in the Songs of the Sabbath Sacrifice.[13]

4Q418 55 8

This line begins with a rhetorical question, a distinctive feature of this fragment (ll. 5, 7) that is part of a larger teaching in lines 8–12 about angels. This section continues the main theme of the passage, the encouragement of the addressees to study, but rhetorically takes a new approach: angels are presented as ideals of pedagogical conduct which the intended audi-ence should emulate. Angels are invoked in a similar way in 4Q418 69 ii 13–14. These lines depict the divine beings improbably declaring that they are too tired to study. This encourages the addressees not to make similar complaints (see commentary below). 4QInstruction teaches its intended audience that they have a special affinity with the angels (e.g., 4Q418 81 4–5; consult section 6 of the introduction). In 4Q418 55 8 this trope is utilized to encourage the addressees to study.

---

12. The word has a definite article in both 4Q418 55 7 and 4Q418 69 ii 5.

13. 4Q405 19a–d 7 reads, for example: "From underneath the wondrous s[hrines] (comes) a sound of quiet stillness (דממת שקט), god-like beings blessing ..." (cf. 4Q400 1 ii 11; 4Q405 20 ii–22 13). Note also Isa 32:17; 1 Chr 22:9; 1QH 20:5.

The construal of angels as eager learners is highly unusual in early Judaism.[14] Several texts depict them not as students but as teachers who impart heavenly knowledge. This is most famously the case in the Book of the Watchers, in which Shemiḥazah and his cohorts "teach" (אלף) illicit knowledge to their human wives (1 En. 8:3; 4QEn[a] 1 iv 1–5). In Jubilees the angels teach Adam how to till the garden of Eden (3:15). The angelology of 4Q418 55 (and 69 ii) is a product of 4QInstruction's reformulation of early Jewish traditions about angels in light of the pedagogical focus that dominates the composition.

Line 8 switches to the second person plural, the common form of lines 8–12. The *mebinim* are asked whether they know that the holy angels belong to God in heaven.[15] The phrasing of the question presumes they should. The question emphasizes the subjection of the angels to God. The *mebin* should praise the angels as well as God (4Q418 81 1), but in general the composition highlights the dominion and mastery of God rather than the independence or prominence of angels (cf. Sir 42:21; Job 4:18).

4Q418 55 9

The reference to angels in line 8 suggests that the ideal students of this line, who pursue after the roots of intelligence, are also angels.[16] This is suggested further by lines 11–12, which also discuss the angels. 4Q418 55 and 69 ii both utilize the theme of the affinity between the angels and the elect, who are encouraged constantly to study the heavenly revelation of the mystery that is to be. A number of terminological links bolsters the similarity of the elect students and the angel students. The latter are "vigilant" over "knowledge" (or an equivalent phrase) in line 9 (cf. 4Q418 69 ii 11). The same root (שקד) is associated with the "we" group of line 3. Line 9 claims that the angels "pursue (ירדפו) after all the roots of understanding" (cf. 4Q418 69 ii 7). The "chosen ones"—the term for the elect in 4Q418 69 ii—pursue after truth, using the same root (l. 10). The angels seek "all the roots of understanding," a unique phrase in 4QInstruction (cf. 4Q300 1a ii–b 3; 4Q301 1 2; Wis 3:15). 4Q418 55 8–9 appeals to the angels to spur on the addressees' devotion to the pedagogical ideals of the composition.

---

14. For studies on angels, consult Tuschling 2007; Sullivan 2004.

15. Following an interrogative *he*, the term אם in l. 8 can mean "or." The line contains a question that consists of two statements, both of which are negated (cf. Josh 5:13; Gen 17:17).

16. *Contra* Wold 2005b, 181.

4Q418 55 10

On the basis of his knowledge "each one" is glorified more than the next. The key question is whether those who are glorified are the elect or angels. The editors of DJD 34 incline toward the former, suggesting that line 10 is about humans.[17] Much of 4Q418 55 10 is found verbatim in the Hodayot.[18] In this composition the key phrase clearly refers to the elect, the "children of your truth." 4Q418 55 10 is better interpreted as an assertion that the angels are being rewarded for their devotion to the pursuit of knowledge.[19] Both lines 9 and 11 are about angels, and it stands to reason that line 10 should be understood in a similar way. This also produces a good reading. Lines 10 fits with the general theme of the fragment of encouraging the addressees to study. The angels are being glorified because they seek knowledge and intelligence (cf. 4Q418 81 9). 4Q418 69 ii 14 supports this interpretation, asserting that "glory" and "splendor" are with the angels, using the same roots as 4Q418 55 10 (cf. 4Q418 81 13). It follows that the imperfect verbs (ירבה, יכבדו) are better understood not as referring to glorification that will take place in the future; rather, the angels currently enjoy their rewards. Knowing that the angels are being glorified as a result of their study would inspire the addressees to study like the angels. Elsewhere, "glory" (כבוד) is associated with the elect status of the addressee and the blessed afterlife that he can attain (e.g., 4Q416 2 iii 11–12; 4Q417 2 i 11). The "glory" of the angels in 4Q418 55 10 accords with 4QInstruction's theme of portraying the elect as similar to the angels.

4Q418 55 11

This line contains two rhetorical questions that emphasize that angels are not like humans: "Are they like a man? For he is slothful. Or a human? For he is still." The obvious answer to both is "no." Line 11 fits with line

---

17. Strugnell and Harrington 1999, 267, 271.

18. 4Q418 55 10 and 1QH 18:29–30 share the text לפי דעתם יכבדו איש מרעהו. This suggests some form of direct relationship between the two compositions, as do numerous other similarities of theme and terminology. Elsewhere I have argued that the Hodayot show reliance upon 4QInstruction as a source. See Goff 2004, 263–88. Consult also section 10 of the introduction of this book.

19. For this interpretation one has to grant that the term איש in 4Q418 55 10 has an impersonal, generic meaning, referring to "each" angel, rather than a "man" in a literal sense. The word can have this meaning. See *HALOT*, 1.44 (e.g., Gen 40:5; Exod 32:27).

9, which stresses that the angels study. Line 11 distinguishes them from humans by describing the latter as lazy.[20] 4Q418 69 ii 13 also affirms that the angels are not slothful (see commentary below). The root of the verb for "being slothful" (עצל) in 4Q418 55 11 occurs extensively in the book of Proverbs to denote a lazy or sluggish person.[21] Since the "we" group of line 3 toils hard for knowledge, they are more like angels than other humans. 4Q418 55 10 portrays humans as both "lazy" and "still" (ידמה). While the root דמה has several meanings, the parallelism of the two כי-phrases in line 11 suggests that people are "still" in the sense of being at rest and not working.[22]

4Q418 55 12

"They" will receive an "eternal possession" (אחזת עולם). As with line 10, the main issue is whether the pronoun refers to angels or the elect.[23] A legitimate case can be made for either reading. The "eternal possession," a phrase which in the Hebrew Bible refers to land (Gen 17:18; 48:4; Lev 25:34), could signify the reward the angels receive for their devotion to the pursuit of knowledge.[24] This reading is plausible, but I prefer the view that the statement refers to the elect. This is supported by a strong parallel in 1QS 11:7–8: "To those whom God has selected he has given them as an eternal possession (אחזת עולם); he has given an inheritance in the lot of the holy ones" (cf. 1QH 19:14–15; 4Q369 1 ii 4). In the Community Rule the phrase refers to the special dispensation given to the elect, which includes their affinity with the angels. The quoted text describes their elect status with the root "to inherit" (נחל). This root, which is prominent in 4QInstruction, is also in 4Q418 55 12 (cf. l. 6; see the excursus in chapter 4). Like the Community Rule, the wisdom text portrays the elect as being in the "lot" of the angels (4Q418 81 4–5). Since 4QInstruction declares that the elect are like the angels, it would be reasonable, after asserting that the angels study intensely and are not like lazy humans, to move next to the

---

20. Stuckenbruck 2004, 65.

21. E.g., Prov 6:6–9; 10:26; 13:4; 15:19 (cf. 4Q418 57 2; 4Q424 1 6).

22. The verb can also express, for example, that people are "silent" or, as in the translation in Strugnell and Harrington 1999 (267), that they "come to an end." Note the translation in Rey 2009a (305) that man "est passager" ("is transitory"). Consult further Tigchelaar 2001, 209; Kampen 2011, 125.

23. Strugnell and Harrington 1999, 272.

24. So Stuckenbruck 2004, 65.

"eternal possession" the elect addressees will inherit if they study like the angels. Like the expression "inheritance of glory" in 4Q416 2 iii 11–12, the term "eternal possession" probably refers to the reception of the rewards that the addressees will receive after death (see section 6 of the introduction).

Parallel text: 4Q417 5 (underline)

Text[1]

[ ] פֿחכה	1
[ותשכיל] [ ] מות עם	2
[בֿ]עֿ[בֿ]וֿ[דתם הלוא] באמת יתהלכו	3
כול] משברי[הם ובדעה כול גליהם vacat ועתה אוילי לב מה טוב ללוא	4
נוצרֿ[ומה] השקט ללוא היה ומה משפט ללוא נוסד ומה יֿאנחו מתים על כֿ[ול יומ]ֿם	5
אֿתֿםֿ [לשֿאֿ]וֿל נוצרתם ולשחת עולם תשובתכם כי תקיֿץֿ וֿתֿ[ראה ב]חֿטֿאֿכֿמֿהֿ וֿיושביֿ	6
מחשכיֿהֿ יֿצרחו על רֿיֿבכם וכול נהיה עולם דורשי אמת יעֿורו למשפטכֿ[ם ואז	7
יֿשמדו כול אֿוילי לב ובני עולה לוא ימצאו עוֿד] וכ[ו]ֿל מחזיקי רשעה יבשֿ[ו ואז]	8
במשפטכם יריֿעו מֿוֿסדי {ה}ֿרקיע וירעמו כול צֿ[בא [לֿ[ ]ל[ ]ל אהבוֿ] [	9
vacat ואֿתם בחיֿרי אמת ורודפיֿ[בינה] שֿ[וֿקדֿ]ֿים וֿ[מֿשחֿ]ֿרי חוכמה ו[שֿוֿקדֿ]ֿים	10

1. Strugnell and Harrington 1999, 281–83; Tigchelaar 2001, 91–93, 209–11; Rey 2009a, 243–47; Puech 2008b, 157–58; Elgvin 1997a, 248–49. The textual notes section refers to these works.

11 על כול דעת איכה תאמרו יגענו בבינה ושקדנו לרדוף דעת בֹ[כול עת]
אֹו בכול מֹ[קום]

12 ולא עיֹף בכוֹל {נ}שני עולם הלוא באמת ישעשע לעד ודעה] לנצח]
תשרתנו זֹבֹ[ני]

13 שמים אשר חיים עולם נחלתם האמור יאמרו יגענו בפעלות אמת
ויעפ[נו (?) vac]

14 בכול קצים הלוא באור עולם יתהֹל[כו] vac [כ]בֹוד ורוב הדר אתם
[ ]

15 ברקיעֹ[קודש וב]סוד אילים כול]   *vacat* [ואתה בן
[מבין]

bottom margin

TRANSLATION

1   … your …

2   … and you will understand … with

3   … in their [w]o[r]k. Do not all their [*breaking waves*] move to and fro with truth?

4   Or with knowledge all their waves? *vacat* And now, foolish of heart, what is good for one who has not

5   been created? [*And what*] is tranquility for one who does not exist? What is judgment for one who has not been established? Why do people groan about a[*ll*] their [*days*]?

6   You [*for She*]ol were fashioned, and to the eternal pit is your return. For it will awake and re[*veal*] your sin, [*and the inhabitants of*]

7   its dark regions will shout out regarding your case. And all who exist forever, the seekers of truth, will awaken for yo[*ur*] judgment. [*And then*]

8   all the foolish of heart will be destroyed, the sons of iniquity will be found no more, [*and a*]ll those who cling to wickedness will wither aw[*ay. And then*]

9   at your judgment the foundations of the firmament will cry out and every h[*ost*] will thunder forth … they have loved …

10   *vacat* But you, chosen ones of truth, who pursue [*understanding,*] see[*k wisdom and*] wat[*ch*]

11 over all knowledge: how can you say "We are weary of under-
    standing. We have been vigilant in pursuing knowledge in [*every
    time*] or in every p[*lace*]"?
12 But he is not tired of all the years of eternity. Does he not delight
    in truth forever? And (does not) knowledge [*eternally*] serve him?
    And the s[*ons of*]
13 heaven whose inheritance is eternal life, would they really say "We
    are weary of deeds of truth and [*we*] are tired of [*vacat* (?)]
14 all the periods"? Do they not mo[*ve*] to and fro in eternal light?
    vacat [*gl*]ory and an abundance of splendor are with them ...
15 in the firmaments of [*holiness and in*] the council of the divine
    beings are all [...] *vacat* And you, [*understanding*] son ...

Textual Notes

69 ii 1. פֿחכה. This reading follows Rey and Puech. Tigchelaar reads
בֿחכה, and the editors of DJD 34 read מֿחכה. The extant portion of the top
stroke fits more with *pe* than the other suggested options.

69 ii 2. בֿ.[עֿ]בֿ[וֹ]דתם. I tentatively follow Rey and Puech. The editors
of DJD 34 suggest this possibility, but do not use it in their edition of the
column.

69 ii 4. כוֹל[מֿשֿבֿרֿיֿ]הם. This reading also accords with Rey and Puech.
The word כול is located on 4Q418 60, which Tigchelaar has plausibly
joined to fragment 69. This is also the case with the first word of line 5.

69 ii 5. ללוֹא; 4Q417 5 2: ללוֹ.

69 ii 6. וֹתֿ[ראֿה]. Again Rey and Puech provide a plausible reading,
in both a physical and a semantic sense. Tigchelaar suggests that the first
trace is from a *lamed*. The traces are slight, but can be read as a *waw* that
does not descend very far.

69 ii 7. רֿיֿבכם; 4Q417 5 4: רבכמה.

69 ii 7. למשפטבֿ[ם]. Elgvin reads למשפטיֿ[ם] as part of the phrase "the
judgments [of God]." I follow here the editors of DJD 34, as do most commentators (Rey, Puech, Tigchelaar).

69 ii 11. בֿ.[כול עת אֿוֹ בכול מֿ[קום]. For this supplement see Puech
and Rey. Little survives of the first letter of the phrase. In this column the
kaf descends further than the *bet* (see בכול in this line), suggesting that the
letter in question is a *bet* (*contra* Strugnell and Harrington).

69 ii 12. ולא. The editors of DJD 34 suggest that an original הלא was
corrected to ולא. This is endorsed by Rey and Puech, but I do not see
enough traces on the fragment to support this claim (so also Tigchelaar).

COMMENTARY

4Q418 69 ii contains a brief but vivid description of theophanic judgment. Along with 4Q416 1, the text is important for understanding the eschatology of 4QInstruction.[2] The column revolves around an opposition between "the foolish of heart" who will be eradicated when judgment occurs and the "chosen ones of truth," the elect whom the fragment associates with the angels. Lines 4–9 are addressed to the former and lines 10–15 to the latter. 4Q418 69 ii relies upon the second person plural more than is normally the case in 4QInstruction. 4Q418 55 does as well and these two texts have several other features in common, such as a penchant for rhetorical questions (see the introduction to the previous chapter for more detail). The editors of DJD 34 speculate that 4Q418 69 ii 4–15 has a different provenance from the rest of 4QInstruction and was added to the composition secondarily.[3] This thesis cannot be ruled out entirely but there is not enough evidence to endorse it. While several distinctive rhetorical forms and terms in 4Q418 69 ii (and frg. 55) are not in the rest of 4QInstruction, the fragment has much in common with 4QInstruction in general, as discussed below (and in the commentary to frg. 55). 4Q418 55 and 69 ii probably do not have a provenance that is separate from the rest of 4QInstruction.

Elgvin has argued that 4Q418 69 ii shows direct reliance upon 1 Enoch 91 and 103:1–104:6.[4] Both this column of 4QInstruction and chapters 103–104 of 1 Enoch address in sequence the wicked and the righteous, using the second person plural. First Enoch 91 refers to resurrection, and Elgvin claims that this is also the case in 4Q418 69 ii 7 (a position critiqued below). He has gone so far as to claim that 4QInstruction is the "bridge" that connects 1 Enoch to the Dead Sea sect.[5] But the parallels in question are rather general and are not sufficient to conclude that 4Q418 69 ii contains direct literary borrowing from the Epistle of Enoch. It is reasonable, however, to understand that 4QInstruction displays some awareness of Enochic traditions. For example, both 1 Enoch and 4QInstruction use the phrase "eternal planting," and this may indicate some familiarity on the part of 4QInstruction with Enochic literature (see the commentary on

---

2. Collins 2004, 49–65; Elgvin 1996, 126–65.
3. Strugnell and Harrington 1999, 14. See also Tigchelaar 2001, 221–22.
4. Elgvin 1996, 132; 1997a, 169. See also Tigchelaar 2001, 212–17.
5. Elgvin 1996, 164.

4Q418 81 13). The texts that comprise 1 Enoch were popular in the late Second Temple period, and one can suggest that some exposure to Enochic material shaped the apocalyptic worldview of 4QInstruction, especially in its emphasis on eschatological judgment.[6]

This commentary will deal first with the poorly preserved material in 4Q418 69 ii 1–4, the text directed at the foolish of heart in lines 4–9, and then the material addressed to the chosen ones of truth in lines 10–15.

4Q418 69 ɪɪ 1–2

A *vacat* in line 4, followed by the address to the foolish of heart, indicates that the preceding lines constitute a separate section. The only visible letters in line 1 are remnants of a word that has a second person singular suffix. The word תשכיל of line 2 is understood as being in the second person singular ("you will understand").[7] After the *vacat* in line 15, which concludes the section directed at the chosen ones of truth, is an exhortation in the second person singular. Lines 1–2 and 15 indicate that the central text of the fragment (ll. 4–15) reverted from the second person singular, the common mode of address in 4QInstruction, to the plural, and then switched back to the singular. This does not prove that lines 4–15 originate from a separate source, but it does indicate that they constitute a distinctive text of the composition. The emphasis on study and the affinity of the *mebin* with the angels are fully in keeping with the rest of 4QInstruction (see below on ll. 13–14).

4Q418 69 ɪɪ 3–4

These lines assert the regularity of the natural order and are posed in the form of a rhetorical question (cf. l. 12). The addressee is to infer that the regular motion of the waves of the sea (presumably the Mediterranean) reflects God's truth and knowledge.[8] The *mebin* is to discern the predictable and ordered structure of the natural world. 4QInstruction affirms that God fashioned the cosmos according to a comprehensive plan (e.g., 4Q417

---

6. Stuckenbruck 2002, 261. See also Tigchelaar 2001, 212–17.

7. Note the intriguing but hypothetical supplement by Rey (2009a, 244) and Puech (2008b, 157): after תשכיל they append בעינות תהו[מות], producing "you will understand [the sources of the dep]ths." See also Strugnell and Harrington 1999, 283; Tigchelaar 2001, 210.

8. In 4Q418 126 ii 11 the elect addressee is to "move to and fro in truth" (באמת התהלך), using the same terminology as in 4Q418 69 ii 3.

1 i 8–9; 4Q418 126 ii 4–5). This knowledge is available primarily through the study of the revealed mystery that is to be, but it can also be acquired to some extent through observation of the natural world (cf. 4Q417 1 i 27).

Since it precedes an account of eschatological judgment (ll. 7–9), the assertion of order in the world in lines 3–4 brings to mind 4Q416 1. This column's account of the final judgment follows a description of the structured nature of the cosmos. 4Q416 1 emphasizes the inevitability of eschatological judgment by presenting it as a feature of the natural order of the cosmos established by God. 4QInstruction does much the same thing in 4Q418 69 ii, although little survives of its account of the orderly character of the world.

4Q418 69 ii 4–5

A *vacat* in line 4 demarcates a new section. Lines 4–9 are addressed to the "foolish of heart" (אוילי לב), who are mentioned in lines 4 and 8. The core message to them is that they will be destroyed in the final judgment. There is no evidence that they should be understood as a specific community or a group that rivals the intended audience of 4QInstruction. The phrase is better understood as a general designation for the wicked. 4Q416 1 affirms that such people will be destroyed, but does not use the phrase "foolish of heart." The expression occurs in 4Q418 58 1 and 4Q418 205 2 in unfortunately fragmentary contexts.[9] Outside of 4QInstruction, the phrase is attested only in 4Q425 1 + 3 8, perhaps in the context of judgment, and possibly in 1QH 9:39, although the key text is fragmentary.[10] The book of Proverbs frequently uses the term אויל, but never attests "foolish of heart."[11]

Lines 4–5 ask the "foolish of heart" a series of four questions, all of which begin with מה ("what?"). The first three questions have a similar structure.[12] Each follows the sequence (1) מה; (2) a positive word such

---

9. Contrast the phrase "wise of mind [lit. heart]" (חכמי לב) in 4Q418 81 20.

10. 4Q425 1 + 3 is fragmentary, but line 6 mentions judgment. In 1QH 9:39 one can reasonably reconstruct או[יל]י לב לא יבינו ("[the fool]ish of heart do not understand"). The synonymous phrase [כס]ילי לב is also possible. See Goff 2007, 280; Stegemann et al. 2009, 129.

11. Proverbs 10:21 states that fools who are without sense will die (אוילים בחסר־לב ימותו), not unlike the "foolish of heart" of 4Q418 69 ii.

12. Strugnell and Harrington 1999, 285. See also their discussion of the form ללא plus a perfect verb.

as "goodness"; (3) ללוא; (4) a verb in the perfect tense. The verbs of these questions refer to the existence or creation of a person. The first asks what is good for someone who has not been created. The next asks what is "tranquility" (with a definite article) for one who does not exist (cf. 4Q418 55 7). The third asks what is "judgment" for a person who has not been established, that is, created (l. 5). The implied answer to all of these questions is "nothing." Tranquility or goodness has no value to a person who is not alive or who has never been born. 4QInstruction does not simply lambast the foolish of heart but also, in keeping with the pedagogical ethos of the document, urges them to contemplate the nature of reality.

Why 4QInstrucion poses such questions is clarified by the fourth in the sequence (l. 5). The editors of DJD 34 translate, "And what lament shall the dead make over their own death?"[13] Other commentators likewise understand the question as being about the dead; this is indeed the standard translation of the word מתים.[14] Should we imagine the dead lamenting their own deaths in Sheol? That would not fit well with the three other questions. A better reading is produced by understanding מתים as having the less common but attested meaning of "people," although the word clearly conveys an allusion to the theme of death.[15] Above I translate the question as, "Why (מה) do people groan about a[ll] their [days]?"[16] This rendering of the question accords well with the three preceding ones. A person who is alive can experience goodness and justice. A person who is

---

13. Strugnell and Harrington 1999, 283.

14. Rey 2009a, 244; Tigchelaar 2001, 210; Kampen 2011, 128.

15. E.g., Gen 34:30; Sir 7:16; 15:17; 4Q162 2 4; 4Q408 3 + 3a 10.

16. Kister has also suggested that this statement has not yet been correctly translated. He proposes "what (can) the dead groan over their own de[ath]?" So understood, the text means that the wicked can in a sense already be considered dead, a motif he compares to a logion of Jesus in Matt 8:21–22 and Luke 9:59–60 ("Let the dead bury their own dead."). This proposal is intriguing, but his novel reconstruction of the final portion of text cannot be endorsed: על מ[ות]ם ("over their own de[ath]") instead of כ]ול יומ ם ("about their [days]") used above. The lacuna is too large to insert only two letters, and the last angular shape of the letter before the gap fits a *kaf* much more than a *mem*. Nevertheless, his understanding of the meaning of the question is insightful, as discussed below. See Kister 2009a, 198–99.

For מה having the sense of "why?" see, for example, Exod 14:15; Job 7:21. The question literally has "day," not "days." The reconstructed phrase כ]ול יומ ם cannot have the adverbial, temporal sense of "every day" (e.g., Ps 1:2) because it is preceded by a preposition על, requiring a noun to follow.

dead cannot. Thus, the argument goes, someone who is living should not groan or complain.[17]

The last of the four questions asks why people in general complain. But since it is posed to the foolish of heart, the clear implication is that *they* groan about their days. Since the three previous questions deal with people who do not exist, this question, in a wordplay with מתים, meaning both "people" and the "dead," portrays those who groan and complain as more dead than alive, as Kister discerns.[18] 4QInstruction ascribes to these fools a form of reasoning that resonates with the bleak assessment of human life found in the book of Qoheleth. The view that one should not complain resonates with the view that the *mebin* is to endure difficult economic circumstances (see section 9 of the introduction). 4QInstruction emphasizes the eschatological destruction of the foolish of heart (l. 8), but has little to say about what they have done to deserve this fate. Line 8 associates them with wickedness, and one can infer that they committed wicked deeds. However, if my understanding of line 5 is correct, the only activity the text associates with the foolish of heart is that they complain about their lives.

It would be hasty to conclude that the foolish of heart constitute a rival sapiential school that continues the teaching of Qoheleth. Above I argued that the expression is a general term for the wicked. It is more reasonable to assert that the characterization of the wicked as complaining excessively is influenced by the author's having read and reflected upon this biblical book.[19] 4QInstruction's criticism of Qoheleth appears to be that those who complain about this world forget that qualities such as goodness and justice are possible for the living, not the dead. With this attitude they consign themselves to death (ll. 7–9), whereas the "chosen ones" can attain eternal life (see the commentary on ll. 6 and 13). The prospect of eternal life for the elect, I suggest, leads the author of 4QInstruction to develop a negative understanding of Qoheleth, and this influences his description of the "foolish of heart."

---

17. For the verb להאנח denoting groans that express complaint, see, for example, Exod 2:23; Ezek 9:4; Sir 25:18; 30:20 (cf. Job 3:24).

18. Kister 2009a, 199.

19. Perdue (2003, 231–58) discusses Qoheleth in relation to the Qumran wisdom texts but does not engage 4Q418 69 ii.

4Q418 69 ɪɪ 6

Line 6 accords with the interpretation of lines 4–5 given above. 4Q418 69 ii 6 affirms the inexorable death of the foolish of heart. The claim that they were "fashioned" for Sheol construes their demise as a regular feature of the natural order. The phrase "eternal pit" (שחת עולם, which could be rendered "eternal perdition") in line 6 is parallel to "Sheol," with both terms referring to the realm of the dead. 4Q418 126 ii 7 utilizes a mythological image of the gates of Sheol closing upon the wicked, describing a fate for them that is similar to that in the present text (cf. 4Q423 5 1). In 4Q418 69 ii the foolish of heart descend into the netherworld.

Ben Sira and Qoheleth stress that death is inescapable for all people.[20] This is also the case in 4QInstruction, with some important modifications. This composition affirms that the wicked die and go to Sheol. 4QInstruction asserts that the elect addressee will experience physical death (see the commentary to 4Q418 103 ii 9). But the *mebin* also enjoys the prospect of life after death (refer to section 6 of the introduction). The addressee's "inheritance of glory" includes life after death (4Q416 2 iii 11–12). The fragmentary text 4Q418 162 4 reads: "eternal pit, and you will have glo[ry]." The contrast between the pit and glory favors the reconstruction by the editors of DJD 34, who read, "[You will be saved from] the eternal pit."[21] Regarding the death of the addressee, 4QInstruction resembles the Wisdom of Solomon more than Qoheleth.[22]

That 4QInstruction operates with the view that there are two opposing fates for the wicked and the elect, Sheol and a blessed afterlife, respectively, is suggested by the terminology it uses. After physical death the wicked go to the "eternal pit" (שחת עולם), whereas the elect experience "eternal joy" (שמחת עולם), eternal life with the angels (see commentary on 4Q417 2 i 10–11). While no passage of 4QInstruction explicitly contrasts the two expressions, they are contrasted in the Treatise on the Two Spirits (with עולם in the plural; 1QS 4:6–14; cf. 4Q286 7 ii 5; 4Q287 6 4). In the Treatise (and in 4QBerakhot), as in 4Q418 69 ii, the "eternal pit" denotes the ultimate fate of the wicked. There is no evidence in 4QInstruction that the

---

20. They both express this point by using the root "to return" (לשוב), as does 4Q418 69 ii 6 (e.g., Sir 40:11; Qoh 3:20). Genesis 3:19 asserts that humans were made from the dust of the earth, to which they return (also using לשוב).

21. Strugnell and Harrington 1999, 386. Note the parallel in 1QH 11:20: "I thank you, Lord, that you have redeemed my life from the pit" (cf. 1QS 11:13).

22. Goff 2010a, 1–21.

"pit" is a place of eternal torment, but this possibility cannot be dismissed. Contemporary texts do envision some sort of everlasting punishment for the wicked after death (1QS 2:7–8; 1QpHab 10:5; 1 En. 90:25; 108:5; Dan 12:2).[23]

The latter part of 4Q418 69 ii 6 is highly fragmentary. The text probably states that "it will awake" and "re[veal] your sin." The antecedent of the verbs is most likely the twin nouns that occur earlier in the line, Sheol and pit.[24] So understood, the netherworld does not simply receive the foolish of heart but is also actively engaged in their condemnation.[25] The reaction of Sheol is continued in line 7.

4Q418 69 ii 7

The first part of this line stresses the active role of Sheol in the destruction of the foolish of heart. Inhabitants of the realm shall "shout out" regarding their case (cf. 1QS 4:13).[26] The netherworld is in a state of tumult, eager to receive the fools. Similarly, in line 9 the "foundations of the firmament" cry out against them. This provides an impression of cosmic and theophanic judgment, in which various elements of the natural order react to the condemnation of the foolish of heart. The judgment scene of 4Q416 1 also describes aspects of the cosmos responding to eschatological events. The seas and the depths, for example, fear and tremble in the face of God's judgment (l. 12).

4Q418 69 ii never refers to all people being judged or suggests that "all iniquity" will be destroyed, as in 4Q416 1 13 or other early Jewish judgment scenes (e.g., 1Q27 1 i; 1 En. 10:16–22). This is nevertheless implied by 4Q418 69 ii 8, which asserts the elimination of the wicked. The term ריב ("case") of line 7 is a legal word, suggesting that God renders a verdict upon the foolish of heart, who are sentenced to Sheol (cf. 4Q417 2 i 14; 4Q418 81 7).

---

23. Puech (2003a, 142) endorses this possibility. Consult also the commentary on 4Q418 126 ii 7.

24. Rey 2009a, 246; Strugnell and Harrington 1999, 286.

25. The verb תקיץ is probably a II-yod verb ("to awake"; קיץ), but there is likely also a double meaning based on the form's similarity to the II-waw root (קוץ), which can mean "to frighten" or "horrify" (Isa 7:6).

26. The term "inhabitants" is reasonably reconstructed, but who in Sheol is shouting is unclear. It could be the souls of the wicked who are already there. One could posit that they are demons, but 4QInstruction contains no explicit reference to evil spirits.

The main text of line 7 has aroused a great deal of interest. The key phrase reads, "And all who exist forever, the seekers of truth, will arise for yo[ur] judgment." Elgvin has argued that this refers to the resurrection of the righteous.[27] He suggests further that the line relies upon 1 En. 91:10, which envisages the resurrection of the elect ("And the righteous will arise from his sleep"). He translates, "The seekers of truth will wake up to the judgments [of God]," reading למשפטי, although the term is better read as למשפטכ[ם] ("yo[ur] judgment"; see textual notes above). Even though Puech uses the latter transcription of 4Q418 69 ii 7 rather than Elgvin's, he has vigorously asserted in several publications that the line does indeed assert the resurrection of the elect. He has written, for example, that the eschatology of this verse is identical to that of Isa 26:19 and Dan 12:2, both of which assert a form of resurrection.[28]

The opinion that 4Q418 69 ii 7 asserts the resurrection of the elect has been successfully critiqued by Tigchelaar and Collins.[29] There is no compelling reason to understand 4QInstruction as affirming a doctrine of resurrection. The line in question is part of the address to the foolish of heart, not the truly chosen ones. If the column contained a reference to resurrection, it would make sense in the section directed toward the latter group, not the former. The key verb of line 7 (יעורו) alludes not to the awakening or rising of the dead but rather to a group that becomes aroused about the judgment of the foolish of heart (cf. Zech 2:17 [Eng. 2:13]). The subject of the verb in question is "all who exist forever, the seekers of truth." This should be understood as a reference to the angels rather than the righteous (who "awake" at the resurrection).[30] The term translated "who exist" is נהיה, the niphal participle that forms part of the mystery that is to be. The word is ambiguous but, combined with the term "forever," denotes beings who live eternally. (For discussion of the participle, see section 5 of the introduction and the commentary on 4Q417 1 i 3–5.) This accords with angels, who have eternal life, as line 13 of the column asserts. The view that angels are "seekers of truth" fits perfectly with the view in 4Q418 55 9 and 4Q418 69 ii 13–14 that the angels ceaselessly pursue knowledge. Understanding line

---

27. Elgvin 1996, 143–44.
28. Puech 2003a, 143. See also 2008a, 159; 2005, 100–1; 2006, 90–92; 2003b, 229; 2004a, 428–35.
29. Collins 2004, 56–57; Tigchelaar 2001, 211. See also Goff 2003b, 176–79.
30. Fletcher-Louis (2002, 118–21) also reads this phrase as referring to the righteous.

7 as discussing angels rather than the righteous also produces a nice parallelism. First the inhabitants of Sheol cry out regarding the condemnation of the foolish of heart (ll. 6–7), and then the angels arise in response to the same event (l. 7). Both the netherworld and heaven react dramatically to the judgment of the foolish of heart. Line 9, if reconstructed correctly, also describes the angels making noise and being in an uproar.

Moreover, the ultimate rewards of the elect in 4QInstruction leave little need for resurrection. As discussed above, the *mebin* will die physically, and enjoys the prospect of eternal life after death. The non-physical aspect of the elect simply continues to exist, enjoying a blessed postmortem life with the angels. The system has no need for resurrection in either bodily or spiritual form. This is also the case in the Treatise on the Two Spirits.[31]

4Q418 69 ii 8

This line proclaims the elimination of the foolish of heart, "the sons of iniquity" and "[a]ll those who cling to wickedness."[32] These are synonymous terms that denote the wicked in a general sense rather than specific groups. Since line 6 proclaims that the fools are destined for Sheol, the assertion that the wicked will be "found no more" probably does not mean that they will be utterly eliminated, but rather that they will not be found *on earth* but instead in Sheol. 4Q416 1 13 claims that "all iniquity will come to an end forever" and associates their destruction with a "period of tru[th]," a distinct moment of eschatological judgment. 4Q418 69 ii 8 does not mention a moment of final retribution and never uses the key term קץ ("period") in an eschatological sense (see l. 14). However, line 8 most likely alludes to the same eschatological event proclaimed in 4Q416 1 13. This would explain why 4Q418 69 ii 8 refers to the elimination of "all" the foolish of heart and "all" who seize wickedness.[33] The tumultuous reaction of elements of the cosmos to the destruction of the wicked implies that

---

31. See, for example, 1QS 4:11–14. Consult Collins 1997b, 116–17.

32. The verb [ו]יבשו associated with "[a]ll those who cling to wickedness" can be understood as from the root יבש, "to wither away, dry up," or בוש, "to be ashamed." *Contra* Tigchelaar (2001, 210), the parallelism of the two previous verbs in l. 7 suggests the former option rather than the latter.

33. The same should be assumed for the "sons of iniquity," a phrase not accompanied by the word "all."

at issue is an outburst of overwhelming divine power. This suggests that judgment is to occur in a distinct moment, as in 4Q416 1.

4Q418 69 ɪɪ 9

Line 9 describes judgment in cosmic and theophanic terms, declaring that when the foolish of heart are judged "the foundations of the firmament" cry out.[34] This complements the claim of lines 6–7 that denizens of the netherworld shout when the fools are given recompense. Theophanic judgment places the cosmos in a state of agitation and tumult (cf. 4Q416 1 11–12).

The key term is fragmentary, but line 9 may mention the "h[ost]" ([צ[בא]), a reference to angels.[35] The term "host" is also prominent in 4Q416 1 (ll. 4, 6). 4Q418 69 ii 9 emphasizes the totality of the cosmos's clamorous reaction to divine judgment, with both elements from below ("the foundations of the firmament") and above (the angels of heaven). The exact nuance of the verb "thunder forth" (ירעמו) associated with the "h[ost]" is not fully clear. In 4Q416 1 4 the "host" are linked with the stars of heaven; 4Q418 69 ii 9 may connect the angels to thunder (cf. 1QH 11:36).[36]

4Q418 69 ɪɪ 10–11

The introduction of a new section in line 10 is marked with a *vacat* followed by a disjunctive *waw*. The unit of lines 10–15 is addressed to the "chosen of truth." Like the preceding section (ll. 4–9), this passage is in the second person plural. As line 8 has three separate synonymous phrases to denote the wicked, line 10 has four to describe the righteous. They are called the "chosen ones of truth" and the ones "who pursue [understanding and] see[k wisdom and] wat[ch] over all knowledge" (ll. 10–11). The expression the "chosen ones of truth" (בחירי אמת) is not found elsewhere, but בחיר ("chosen") is an attested term for the elect (e.g., CD 4:3–4; 1QS 8:6).[37] All four expressions of 4Q418 69 ii 10 are roughly synonymous, and

---

34. The verb יריעו is probably a hollow *hiphil*.

35. Puech 2008b, 157; Kampen 2011, 128.

36. Note the parallelism of angels, thunder, and stars in 1 En. 8:3: "Baraqel taught the signs of the lightning flashes. Kokabel taught the signs of the stars." See also Rey 2009a, 251.

37. 1QH 6:13–14, like 4Q418 69 ii, associates this term with "truth" and those

signify the elect audience of 4QInstruction.[38] The phrases also convey that
members of this group should strive to seek knowledge—a major topos
of the composition. The angels are similarly portrayed as ideal students in
this column (e.g., ll. 13–14) and in 4Q418 55 8–11.

The rhetorical question of 4Q418 69 ii 11 imagines the "chosen ones
of truth" making an improbable statement—that they would say "we are
weary (יגענו) of understanding." Line 13 similarly doubts that angels would
ever say that they are "weary (יגענו) of deeds of truth."[39] In both rhetorical questions the verb is in the first person plural. The second question is
uttered by angels, depicting what they would say (יאמרו); the first is placed
in the mouth of the plural addressees, in the second person ("How can you
say …"; תאמרו). The difference in person demonstrates that the "chosen
ones of truth" are the addressees, who should look to the angels as models
of pedagogical conduct. Angels never tire of seeking knowledge, and neither should they. The rhetorical questions of 4Q418 69 ii 11–13 are similar
to those of 4Q418 55 8–9, which ask if the *mebinim* know that the angels
pursue truth (see commentary above).

4Q418 69 ii 10–14, like 4Q418 55 8–11, takes the trope that the addressees have a special affinity with the angels and applies it to the overarching
pedagogy of 4QInstruction. The angels embody an educational ideal that
the students should follow. Their bond with the angels is expressed by an
overlap of terminology. The elect are the "chosen ones of truth (אמת)"
(4Q418 69 ii 10), and in line 7 the angels are "seekers of truth (אמת)." The
term is also used in lines 12 and 13 (see below; cf. 4Q416 1 10). The elect
keep "watch" over knowledge (4Q418 69 ii 10), using the root שקד. In
4Q418 55 9 this root describes the devotion of the angels in their search
for knowledge (cf. l. 4; 4Q416 2 ii 14). The use of שקד in 4Q418 69 ii 11 is
somewhat different from these other examples. Here the root is in parallelism with the verb יגע. This word can mean "to be weary," but also "strive" or
"labor." While the latter meaning does fit with שקד, the statement in line
13 that the angels would never say that they are יגענו, paired with יעף ("to
be tired"), suggests that the word has a negative valence ("to be weary"),

---

who seek understanding: "men of truth and the elect of ri[ghteousness, those who
see]k insight and those who search for understanding."

38. Collins 2004, 55.

39. Note Sir 43:40: "Lift up your voices to glorify the Lord as much as you can, for
there is still more. Extol him with renewed strength, and weary not (אל תלאו), though
you cannot fathom him."

not a positive one ("to strive").[40] This makes the combination of יגע and
שקד somewhat unusual. The verb שקדנו ("we have been vigilant"), associated with the claim that they are too weary to study (יגענו), conveys the
(erroneous) viewpoint of the elect that their learning is sufficient and they
no longer need to study. Line 11 uses שקד in the perfect tense, denoting
a completed action.[41] They *have been* vigilant in seeking knowledge and,
it is implied, that they no longer do so. The chosen of truth are taught not
to think like that.

4Q418 69 II 12–14

As mentioned above (ll. 10–11), these lines provide an incentive for
the addressees to continue their studies. Explaining the claim in line 11
that they should not tire of understanding, line 12 asserts that God is
never exhausted (עיף; cf. l. 13), and that he delights eternally in knowledge and truth. The intended audience of 4QInstruction should look not
only to the angels for inspiration to continue their studies. God himself is
a lover of truth. The text may allude indirectly to Woman Wisdom, who
never explicitly appears in 4QInstruction, since God "delights" (ישעשע)
in truth, a verb that is prominent in Prov 8:30–31.[42]

The end of line 12 begins a statement about angels. Line 13 asserts
explicitly that the "inheritance" of the angels is eternal life. This claim is
important for understanding that the *mebin*, who is repeatedly likened to
the angels, has the prospect of eternal life as well (see section 6 of the introduction). The line poses a rhetorical question that depicts the angels as
saying, incredulously, that they have become weary of the truth. They also
claim, in parallelism, that they are tired of "all the periods," or eternity.[43]
The rhetorical question of this line parallels the one uttered by the elect in
line 11 (see commentary above).

---

40. For the former, see 2 Sam 23:10; Jer 45:3; for the latter, note Josh 24:13; Isa
49:4.

41. The root is in the form of a participle in l. 10 and an imperfect in 4Q418 55 9,
and in both cases clearly has a positive sense, denoting seeking for knowledge.

42. The claim that knowledge serves God can be understood as an assertion that
Woman Wisdom is not a co-creatrix but rather unambiguously subservient to God
(cf. Sir 42:21). Wisdom ministers before the deity in Sir 24:10. See Fletcher-Louis
2002, 121.

43. Line 12 similarly stresses that God tires of neither all the years of eternity nor
truth.

4Q418 69 II 14

The discussion of the angels continues in 4Q418 69 ii 14–15, but much of the text has not survived. Line 14 extols them, asserting that they move in eternal light and possess "[gl]ory and an abundance of splendor." This praise, coming after rhetorical questions that encourage the addressees to study like the angels, provides further incentive for them to do so. The terms "[gl]ory" (כ[בוד]) and "splendor" (הדר) occur in 4Q418 55 10 (הדרו; יכבדו), where they describe rewards given to the angels for their ceaseless study. The words likely have a similar function in 4Q418 69 ii 14. The ultimate reward of the *mebin*, his "inheritance of glory" (4Q416 2 iii 11–12), involves joining the company of angels in eternal life after death. To fulfill this fate, he is to study the mystery that is to be during his life. Being reminded of the blissful existence that the angels enjoy spurs the *mebin* to remain devoted to this pedagogical goal.

4Q418 69 II 15

Line 15 mentions the "firmament" (in the plural), a reference to the celestial realm of the angels. This is reminiscent of 4Q416 1 1–4, in which the host of heaven are associated with the stars. 4Q418 69 ii 15 also states that they are in "the council of the divine beings (סוד אילים)," presumably a reference to the angelic retinue that stands before God in heaven (4Q286 1 ii 6; 4Q400 1 ii 9; Ps 82:1).[44] The *vacat* in the line marks the end of the address to the chosen ones of truth. The text then switches to the second person singular, preserving the beginning of an exhortation, the body of which has not survived.

---

44. Strugnell and Harrington 1999, 291.

11.
4Q418 81 + 81A

Parallel texts: 4Q423 8 (underline); 4Q423 23 (dotted underline)

Text[1]

top margin

שפתיכה פתח מקור לברך קדושים ואתה כמקור עולם הלל [שמו כי]אֿ   1
הבדילכה מכול

רוח בשר ואתה הבדל מכול אשר שנא והנזר מכול תעבות נֵפֿשֿ[כי]אֿ   2
הוא עשה כול

ויורישם אֵיֶשׁ נחלתו והוא חלקכה ונחלתכה בתוך בֵנֵי אדם[ובנ]חֿלֿתֿו   3
המשילכֿה ואתה

בזה כבדהֻו בֵהֻתֵקֵדשכה לו כאשר שמכה לקדוש קֻודשים[לכֿול בני   4
תֻבל ובכוֹל מ]ל[אכֿים]

הפיל גורֵלֵכֵה וכבודכה הרבה מואדה ויֵשׁימכה לו בכור בֵ[5
לֿ]   [

וטובתֵי לֵכֿה אתן זֿאתה {ל}הלוא לכה טוֹבֿ ובאמונתוֹ הלך תמיד   6
]   [

מעשיכה ואתה דרוש משפטיו מיד כול יֵריבֿכֵֿהֿ בכול מזֻ[ם○   7
[

אהבהו ובחסד {עֿוֿלֿםֿ} וברחֻמֿים על כול שומרי דברו וקנאתֿוֿ]   8
[

ואתה שכלֿ[פ]תח לכה ובאוצרו המשילכה ואיפת אמת פיקד[ה לכה   9
משפט וצדקֿ]

---

1. Strugnell and Harrington 1999, 300–3; Tigchelaar 2001, 94–96, 230–34; Rey 2009a, 307–9; Puech 2005, 108–10; Elgvin 1997a, 268–69; 1998, 119. The textual notes section refers to these works.

אתכה המה ובידכה להשיב אף מאנשי רצון ולפקוד עֹל[10
[

עמכה בֹּטֹרֹם תקח נחלתכה מידו כבד קדושיו ובט[רם 11
[

פתח[מ]קֹור כול קדֹושים וכול הנקרא לשמו קודשי[ם 12
[

עם כול קצֹים הדרֹז פארתו למטעת עוֹ[לם 13
[

[ ]הֹ תבֹ[ל]ֹ בֹֹו יֹתהלכו כול נוחלי ארץ כי בשמ[ים 14
[

ואתה מבין אם בחכמת ידים המשילכה וֹדעֹ[ת 15
[

אוֹט לכול הולכי אדם ומשם תפקוֹד טרפכה וֹ[16
[

התבונן מודה ומיד כול משכילכה הוסף לקחֹ[17
[

הוצא מחסורכה לכול דורשי חפץ ואז תכֹ[ין 18
פֹיֹד[

תמלא ושבעתה ברוב טוב ומחכמת ידיכֹהֹ[19
[

כי אל פלג נחֹלֹתֹ[כֹו]ל[חיֹ] וכול חכמי לב השכֹלֹוֹ[ן 20
[

Translation

1. Your lips he has opened as a spring to bless the holy ones. So you, as an eternal spring, praise [*his name, beca*]use he has separated you from every

2. fleshly spirit. And you, separate yourself from all that he hates and keep away from all abominations of the soul, [*beca*]use he has made everyone

3. and has bequeathed to each man his inheritance. He is your portion and your inheritance among humankind, [and over] his [in]heritance he has given you dominion. So you

4   in this way glorify him, by making yourself holy to him, as he has established you as most holy [of all *the people of the*] world. And among all the [*a*]n[*gels*]

5   he has cast your lot and your glory he has greatly magnified. He has established you for himself as a firstborn son among ...

6   "and my goodness I give to you." And you, is not his goodness for you? So in his faith walk constantly ...

7   your deeds. So you, seek his judgments from every opponent of yours in all ...

8   love him, and with piety and with compassion upon all who keep his word. And zeal for him ...

9   And you, he has [*op*]ened up intelligence for you and over his treasury he has given you dominion, and a measure of truth is stipul[*ated for you ... judgment and righteousness,*]

10 they are with you and it is in your hand to turn away wrath from the men of (God's) pleasure and to visit upon ...

11 with you. Before you receive your inheritance from him glorify his holy ones. And be[*fore ...*]

12 open a [*sp*]ring (for) all the holy ones and thus everyone who is called by his name (will become) holy [*ones ...*]

13 with all periods (is) his splendor, his grandeur (is) with the eter[*nal*] planting ...

14 ... the wor[*ld*]. In it all those who inherit the earth shall walk to and fro, for in heav[*en ...*]

15 And you, understanding one, if he has given you dominion over manual skill and knowl[*edge ...*]

16 resources for all humankind and from there you will attend to your nourishment and ...

17 Improve greatly in understanding and from all of your teachers get ever more learning ...

18 Bring forth what you need to all who seek business. And then you will make ready [*... your mouth*]

19 you will fill and you will be sated with much goodness. And from your manual skill ...

20 for God has distributed the inheritance of [*eve*]ry [*living thing*] and all the wise of mind have gained intelligence ...

Textual Notes

81 1. אׄ[כׄ]. Following Rey and Puech. The visible traces could also be from a *zayin*. The editors of DJD 34 reconstruct יׄ[א], and Tigchelaar, יׄ[מא]. The reconstruction כיא works better than the other options if one includes the reasonable supplement "his name." For an *aleph* with the straight stroke one finds here, see line 14.

81 3. איׄש; 4Q423 23 1: האיׄש. So Tigchelaar. Rey reads the final *he* as being a part of the preceding verb, ויורישׄ[מׄה. The trace before the *he* is extremely faint and not necessarily from a *mem*.

81 4. לקדוש; 4Q423 8 3: דשׄ◦[. In the commentary I discuss ways the variant in 4Q423 8 can be understood.

81 6. הלוא{ל}. The initial top stroke of a *lamed* has no cancellation dot and shows no sign of erasure. Rather, the letter was never completed. As Tigchelaar suggests, the scribe probably began to write לוא and then realized that the correct form is הלוא.

81 8. וקנאתׄו. This phrase is preserved in PAM 40.618, as are the final letters in lines 7 and 9. Rey and the editors of DJD 34 give in their transcriptions the reading I use (so too Elgvin), but in their discussions of the line they transcribe וקנאהו. In 40.618 the traces are faint, but support reading וקנאתׄו.

81 12. מׄ[קוׄר]. The editors of DJD 34 read *shin* instead of *qof*. The material evidence for this word, which is sparse, allows for both options. The reading used here has the advantage of producing a phrase also used in line 1 (פתח מקור).[2] The word in question is the first on a small scrap that has been joined to the rest of 4Q418 81. Tigchelaar calls into question the legitimacy of attaching this fragment (which he calls 4Q418 81b) to the text. The pieces do fit together nicely, which he grants. They neatly form the word יׄתהלכו in line 14, for example. One must also acknowledge that several oddities are created by this placement. For example, the bottom of the word בטרם of line 11 should appear on the attached fragment (Tigchelaar's 4Q418 81b), but it does not.

81 12. לשמו. The final *mem* in medial position suggests that the scribe thought he had finished the word after writing לשם and then realized he had not written the suffix, which he then added, as the editors of DJD 34 discern.

---

2. This reading is also endorsed by Stuckenbruck 2004, 63; Wold 2005b, 162.

81 14. בֹ֗ו [ל]תֹּבֹ. The text here is highly uncertain. Materially,כי
instead of בו is possible. תבל is a feminine word, but בו has a masculine
suffix, suggesting that it refers to a word now lost from line 13.

COMMENTARY

4Q418 81 is a major text for understanding the addressee's elect status
and his relationship with the angels. One of the major debates regarding
this column is whether its intended addressee is a priest or not. (In my
opinion, as I discuss below on l. 3, he is not.) The overall goal of 4Q418
81 is to help the *mebin* understand that he is different from the rest of
humankind because God has given him elect status. This theme is the
main focus of the first fourteen lines of the column. These lines can be
broken down further into subunits.[3] Lines 1–2 encourage the addressee to
bless the angels, and they claim that he has been separated from the rest
of humanity. In lines 3–8 the author expounds on the "lot" of the *mebin*,
a reference to his elect status, including his affinity with the angels. Lines
9–14 discuss various things that the addressee, because of his elect status,
can or should do. He should, for example, bless the angels (ll. 11–12). Lines
15–20 of 4Q418 81 deal primarily with economic issues that relate to the
mebin. Attention is given to his skill in craftsmanship (ll. 15, 19), referring
to some sort of work as an artisan by which he supports himself.

4Q418 81 1
The addressee is to bless the "holy ones" (קדושים). The line twice likens
the praise coming forth from his mouth to a spring of water (מקור). God
has opened his mouth as a spring to praise the angels, and the *mebin* is
metaphorically described as an "eternal spring." Line 12, using similar language, exhorts him to open a spring to bless the holy ones (פתח [מ]קור; see
below). There is a tradition in both the Hebrew Bible and Second Temple
literature of describing the Torah as a nurturing stream (e.g., Ps 1:3; CD
6:4; Sir 24:30–34).[4] Good or proper speech is also likened to a flowing
stream of water.[5] In 4QInstruction the metaphor may allude indirectly to
the Torah, but the emphasis of 4Q418 81 1 is on praising the angels. In Ben

---

3. Strugnell and Harrington 1999, 14–15.

4. Fishbane 1992, 3–16.

5. Several sayings in Proverbs describe the words of the wise as a "spring of life."
Proverbs 10:11, for example, states: "The mouth of the righteous is a spring of life

Sira the wise person understands the dominance of God, and thus a sign of a person's wisdom is his praise of God (15:9–10). In language similar to that of 4QInstruction, 4QSongs of the Sage discusses opening the lips into a "spring" of divine praise.[6] The image of flowing water also evokes the description of the temple in Ezek 40–48, and this text may inform the line at hand. 4Q418 81 does allude to the holy of holies in line 4 to describe the holiness of the addressee (see below). Like the temple, the ideal addressee is a holy entity from which divine praise comes forth.

The praise of God is a trope in 4QInstruction. Elsewhere the composition exhorts the *mebin* to extol the deity. 4Q416 2 iii 11 urges one to praise his name constantly (שמו הלל תמיד; cf. 4Q417 1 ii 6, 9). This motif supports the supplement of similar terminology in 4Q418 81 1: "praise [his name]" (הלל [שמו]). The extolling of God in this line is reasonably reconstructed. The praise of the "holy ones" (קדושים) is explicit, as in lines 11–12. The phrase "holy ones" is a common term for angels in early Judaism.[7] The blessing of angels is relatively uncommon, but it is attested.[8] In Tob 11:14, Tobit extols God and the angels, as does the Cave 11 version of the War Scroll (11Q14 1 ii 2–6). The Songs of the Sabbath Sacrifice includes praise of the angels, who in turn praise God.[9] A call to bless angels is not found elsewhere in 4QInstruction. However, the idea that the addressee is like the angels is important throughout the composition. It is a central motif, for example, in the "vision of meditation" passage of 4Q417 1 i 13–18 (consult commentary above). Lines 4–5 of 4Q418 81 contain an important wordplay regarding the root קדש, in which the addressee

---

(מקור חיים), but the mouth of the wicked conceals violence." See also 13:14; 14:27; 16:22; cf. 18:4; 4Q418 103 ii 6; 4Q418 127 1.

6. 4Q511 63 iii 1–2: "As for me, my tongue will extol your justice because you have unfastened (פתחתה) it. You have placed in my lips a spring of praise (מקור תהלה)." The Community Rule and the Hodayot employ the image of opening a spring to describe the transmission of supernatural revelation (e.g., 1QS 11:3; 1QH 10:20). See Rey 2009a, 310; Strugnell and Harrington 1999, 303.

7. See Strugnell and Harrington 1999, 304; Stuckenbruck 2004, 64–65. For a different interpretation of the term "holy ones," see Fletcher-Louis 2002, 178, 186. Consult also Puech 2005, 110–11.

8. See the material discussed in Stuckenbruck 2004, 52–67. Consult also Sullivan 2004.

9. 4Q400 2 2–3: "They [the *elim* of knowledge] are honored among all the camps of the *elohim* and revered by councils of humans … they declare the splendor of his kingship" (cf. 4Q403 1 i 32–33). See Stuckenbruck 2004, 61.

is described as a "most holy one" (see below). Both the intended audience of 4QInstruction and the angels are "holy ones" (קדושים). Because of the composition's conception of the elect as resembling the angels, there is intentional ambiguity between the two groups. Several early Jewish texts, in particular the Songs of the Sabbath Sacrifice, depict the angels as singing in heaven and extolling God (e.g., 4Q403 1 i; 1 En. 40:1–5). The *mebin* is to act in a similar way. 4Q418 81 1, by having him bless God and the holy ones, gives concrete expression to the idea that he is like the angels and has a special relationship with them.

The addressee is to praise God "like an eternal spring (מקור עולם)." The phrase is similar to the "eternal planting" of line 13, which designates elsewhere in early Jewish literature an elect community (see below). 4QInstruction asserts that the angels have "eternal life" (4Q418 69 ii 13; cf. 4Q418 55 12). The addressee has the prospect of eternal life with the angels if he follows the teachings of 4QInstruction (see section 6 of the introduction). By praising the holy ones, he is acting in a way that will help him attain the full realization of his elect status so that he can join the angels in eternal fellowship after death (cf. 4Q418 81 11–12).[10]

4Q418 81 1–2

Lines 1–2 elaborate the view that the addressee is like the angels. God has separated him from the "fleshly spirit" (רוח בשר). The *mebin* should thus separate himself from this spirit and, in parallelism, he is to keep away from what God hates and abominations of the soul. The phrase "fleshly spirit" denotes humanity in general, the non-elect who do not possess the potential to achieve life after death, in contrast to the addressee. The fleshly spirit is opposed to the "spiritual people" in the vision of meditation passage (4Q417 1 i 13–18). 4Q416 1 12 envisages the destruction of the fleshly spirit in the final judgment.[11] Because of his elect status, the *mebin* is in a sense more like the angels than other humans.[12]

The separation of the addressee from humankind is theological rather than physical. Throughout 4QInstruction he is engaged socially and economically in the affairs of ordinary life (e.g., 4Q417 2 i 17–19). He does

---

10. Stuckenbruck 2004, 65.

11. See the discussion in the commentary below on the phrase "spirit of life" in 4Q418 126 ii 8.

12. Tigchelaar (2001, 232) puts forward a similar interpretation. See also Rey 2009a, 315–16.

not live a cloistered existence. This tempers the force of the claim that the *mebin* should stay away from the fleshly spirit. He is not encouraged to be a misanthrope. God's hatred of the fleshly spirit is expressed in the eschatological judgment. No effort is made to express this hatred in terms of how the *mebin* approaches the world around him in his daily life. He is to understand that he is holier than most other people. 4Q418 81 1–2 expresses this with regard to his conduct not toward humankind (the fleshly spirit) but rather toward the angels, which he is to bless. Language of "abomination" (תועבה), describing what the *mebin* should avoid, is a cultic metaphor in keeping with the allusions to the temple in the column, and helps convey the holiness of the addressee (see further on l. 4).[13]

4Q418 81 2–3

God created all people and bestowed to each person his particular "inheritance" or allotment in life (cf. l. 20; 4Q416 3 2; 4Q423 5 3). The "inheritance" of the *mebin* is much better than what God bequeaths to most people (see the excursus in chapter 4). Line 3 makes the extraordinary claim that God himself is the "inheritance" of the addressee: "But he is your portion and your inheritance (חלקכה ונחלתכה) among humankind."[14] This is a patent allusion to Num 18:20.[15] The interpretation of this reference has been much debated. The biblical verse asserts that God has allocated to the Aaronic priests control over the temple sacrifices. Several commentators have concluded that the intended addressees of line 3 could be or in fact are priests.[16] The holiness of the *mebin* is indeed an important motif in 4Q418 81, and to this end priestly language is used (see below on l. 4). As Elgvin has argued, the envisioned addressee is probably

---

13. Regarding the phrase "abominations of the soul," it is likely that the phrase refers to God's "soul" (נפש; cf. Lev 26:11, 15). See Strugnell and Harrington 1999, 304.

14. Strugnell and Harrington (1999, 516–18) supplement this phrase in 4Q423 4 3a–3, cast in the first person rather than the third, on the basis of the parallel text 1Q26 1 7, which does in fact read "And he (God) said to him 'I am [your] por[tion].'" This reconstruction of 4Q423 4 3a–3 is not endorsed in Tigchelaar 2001, 142. Note the divine speech in the first person in 4Q418 81 6 (see below).

15. Num 18:20: "Then the Lord said to Aaron: 'You shall have no allotment in their land, nor shall you have any share among them; I am your share and your possession (חלקכה ונחלתכה) among the Israelites'" (cf. Pss 16:5; 73:26). See Strugnell and Harrington 1999, 305; Puech 2005, 111; Rey 2009a, 317.

16. Strugnell and Harrington 1999, 20; Tigchelaar 2001, 236; Fletcher-Louis 2002, 178; Lange 2000, 40.

not an actual priest.[17] There are references to cultic and halakhic issues in 4QInstruction. Participation in the temple cult is mentioned in 4QInstruction, for example, in 4Q423 3 4–5 (cf. 4Q423 5 1a). Two halakhic traditions are invoked in the composition (4Q416 2 iv 7–10; 4Q418 103 ii 6–9). If the *mebin* were a priest, one would expect much more of this kind of material. Ritual purity is not a major theme of 4QInstruction. The fact that the intended addressees include women (4Q415 2 ii) problematizes further the opinion that they are priests. The priestly traditions in 4Q418 81 3 are better understood as being invoked metaphorically, to explain the elect status of the addressee. The claim in Num 18:20 that God is the special portion of the priests signifies their authority over the temple and its sacrifices. In 4QInstruction this biblical claim is applied to the *mebin*, denoting the special inheritance that God has established for him: that the *raz nihyeh* has been disclosed to him, that he is in the lot of the angels (l. 5), and that he has the potential to attain eternal life. There are various professions represented by the intended audience of 4QInstruction (see section 9 of the introduction). It is not impossible that some of them were priests. The group as a whole, however, is not a community of priests.

The manner in which 4Q418 81 3 reformulates Num 18:20 also suggests that the column is not addressed to priests. The biblical verse describes the inheritance of the priests from the tribe of Levi as being God himself to distinguish their dispensation from that of the other tribes of Israel, which receive land. The deity is "your portion and inheritance *among all the sons of Israel* (בתוך בני ישראל)." 4Q418 81 3 asserts that God is "your portion and inheritance *among humankind* (בתוך בני אדם)."[18] Language from Num 18:20 is removed from its scriptural context concerning priests and adapted to the dominant theme of the pericope (ll. 1–5): the superiority of the inheritance of the *mebin* over that given to the "fleshly spirit," that is, humankind in general.[19] Also, since the Aaronids are not given land, the author of 4QInstruction may have been drawn to this tradition because its envisioned addressee is poor. He can be easily understood as not owning land, but possessing an endowment of a special status from God. In both respects he resembles the Aaronid priests. Note also that 4QInstruction shifts the person of Num 18:20, in which God directly speaks to Aaron.

---

17. Elgvin 2004, 82–83. Consult also Wold 2005b, 179.

18. Rey 2009a, 318. See his valid criticism (2009a, 311) of Puech (2005, 112), who argues that the phrase "sons of Israel" should be added to 4Q418 81 5.

19. Tigchelaar 2001, 232; Wold 2005b, 169.

In 4Q418 81 3 the speaker is not God, but the implied teacher-author of
4QInstruction.

The end of line 3 uses terminology that elsewhere in 4QInstruction
describes the bestowal of elect status to the *mebin*—להמשיל (cf. l. 9).
4Q416 2 iii 11–12 uses this verb to assert that he has been given an "inheritance of glory." 4Q423 1 2 employs להמשיל to describe the addressee's
control over Eden. 4Q418 81 3 claims that God has given him "his" inheritance. The editors of DJD 34 suggest that the suffix refers to either Adam or
God.[20] The stress of the column on God being the inheritance of the *mebin*
suggests the latter option.

4Q418 81 3–4

These lines are critical for understanding the holiness of the addressee.
He is to "glorify him" (God; כבדהו). In line 11 he is to "glorify" the holy
ones. According to line 4 the *mebin* is to honor God by consecrating himself (בהתקדשכה) to him. The addressee is to honor the deity because of
the special inheritance which he gave to him. He is to do this not only with
praise, but also by maintaining his own holiness. 4Q418 81 4 makes rich
use of the root קדש ("to consecrate, make holy"). The claim that he should
make himself holy is explained by the assertion that God established the
addressee "as a most holy one." The Hebrew here is קדוש קודשים. The
phrase is rather unusual. This exact spelling of the phrase occurs nowhere
else in the Hebrew Bible or Second Temple Jewish literature.[21] The expression is most likely a misspelling of קודש קודשים. This can be supported by
the variant in 4Q423 8 3.[22] 4Q418 81 4 has been understood as a direct reference to the holy of holies, with the elect *mebin* metaphorically described
as the sanctuary itself.[23] This usage would not be unlike the description in

---

20. Strugnell and Harrington 1999, 302.

21. Note the phrase "the holy ones of the Holy of Ho[lies]" (קדושי קודש
[קוד]שים) in the Songs of the Sabbath Sacrifice (4Q400 1 ii 6), and the unfortunately
fragmentary expression קדושי קודש[in 4Q267 15 3 ("the holy ones of holiness"; cf.
4Q381 76–77 7; 4Q511 35 2–3; 11Q5 26:9; 4QMMT B 79). See Tigchelaar 2001, 233.

22. 4Q423 8 3 reads דש○ קודשים. The letter trace preceding the *dalet* could be
from a *qof*, as Tigchelaar (2001, 143) suggests, but it could also be from a *waw* (so Rey
2009a, 308). 4Q423 8 3 can be reconstructed as either לקו[דש קודשים] ("[as a mo]st
holy one") or לק[דש קודשים], which can be rendered "[to san]ctify the holy ones" (or
as a defective spelling of the first option). Consult Strugnell and Harrington 1999, 525;
Puech 2005, 112.

23. Strugnell and Harrington 1999, 15, 302; Stuckenbruck 2004, 63.

the Community Rule of the *yaḥad* (or an elite subgroup within this sect) as a "foundation of the holy of holies" (1QS 8:5–6; cf. 9:5–6; 1QSb 4:28).[24] Elgvin has observed that if the holy of holies were the line's intended referent, the spelling in 4Q418 81 4 would be somewhat different (קודש קודשים instead of קדוש קודשים).[25] Elgvin is on the mark, but there is not a major semantic difference between his two options.[26] קודש is typically a noun and קדוש an adjective.[27] Since קדוש is the first member of a construct chain in 4Q418 81 4, it is likely a substantized adjective functioning as a noun (cf. Num 16:5; Ps 34:10). The phrase קדוש קודשים of line 4 is reasonably understood as a variant spelling of קודש קודשים. As Elgvin has rightly discerned, however, line 4 does not primarily refer to the temple. The expression is used numerous times in the Hebrew Bible in a superlative sense. Exodus 30:10, for example, describes an atonement ritual by asserting that "it is most holy (קֹדֶשׁ־קָדָשִׁים) to the Lord."[28] Understanding the key phrase of 4Q418 81 4 in a superlative sense ("most holy") yields a plausible interpretation. The *mebin* is a "most holy one."[29] This interpretation fits well with the assertion that he is most holy "[of all the people of the] world." Language of holiness describes the elect status of the addressee, his special inheritance from God.[30] The root קדש also evokes the angels, "the holy ones" (ll. 1, 11–12), expressing the key theme that his

---

24. The Dead Sea sect is presented in this text as an interim temple that atones for the land, a view buttressed by the group's criticism of the temple (e.g., CD 6:14–16).

25. Elgvin 1997a, 136.

26. Since the expression is prefaced by a *lamed*, one could read לקדוש as a *qal* infinitive, in which case the phrase means that the *mebin* has been established "to sanctify" the holy ones. This meaning of the root, however, is generally conveyed in the *piel* rather than the *qal* (in which case one would expect לקדש, as mentioned above). See Elgvin 1998, 119.

27. For the former see, for example, Lev 22:3; Ps 77:14; for the latter, Deut 7:6; 2 Kgs 19:22.

28. Note also, for example, Exod 29:37; 30:29; 40:10; Lev 2:10.

29. So too Strugnell and Harrington (1999, 15), but in their translation of 4Q418 81 they translate instead "holy of holies" (302). The superlative option is also endorsed in Kampen 2011, 132; Tigchelaar 2001, 231; Wold 2005b, 107, 162. Note the translation by Elgvin (2004, 81), "he set you as holy among the holy ones," and Rey 2009a, 309, "il t'a établi saint des saints."

30. 4Q416 2 ii 6 mentions the "holy spirit" of the addressee (cf. 4Q418 76 3). 4Q418 234 1 contains a fragmentary reference to "an inheritance of holiness." 4Q418 236 3 refers to "your heart of holiness," in reference to the *mebin*. Note the discussion of 4Q415 2 i + 1 ii in Tigchelaar 2001, 225–30.

elect status makes him like the angels (ll. 4–5). The phrase לקדוש קודשים of line 4 clearly alludes to the temple, but the main point of the phrase is to express the holiness of the addressee. To this end, the line uses terminology that evokes the temple.

4Q418 81 4–5

God gave the *mebin* a "lot" (גורל) among the angels.[31] The term "lot" reflects a deterministic mindset, asserting that this dispensation is part of the inheritance God established for him.[32] 1QS 11:7–8 describes the elect status of the members of the Dead Sea sect by claiming that God "has given them an inheritance in the lot of the holy ones (ינחילם בגורל קדושים)" (cf. 2:2). The Hodayot similarly portray the elect as "in the lot of your holy ones" (בגורל עם קדושיכה; 1QH 19:14–15). The Rule of Benedictions also claims that the elect have been placed among the lot of the angels (1QSb 4:26). Fragments 55 and 69 ii of 4Q418 assert that the *mebin* should be like the angels. 4Q418 81 4–5 provides a rationale for this view. He should act like the angels because he was fashioned by God in a way that makes him similar to them. 4Q418 81 4–5 thus elaborates the claim of lines 1–2 that God has separated the addressee from the rest of humankind. The vision of meditation passage (4Q417 1 i 13–18) teaches him to be like the spiritual people, who were created in the likeness of the angels. His affinity with the angels undergirds the view that he will attain eternal life in fellowship with the holy ones.

4Q418 81 5 asserts that God has magnified the "glory" (כבוד) of the addressee. 4Q418 81 uses this root as an imperative to declare that he should "glorify" God and the angels (ll. 1, 11). "Glory" is at times in 4QInstruction a quality possessed by God (4Q417 1 i 13; 4Q418 126 ii 9), but more often it is an aspect of the *mebin*, denoting his elect status. 4Q416 2 iii 11–12, for example, claims he has an "inheritance of glory."[33] In 4Q418 81, both "glory" and "holiness" signify the elect status of the addressee.

---

31. Given the theme in 4QInstruction of his special relationship with the angels, the reconstruction "all the [a]n[gels]" (ל[מ]לאכים]) makes sense, but one should note that the word "angels" does not have a strong material basis and is reconstructed on the basis of a single visible letter, a *lamed*. The reconstruction is supported by l. 5, which states that the addressee is a son of God (see below). See Rey 2009a, 311.

32. The highly deterministic Treatise on the Two Spirits states that God has "cast the lots" of all people (1QS 4:26). See further Lange 2000, 39–48; Elgvin 1998, 121.

33. 4Q416 2 ii 18; 4Q416 2 iv 11; 4Q418 159 ii 6.

4Q418 81 5 also claims that God established the *mebin* "for himself as a firstborn son (בכור)." The editors of DJD 34 find it "a little surprising" that the text describes the addressee as God's firstborn son.[34] 4QInstruction itself contains some hesitation regarding this assertion. 4Q423 8 4 does not affirm that he is the firstborn son of God (בכור), but rather that he is *like* his firstborn (כבכור).[35] There is not enough evidence in 4QInstruction to argue that 4Q418 81 5 describes the apotheosis of the addressee or makes claims that are as extreme as those of the Self-Glorification Hymn (see also the commentary on 4Q416 2 iii 11–12). Elgvin argues that 4QInstruction draws upon national traditions, since Israel is called the son of God (e.g., Exod 4:22), as is David (2 Sam 7:14).[36] However, such biblical traditions are not at all prominent in 4QInstruction. 4Q418 81 5 is better understood in terms of major themes of the composition. The *mebin* is called a son of God, a common term for angels. This accords with the claim that he is in the lot of the angels. Being the firstborn son expresses further the superlative or exceptional nature of the addressee's holiness.[37] Being the firstborn son also expresses that he is entitled to the special inheritance that God has allotted to him (see above on l. 3).

4Q418 81 6

Line 6 begins with first person speech. The speaker declares that he has given "my goodness" (טובי) to the addressee, and the line reiterates the point in the third person, asserting that he has offered "his goodness" to him. The first statement is most likely a report of divine speech that began at the end of line 5.[38] In keeping with the tenor of 4Q418 81, God claims that he has bestowed unusual privileges, here described as "goodness," upon the addressee. The fact that God makes this assertion in the first person (as secondary speech relayed by the author of the composi-

---

34. Strugnell and Harrington 1999, 305. See also Tigchelaar 2001, 233–34; Elgvin 2004, 82.

35. 4Q423 8 4 can also be read as stating that God established him *as* his firstborn son. See further Fletcher-Louis 2002, 198.

36. Elgvin 1998, 122. He has also argued that 4Q418 81 1–14 is similar to Solomon's prayer in 1 Kgs 3:6–14 to receive wisdom. See Elgvin 2004, 81. Consult further Tigchelaar 2001, 233.

37. Joseph is described as "the firstborn son of God" in Jos. Asen. 21:4.

38. Strugnell and Harrington (1999, 302, 306) suggest the divine speech of l. 6 was fronted by this supplement at the end of l. 5: "saying, 'I will bless you] and my goodness to you I will give.'"

tion) emphasizes his special relationship with the *mebin*. The end of line 6 emphasizes that God has bequeathed him with a special status to encourage him to be upright and faithful (cf. 4Q418 126 ii 10; 4Q418 148 ii 8). The overarching goal of 4Q418 81 is not simply to make the addressee aware of the elect status that God gave him, but also to convince him to act accordingly. The focus on the ethics of the *mebin* continues into the lost second half of line 6. This is suggested by the first phrase of line 7, "your deeds."

4Q418 81 7

The line discusses the topic that the *mebin* should be ethical (l. 6), but the exact sense of line 7 is not clear. He is told to "seek his judgments," presumably those of God. The phrase לדרוש משפט can denote investigating a case (4Q424 3 4), explaining or applying a regulation (1QS 6:7; 8:24), or to practice justice (Isa 1:17). In 4Q418 81 7 he is to seek judgments from all of his opponents (כול יריבכה) (cf. 4Q417 2 i 12, 14). The *mebin* may be urged to seek redress from God when he has been wronged by someone. What sort of adversary is envisioned by the text is not clear. 4Q417 2 i 1–6 gives the addressee advice for resolving conflicts with someone who has a higher social standing. This may be the case in 4Q418 81 7 as well, but there is not enough evidence in the line to support this view conclusively.

4Q418 81 8

The *mebin* is to love God and treat other members of the elect community with compassion. He is urged to love "him" (God) and, in parallelism, to show zeal towards him. This call for devotion corresponds to the instruction in line 4 to glorify the deity. The *mebin* is to display "piety" and "compassion," attributes often associated with God, toward people, in particular "all who keep his word (שומרי דברו)." This expression refers to the elect *mebinim*. The same phrase occurs in the vision of meditation passage, describing those for whom the book of remembrance is written (4Q417 1 i 16; cf. 4Q418 169 + 170 3). The elect are described as "men of (God's) pleasure" in 4Q418 81 10 (see below).

4Q418 81 9

God has made supernatural revelation available to the addressee as part of his elect status. The column of 4Q418 81 never mentions the mystery that is to be, but line 9 alludes to it. He has "[op]ened up intelligence" to him (שכל [פ]תח). The verb פתח elsewhere in the column describes

God's opening the addressee's mouth to praise the angels (cf. ll. 1, 12). The word "to open" signifies the disclosure of revelation in the book of Mysteries and the Community Rule (4Q299 3a ii–b 13; 1QS 11:3–4).[39] 4Q418 55 10 refers to the "intelligence" of the angels, also suggesting that the term in 4Q418 81 9 refers to heavenly knowledge (cf. 4Q417 1 i 25).

God has given the *mebin* dominion over his "treasury" (אוצר). Elsewhere in 4QInstruction God's "treasury" denotes his abundance and ability to provide food for humankind (4Q417 2 i 19). In 4Q418 81 9 the term probably refers to the revelation of supernatural knowledge to the *mebin* (cf. 4Q286 1 ii 7; 4Q298 3–4 i 9; Sir 1:25).[40] This is suggested by the parallelism of the line. Line 9 also associates the term "treasury" with the verb להמשיל ("to put in charge," "give authority"). 4QInstruction uses this verb several times to signify that God established the *mebin* to have elect status. 4Q418 81 3, for example, employs the term in connection to his special inheritance (see above).

A "measure of truth" (איפת אמת) has been allocated to the addressee. Parallelism suggests that the phrase also alludes to the knowledge he can attain through the disclosure of revelation given to him, a key element of his elect status.[41] 4Q416 1 10 describes the elect who will be rewarded at the final judgment as the "sons of his truth," associating God's "truth" with the elect.[42] 4Q418 81 9 connects this word to "ephah," a biblical unit of measurement. Elsewhere in 4QInstruction the term signifies God's just and orderly creation of the world (4Q418 126 ii 3–5; cf. 4Q416 1 4; 4Q418 127 6).[43] This suggests that the word in 4Q418 81 construes the bestowal of elect status to the addressee as an inherent part of God's plan for the cosmos. These other attestations of the term "ephah" in 4QInstruction also suggest that the revealed knowledge mentioned in line 9 includes comprehension of the divine structure of the world.

---

39. The key phrase of 4Q299 3a ii–b 13 is "the [p]lan of the time of birth he opened before them." 1QS 11:3–4 uses the verb "to open" in connection to the mystery that is to be: "For from the source of his knowledge he has opened up his light, and my eyes have observed his wonders, and the light of my heart the mystery that is to be." See Wold 2005b, 165.

40. Tigchelaar 2001, 234.

41. Kister 2005, 169–70.

42. 4Q416 4 3; 4Q418 55 6; 4Q418 88 ii 8.

43. Rey 2009a, 312; Strugnell and Harrington 1999, 307.

4Q418 81 10

Line 10 begins by stating that "they" are with the *mebin*. The anteced-
ents of the pronoun have not survived. The editors of DJD 34 supplement
"judgment and righteousness" at the end of line 9.[44] This is reasonable
because of the prominence in the column of the theme of divine favor
toward the addressee. He turns wrath away from the אנשי רצון, literally
"men of pleasure." The term רצון often refers in early Jewish literature to
God's will or pleasure (e.g., 1QS 5:1; CD 3:15; Sir 39:18).[45] This is also
the case in 4Q418 81 10 and elsewhere in 4QInstruction.[46] The "men of
pleasure" carry out God's pleasure or will and, it is implied, have received
divine favor. The phrase signifies the elect.[47] Similar expressions in early
Jewish and Christian literature denote the elect. The Hodayot, for example, state that God shows compassion to "all the sons of his will" (כול בני
רצונו) (12:33–34; cf. ll. 28–29).[48] Writing before the official publication of
4QInstruction, Wolters observed that the phrase "men of (God's) pleasure" in 4Q418 81 10 is similar to Luke 2:14.[49] This verse depicts a mul-
titude of angels giving praise, giving glory to God and peace to "men of
good pleasure" (ἀνθρώποις εὐδοκίας). In the passage this expression denotes
people who will receive salvation. This resonates with 4Q418 81, as does
the Lucan text's emphasis on glory (e.g., ll. 4–5). The allocation of praise to
both God and the elect in Luke 2 is similar to 4Q418 81, which urges the
praise of God and angels with whom the elect are associated. The phrase
"men of (God's) pleasure" in 4Q418 81 10 supports the opinion, voiced

44. Strugnell and Harrington 1999, 303. So also Puech 2005, 109.

45. For a useful survey of the use of the term in Ben Sira and the Dead Sea Scrolls,
see Aitken 2002, 282–301.

46. 4Q416 2 ii 12; 4Q416 2 iii 12; 4Q418 126 ii 5; cf. 4Q416 2 iv 7–9; 4Q416 2 ii
7. See Rey 2009a, 38.

47. Rey (2009a, 313) is justly critical of the view that the term signifies the *yaḥad*.
For the relation between the Dead Sea sect and the group to which 4QInstruction is
written see section 10 of the introduction.

48. See also 1QH 19:12; 1QS 8:6; 4Q545 4 18.

49. Wolters 1994, 291–97. His article incorrectly identifies 4Q418 81 as 4Q416.
He used Eisenman and Wise 1992, 241–55. They include ten texts of 4QInstruction,
which they label as being from 4Q416 and 4Q418. However, they never clarify which
fragments are from which manuscript (hence Wolters's confusion that the text in question is from 4Q416). See also Elgvin 1998, 124; Harrington and Strugnell 1993, 493.

earlier by Fitzmyer and Wolters, that the soteriology of Luke 2 draws upon early Jewish conceptions of the elect.[50]

The addressee has the power to turn wrath away (להשיב אף) from the "men of (God's) pleasure." In 4Q417 2 i 15 God turns wrath away from the elect and forgives sins. In the Hebrew Bible it is not only God who can do this, but some people as well. In Ps 106:23 Moses does so when he intercedes on behalf of Israel, whose people God wants to destroy because of their sins (cf. Exod 32:11–13; Num 14:13–18). In a reference to his prophetic activity, Jeremiah turns away wrath (Jer 18:20). Through his zeal Phineas defuses God's anger, and God decides not to punish Israel (Num 25:11; cf. Prov 29:8).[51] In these biblical examples a person performs actions that please God, and because of this a group of people is spared punishment. In 4Q418 81 10 the *mebin* can turn God's anger away from other elect addressees by doing what God favors (in accordance with his רצון). He helps his fellow elect be accepted by God, I suggest, by encouraging them to do what he himself is urged to do: to be ethical and to carry out the pedagogical ideals of the composition (see also below on l. 12).[52] In this way God's wrath would turn away from them when they are judged.

4Q418 81 11–12

These lines hearken back to the core issue of line 1, that the addressee should bless the holy ones. Line 11 asserts that before the *mebin* receives his inheritance he is to "glorify" (כבד) the angels. "Inheritance" (נחלה) in 4QInstruction often denotes the elect status of the addressee (see ll. 2–3). The full manifestation of this status occurs when he attains life after death with the angels. This suggests that line 11 discusses the *fully realized* inheritance of the addressee, received after the expiration of the body. In order to attain this goal he should praise the angels. Line 4 encourages him to "glorify" God. As discussed above, lines 4–5 exhort the addressee not only to praise God, but also to understand that he is holy and in the lot of the angels (the "holy ones"). It is reasonable to interpret line 11 in a similar way. By glorifying the angels, he comes to realize that he is like them, since they too give glory to God. To achieve fully the rewards of his elect status, the addressee needs to be pious and ethical, and to understand that he is like the angels.

---

50. Fitzmyer 1958, 225–27; Wolters 1994, 292.
51. Strugnell and Harrington 1999, 307; Tigchelaar 2001, 234.
52. Wold 2005b, 179.

Like line 11, 4Q418 81 12 accords with line 1 of the column. The language of opening a spring (פתח [מ]קור) is also in line 1 (see above). There the spring refers to one opening his mouth to bless the holy ones. Given the importance of divine praise in the column (ll. 1, 4, 11), there is no reason to doubt that this is the case in line 12 as well.[53] The line, however, never mentions the motif of praise directly.

The second half of 4Q418 81 12 is ambiguous. After the reference to the holy ones, the text refers to "everyone who is called by his name," followed by the word "hol[y ones]" (קודשי[ם]; cf. 4Q417 13 2). The key interpretive problem is how to understand the waw that begins the phrase (וכול הנקרא). Line 12 could be understood in terms of parallelism—one should glorify the holy ones *and* all who are called by his name holy ones. The waw may instead denote a result clause: by glorifying the angels, *then* all those who are called by his name will become holy ones. I prefer the second option.[54] The first reference in line 12 to the "holy ones" denotes the angels, as in lines 1 and 11, and the phrase "everyone who is called by his name" in line 12 signifies the elect (cf. 11Q14 1 ii 14–15).[55] By honoring God, the addressee is able to turn the deity's wrath away from the elect (l. 10). The second half of line 12 clarifies how this is done. By praising the angels, the *mebin* becomes a model that the other members of his community can emulate. This helps them understand that they have been given special divine favor and are like the holy ones.

4Q418 81 13

God's splendor is eternal, existing throughout all the "periods." The demarcation of history into periods is not elaborated upon, but 4QInstruction assumes a schematization of history that is similar to that of the Apocalypse of Weeks (1 En. 93:1–10; 91:11–17) or Dan 9.[56] 4Q418 81 13 also states that God's grandeur is with "the eter[nal] planting" (מטעת [עו]לם). As is well known, in early Jewish literature the phrase and simi-

---

53. Stuckenbruck 2004, 65.

54. Strugnell and Harrington (1999, 303) translate: "Begin with a song for all the Holy Ones. And everyone one who is called by <his> name will be made/called holy." For assessment of the transcription upon which this translation is based, see the textual notes section above.

55. Elgvin 1998, 125.

56. For קץ in the plural elsewhere in 4QInstruction, see 4Q415 2 i + 1 ii 8; 4Q416 1 14; 4Q417 1 i 7; 4Q418 69 ii 14; 4Q418 77 4; 4Q418 123 ii 2.

lar language conveys a botanical metaphor that signifies the flourishing of the elect and that they have God's favor.[57] The Community Rule uses the expression מטעת עולם to describe an elect group of the *yahad*, the Community council (1QS 8:5–6; cf. 11:8). 1 Enoch uses similar language for those who will receive eschatological rewards (e.g., 10:3, 16; 93:10; cf. Jub. 1:16; 36:6). The Damascus Document calls God's establishment of the Dead Sea sect a "root of planting" (CD 1:6–7). Elgvin has suggested that the "eternal planting" of 4Q418 81 refers to the "remnant community."[58] As Stuckenbruck has pointed out, the idea of a righteous remnant is not prominent in 4QInstruction.[59] Elgvin is correct, however, that the term denotes the elect community to which the composition is addressed. This is suggested by the claim that God's grandeur is with the eternal planting. 4Q423 1 also supports this interpretation, since it describes the addressee as having stewardship over the garden of Eden, a botanical metaphor for his acquisition of wisdom (see commentary on this text). This fragment uses the word "planting" (מטע) in an unfortunately fragmentary context (l. 7). Moreover, line 13 of 4Q418 81 fits well with the rest of the column. The text does not emphasize the holiness of the addressee alone, but also that of the elect group of which he is a member (l. 12). Together they comprise God's "eternal planting."

4Q418 81 14

This line contains a fragmentary reference to the eschatological rewards to the elect. All who inherit the earth (נוחלי ארץ) will walk in "it," presumably a reference to "the wor[ld]"; this statement is followed by a fragmentary reference to heaven. The phrase "all those who inherit the earth" uses the key root נחל, which often in 4QInstruction denotes the special status of the addressee (e.g., l. 3; 4Q416 2 iii 11–12). 4Q418 55 6 refers to those who inherit truth, a virtue commonly associated with the elect in 4QInstruction (see the commentary to 4Q416 1 10; cf. 4Q423 4 3). The Sermon on the Mount famously utilizes the motif of inheriting the earth, in tandem with the claim that the poor in spirit shall receive the kingdom of heaven. Both phrases likely signify the eschatological

---

57. This metaphor may derive from Third Isaiah, where it describes the glory of restored Zion (60:21; 61:3; cf. 65:22; see also the excursus in chapter 8). Consult Stuckenbruck 2002, 249–57; Tiller 1997, 312–35.

58. Elgvin 1998, 125.

59. Stuckenbruck 2002, 251.

rewards that are allocated for the pious (Matt 5:3, 5; cf. m. Sanh. 10:1).[60]
The Hebrew Bible also describes the righteous as inheriting the earth (Isa
57:13; Ps 37:22).[61] In the book of Mysteries and the Book of the Watchers
wickedness is vanquished from the earth, leaving the righteous to enjoy a
utopian, blessed existence on earth (1Q27 1 i 5–7; 1 En. 10:16–11:2; cf. 1QS
4:18–25). As the sole people remaining after the judgment, they inherit the
earth. First Enoch 5:7 describes the inheritance of the earth as a reward the
elect shall receive, along with light and joy and peace. The eschatological
judgment scene of 4Q416 1 asserts that "all iniquity" will be destroyed (l.
13), not unlike the book of Mysteries and 1 En. 10. However, unlike these
texts, 4QInstruction never describes the purified, restored earth in which
the righteous shall lead a blessed existence. Since the text proclaims final
judgment, it is reasonable to posit that such a transformation of the world
is implied. But, reflecting ambiguity in the composition regarding when
eternal life is attained, 4QInstruction lays out the possibility that the elect
can attain life after physical death, not simply at the moment of final judgment (see section 6 of the introduction). This complicates the view that
inheriting the earth in 4Q418 81 14 signifies the ultimate rewards of the
elect on a transformed earth after the ultimate destruction of wickedness.
It is possible that the elect one attains positive recompense from God after
the death of the individual *mebin* and that the text also proclaims a universal eschatological judgment in which the earth is cleansed of evil. The
full text of line 14 may have originally described inheriting the earth as a
reward of the elect after the final judgment.[62] Given the use of this trope
elsewhere in early Judaism, this is a plausible interpretation, but it cannot
be endorsed with certainty.

---

60. Elgvin 1998, 126.

61. Strugnell and Harrington 1999, 309.

62. Another possibility is that the expression (literally, "the inheritors of the
earth") denotes the elect who are on the earth now—those who have a special inheritance are on the earth (cf. 4Q418 126 ii 16). This can be supported by the admittedly
fragmentary reference to them walking in the world. The verb in question is in the
hithpael (יתהלכו). Elsewhere in 4QInstruction this verb in this *binyan* denotes conduct. 4Q416 2 iii 9 connects this verb in the *hithpael* to the *mebin* being restored to
glory, a reference to his elect status (see commentary above; cf. 4Q418a 18 4). 4Q423
3 2 is fragmentary but similarly relates an urge to "walk" in the *hithpael* with the mystery that is to be (cf. 4Q417 19 4). The full line may have emphasized that by living on
earth with humility, piety, and righteousness the *mebin* can join the angels after death.

4Q418 81 15

Line 15 begins a new section (ll. 15–20), demarcated with ואתה מבין ("And you, understanding one"). This pericope focuses on practical issues, such as the addressee's ability to earn a living. Line 15 asserts that God may have given him "manual skill" (חכמת ידים). The Hebrew is literally the "wisdom of the hands," and refers to some sort of craftsmanship that allows the *mebin* to earn a wage and support himself.[63] The phrase also occurs in line 19 in connection with the assertion that the addressee can obtain enough food (cf. l. 16). 4Q418 137 2–4 also attests the expression, along with references to "wages" (reconstructed) and "long life."[64] 4Q418 81 15 describes the technical skill of the *mebin* as God-given through the verb המשילכה ("he has given you dominion"), a verb that in 4QInstruction denotes God's bestowal of elect status to the addressee (see 4Q416 2 iii 11–12). 4Q418 137 2 also appears to portray "wisdom of the hands" as expertise given by God (cf. Wis 7:16). 4Q418 81 15 supports the view that the *mebin* should not be situated in an upper-class scribal milieu, à la Ben Sira. The Jerusalem sage, whose instruction attests a variant of the phrase "wisdom of the hands" in Sir 9:17, extols the "wisdom of the scribe" (חכמת סופר) and argues that this profession is superior to menial jobs such as working as a potter or a smith (38:24–34).[65] 4QInstruction, by contrast, addresses people who hold such jobs. The members of the intended audience of the composition possess a range of humble, subsistence-level professions such as farming (e.g., 4Q423 5; see section 9 of the introduction).

4Q418 81 16

This line refers to God's creation of food for humanity and the addressee's acquisition of his own provisions. The word אוט, translated here as "resources," is enigmatic, but is reasonably understood as referring to material that has a practical benefit for the *mebin* (see the commentary on 4Q416 2 ii 1). The term probably signifies food in 4Q418 81 16, as suggested by the parallel reference to "nourishment" (טרף). These two terms

---

63. Leibner 2010, 264–96.

64. The phrase is also attested in 4Q418 102a + b 3 and 4Q418 139 2 in fragmentary contexts (cf. 4Q424 3 7).

65. Ben Sira 9:17 regards the work of craftsmen as valuable, but considers the wisdom of the sage more important: "In skilled artisans (בחכמי ידים) their deftness is esteemed, but the ruler of his people is the skilled sage (חכם)." This is also the case in Ben Sira 38 (vv. 31–32).

are also combined in 4Q416 2 ii 1. The latter text asserts that God has made food available for all humankind. The expression הולכי אדם in 4Q418 81 16, literally "walkers of man," may refer to humanity in general, conveying that people are mortal and "go the way of the earth."[66] The resources are thus "for" (with a *lamed* preposition) humankind. The line, like 4Q416 2 ii 1, asserts that God makes available for humans the food they need to survive. The second half of 4Q418 81 16 asserts that the *mebin* can acquire the food he needs. This presumably refers to his ability to earn a living, since line 15 understands his artisan skill as having been given by God.

4Q418 81 17

Line 17 expresses the pedagogical ethos of 4QInstruction. The addressee is to acquire understanding and to learn from his teachers. 4Q418 221 similarly exhorts the *mebin* to get learning. The two texts are similar in terms of theme and terminology. The two fragments are in continuity with the wisdom tradition, which constantly encourages students to study and obtain knowledge. The poem that introduces the book of Proverbs urges one "to get ever more learning" (יוסף לקח; 1:5; cf. 9:9, 16:21, 23). The same language is employed in 4Q418 81 17 (הוסף לקח) and in 4Q418 221 3 (cf. 4Q298 3–4 ii 5; 4Q436 1a–b i 2). The phrase "improve in understanding greatly" (התבונן מודה) is only found in 4QInstruction among the Dead Sea Scrolls (4Q415 11 12; 4Q417 3 3; cf. Jer 2:10).[67] 4Q418 81 17 assumes that the *mebin* is not under the authority of a single teacher, but rather can learn from several people ("all your teachers"; cf. m. 'Avot 4:1).

4Q418 81 18

The addressee is to meet his basic needs by engaging in trade. It is assumed that he has sufficient resources to do so. This is similar to 4Q417 2 i 17–18, which advises the addressee to trade his surplus. 4Q418 81 18 never mentions any sort of hardship experienced by the *mebin*. The line uses the word מחסור to describe his lack of wherewithal for his basic needs; this is a characteristic term of 4QInstruction (see the commentary on 4Q417 2 i 17–18). He addresses this lack by going to "all who seek business," likely a reference to people who trade. The term translated "busi-

---

66. The argument is based on Qoh 12:5, which stresses human mortality: "because all must go (הלך האדם) to their eternal home." See Strugnell and Harrington 1999, 310; Seow 1997, 364.

67. Kampen 2011, 133.

ness" is חפץ, which often means "delight" (e.g., Ps 1:2; Qoh 5:3). The word can also mean "business" and this is clearly the sense in 4QInstruction (see the commentary on 4Q418 126 ii 12).[68] The term signifies commerce in 4Q417 2 i 17–18, denoting the place at which the addressee barters his surplus. In 4Q418 126 ii 12 the *mebin* is told "from your basket he will seek what he desires (ידרוש חפצו)," using the same words as 4Q418 81 18 (דורשי חפץ). Line 13 of 4Q418 126 ii mentions the addressee's "need" (מחסור), suggesting that he will help satisfy his basic needs through the transaction, as in 4Q418 81 18. The pairing of the terms חפץ and דרש is rare in other early Jewish texts but surprisingly common in 4QInstruction (4Q418 102a + b 4; 4Q418 126 ii 4; 4Q418 127 4; 4Q418 158 3; cf. Sir 32:14).

4Q418 81 19

Through industry and trade the addressee can provide for himself. He will be sated with goodness. Line 19 fits well with the emphasis on trading in the previous line, and presumes a business transaction that was successful. The incomplete reference to "manual skill" at the end of this line (see above on l. 15) suggests that the trade involves items that the *mebin* himself fashioned. He meets his basic material needs through skill in craftsmanship.

4Q418 81 20

God has established the "inheritance" (נחלה) of all creatures. The term refers to the allotment in life that God has established for each person. Lines 2–3 of the column similarly declare that he has given each person his inheritance (cf. 4Q416 3 2; see the excursus in chapter 4). 4Q418 81 20 puts forward a deterministic perspective. The line does not explicitly address the themes of trading and self-sufficiency that are prominent in lines 15–19. Whatever the *mebin* can earn through trade is presumably understood as part of the inheritance that God has established for him.

The second statement of 4Q418 81 20 is frustratingly incomplete. All the "wise of mind (חכמי לב) have been made intelligent." The expression "wise of mind" (literally "wise of heart") occurs nowhere else in 4QInstruction. (Contrast the "foolish of heart" of 4Q418 69 ii 4–9.) The phrase

---

68. Strugnell and Harrington 1999, 310; Puech 2005, 117.

and variant forms occur frequently in Proverbs and Ben Sira.[69] Elsewhere in the Dead Sea Scrolls the expression is rare (4Q424 3 6; 4Q468a 2). Appealing to Exod 31:6 ("And in the heart of everyone wise of heart I have put wisdom"; cf. 28:3), Michael Fox argues that being "wise of heart" in the Hebrew Bible refers to a person's potential to acquire wisdom.[70] 4Q418 81 20 accords with this interpretation, since like Exod 31:6 it states that intelligence has been given (by God) to the wise.[71] The "wise of mind" clearly include the intended audience of 4QInstruction. The *mebin* possesses wisdom of the heart (intelligence; l. 20) and wisdom of the hands (technical skill; ll. 15, 19).

---

69. See for example Prov 16:21: "The wise of mind (lit. "heart") is called perceptive, and pleasant speech increases persuasiveness" (cf. 10:8, 11:29; 16:23; Sir 45:26; 50:23).

70. The person who receives wisdom from God has, in somewhat circular logic, a predisposition for it in the first place (cf. Wis 7:7). See Fox 2000, 109.

71. The verb associated with the wise of heart, השכלו, is most likely a defective *hiphil*. It could be a *hophal*, but the form is unattested. One could also understand the verb as a *hithpael* with an assimilated *tav*. This root in the *hiphil* often has an intransitive sense (e.g., Ps 2:10; Isa 41:20) and this is probably the case in this line. Puech (2005, 118) supplements the line so that the wise of mind are given knowledge of "the mystery that is to be." See also Strugnell and Harrington 1999, 311.

12.
4Q418 103 II

Parallel text: 4Q418a 4 (underline)

TEXT[1]

	]○○○[	1
	[	
]אכרים עד כול א֯[	○]◌	2
	[כבוא]	
ד֯[ש הבא בטנאיכה ובאסמיכה כול֯] פרי אדמתכ֯ה		3
	[	
]ב֯ודו ולוא	ישוה עת בעת דורשם ואל תדם ב֯]ע֯○	4
	ת[	
]○כה ו֯מצא	כ֯י כולם ידרשו לעתם ואיש כפי חפצ֯[ו	5
	]○י֯ הליב֯י	
ב֯]מסחורכה אל תערוב	כמקור מים ח֯יים אשר הכ֯יל א֯[ו֯]ט֯ו֯[ן	6
	אשר] לרעכה [	
]בצמר ובפשתים	למה יהיה כלאים כ֯בפרד והייתה כלוב֯[ש שעטנז	7
	ועבודתכה כח֯ור֯[ש	
]ז֯ורע כלאים	בשור ובח֯[מו֯]ר֯ [י֯]ח֯ד֯[ו]וגם תבואתכה תה֯[יה לכה כ֯]	8
	אשר הזרע והמלאה ותבוא֯[ת	
ב֯]ח֯ייכה יתמו	ה֯[כרם]י֯קד֯[ש יחד֯ו] הונכה עם בשרכה]	9
	יחד ובחייכה לוא תמצא	

bottom margin

1. Strugnell and Harrington 1999, 329–31; Tigchelaar 2001, 99–100; Rey 2009a, 112–13.

TRANSLATION

2   ... farmers, until all [... *when*]

3   [*new gr*]ain [*comes in*], gather in your baskets and your store-
      houses all [*the fruit* of yo*ur* land ...]

4   season will resemble season when examining them. And do not
      be like ... his ... and you shall not ...

5   for all of them will be examined at their season, each according to
      [*his*] desire ... and find the paths of ...

6   like a spring of living water that includes his re[*so*]urces ... your
      merchandise do not mix [*with*] that which [*belongs to your neigh-
      bor,*]

7   lest it be of diverse kinds like a mule, and you be like one who
      wea[*rs sha'aṭnez*], with wool together with flax, and your work like
      one who plo[*ws*]

8   with an ox and a do[*nk*]ey [*to*]geth[*er*]. And also your produce will
      bec[*ome for you like*] one who sows diverse kinds, who forfe[*its
      together*] the seed, the ripe fruit, and the produce [*of*]

9   the [*vineyard*]. Your wealth with your flesh ... [*in*] your life they
      will be finished together, but in your life you will not find ...

TEXTUAL NOTES

103 ii 3. שׁׄ[ח]דׄ. See the discussion of this reconstruction in the commentary below.

103 ii 4. דורשׁם; 4Q418a 4 2: [דׄורשׁמׄ]ה.

103 ii 4. וׄאל; 4Q418a 4 2: אל.

103 ii 5. יׄדרשׁו; 4Q418a 4 3: דרוש אׄדׄרׄ[שׁו].

103 ii 7. בּׄכפרד. The supralinear *kaf* preposition is best understood as
a correction for the *bet* preposition. Not enough survives of the *bet*, however, to know whether a correction dot was placed over it.

103 ii 9. הונכה. The editors of DJD 34 read the trace of a *mem* before
this word, from which they reconstruct םׄ[גׄו]. As Tigchelaar explains, what
they discern as a letter trace is more likely a niche or recess in the edge of
the fragment (notice how the shadow in the photo of PAM 43.475 has the
same shape as the location in question). Also there is not enough space in
the lacuna for this supplement. See plate VI in Rey.

COMMENTARY

This fragment is important for two reasons. First, its envisioned addressee is a farmer, as in other 4QInstruction texts (see the commentary on 4Q423 5). 4Q418 103 ii supports the view that the document envisages an audience that comprises people with a range of humble and modest professions (see section 9 of the introduction). Second, the instruction of 4Q418 103 ii is halakhic. The text utilizes the prohibitions against "diverse kinds" (כלאים) in Lev 19 and Deut 22.[2] The other major instance of halakhah in 4QInstruction is the teaching on annulling vows in 4Q416 2 iv. 4Q418 103 ii and 4Q416 2 iv both illustrate that while legal concerns are in general not prominent in the composition, biblical law influences how 4QInstruction guides the *mebin* in his ordinary life. Structurally, three units can be discerned in the fragment: lines 2–3, which use a second person imperative when discussing the gathering of crops; lines 4–6, which favor the third person and also give agricultural advice, and lines 6–9, which revert back to the second person.[3] This third section is the main text for the halakhic issue of diverse kinds.

4Q418 103 ii 2

Of the three intact words in this line, one deserves mention—"farmers" (אכרים). Given the agricultural advice of the fragment, the term probably refers to the text's intended audience. It has been argued that in biblical Hebrew the word refers to agricultural laborers who do not own the land they work.[4] This is possible. This meaning would be consistent with the general emphasis in 4QInstruction on the poverty of the addressee. Some biblical verses imply that an אכר is a landless "farmhand," but other instances of the word do not necessarily demonstrate this precise meaning.[5] The term is likely a broad designation that can encompass various kinds of agricultural workers, including both small landowners and land-

---

2. Schiffman 2004, 94–99.

3. Rey 2009a, 117.

4. Gese 1962, 432–34.

5. See for example Isa 61:5; Jer 14:4; 31:24; Amos 5:16. In 2 Chr 26:10 King Uzziah hires out many "farmers" to work the lands, without any sense that they are cultivating land they own. Early Jewish literature never attests the word אכר outside of 4QInstruction. The word is also in the fragmentary text 4Q418 133 2 (in the plural, as in 4Q418 103 ii 2). See also Paul 1991, 179.

less workers. The intended audience of the composition probably includes both groups.

4Q418 103 ii 3

Line 3 retains part of an exhortation that involves the harvesting of crops. I reconstruct the word "new" (חד[ש]), understanding the term as denoting new grain or some other type of produce to be harvested.[6] The editors of DJD 34 prefer "[that which is con]secrated," transcribing [מקו]דש[7] (cf. Lev 27:16–25).[7] There is, however, not enough space for these letters, even if the word were spelled defectively. The relatively rare words "basket" (טנא) and "storehouse" (אסם) refer to harvesting in the Hebrew Bible, suggesting that this is also the case in 4Q418 103 ii.[8] "Basket" occurs in 4Q418 126 ii 12, in the context of bringing items to market, presumably agricultural produce (cf. 4Q284a 1 2, 4; Sir 31:14).[9] Since both terms are in the blessings of Deut 28 (vv. 5, 8), the bounty of the harvest may be understood as a consequence of the addressee's piety.

4Q418 103 ii 4–5

Not enough survives of these lines to interpret them successfully. I tentatively understand the first attestation of עת in line 4 as the subject of the verb שוה (meaning "to resemble"), but other options, in terms of the syntax and the meaning of the verb, are possible.[10] Lines 4 and 5 stress

---

6. Rey 2009a, 113. This has the support of Lev 26:10, which recommends that the stored grain be eaten to make room for the new (cf. 23:16; Num 28:26). For the supplement of the verb "to come" at the end of l. 2 to denote the arrival of harvest time, see, for example, Lev 25:22.

7. Strugnell and Harrington 1999, 330–31. They grant the reconstruction "new (crop)" as a possibility. See also the discussion of the root קדש in l. 9.

8. For "basket," note Deut 26:2–4 (cf. 28:17); for "storehouse," see Prov 3:9–10. That 4Q418 103 ii 3 discusses harvesting is also indicated by the term "land" in the parallel text 4Q418a 4 1. For the reconstruction "all [the fruit of your land]" used above for 4Q418 103 ii 3, see Strugnell and Harrington 1999, 480.

9. The term "storehouse" occurs nowhere else in early Jewish literature.

10. The verb could be a *hiphil*, meaning "to compare." It is also possible that עת is the object and that the subject of the verb was at the end of l. 3 and has not survived. The above translation assumes that "season," normally a feminine word in the Hebrew Bible, is understood as masculine, which occurs in later Hebrew. So also Strugnell and Harrington 1999, 330–31.

the act of examining (לדרוש) things in their "season" (עת).[11] In line 4 the seasons themselves may be examined, whereas in line 5 other things, perhaps the crops, are evaluated in their season. 4Q418 103 ii 4–5 may retain remnants of instruction about correctly observing the seasons and about inspecting the crops in order to know the right time when they should be harvested. This teaching is in 4Q423 5 5–6 (see commentary on this text). The word הליכי ("paths of") at the end of 4Q418 103 ii 5 is probably a construct plural of הליך, a *hapax* in the Hebrew Bible (Job 29:6).[12]

4Q418 103 ii 6

The first half of line 6 makes an enigmatic reference to "a spring of living water" (מקור מים חיים). The biblical metaphor of a spring of water is instructive for understanding the line. The metaphor often expresses that God or the Torah is nurturing and allowing life to flourish.[13] In 4Q418 81 1 the addressee's mouth is described as an "eternal spring" that blesses the angels. In 4Q418 103 ii 6 the key expression is a metaphor, as indicated by the *kaf* preposition. The metaphor, I suggest, refers to the harvest that is to be reaped by the addressee. The crops are like a "spring of living water" in that they provide sustenance to the *mebin* and give him life. That the metaphor denotes crops is also suggested by the enigmatic word אוט, translated here "resources." The term probably refers to some sort of material asset which cannot be precisely identified (see the commentary to 4Q416 2 ii 1).

---

11. 4Q418 103 ii 5 reads ידרשו and 4Q418a 4 3 [דרוש אדר[שו. The latter has an infinitive absolute, whereas 4Q418 103 ii does not. The main verb of the 4Q418a text can be understood as being in the first person. The editors of DJD 34 suggest that the spelling may be derived from the phonetic similarity of *aleph* and *yod*, and that אדר[שו] should be interpreted as if it were written with a *yod*, as in 4Q418 103 ii 5 (Strugnell and Harrington 1999, 481). Note the spelling of Jesse (normally ישי) as אישי in 1 Chr 2:13. See further Joüon and Muraoka 2008, 85 (§26e).

12. The only other occurrence of this word in early Jewish literature is also in 4QInstruction (4Q418 127 4). See Strugnell and Harrington 1999, 332.

13. The phrase "spring of living water" (מקור מים חיים) is used by Jeremiah to refer to God, whom the people of Judah have abandoned (2:13; 17:13; cf. 4Q504 1–2 v 2). The book of Proverbs uses a similar expression, "spring of life" (מקור חיים), several times. Proverbs 14:27, for example, states that the fear of the Lord is a spring of life (13:14; 16:22; cf. 18:4). See further the commentary on 4Q418 81 1.

4Q418 103 ɪɪ 6–9

The second half of line 6 begins the section that utilizes the biblical law of "mixed kinds" (cf. 4Q418 29 1). The passage starts with a reference to the "merchandise" (מסחור) of the *mebin* which should not be mingled, presumably with material that belongs to someone else (the phrase "your neighbor" is supplemented; cf. 1QS 6:22). The editors of DJD 34 speculate that מסחור may be an error for מחסור, a characteristic word frequently appearing in 4QInstruction that denotes one's lack or material need (e.g., 4Q417 2 i 19).[14] The "merchandise" reading, however, provides a plausible interpretation, and there is no compelling need to amend the text.[15] The merchandise is reasonably understood as the harvested produce of the preceding lines (ll. 3, 6). It is an agricultural surplus that the *mebin* can take to sell or trade, as in 4Q417 2 i 17–18 (see commentary above).

Line 7 explains the consequences of mixing one's merchandise with that of another person. "It" (the merchandise) would then be considered כלאים and is compared to a mule, a mixed animal (the product of a donkey and a horse).[16] The addressee is then compared to one who wears *sha'atnez* (שעטנז), a term that refers to prohibited cloth made of mixed textiles.[17] The labor of the *mebin* is likened to one who plows with an ox and donkey hitched together (ll. 7–8). The crop yield produced by such means would be considered כלאים and thus rendered unusable (see below on l. 8).

The instruction on farming in 4Q418 103 ii 6–9 adapts legal material from Lev 19:19 and Deut 22:9–11.[18] These verses strive to ensure that a principle of separation of different kinds of things is applied to one's daily

---

14. Strugnell and Harrington 1999, 332. These two terms occur together in 4QInstruction (4Q418 107 3–4).

15. Also, it is not clear what it would mean if the addressee were told not to mix his "lack" of material needs with that of someone else.

16. Mules are never mentioned in the biblical laws about diverse kinds, but this warning is presumably based on Lev 19:19, which prohibits one from breeding two different kinds of animals together (cf. m. Kil. 1:6; 8:2–6).

17. The word שעטנז is safely reconstructed in l. 7 because of the theme of improper mixing in the passage and the line's reference to flax and wool. The term *sha'atnez* has been understood as an Egyptian loanword (cf. m. Kil. 9:8). See Milgrom 2001, 1664; Lambdin 1953, 155, following a suggestion by Albright. Consult also Görg 1980, 13–17.

18. Strugnell and Harrington 1999, 333; Rey 2009a, 116–118; Kampen 2011, 141; Milgrom 2000, 1656–65; Carmichael 1995, 433–48; Shemesh 1998, 244–63; 2001, 181–203.

life, in terms of what a person wears and how he farms. While all three of these texts present mixing different materials as undesirable, they all differ from each other, as illustrated by the following chart:

The Law of Diverse Kinds in Leviticus, Deuteronomy and 4QInstruction

4Q418 103 ii 6–9	Deut 22:9–11	Lev 19:19
6b. your merchandise do not mix [with] that which [belongs to your neighbor]		
7a. lest it be of diverse kinds (כלאים) like a mule		19:19a. You shall not let your animal breed with a different kind (כלאים)
7b. and you be like one who wea[rs *sha'aṭnez*], with wool together with flax (בצמר ובפשתים)	22:11. You shall not wear *sha'aṭnez*, wool and flax, together (שעטנז צמר ופשתים יחדו)	19:19c. nor shall you put on a garment made of two different materials (בגד כלאים שעטנז)
7c–8a. and your work like one who plo[ws] with an ox and a do[nk]ey [to]geth[er] (כחור[ש] בשור] [ובח[מו]ר [י][חד]ו).	22:10. You shall not plow with an ox and a donkey yoked together לא־תחרש בשור־) (ובחמר יחדו)	
8b–9a. And also your produce will bec[ome for you like] one who sows diverse kinds (כלאים), who forfe[its together] the seed, the ripe fruit, and the produce [of] the [vine-yard].	22:9. You shall not sow your vineyard with different kinds of seed (כלאים), or the whole yield will have to be forfeited, both the crop that you have sown and the yield of the vine-yard itself.	19:19b. you shall not sow your field with two kinds of seed (כלאים)

The table demonstrates several points. First, the version of the law in Deuteronomy appropriates and reworks the version of the law in Leviticus, which is therefore older.[19] The prohibition regarding sowing different kinds of seeds together is limited in Deut 22:9 to the vineyard; this is not the case in Leviticus. Deuteronomy provides clarification that is not in Leviticus. Deuteronomy 22:11, for example, specifies that the enigmatic term שעטנז refers to wearing wool and flax together. Leviticus does not explain the term. Deuteronomy 22:10 prohibits yoking an ox and a donkey together in the field, whereas Lev 19:19 is against breeding different kinds of animals in general, without naming any specific type of animal.[20] Second, the passage in 4QInstruction is closer to the version of the law in Deuteronomy than to that of Leviticus.[21] The reference to plowing with an ox and donkey together in 4Q418 103 ii 7–8 accords with Deut 22:10. 4Q418 103 ii 7 mentions flax and wool, as does Deut 22:11. The proximity of the 4QInstruction text to Deut 22 explains the supplement of the word "vineyard" in 4Q418 103 ii 9 (cf. Deut 22:9).

Both Lev 19 and Deut 22 are framed as prohibitions. They rely upon the לא־תקטול form—"You shall not …" The only prohibition in 4Q418 103 ii 6–9 occurs in line 6, which urges the *mebin* not to mix his merchandise with that of his neighbor. He is not told to avoid sowing different kinds of seed together; rather his merchandise, if mingled, will be treated *as* produce farmed in this prohibited manner. He is not commanded to avoid wearing fabrics of different kinds together; rather he will be *like* someone who does this if he mixes his merchandise. The legal principle that diverse kinds are prohibited is applied to his merchandise (his crops).[22] 4QIn-

---

19. Milgrom 2000, 1658; Fishbane 1985, 58–63. See also Shemesh 1998, 263.

20. Shemesh 2001, 186–87.

21. Rey 2009a, 118.

22. 4QMMT and the Damascus Document make a similar move in that they invoke the biblical legislation of diverse kinds to argue against exogamy. 4QMMT B 75–82 reads "And concerning the practice of illegal marriage that exists among the people: (this practice exists) despite their being so[ns] of holy [seed], as is written, Israel is holy. And concerning his (i.e., Israel's) [clean ani]mal, it is written that one must not let it mate with another species; and concerning his clothes [it is written that they should not] be of mixed stuff; and he must now sow his field and vine[yard with mixed specie]s … But you know that some of the priests and [the laity mingle with each other and they] unite with each other and pollute the [holy] seed (as well as) their own [seed] with women whom they are forbidden to marry …" 4Q271 3 9–10 explains that a father should not give his daughter in marriage to an unsuitable man "for [that is

struction's appeal to biblical law assumes that combining diverse kinds should not be done. From this one can conclude that the *mebin* did in fact follow כלאים rules in his farming, but this is not explicit in the text.

The prohibition against mixing one's merchandise of 4Q418 103 ii 6 may mean that in the marketplace and on the way to the site of trade, the *mebin* should not store his material with that of another person. Perhaps he is to trade his merchandise himself and not in a joint venture with another person. The emphasis on not mixing his surplus with that of others is consistent with the general attitude of caution the composition adopts towards business and financial practices. 4Q416 2 ii 3–7, for example, recommends that the *mebin* not make a pledge for a loan for a neighbor, in effect mixing his own finances with that of another person.

4Q418 103 ii 8–9 asserts that the crop yield of the addressee would be rendered unfit, using the verb לקדוש and other terminology from Deut 22:9. This is another consequence of the *mebin's* mixing his merchandise (גוג; l. 8). This biblical verse urges one not to sow his vineyard (כרם) with diverse seeds "lest you forfeit the whole yield (פן־תקדש המלאה)," both the seeds (הזרע) that you have sown and the produce of the vineyard (תבואת הכרם) itself." If one mixes different seeds the full yield, including the seeds sown and the harvested crops, is rendered unusable. Deuteronomy 22:9 uses the verb לקדוש in the *qal* to denote that they are removed from ordinary use.[23] *Contra* the editors of DJD 34, the term [ש]יקד in 4Q418 103 ii 9 does not mean that crops sown with diverse seeds are to be consecrated to the sanctuary (which would probably be in the *piel*) (cf. m. Kil. 5:8; 7:2–4).[24] Offerings of produce grown in violation of כלאים legislation would not make an appropriate offering. As in Deut 22:9, the verb means in the *qal* that the harvest is forfeited and cannot be used. In this verse the references to seeds and produce explicate the term "whole yield" (מלאה), referring to the entire harvest (cf. Num 18:27). In 4Q418 103 ii 8–9 the refer-

---

כלאים, (plowing with) o]x and ass and wearing wool and linen together" (cf. 4Q481 1 2). Josephus writes that disregard for the law of diverse kinds could affect how people regard sexual reproduction (*Ant.* 4.228–230). 4Q418 81 2–3 asserts that God has separated the addressee from the fleshly spirit, a term for humanity writ large, the nonelect. As I argue in the excursus on marriage in chapter 1, this principle of separation informs the text's approach to marriage. Shemesh 1998, 263; 2001, 184–85; Schiffman 2004, 96–97; Baumgarten 1996, 175–77; Qimron and Strugnell 1994, 55–57.

23. Christensen 2002, 507–8; Fishbane 1985, 61.

24. Strugnell and Harrington 1999, 331, 333. Schiffman (2004, 94) also criticizes this point.

ences to seeds and the yield do not explain the meaning of המלאה. Rather, this word is the second entry in a three-item list—the seed, המלאה, and the yield (תבואה, a term that also occurs in Deut 22:9). This suggests that, in contrast to Deut 22:9, in 4Q418 103 ii 8 המלאה does not refer to the entire harvest but rather part of it, namely, the ripe fruit (or grain) that was produced. However, the basic idea is the same as in Deut 22:9: the entire harvest becomes unusable when diverse seeds are mixed.

4Q418 103 ii 9

The second half of line 9 begins a new topic: the finitude of wealth and of the physical body. The editors of DJD 34 suggest that the initial words of this portion be translated "your wealth together with your cattle (בשר)," arguing that both nouns denote forms of property and wealth.[25] However, the line emphasizes the "life" of the addressee and finitude, denoted by the verb "to be finished" (יתמו; cf. 4Q416 1 13). This suggests understanding בשר in the conventional sense of "flesh," referring to the body of the addressee, which will expire (cf. 4Q418 127 1–3).[26] The basic point is reminiscent of Qoheleth—both one's wealth and physical body come to an end. Not enough of the text survives to know why this theme is brought up (see also the commentary on 4Q418 69 ii 4–5).

25. Strugnell and Harrington 1999, 334.
26. Rey 2009a, 116.

13.
4Q418 126 II + 122 II

T<small>EXT</small>[1]

1   ]   ל[וֹא ישבוֹת אחד מכול צבֹאם ה]
            [

2   וא[תה מב]יֹן באמת מֹוד כול אוט אנשים א]
            [

3   כי בֹא[פֹ]תֹ אמת ומשקל צדק תכן אל כול מֹ[עשיהם
            [

4   פֹרשם באמת הוא שמם ולחפציהם ידרש[וּ
         מֹאל לוֹא]

5   יֹסתר כול וגם לוא נהיו בלוא רצונו ומחוכֹ[מתו
         יתֹן]

6   משפט להשיב נקם לפעלי און ופקודת שֹ[לום
            [

7   ולסגור בעד רשעים ולהרים ראוש דלים]
         ולהֹבֹיֹאֹם[

8   בכבוד עולם ושלום עֹד ורוח חיים להבדיֹלֹ[מבֹשֹר

9   כול בני חזה ובכוח אל ורוב כבודו עם טובו]
            [

10   ובאמונתו ישיחו כול היום תמיד יהללו שמו זֹ[הֹ]
            [

11   ואתה באמת התהלך עם כֹול דֹוֹרשיֹ [בֹינֹהֹ   vacat
            [

1. Strugnell and Harrington 1999, 349–52; Tigchelaar 2001, 102–3; Rey 2009a, 255–57 (covering ll. 1–10). The textual notes section refers to these works.

וּבידכה אוטֹהׁ ומטנאכה ידרוש חפצו ואתה מֹ[בין   12
[

ואם לוא תסׄיׄג ידו למחסורכה ומחסור אוטֹו]   13
[

או[טֹהו ואל ישׂיֹם מחפצֹו כי אל יׄס]ׄ   ] 14
[

ב]ׄידכה למֹתר ופרץ מקניב]ׄה   ] 15
[

עׄוׄלֹם בֹנֹוֹחֹלֹיׄכה]   [   ] 16
[

TRANSLATION

1   [... n]ot one of all their host ever rests ...

2   And y[ou, understandi]ng one, truthfully measure all resources of
men ...

3   for with an eph[a]h of truth and a measure of righteousness God
apportions all [their] d[eeds ...]

4   He has spread them out, in truth he has established them and by
all who delight in them [they] are studied [... From God nothing]

5   is hidden. And also, nothing exists without his good will and apart
from [his] wis[dom ... He will dispense]

6   justice to repay vengeance towards the evil-doers and the punishment of re[compense ...]

7   to lock up the wicked and to lift up the head of the poor [... to
lead them]

8   to eternal glory and everlasting peace and a spirit of life to separate[from the flesh ...]

9   all the children of Eve. And in the strength of God and an abundance of his glory with his goodness ...

10   and in his faithfulness they will extol all day. Constantly they will
praise his name and ...

11   vacat And you, in truth walk with all who seek [understanding ...]

12   and in your hand are his resources and from your basket he will
seek what he desires. And you, un[derstanding one ...]

13   and if his means are not sufficient for what you lack or the lack of
his resources ...

14   ... his [*reso*]urces. And God will arrange because of his desire, because God will ...

15   [... *in*] your hand with a surplus and you[*r*] livestock will increase ...

16   ... forever, according to your inheritors ...

TEXTUAL NOTES

126 ii 2: וא[תה מב]זֹּן. The first two letters of this phrase are from 4Q418 122 ii 5 (the first word of line 3 and part of the first letter in line 4 are also from this fragment). The join of fragments 122 ii and 126 ii of 4Q418, proposed by Tigchelaar, is plausible (see Rey, pl. 11). For the last two letters of וא[תה מב]זֹּן, consult PAM 41.909.

126 ii 2: מזֹד. The editors of DJD 34 and Tigchelaar read מיד. I follow Rey, who suggests מזֹד, understood as an imperative of מדד ("to measure"). The phrase "And you, understanding one" typically begins exhortations in 4QInstruction, in which case one would expect an imperative.

126 ii 8: להבדֹיל. See PAM 41.909.

126 ii 12: אוטה. This was the original word that was written. A second hand placed a cancellation dot over the *he* and added a supralinear *waw*, correcting the word to אוטו.

126 ii 13: תסיג. A second hand placed a cancellation dot over the *samek* and corrected it to a *sin*.

126 ii 14: [א]טֹהו. For this reading, see Tigchelaar. The editors of DJD 34 reconstruct פֹיהו but allow that the transcription used here is a possibility.

126 ii 16: בֹנוֹחֹלֹיֹכֹה. This reading is endorsed by Tigchelaar and was proposed by Strugnell in the Preliminary Concordance. In DJD 34 he and Harrington tentatively read וֹ[ ]זֹיֹֹ לֹיכה. They grant that the reading favored here is possible. Of these two options, בֹנוֹחֹלֹיֹכֹה is to be favored, but the paucity of the letter traces forces suggestions to remain tentative.

COMMENTARY

4Q418 126 ii divides into two distinct sections. Lines 1–10 praise God's creation of the world and assert his distribution of eschatological recompense to the righteous and the wicked. The first five lines are about the deterministic, structured nature of the created order, and lines 6–10 focus on eschatology. Lines 11–16 discuss the financial and material needs of the *mebin*. 4Q418 126 ii itself was preceded by at least one other column, of which only a single letter is extant. A better impression of this preceding column is now available by joining 4Q418 126 with fragment 122 of 4Q418 (see textual notes section). The join helps fill out part of 4Q418 126 ii 2–4 and provides approximately twenty words of 4Q418 126 i.

4Q418 126 ii 1

The first line of the column is fragmentary, but it asserts that all "their host" (צבאם) never ceases. Given the emphasis in lines 1–5 on the divinely established structure of the cosmos (see esp. ll. 4–5), line 1 probably declares that the angels, associated with stars, obediently follow their heavenly courses which God established for them. The line would thus be similar to 1 En. 2:1, which states that the luminaries of the heavens move according to their appointed order (cf. 41:5; 69:20; 72–82 *passim*).[2] 4Q418 126 ii 1 employs the form לא יקטול, denoting a general prohibition, conveying that the activity of the stars is not only in the future but is ongoing and constant. 4Q416 1 supports reading "host" in 4Q418 126 ii in a cosmological sense. The former text uses this word several times when emphasizing the regularity of the natural order. 4Q416 1 3, following the join with 4Q418 229, states that the stars do not cease (לדמות), and line 4 mentions "their host," suggesting that the stars are associated with the angels, as in 4Q418 126 ii 1 (see commentary above on 4Q416 1).[3]

4Q418 126 ii 2

The addressee is to "measure all resources of men." The goal is not simply to praise God as the creator of a structured cosmos, but also to encourage the *mebin* to assess and comprehend the orderly nature of the world. This is stressed elsewhere in 4QInstruction (e.g., 4Q416 1 1–9; 4Q418 69 ii 3–4; 4Q423 5 5–6). This is most likely the basic idea in 4Q418 126 ii 2 as well. However, the line is ambiguous in terms of what the *mebin* is to measure. The word אוט (translated here as "resources") probably refers to material resources or assets, the exact nature of which cannot be determined (see the commentary on 4Q416 2 ii 1).[4] Line 3 claims that God has arranged things with truth and balanced scales and line 4 that he fashioned the world according to his will (see below). Perhaps line 2,

---

2. Nickelsburg 2001, 155; Lelli 1999, 809–15.

3. Rey 2009a, 258.

4. 4Q418 127 5–6, like 4Q418 126 ii 2–4, combines the term אוט with a description of God's just scales.

in conjunction with the material that follows, relies upon some sort of microcosm/macrocosm parallelism, in which God's orderly creation can be discerned in both the natural cosmos and the world of the addressee, which includes resources such as food and shelter.

4Q418 126 ɪɪ 3

When God established the way things are, he did so "with an eph[a]h of truth and a measure of righteousness." An ephah (איפה) is a measurement of weight in the Hebrew Bible, and the term "measure" (משקל) also denotes weight (e.g., Lev 26:26; Ezek 4:16). God displayed a sense of balance and proportion when he created the world. This creation theology resonates with the theme of determinism in 4QInstruction. In 4Q418 81 9 the phrase "ephah of truth" refers to the divine disclosure of heavenly revelation to the *mebin* (which presumably included knowledge about the cosmos).[5] The expression "ephah of righteousness" (איפת צדק) appears in the Hebrew Bible (Lev 19:36; Ezek 45:10; cf. Job 31:6). 4Q418 126 ii may adapt this biblical phrase. The association in line 3 of the ephah with truth is consistent with a preference for the word אמת throughout this section of 4Q418 126 ii (ll. 2–4) and other texts that emphasize God's creation of the world (e.g., 4Q416 1 10, 13, 14; 4Q417 1 i 8). 4Q418 127 6, like 4Q418 126 ii 2, depicts God using balanced scales to assert the proper apportionment of elements of the created order: "With righteous balances he has weighed (שקל) all their measurements."[6]

While the just scales of 4Q418 126 ii 2 evoke the theme of creation, the fragmentary nature of the column prevents knowing what precisely God measures with his just scales. The surviving final letter of line 3 is probably a *mem*, and Rey, on the basis of Ps 90:17, plausibly reconstructs "their deeds" (מעשיהם).[7] So understood, the line emphasizes that God has established the ways of human beings with balance and just proportion.[8]

---

5. For "ephah," see also, for example, 4Q418 167a + b 4; 4Q418 15 4; for "measure," 4Q418 77 3–4; 4Q418 87 12.

6. Strugnell and Harrington 1999, 358–60; Puech 2005, 105–8.

7. Psalm 90:17 requests, "The deed of our hands establish (כוננה) for us." See Rey 2009a, 257.

8. 1 Enoch 43:2 employs imagery of the scale in a cosmological context: "And I saw a righteous balance, how they are weighed according to their light, according to the breadth of their spaces and the day of their appearing."

This reading provides a deterministic rationale for the call in line 2 for the addressee to measure the "resources" of human beings.

4Q418 126 ii 4

Lines 4–5 place the motifs of determinism and the ordered nature of God's creation in a cosmological context. He has "spread" (פרש) "them" out (l. 4). The antecedent of "them" has not survived. This is also the case with the second verb of the line (שמם). Rey suggests that these pronouns refer to the creation of humankind.[9] He bases this view on the second half of line 4, which he reconstructs as stating "they seek [knowledge]." This is possible, but I favor a different understanding of this text. The emphasis on the created order in the column suggests to me that the pronouns of line 4 refer to the elements of creation that God arranged properly (cf. 4Q417 2 i 19–20). 4Q418 126 ii 1 mentions the correct and unceasing motion of the stars. The verb פרש, used in line 4, denotes God's fashioning the world in 4Q417 1 i 8–11, a crucial passage for the creation theology of 4QInstruction. In 4Q417 1 i "truth" is a key term (l. 8), as in 4Q418 126 ii 2–4. It is likely that line 3 describes how God arranged the deeds of humanity, and that line 4 places this assertion in the broader, cosmological context of his deterministic creation of the world. The Treatise on the Two Spirits makes a similar interpretive move (e.g., 1QS 3:13–24).

The major issue for interpreting the second half of 4Q418 126 ii 4 is its use of the term חפץ. The term is prominent in this column and in 4QInstruction in general (see further below on l. 12). The term has a wide semantic range but denotes desire or an object that is desired. The word often refers to desires that relate to one's basic material needs, and thus can also mean "business," "concern," or "matter." It is normally pointed in the Hebrew Bible as חֵפֶץ. There is a different noun of the same root, חָפֵץ, which signifies not delight or joy itself but rather a person who delights.[10] This is probably the form of the root intended here, whereas the former meaning is more common in 4QInstruction (e.g., 4Q416 2 ii 8; 4Q417 2 i 12; 4Q418 158 3). This is suggested by Ps 111:2: "Great are the works of the Lord, studied by all who delight in them (דרושים לכל־חפציהם)."[11] The verse has the same vocabulary as 4Q418 126 ii 4 (לחפציהם ידרש[ו]). So understood, the line states that they—referring to the plural suffixes of the two previous

---

9. Rey 2009a, 258.

10. *HALOT*, 1:340.

11. Strugnell and Harrington 1999, 353.

verbs—are studied by those who delight in them (literally, "their delight-
ers"). The suffixes likely denote the elements of the created order. Aspects
of the cosmos are studied by those who take pleasure in apprehending their
structured and ordered nature. This sentiment in 4Q418 126 ii is similar to
that of the hymns of creation in Ben Sira (39:12–15; 42:15–43:33)—one can
better appreciate the nature of God by understanding the regularity and
structure of the cosmos. The third person suffix appended to חפץ probably
denotes anyone who delights in God's works, but it clearly includes the
community to which 4QInstruction is addressed.

4Q418 126 ii 5

This line makes explicit that the preceding material should be understood against the backdrop of a broad, cosmological context—nothing
comes into being that does not reflect God's will and wisdom. The creation theology of this section of 4Q418 126 ii supports my supplement
to the extant part of the sentence in lines 4–5: "[From God nothing] is
hidden." The trope that nothing escapes the notice of God is consistent
with the emphasis on his wisdom. Note the parallel in Sir 42:20–21: "No
understanding does he lack; no single thing escapes him. He regulates the
mighty deeds of his wisdom."

4Q418 126 ii 5 affirms that everything in existence testifies to God's
"good will" (רצון) and "wisdom" (חכמה). The word רצון can denote favor
or pleasure, but here it signifies the will of God. The term has this meaning
elsewhere in 4QInstruction. 4Q416 2 iii 12 urges that one constantly seek
to understand God's will. The elect in 4Q418 81 10 are called the "men
of (God's) pleasure (רצון)" (cf. Pss 40:9; 143:10; 1QS 9:24). The Hodayot
use the same term to assert God's control over creation: "without your
will nothing comes to pass" (1QH 18:4; cf. 9:10). Ben Sira also stresses
that God's will is evident in creation (42:15; 43:26). The reference to God's
wisdom resonates with 4Q417 1 i 8–9, which affirms that God fashioned
the world by means of the mystery that is to be and through his wisdom
(see commentary above). 4Q418 126 ii, in contrast to 4Q417 1 i, never
mentions the mystery that is to be. Given the importance of the *raz nihyeh*
in 4QInstruction, one can reasonably posit that it is assumed in 4Q418 126
ii that the rational nature of the cosmos can be apprehended through contemplation of this mystery. 4QInstruction agrees with Ben Sira that God's
will can be comprehended through observation. The Qumran wisdom text
diverges from Ben Sira in its assertion that esoteric, supernatural revelation should be studied (Sir 3:21–24). In 4QInstruction the mystery that is

to be provides a fuller impression of the nature of God than what can be achieved through perception of the world (see also the commentary on 4Q417 1 i 27).

4Q418 126 ii 6

The focus shifts in lines 6–10 to eschatological concerns. As in lines 1–5, the overall point is that reality is arranged according to a divine plan. The transition from cosmological speculation to eschatology is also found in 4Q416 1 1–14. 4Q417 1 i similarly includes both deterministic descriptions of the created order and assertions of divine judgment (ll. 11–12, 14–15). 4Q418 126 ii 6 asserts that God will dispense justice upon the wicked. Divine judgment is construed as inevitable. The line employs the phrase "to repay vengeance" (להשיב נקם), which describes in Deuteronomy God's judgment against the iniquitous (32:41, 43; cf. Sir 12:6; 35:23). The expression "evildoers" (פעלי און) is also biblical and may reflect reliance upon the Psalms, which frequently use the expression (e.g., 28:3; 94:4; 101:8). Parallelism suggests that after declaring vengeance upon the evildoers, 4Q418 126 ii 6 calls for "punishment of recompense" (פקודת [ש]לום) upon the wicked, or some other equivalent phrase.[12] A similar expression occurs in the Hodayot (פקודת שלומם) and can be plausibly reconstructed elsewhere in 4QInstruction (1QH 9:19; 4Q418 113 2; cf. 4Q416 1 13).

4Q418 126 ii 7

Line 7 preserves two infinitive phrases that contrast the eschatological fates of the righteous and the wicked. The expression "to lock up the wicked" combines the verb לסגור ("to close") with the preposition בעד; together they denote closing something, often a door. The words are used together when God shuts the doors of the ark in Gen 7:16 (cf. Judg 3:22). The Hodayot also help explain 4Q418 126 ii 7. In these thanksgiving hymns the wicked are sent to the netherworld: "The doors of the pit close behind (ויסגרו דלתי שחת בעד) the one who is pregnant with iniquity" (11:19; cf. 13:11; 4Q432 5 6). Similar imagery occurs in a fragmentary text of 4QInstruction: "and it was shut upon (ויסגר בעד) all the sons of in[iquity]"

---

12. The reconstructed word could either be שלום ("recompense") or the more common שלום, which would here mean "completion" (cf. l. 8). See Strugnell and Harrington 1999, 354.

(4Q418 201 2).[13] 4Q418 127 2, in the context of describing God's judgment, addresses the wicked who are to pass through gates toward death: "And your soul will desire that you enter into its gates (פתחיה) and that (the earth) bury and cover you."[14] 4Q418 126 ii 7 describes the ultimate fate of the wicked after God's judgment. They will go to Sheol. The image likely utilizes the mythological trope of the gates of the netherworld shutting upon them.[15]

Several other texts of 4QInstruction assert that the wicked will go to the netherworld. 4Q418 69 ii 6 affirms that the "foolish of heart" will go to the "eternal pit," a phrase that probably denotes Sheol (see commentary above). The word "pit" is elsewhere combined with Abaddon, indicating that the term signifies the netherworld (4Q418 177 2). 4Q418 102a + b 1 mentions the "pit" in the context of eschatological judgment (cf. l. 5). The "judgment of Korah" in 4Q423 5 1 may allude to the tradition that the wicked will go to Sheol, since the text alludes to the failed rebellion in the wilderness by Korah, who was swallowed up by the earth (Num 16). One can posit that 4QInstruction envisages some sort of eternal punishment for the wicked in Sheol. Conceptions of a cursed afterlife are present in Judaism by the second century B.C.E. (see the commentary on 4Q418 69 ii 6).[16] The word "pit" (שחת) can denote destruction or perdition. However, regarding what happens to the wicked in the "pit," 4QInstruction provides no detail and shows no interest. The focus is on their removal from this world, not their ultimate fate.

The next section of 4Q418 126 ii 7 describes the exaltation of the poor (להרים ראוש דלים). Given the contrast with the first half of this line, the text likely describes the eschatological recompense of the elect. This is also suggested by line 8, which mentions "eternal glory" and "everlasting peace." The emphasis on the "poor" (דלים) suggests that the term denotes the intended audience of 4QInstruction. 4Q416 2 iii 11–12 proclaims the elect addressee's reception of an "inheritance of glory" along with his elevation out of poverty, using the same key terms that are in 4Q418 126 ii 7 (ראוש, להרים). This line, however, unlike 4Q416 2 iii 11–12, refers to the

---

13. The verb "to close" is also associated with the fate of the wicked in the book of Mysteries (1Q27 1 i 5–6; cf. 4Q299 8 9). See further Goff 2007, 87.

14. Puech (2005, 105–6) reasonably understands this text as discussing Sheol. See also Strugnell and Harrington 1999, 358–59.

15. Paul 2010, 163–69.

16. Goff 2003b, 200–4. See also Collins 2001, 119–39.

"poor" in the third person and does not directly address the *mebin*. The assertion that God will raise up the "poor" during eschatological judgment probably provides motivation for the addressee to understand that he is poor. Poverty in this context does not simply denote economic standing. It metaphorically signifies a person's humility and piety, and his future favor by God during judgment (see section 9 of the introduction).

4Q418 126 ii 8

This line refers to eschatological rewards. The expressions "eternal glory" (כבוד עולם) and "everlasting peace" (שלום עד) denote the eternal life that the "poor" of line 7 are to receive. The expressions signify the ultimate rewards of the elect elsewhere in the Qumran scrolls.[17] This is clearly the case in the Hodayot, which attests these phrases in a form that is quite similar to line 8: "Your truth will shine forth for everlasting glory (כבוד עד) and eternal peace (שלום עולם)" (1QH 19:29–30). In this text, as in 4Q418 126 ii 8, the emphasis is on the eschatological future.[18] This supports the view discussed above that the "poor" of line 7 should be associated with the elect *mebin*.

4Q418 126 ii 8 ends with an intriguing phrase: "and a spirit of life (רוח חיים) to separate." In the Qumran scrolls the phrase "spirit of life" occurs only in the 4QD texts (not in CD). There the expression refers to the physical vitality of a living person. In the context of telling the priests to examine the hair of an afflicted person, it states, "the blood vessel is filled with bl[ood] and the sp[ir]it of life pulsates up and down in it" (4Q266 6 i 12 [par. 4Q269 7 8; 4Q272 1 ii 1; 4Q273 4 ii 3]). The text expounds on the subject of skin maladies (cf. Lev 13–14).[19] In the Hebrew Bible the expression is associated with "flesh" in the sense of creatures that are alive. In Gen 6:17, for example, God claims that he will send a flood that will destroy "all flesh in which is the spirit of life (רוח חיים)" (cf. 7:15; Job 7:7). Since 4Q418 126 ii 8 enumerates the eschatological rewards allocated to the elect, it

---

17. For the former phrase, note 1QH 5:23; 11:5; cf. 1QS 2:4; 1QSb 3:4; Sir 49:12; for the latter, see 1QH 7:29. Refer above to the reconstruction of שלום in 4Q418 126 ii 6.

18. The Hodayot emphasize a distinct moment of eschatological judgment in the future, but understand the elect person's fellowship with the angels as to some extent realized in the present. See Goff 2004, 284; Nitzan 2003, 131; Nickelsburg 2006, 188–93.

19. Baumgarten 1996, 53–54; 1990, 153–65; Rey 2009a, 259.

is reasonable to understand the key phrase as discussing the separation of the spirit from the body—that is, the moment of physical death after which the *mebin* will attain eternal life. I am inclined toward this interpretation, but the fragmentary state of the line prevents firm conclusions. Following my reading, one should supplement the line so that it states that the spirit of life is separated "from the flesh" (מבשר) rather than "from every spirit of darkness," as in DJD 34.[20]

4Q418 126 ii 8 merits comparison to 4Q418 81 1–2. In this text the *mebin* is separated from the spirit of flesh. This expression does not exclusively denote the wicked, but rather people who do not possess the knowledge required for salvation (see commentary above). Whereas "spirit of flesh" refers to humanity writ large, the mass of people who are not among the elect, "spirit of life" denotes the vitality of people who are living, encompassing the elect and the non-elect. The *mebin* is not among the spirit of flesh. He is not separated from the "spirit of life," it seems, until he dies.

4Q418 126 II 9

Line 9 praises God. In its original form, the text presumably declared that the allocation of eschatological rewards and punishments testifies to the dominion of God. The line mentions "an abundance of his glory (כבודו)." Line 8 refers to "glory" when describing the postmortem rewards of the *mebin*. "Glory" is elsewhere associated with the holiness or elect status of the addressee (e.g., 4Q416 2 iii 11–12; 4Q418 81 4–5). But here "glory" is an attribute of God, conveying his majesty and power, as does the word "strength" (כוח). Both motifs describe God in 4Q417 1 i 13 (which uses גבורה instead of כוח). The editors of DJD 34 reconstruct line 9 as stating that "they shall muse" upon the strength and glory of God. (Below I discuss who could be praising God.) So understood, divine praise is a topic in both lines 9 and 10. This is explicit in the latter case and a reasonable conjecture in the former. The original text of 4Q418 126 ii 9 may have asserted that when the *mebin* receives his allotted eschatological recompense (ll. 7–8), he will observe God's power and thus know his strength and glory, and praise him accordingly.

4Q418 126 ii 9 contains a fascinating but obscure reference to "all the children of Eve" (כול בני חוה). The figure of Eve is not prominent in early Jewish literature, although there is some discussion of this matriarch (e.g.,

---

20. Strugnell and Harrington 1999, 352.

Sir 25:24; Tob 8:6).[21] The phrase "children of Eve" (literally "sons") is rare in ancient Judaism, in contrast to the expression "son of Adam," a common phrase that signifies a human being, as in, for example, the book of Ezekiel. I have previously suggested that "all the children of Eve" may refer to the elect community to which 4QInstruction is addressed.[22] The rationale for this view is that elsewhere the *mebin* is associated with Adam (see below on 4Q423 1). Upon further reflection, a better interpretation is that "all the children of Eve" signifies humankind in a general sense. This is supported by a similar phrase in Ethiopic.[23] If one reads 4Q418 126 ii 8 as discussing the moment of death (the separation of the "spirit of life") and the reception of eternal life by the "poor," the text may have continued by stating that they *will no longer be among* "all the children of Eve." The elect addressee, who is in the lot of the angels (4Q418 81 4–5), would no longer be among humankind ("the children of Eve") because, having received a blessed afterlife, he is among the angels.

"They" will constantly exalt God's faithfulness and "praise his name." The latter phrase uses terminology that is very similar to 4Q416 2 iii 11, which exhorts the *mebin* to extol God. The key issue is who is praising God. An obvious possibility is the angels, since their adoration of God is a well-known trope in early Judaism (see the commentary to 4Q418 81 1). The antecedent is better understood as the elect who have joined the angels. This is suggested by the context of 4Q418 126 ii 8–10. These lines provide an account of the allocation of eschatological rewards that focuses on the elevation of the "poor." They receive "eternal glory" when they experience physical death. They will no longer be found with "all the children of Eve," or humankind, because they will be with the angels. There they will comprehend aspects of God such as his glory, strength, and faithfulness and, as a result, praise him constantly.

4Q418 126 II 11

This line demarcates a new section, beginning with a *vacat* and ואתה ("And you ..."). The addressee is to "in truth walk" (באמת התהלך). He is

---

21. Andrews 2007, 1–22; Rey 2009a, 260.

22. Goff 2003b, 220.

23. In Ethiopic the messianic title "the Son of Man" is *walda ʾegʷāla ʾemma-ḥeyāw*, literally "son of the offspring of the mother of the living," a reference to Eve. The segment *ʾegʷāla ʾemma-ḥeyāw* denotes humankind. See Caquot 1996, 27; Wold 2005b, 232–34.

told several times to "walk" in the *hithpael* elsewhere in 4QInstruction, typically in the sense that he should live in an upright and ethical manner (e.g., 4Q416 2 iii 10, 21; 4Q417 1 ii 10, 12; 4Q418 69 ii 3). This is presumably also the case in the line at hand. The elect are elsewhere associated with truth in 4QInstruction. For example, they are called "the sons of his truth" in 4Q416 1 10 and the "chosen ones of truth" in 4Q418 69 ii 10. In 4Q418 126 ii 11 the *mebin* is to walk with "all who seek [understanding]." The line provides encouragement, typical of sapiential instructions, for a student to ally himself with those who thirst for knowledge. 4Q418 69 ii 7 depicts the angels as those who seek after truth (דורשי אמת). Both the ideal student-addressee and the angels are presented as tireless seekers of knowledge. 4Q418 126 ii 11 urges the *mebin* to act like the angels.

4Q418 126 ɪɪ 12

This line, along with line 13, gives practical instruction to the addressee about meeting his basic material needs. Lines 12–13 (and perhaps 14) describe some sort of mercantile encounter between the *mebin* and another person. In line 12 "his" resources are in the hand of the *mebin* and this other person seeks his "desire" from the basket of the addressee.[24] The term "resources," which is also in lines 13 and 14, translates the enigmatic term אוט. The word probably denotes some type of material or financial asset (see the commentary to 4Q416 2 ii 1). The other person wants something *from* the addressee's "basket," presumably some sort of produce that he has grown and is attempting to sell or barter. The word טאנא has an agricultural meaning in the Hebrew Bible and 4Q418 103 ii 3 (see the commentary on this text). He seeks his "desire" (חפץ) from the basket of the *mebin*. The term "desire" elsewhere in 4QInstruction refers to items that are desired in the context of trade. In 4Q417 2 i 18, for example, the addressee is urged to sell his surplus, which is also a topic in 4Q418 126 ii 15, at a trading place (מחוז חפצו). The combination of the verb "to seek" (לדרוש) with the word "desire" is frequent in 4QInstruction, but it occurs nowhere else in the Dead Sea Scrolls. The two words describe people who seek to do business with the addressee in 4Q418 81 18 (see commentary there).[25] The "resources" of the third party are in the hand of the addressee.

---

24. For the suffix on "resources" in l. 12, see the textual notes section above.

25. The word חפץ is attested over twenty times in 4QInstruction, typically denoting a person's "desire" in relation to trade or meeting material needs. In addition to the texts mentioned above, consult 4Q416 1 2; 4Q416 2 ii 8; 4Q417 2 i 12; 4Q418 46 3;

This other person secures his basic needs through trade with the *mebin*. Through this exchange both parties meet their material needs.

4Q418 126 ɪɪ 13

Line 13 focuses on the addressee meeting his basic needs through what he receives from the third party. The transaction may not fully satisfy the *mebin*: "and if his means are not sufficient for what you lack (מחסורכה) ..."[26] The Hebrew of the beginning of this phrase literally states "And if his hand does not attain" (ואם לוא תשיג ידו). This phrase denotes poverty in Lev 5:11, which asserts that if one cannot afford (ואם לא תשיג ידו) two turtledoves or pigeons for the sin offering, one may substitute a tenth of an ephah of choice flour.[27] The expression is used in the penal code of the Community Rule in the case of a person who is unable to replace possessions that are lost (1QS 7:8). The trading arrangement may be unsuccessful in terms of helping the *mebin* meet his material needs. Both participants in the exchange are likely subsistence farmers who, in a good season, have produced enough crops to sell a surplus at market (cf. l. 15). The *mebin* is poor and elsewhere assumed to be a farmer (see the commentary to 4Q423 5). The fact that the other person is trying to meet his own material needs by trading with the addressee suggests that he is from the same low economic stratum as the *mebin*. 4Q418 126 ii 13 mentions the lack of *his* resources, referring to the trading partner (cf. l. 14), and the "lack" of the *mebin* (מחסורכה).[28] Both participants in the trading scenario of 4Q418 126 ii 12–13 are at a mid- to low financial level.[29]

4Q418 126 ɪɪ 14

This line contains an incomplete reference to "his" resources, presumably those of the trading partner of the *mebin*, since this suffix refers to

---

4Q418 88 ii 1; 4Q418 94 3; 4Q418 102a + b 2; 4Q418 103 ii 5; 4Q418 106 1; 4Q418 107 4; 4Q418 127 4; 4Q418 128 + 129 3; 4Q418 138 4; 4Q423 1 6. The term denotes God's desire in 4Q416 1 2. The word is used together with דרש in 4Q418 102a + b 4; 4Q418 126 ii 4; 4Q418 127 5; 4Q418 158 3 (cf. 4Q418 46 3; Sir 35:14). See also Strugnell and Harrington 1999, 356; Rey 2009a, 34; Tigchelaar 2001, 237–38.

26. For more on the term מחסור, see the commentary on 4Q417 2 i 17–18.

27. The expression appears to have a similar meaning in the fragmentary 4Q266 6 ii 12 (cf. Lev 14:32; 25:26; Num 6:21). See Murphy 2002, 173.

28. In 4Q416 2 ii 1 (par. 4Q417 2 ii 3) God fulfills the addressee's "lack of resources" by making food available (cf. 4Q418 107 4).

29. Goff 2003b, 158.

this person in lines 12 and 13. In line 14 God is to "arrange" something, but it is not clear what; this action is connected to "his desire" (חפצו; cf. l. 12).[30] Given that line 13 discusses the possibility that the trade may not be successful, line 14 should perhaps be interpreted along the lines of 4Q417 2 i 19–20. This text encourages one to rely on God if he cannot support himself (see commentary above). 4Q418 126 ii 14 may have analogously asserted that God will arrange that the addressee's material needs will be met even if his efforts at trade are unsuccessful, because of the deity's "desire" to do so (cf. 4Q416 2 ii 1).

4Q418 126 ii 15

Line 15 contains a fragmentary reference to the "surplus" of the *mebin*. This presumably refers to crops he does not need for himself but can trade. He is also given instruction on trading a surplus in 4Q417 2 i 17–18. 4Q418 126 ii 15 has a parallel reference to the "increase" (פרץ) of his livestock. The verb פרץ often means "to break through" in the sense of a breach, but in the Hebrew Bible it can also signify that one's livestock has increased (Gen 30:29–30; Job 1:10). The term מקנה may mean "property" in 4Q418 126 ii 15 in a general sense rather than "livestock." The term refers to live-stock elsewhere in the scrolls (4Q368 2 11; 4Q422 3 9). Not enough of the line survives to understand why the financial fortunes of the addressee are improving. Line 14 suggests that God will ensure that the economic situation of the *mebin* will improve.

4Q418 126 ii 16

Almost nothing from this line survives. It contains a form of נחל ("to inherit"), which often refers to the elect status of the addressee in 4QInstruction (see the excursus in chapter 4). The word here takes the unusual form of a plural participle with a second person suffix ("your inheritors"; cf. 4Q418 81 14).

---

30. The word אל occurs twice in the line. I take them both to be instances of the word "God," but the first may be a negation of the verb.

14.
4Q423 1

Text[1]

top margin

[עים]ן גן הלוא להשכיל נחמד נעים עץ וכל תנובה פרי וֹכל[   ] 1

ונחמד [

ולשמרו לעבדו המשילכה ובו דֹה[או]מ שֹכֹיל[ה]ל[   ] 2

vac נאות ג[ן   [

לכה תתן לא וכוחה לכה תצמיח ודֹרֹדֹר קיץ [והאדמה]   ] 3

◦[[

vacat   [במועלכה   ] 4

[[

◦ הֹ ◦[ל]ל [הורֹ[ות רחמי וכל ילדה [*vac*   ] 5

[[

לכֹה תצמי]ח כל כי חפציכה בכל [   ] 6

[[

ה ◦]בֹם [ובמטֹעֹ]   ] 7

[

Translation

1   ... and every fruit of the produce and every delightful tree, desirable for making one wise. Is it not a de[*lightful and desirable*] garden ...

2   ... for [*making*] one v[*er*]y wise? He has given you authority over it to till it and keep it. *vacat* A [*lush*] gar[*den* ...]

---

1. Strugnell and Harrington 1999, 507–8; Tigchelaar 2001, 141; Elgvin 1997a, 278–79; Wold 2005b, 113–14. The textual notes section refers to these works. Elgvin is the editor of 4Q423 1 in DJD 34.

3   [... *but the earth*] will make thorn and thistle sprout for you and
    its strength will not yield to you ...

4   ... when you are disloyal. *vacat* ...

5   ... *vacat* she has given birth and all the wombs of pregnant
    [*women* ...]

6   ... in all your desires because it will make everything spro[*ut for
    you* ...]

7   ... and with the planting ...

TEXTUAL NOTES

1 1: וכל. The editors of DJD 34 claim that the same letters were written supralinearly above the second וכל in the line and then erased. The
supralinear traces are too fragmentary to confirm this.

1 2: [נ]ג̇ [נאות]. The editors of DJD 34 reconstruct ג̇ [נ]עו̇ת. So also
Wold. This reading presumes the join of fragments 1 and 2 i of 4Q423.
Below this join is critiqued.

COMMENTARY

This short fragment makes the remarkable claim that the *mebin* has
been given authority over the garden of Eden. To teach him about his elect
status, he is likened to Adam. 4Q423 1 1–3 is important for understanding
the interpretation of Gen 1–3 in early Jewish literature. Lines 5–7 of 4Q423
remain obscure, but deal with childbirth. The complete column may have
originally presented Adam and Eve as a paradigm of ideal marriage that
encourages the *mebin* to marry and have children.

    Text-critically, the main issue is whether fragments 1 and 2 i of 4Q423
are from the same column or not.[2] According to the editors of DJD 34,
they are.[3] So understood, line 7 attests the word "planting" (frg. 1) and,
from frg. 2 i, a reference to good and evil. Wold endorses the join.[4] Tigchelaar, however, expresses caution and presents the two fragments separate-
ly.[5] Skepticism regarding the join is warranted. The putative join between
the fragments is distant, meaning that the two pieces do not directly fit

    2. 4Q423 1 was originally classified as 4Q423 2 and frg. 2 as frg 1.
    3. Elgvin in Strugnell and Harrington 1999, 506. See pl. 30 for the placement of
the two fragments.
    4. Wold 2005b, 113.
    5. Tigchelaar 2001, 141. This move is followed by Kampen (2011, 182–83).

together. Such joins, while possible, should in general be treated with caution. Other physical factors also argue against the join.[6]

4Q423 1 1

The fragment contains a description of the garden of Eden. The language of the column draws directly from the book of Genesis.[7] The statement of line 1 כל עץ נעים נחמד להשכיל ("every delightful tree, desirable for making one wise") accords with Gen 2:9 and 3:6. The first verse from Genesis describes the garden as containing "every tree that is desirable (כל־עץ נחמד) to the sight"; in the second, the tree of the knowledge of good and evil is "desirable to make one wise" (נחמד העץ להשכיל). The author of 4QInstruction apparently connected these two verses on the basis of their common word נחמד ("desirable"). He did not slavishly reproduce the text, but rather creatively reformulated its language. 4QInstruction intensifies the attractiveness of the trees of the garden by using two adjectives, נחמד and נעים ("desirable"; "delightful"). Genesis 1–3 uses the first adjective but not the second. The word "delightful" (נעים) probably conveys that the trees are physically beautiful. The term describes a woman's beauty in the Song of Songs and Sarah's beauty in the Genesis Apocryphon (Song 1:16; 1QapGen 20:2; cf. Sir 45:9). The phrase "every fruit of the produce" in 4Q423 1 1 is not in Genesis and contributes to the column's portrait of the garden as lush and abundant in fruit (cf. 1QS 10:15). The incomplete rhetorical question at the end of line 1 underscores that it should be obvious to the *mebin* that the garden is beautiful and can provide knowledge.

4Q423 1 1 elides Gen 2:9 and 3:6 to emphasize that *all* the trees of the garden provide wisdom. In Genesis itself the two verses are quite differ-

---

6. If one were to grant this join, frg. 2 i would attest the left edge of the column and its margin. One would then have to admit that the first four lines of the reconstructed column are markedly shorter than the following lines (see pl. 30 of DJD 34). I would be more prepared to accept the join if the line lengths of the reconstructed column were more consistent. Furthermore, if one wants to make a distant join, it is not clear that the placement of the two fragments in DJD 34 is correct. Line 2 of the reconstructed column is construed in DJD 34 (507) as attesting the phrase "An [enjoya]ble g[arden]" (ג.[נעו[ן]ח[ת). The reconstruction presumes the distant join, with the first visible letter of the phrase on the end of frg. 1 and the second on frg. 2 i. However, the space allotted between the two fragments in the image in DJD 34 does not leave enough room for the four letters required for this phrase. See also Tigchelaar 1999, 55.

7. Wold 2005b, 114; Elgvin in Strugnell and Harrington 1999, 509.

ent, despite their common terminology. Genesis 2:9 uses the term נחמד
for all the trees of the garden. In 3:6 the word contributes to Eve's realization that the tree of the knowledge of good and evil is desirable. The latter
verse asserts that this tree, not all of them, can make one knowledgeable
(להשכיל).[8] Genesis 2:9 does not claim that all of the trees of Eden can provide wisdom, but rather that they are desirable to look at (נחמד למראה)
and that they produce good food. 4Q423 1 1 applies the phrase "to make
one wise" of Gen 3:6 to the entire garden, a claim not made in Genesis
itself.[9] There is no sense that the knowledge of good and evil is restricted
to a single tree. Furthermore, there is no indication in 4QInstruction of
any prohibition from eating any of the trees, in contrast to Gen 2:17. This
omission is also found in Ben Sira's account of the creation of humankind.[10]

4Q423 1 2

In 4QInstruction Eden functions as a metaphor for the knowledge that
the *mebin* can obtain through his elect status. This is suggested by the striking statement in line 2 that he has been given authority over the garden (בו
המשילכה). He is entrusted to "till" and "keep" the garden (לעבדו ולשמרו;
for more on this phrase see below). This is another adaptation of Genesis
language, utilized to explain to the addressee the nature of his elect status.
According to Gen 2:15, God places Adam in the garden to till and keep
it, using the same verbs as in 4Q423 1 2.[11] The verb "to give authority" is
used elsewhere in 4QInstruction to refer to the special status of the *mebin*.
4Q418 81 3 uses the verb המשיל, also in the *hiphil*, to claim that God has
entrusted him with his special "inheritance" (cf. 4Q416 2 iii 11–12).[12] A
key part of his elect status is access to the mystery that is to be. As argued

---

8. Cf. 4Q265 7 14: "[for] the garden of Eden is holy and all its young shoots which
are in its midst are holy." Consult Eshel 1997, 10–11.

9. The verb להשכיל is repeated in 4Q423 1 2. See also Wold 2005b, 115.

10. Sir 17:7: "He filled them with knowledge and understanding and showed
them good and evil." Cf. 4Q303 8–9; 4Q305 2 2–3. The prohibition against eating the
fruit is mentioned in 4Q422 1 10 and 4Q504 8 7 (cf. 1 En. 25:4). See further Chazon
1997, 14, 20; Kugel 2001, 164–65; Levison 2010, 300–2; Schmid and Riedweg 2008.

11. The verb לעבוד denotes working the soil also in Gen 2:5; 4:2, 12. The verbs
have feminine suffixes in Gen 2:15, but masculine ones in 4Q423 1 2. As Elgvin in
Strugnell and Harrington (1999, 509) suggests, this is probably an intentional change
reflecting the more common masculine gender of the word גן.

12. As discussed in the commentary to 4Q416 2 iv, this verb is used in both that
column and Gen 3 to describe the authority of the husband over the wife.

in the commentary on the vision of meditation passage (4Q417 1 i 13–18), the addressee is to emulate the "spiritual people" who are likened to angels. These people have access to the same heavenly revelation (the vision of meditation) that Adam had in the garden. 4Q423 1 2 implies, by metaphorically placing the *mebin* in the garden, that he has the potential to obtain the same knowledge that Adam once possessed in Eden, a restoration of primordial knowledge.[13] The mystery that is to be is not mentioned in 4Q423 1, but this revelation is likely alluded to in line 2. 4Q417 1 i 6–8 claims that he can learn the knowledge of good and evil through studying the *raz nihyeh*.[14] The *mebin*, like Adam, can attain the knowledge of good and evil. This knowledge is not understood in 4QInstruction as simply knowing right from wrong. As discussed in the commentary on 4Q417 1 i 6–8, this knowledge denotes the acquisition of wisdom in a broader sense, an understanding of the created order and the divine deterministic scheme that guides it. The Treatise on the Two Spirits supports this understanding of the knowledge of good and evil, connecting this trope to its deterministic understanding of creation.[15] The view that both the *mebin* and Adam acquire the knowledge of good and evil, understood as divinely revealed knowledge about the created order, is consistent with several other ancient Jewish texts that associate Adam with angels. The Treatise on the Two Spirits asserts, for example, that God discloses "the wisdom of the sons of heaven" to the elect so that they can attain the "glory of Adam," a phrase that probably denotes eternal life (1QS 4:22–23; cf. CD 3:20; 1QH 4:27). Jubilees presents the angels as teaching Adam (3:15). In 3 Baruch angels plant the garden (4:7–15; cf. Pss. Sol. 14:3).[16]

4Q423 1 2 uses the verb המשיל to describe the authority of the addressee over Eden. The word does not only allude to God's bestowal

---

13. Macaskill 2007, 110. Also observe the intriguing but fragmentary phrase in 4Q418 251 1, "[the inher]itance of Adam" (נח[לת אדם]). It is tempting to speculate that the text originally discussed the addressee's special inheritance (his elect status) as akin to the "inheritance of Adam." It is also possible that אדם refers to humankind and the text stated that God has established the inheritance of all people as in, for example, 4Q418 81 20.

14. Note the fragmentary reference to knowing good and evil in 4Q423 2 i 7.

15. The Treatise concludes its teachings about the nature of the world by stating: "For God has sorted them into equal parts until the appointed end and the new creation. He knows the result of their deeds for all times [everlas]ting and has given them as a legacy to the sons of man so that they may know good [and evil]" (1QS 4:24–26).

16. Additional parallels are discussed in the commentary on 4Q417 1 i 16–17.

of elect status to him, as mentioned above. It also resonates with early Jewish traditions regarding the grant of dominion given to Adam in Gen 1 (vv. 26, 28). This biblical chapter employs the relatively infrequent verb לרדות to denote Adam's power over the creatures of the world.[17] Several ancient Jewish texts that recount God's wish for Adam to rule the world, however, employ not this verb but rather המשיל.[18] This is evident in the Hebrew Bible itself. Psalm 8, which deals with the creation of humankind, claims: "You have given him (man; Adam) dominion (תמשילהו) over the works of your hands" (v. 7 [Eng. v. 6]). 4QWords of the Luminaries uses the same verb to describe Adam's authority over the garden: "[in the gard]en of Eden which yo[u] planted you made [him] rule ([המשלת]ה אותו)" (4Q504 8 6).[19] The Treatise on the Two Spirits uses the key root in a similar way: "He created Adam for dominion over (לממשלת) the world" (1QS 3:18).

The *mebin* is not simply given Eden as a gift. He is supposed to work in the garden. As mentioned above, he is to "toil" and "keep" the garden. The emphasis on toil helps the garden function as a metaphor for his acquisition of wisdom. The addressee obtains knowledge from the study and contemplation of the mystery that is to be, not simply from its disclosure. Eden is not evoked as the ultimate abode of the righteous in the manner of texts such as 1 Enoch 32–33.[20] Eden denotes what the present should entail—the *mebin* studying and meditating upon the mystery that is to be.[21] Given that the intended audience includes farmers (see 4Q423 5), the motif of working the land would have resonated with this community (note the commentary below on 4Q423 1 6).[22]

---

17. Cf. Gen 9:7; Lev 26:17; Sir 44:3.

18. Barzilai 2007, 21–22; Chazon 1997, 16, 22.

19. 4Q422 1 9–10; 4Q287 4 2; 4Q381 1 7. Cf. Wis 9:2.

20. Note, however, that 4QInstruction's emphasis on the beauty of the garden's trees is consistent with this eschatological tradition. See Tigchelaar 1999, 38–49; Shimoff 1995, 145–55.

21. As argued in section 6 of the introduction, the ultimate rewards of the *mebin* probably include life after death with the angels. It is not impossible that this blessed state is understood to take place in a restored garden of Eden. This, however, is never stated in 4QInstruction.

22. Consult also the discussion of 4Q423 5 6 in the following chapter. This line refers to the knowledge of good and evil when discussing the farming practices of the addressee.

4Q423 1 3

"Thorn and thistle" can be produced for the *mebin*. The phrase of line
3 קיץ ודרדר תצמיח לכה ("[the earth] will make thorn and thistle sprout
for you") is found verbatim in Gen 3:18 (cf. Hos 10:8; Isa 32:13). In Genesis 3 the "thorn and thistle" are produced by the earth (האדמה; v. 17).
They exemplify the harsh conditions that the primal couple face upon their
expulsion from Eden. The second part of 4Q423 1 3 reads "and its strength
will not yield to you" (וכוחה לא תתן לכה). This shows additional reliance
upon Genesis. Genesis 4:12 states "it [the earth] will no longer yield to its
strength (לא־תסף תת־כחה לך)." This is part of the description of Cain's
punishment for the murder of his brother. I argued above that the exegetical strategy of 4Q423 1 1 is to combine material from Gen 2:9 and 3:6 on
the basis of their common word נחמד. A similar approach is at work in
line 3, since both Gen 3:18 and 4:12 assert that "the ground" (האדמה) will
be harsh in terms of growing food.[23] Because "the ground" is important for
both verses in Genesis, the word is reasonably supplemented in 4Q423 1
3, understood as the subject of the extant verbs and the antecedent of the
feminine suffix of "strength."[24]

In both Gen 3:18 and 4:12 the harshness of the soil is emphasized in
the context of expulsion—Adam from the garden and Cain from his family.
Expulsion is, by contrast, never a theme in 4QInstruction. The assertion
that the *mebin* has authority over the garden assumes that he has access to
it, not that he is prohibited from it. One should not interpret 4Q423 1 3 as
envisioning the addressee as banished from the garden. A better reading is
that the garden itself can produce "thorn and thistle."[25] This is not the case
in Gen 1–3. 4Q423 1 3 describes a garden that is shoddy and in poor condition. If a flourishing, luxuriant garden is a metaphor for the *mebin*'s successful acquisition of wisdom, its decline symbolizes his failure to achieve
the pedagogical goals of the composition. The garden can symbolize either
the right or the wrong path. If he does not study the mystery that is to
be, he will not attain knowledge, and his elect status will be in jeopardy.
Note also the fragmentary reference to the addressee's being disobedient
in 4Q423 1 4. This suggests the behavior that results in the degradation of
the garden includes not simply a lack of study but of ethics as well.

---

23. The Apocalypse of Moses also conflates Gen 3:18 and 4:12 when recounting
Adam's expulsion from Eden (24:2). See Dochhorn 2002, 351–64.

24. Elgvin in Strugnell and Harrington 1999, 507.

25. Goff 2010a, 7.

The Garden of Eden in 4QInstruction and the Hodayot

The interpretation that in 4Q423 1 3 the garden can yield "thorn and thistle" is supported by the Hodayot. There are several affinities between this composition and 4QInstruction.[26] The Hodayot are written by a teacher who claims to disclose supernatural revelation to his students (e.g., 12:28). They are understood to have elect status. Not unlike 4QInstruction, the Hodayot assert that their envisioned students are in the lot of the holy ones. Both texts use the term "eternal planting" to describe their respective addressees (1QH 14:16, 18; 4Q418 81 4–5, 13).[27] The Hodayot metaphorically portray the flourishing of the elect community with the image of branches of the "eternal planting" being nurtured in the streams of Eden (1QH 14:19; cf. Gen 2:10–14). The authorial voice of the teacher figure in the Hodayot describes himself as being at the center of a luxuriant garden filled with trees (16:5–9). He claims that he has the power to turn the garden into a wasteland: "When I withdraw (my) hand, it (the garden) becomes like a juniper [in the wilderness], and its rootstock like nettles in salty ground. (In) its furrows thorn and thistle (קוץ ודרדר) grow up into a bramble thicket and a weed patch" (ll. 25–26). Language from Gen 3:18 describes not the expulsion of the elect from Eden, but rather the collapse of the garden itself. As in 4QInstruction, the elect are understood as being in a sense in Eden, and this situation is considered somewhat precarious, with the garden vulnerable to decline and ruin. Both compositions describe Eden in this way to make different points. The speaker of the Hodayot is eager to assert his own access to revelation, which he transmits to his students. He emphasizes his own power over the garden. He is in its midst and can change its verdant status if he wishes. By contrast, the teacher-author of 4QInstruction shows much less interest in himself. He does not stress his control over his students. Rather he exhorts them to make the right choices in life. He never praises his own wisdom or access to revelation. Unlike the Hodayot, he does not emphasize that he has the power to turn the garden to a desert. Rather, it is the responsibility of the student-addressee to maintain the verdant condition of the garden through diligence and hard work.

---

26. Goff 2004, 263–88. Consult further Macaskill 2007, 86–88; Hughes 2006, 150–59, 178–81.

27. Note the fragmentary reference to "planting" in 4Q423 1 7 (see below).

4Q423 1 4

Only one phrase is extant in this line, a reference to the disloyalty of the addressee (cf. 4Q416 2 iii 3; 4Q418 101 ii 5; 4Q418 159 ii 2). The lost text in lines 3–4 presumably elaborated upon forms of behavior that would result in the decline of the garden. Line 4 also has a lengthy *vacat*, suggesting that the material that follows begins a new section.

4Q423 1 5

It is unfortunate that little of lines 5–7 survives. These lines apparently made some sort of connection between the authority of the addressee over Eden and childbirth. Line 5 attests the word ילדה, which may be understood as either "she has given birth" or "her child." The line mentions "all the wombs" of pregnant women.[28] There is also an unclear reference to production in line 6, which may also invoke the theme of fertility (see below). Line 5 probably discusses Eve and childbirth. Both semantic options given above for ילדה assume one mother (who has either given birth or whose child is mentioned). Given the focus of the column on Adam and the garden, the woman at issue is likely Eve. The reference to multiple wombs suggests that the line in its original form stated that all women give birth because of Eve, the first woman to give birth. Wold suggests that this line may refer to the curse in Gen 3:16.[29] This verse is indeed significant, since it establishes a connection between Eve and childbirth (she bears her first child, Cain, in Gen 4:1). Unlike Gen 3:16, the extant material of 4Q423 1 5–7 never emphasizes the woman's pain in childbirth (cf. Apoc. Mos. 25:1). The column also never mentions that her husband rules over her, but on the basis of 4Q416 2 iv this can be assumed (see commentary above).

The message of line 5 is probably that as Adam and Eve had children, the *mebin* should do the same. This is consistent with lines 1–2, which stress that he should work and till the garden. He should be productive and fruitful not only in terms of his education but also as a father. The path advocated by 4QInstruction does not only include contemplation of

---

28. Elgvin in Strugnell and Harrington (1999, 510) argues that the plural construct form רחמי means "compassion" or "mercy." He is followed by Wold 2005b, 114. Given the line's clear context of childbirth, the word much more likely denotes the "wombs of" pregnant women. So also Kampen 2011, 182.

29. Wold 2005b, 116. Eve is punished in this verse but, strictly speaking, it contains no curse. The ground is cursed in v. 17.

the mystery that is to be. It also consists of marrying and having children.
Elsewhere the composition stresses childbirth, and it is reasonable to posit
that the male addressee was encouraged to have children.[30]

4Q423 1 6

The theme of fertility may have extended into line 6, which makes a
vague reference to "everything" being produced. The verb ‏[ח]‏‏להצמי‎ has a
feminine subject, as in line 3, suggesting that the implied subject is not the
garden, which in this column is a masculine word (see l. 2). The subject
could be Eve or perhaps the wife of the addressee. Another possibility is
"the earth" (‏האדמה‎), which is the likely subject of this verb in line 3 (see
above).[31] The word "everything" could refer to the idea that all people are,
in a sense, children of Eve. Or if the subject is "the ground," the line may
refer to the production of crops.[32] Conclusions must remain tentative, but
the latter option is supported by several texts of 4QInstruction that understand that the intended addressee could be a farmer (see the commentary
to 4Q423 5). His charge to toil in Eden (l. 2) may have been used to explain
whatever agricultural success he attains.

4Q423 1 7

Only one word is extant in this line, but it is quite significant—
"planting" (‏מטע‎). This evokes both Eden and the phrase "eternal planting,"
an expression that in other early Jewish texts and 4QInstruction signifies
the elect community (see the commentary on 4Q418 81 13). Though the
context of the term has not survived, its presence in 4Q423 1 strengthens
the view, discussed above, that Eden functions in this column as a metaphor for the elect status of the addressee and his potential to obtain knowledge once possessed by Adam in the garden.

---

30. 4Q415 9 2; 4Q415 11 11; 4Q423 3a 3; 4Q423 3 3–4. See also the first excursus
in the chapter on 4Q415 2 ii.

31. So Elgvin in Strugnell and Harrington 1999, 511.

32. The phrase "children of Eve" in 4Q418 126 ii 9 is likely a general designation
for humankind (see the commentary on this text).

15.
4Q423 5

Parallel text: 4Q418a 3 (underlined)

Text[1]

1a	עֿם כול זקני	[והשמר לכה פֿן
	תשׁיֿב ללוֹוֹ כֿוהֿ[ן]	
1	]ֿה את משפֿט קורח	
	ואשֿר גלה אוזנכה	
2	[ברז נהיה]∘∘קוֹ∘[ ]וֹֿהֿ∘ קֿבֿוֹץֿ[ר]וש אבות[∘∘	
	] דֿ ונשיא עמכה	
3	הו]אֿ פלג [נ]ֿחֿלת כל מושלים ויצר כל מעשֿה	
	בידֿו והוא פעולת	
4	מעשׂיהמה ידע וישפו]ט כולם באמת יֿפקוד לאבות ובנים ל[גרֿיֿ]ֿם	
	עם כל אזרחים יֿדבר	
5	אם אתה]אֿיֿש אדמה פקוד מועדי הקיץ ואסוֿף תבואֿתכה	
	בעתה ותקופת	
6	הקציר למועדו ה]תֿבֿונן בכל תבואתכה ובעֿבֿוֿדֿתכה השכֿ[ל למען	
	תדע ה]טֿוב עם הרע	
7	אֿ]יֿש שכל את בעל אולת הֿ] [לֿ[	
	שים כן איֿשׁ	
8	שכל]]ו כול הֿ[ ]ק יאמר]	
	בֿר]וֹב שכלו ∘[ ]	
9	יֿ]הֿיה בכל [דֿר]כֿו אשר בטֿל∘[	
	ללא]	

1. Strugnell and Harrington 1999, 518–19; Tigchelaar 2001, 142–43; Rey 2009a, 119–21; Elgvin 1997a, 290–91; Scott 2001, 194–202. The textual notes section refers to these works. Elgvin is the editor of 4Q423 5 in DJD 34.

$$\text{]ע᷂ בֹּכֹמֹה ואֹףֹ[} \qquad \text{]לֹ[} \qquad \text{]} \quad 10$$

$$[$$

TRANSLATION

1a [...*wi*]th all the el[*ders of* ...] and take care lest you return to Levi
the prie[*st*]

1 ... the judgment of Korah and as he uncovered to your ear

2 [*the mystery that is to be* ...] gather [*the h*]ead of the fathers ...
and the leader of your people

3 [... *H*]e apportioned the [*in*]heritance of all rulers and fashioned
every deed with his hand. As for him, the reward of

4 [*their deeds he knows. He will jud*]ge all of them in truth (and)
visit upon fathers and sons, upon [*sojourner*]s together with every
native-born. He will speak

5 [... *if you are*] a farmer, observe the times of summer and gather
your produce in its time and the season

6 [*of the harvest at its appointed time. Con*]template all your produce
and your work comprehe[*nd so that you may have the knowledge
of*] good and evil

7 [... *a m*]an of understanding with a fool ... thus a man

8 [*of understanding* ...] all ... he will say [... *in the abun*]dance of his
intelligence

9 [... *it will*] be in his entire [*pa*]th which ... without

10 ... with you and even ...

TEXTUAL NOTES

5 1a. עֹם כול זקנֹי. This phrase is from 4Q418a 3 2 and is supplemented
on the basis of the overlap between line 3 of that fragment and 4Q423 5 1.
The exact placement of the text in 4Q423 5 cannot be established.

5 1a. וֹהשמר לכה פֹן תשֹׁוֹב ללוֹיֹ כוהֹ[ן]. This text is superscript in two
scribal hands that are different from the rest of the column.[2] Line 1a was
added secondarily. The first two words of the line are much larger than the
others.

---

2. Elgvin in Strugnell and Harrington (1999, 518) understands the first two words
as cursive and the rest as semicursive. The *shin* of וֹהשמר could be understood as semicursive. See Rey. Consult also Yardeni 2002, 181, 187; Cross 1961, 149, 162.

5 2. קְבֹוֹצֵ. I follow Rey (who reads קְבֹוֹצֵ○○). קְבֹה○○ is transcribed by Elgvin (in DJD 34 and 1997a) and Tigchelaar. Rey's reading is compatible with the traces (the visible descender, for example, could be from a final *ṣade*) and produces a coherent reading. The first letter trace that commentators discern appears to go with the preceding word. The second, while perceptible on PAM 42.592, is more likely shadow (compare 43.535).

5 2. וש[ר]. Before this word both Elgvin (in DJD 34 and 1997a) and Tigchelaar supplement כל ("every"). So also Scott. This addition is reasonable semantically. However, there is no visible upper stroke of the *lamed* where one would be expected. The space between the words "gather" and "[h]ead" may simply be greater than normal.

5 3. כל מעשׂה. These words are visible on a scrap that is joined to the fragment in PAM 43.535, not 42.592. The *lamed* of ל[גור]מֹ from the following line is also on this piece.

5 9. ללא. Commentators discern an illegible letter-trace after this word. But the mark in question appears to be shading rather than from ink. The letters of this section in lines 6–9 are faded and in general difficult to read.

COMMENTARY

This poorly preserved text falls into three sections. Lines 1a–4 refer to leaders of some sort and stress that all people will face judgment. Lines 5–6, which contain a substantial amount of text, likely understand the intended addressee as a farmer. Very little of lines 7–10 have survived. They contrast "a man of understanding" with a fool.

4Q423 5 1A

This line refers to "Levi the prie[st]" (see textual notes section). Priestly tradition is also invoked in line 1, which mentions the judgment of Korah. There is not enough text to interpret the reference to Levi sufficiently. The priestly patriarch appears nowhere else in 4QInstruction. Since the addressee is to "take care" lest he return to Levi, this action is discouraged (cf. 4Q416 2 ii 8; 4Q418 88 ii 3).[3] This is consistent with the judgment of Korah in line 1, in that this invokes a biblical tradition of priests who should not be emulated (see below). It has been argued that at least some

---

3. The root שוב may signify returning something (which is not preserved in the extant text) to Levi.

portions of 4QInstruction understand the *mebin* to be a priest. As I argue in the commentary on 4Q418 81 3, the document's general lack of interest in ritual purity or cultic affairs suggests that the envisioned addressee is not a priest.

4Q423 5 1–2

While relatively little of this line is extant, it contains two noticeable features: a reference to the "judgment of Korah" and an assertion (which continues into line 2) that the mystery that is to be was revealed to the *mebin*. The judgment of Korah evokes Num 16, in which the priest Korah and his supporters rebel and are then swallowed by the earth.[4] Scott understands 4Q423 5 1 as alluding to a split in the early days of the *yaḥad*.[5] However, there is little evidence in 4QInstruction to suggest that it was authored by the movement associated with the Teacher of Righteousness (see section 10 of the introduction). 4QInstruction contains no explicit reference to a splinter group that is regarded polemically. One could interpret the appeal to Korah as some sort of criticism of the priesthood, but critique of this institution is never unambiguously a theme in 4QInstruction.[6] 4Q423 5 stresses not the punishment of a single group, but rather that all will be judged (see below on l. 4). This suggests that the author of the column turned to the story of Korah to assert that God will punish the wicked in general when he judges humankind.[7] Korah is emblematic of a person who goes against God's will and is consequently punished.

4Q423 5 1 reminds the *mebin* that the mystery that is to be has already been revealed to his "ear," an assertion found elsewhere in the composition (4Q416 2 iii 18; 4Q418 123 ii 4; 4Q418 184 2; 4Q423 7 6). I tentatively suggest that the original text of 4Q423 5 1–2 affirmed that God revealed to the addressee through the *raz nihyeh* that he will judge all of humankind and punish the wicked. The lines can be understood in terms of parallelism,

---

4. There may be a reference to Dathan, one of Korah's rebellious accomplices (e.g., Num 16:2), in 4Q418 290 1. Very little survives of this fragment, however, and firm conclusions about it cannot be established. 1QM 17:2 mentions "the judgment [of Nadab and] Ab[ihu]" (cf. 4Q491 1–3 1).

5. Scott 2001, 202.

6. Kampen (2011, 185) suggests that lines 1–2 may have discussed how one evaluates the priesthood.

7. Elgvin in Strugnell and Harrington (1999, 519) understands the phrase "judgment of Korah" as directed against unjust leaders. See also Fletcher-Louis 2002, 185.

with the first foot saying that God has revealed to the *mebin* knowledge of the judgment of Korah and the second that he disclosed through the mystery that is to be that he will judge all of humankind. The inevitability of divine judgment is a topic elsewhere in the composition (e.g., 4Q417 1 i 14–15). Contemplation of the *raz nihyeh* helps one understand God's plan that guides the entirety of creation and history, and this includes the final judgment (see section 5 of the introduction).

4Q423 5 2

The poor material condition of line 2 is unfortunate. The line contains the only reference in 4QInstruction to political leaders. The "[h]ead of the fathers" (ר[ר]וש אבות) and the "leader of your people" (נשיא עמכה) are mentioned. These expressions occur nowhere else in the document. Elgvin suggests that the phrases denote lay leadership in Israel.[8] Similar phrases have this sense in the Bible.[9] The focus on such leaders contrasts with the emphasis on priestly tradition in 4Q423 5 1a–1. The references to rulers and priests may point toward leaders in the Hasmonean court, since these kings combined the two offices in the same person. The precise kinds of leaders cannot be sufficiently recovered. On the basis of lines 3 and 4 (see below), one can speculate that line 2 may have emphasized the subservience of political authorities to God and/or that he will judge them.

4Q423 5 3

This line sheds some light on the column's interest in political leaders. Line 3 affirms that God established "the [in]heritance of all rulers (מושלים)." God is praised because he fashioned all deeds and knows their outcome.[10] The authority of human rulers is far exceeded by that of God.[11] He established their powerful station in life. Their dominion is under-

---

8. Elgvin in Strugnell and Harrington 1999, 530; Scott 2001, 196.

9. Note, for example, Num 7:2: "the leaders of Israel (נשיאי ישראל), heads of their ancestral houses (ראשי בית אבתם), the leaders of the tribes, who were over those who were enrolled, made offerings." The phrase "leader of your people" is in Exod 22:27 [Eng. v. 28]. For expressions similar to רוש אבות, see Exod 6:14, 25; Josh 19:51; 22:14; Ezra 2:68; 1 Chr 7:11 (note also 1QSa 1:16, 25; 1QM 2:7; 11QT 57:12).

10. Lines 3–4 are reconstructed as stating that God knows the reward of all the deeds of the rulers. Context suggests that this refers to what they shall receive during the final judgment (cf. 1QS 4:15, 16, 25). See Elgvin in Strugnell and Harrington 1999, 521.

11. Scott 2001, 199–201, understands this line in terms of the dynamics of the

stood against the backdrop of the deity's ultimate power.[12] 4Q416 1 4–6 emphasizes that all kingdoms and provinces are under his control. The reference to judgment in 4Q423 5 4 may denote dissatisfaction with rulers, but 4QInstruction contains no explicit political critique of Israel's leaders (contrast, for example, CD 8:10).

4Q423 5 4

God will judge "all of them" (כולם). Much of the verb "to judge" must be supplemented. This reconstruction is reasonable.[13] The line uses the root פקד, which elsewhere in the composition refers to eschatological judgment (פקודה; see the commentary to 4Q417 1 i 7–8). The contrasting pairs of 4Q423 5 4—fathers and sons, aliens and native-born—are merisms, denoting universality.[14] Referring to these different groups helps establish that all people will be judged, a trope found elsewhere in 4QInstruction (4Q417 2 i 15–16; 4Q418 77 3). Although the relevant material is fragmentary, the most immediate antecedent of "all of them" is "rulers." All human leaders will be judged. When judgment is presented as affecting all people, rulers are not special, but rather are like the rest of humankind. As in line 3, human power is understood against the backdrop of God's superiority. The assertion that people will be judged "in truth" (l. 4) resonates with other accounts of judgment in 4QInstruction in which the term is used. The judgment scene of 4Q416 1 states that the "sons of his truth" will be spared (l. 10), and the righteous who will be spared in 4Q418 69 ii are similarly called the "chosen ones of truth" (l. 10).

Dead Sea sect, arguing that the term "rulers" alludes to Isa 28 and those who followed the "man of mockery" (e.g., CD 1:4; 20:11). See also Rey 2009a, 122.

12. Note the parallel in Sir 10:4–5: "Sovereignty over the earth (ממשלת תבל) is in the hand of God, who raises a man over it for a time. Sovereignty over everyone is in the hand of God, who imparts his majesty to the ruler" (cf. Wis 6:1–3).

13. See, for example, Kampen 2011, 185; Rey 2009a, 119; Elgvin in Strugnell and Harrington 1999, 518.

14. The term "aliens" is reasonably reconstructed, despite the lack of surviving text (גרי[ם]). The pair "fathers and sons" implies that some sort of group contrasting with the "native-born" should be supplied. Elgvin in Strugnell and Harrington (1999, 521) translates the term "proselytes." The emphasis on the native-born in the text, however, suggests that גר refers to resident aliens rather than converts to Judaism. See further Berthelot 1999, 177; Rey 2009a, 122–23.

4Q423 5 5–6

These lines are significant for understanding the social background of the intended audience of 4QInstruction. This pericope understands that the *mebin* is a farmer or, depending on how the line is reconstructed, that he could be one.[15] Elgvin understands line 5 as beginning with the phrase "[if you are a fa]rmer." The Hebrew is איש אדמה, literally "a man of soil" (cf. 4Q423 5a 2).[16] The expression denotes Noah, the first vintner, in Gen 9:20 (cf. Zech 13:5).[17] 4Q423 5 5 exhorts the *mebin* to "observe the times of summer" and "gather your produce in its time." Rey suggests that this should not be understood as referring to actual agricultural practices.[18] Rather, he argues, the text appeals to farming as a metaphor. He reconstructs the beginning of the line as [כא]יש אדמה—one should observe the seasons "[*like* a fa]rmer" (emphasis mine). To support this interpretation he invokes Sir 6:18–19, which refers to farming in a metaphorical sense.[19] The author of 4QInstruction would agree, I think, that farming could function as a metaphor that teaches the *mebin* about other subjects. But 4QInstruction acknowledges that its addressee could be an actual farmer. This is suggested in 4Q423 5 and the rest of 4QInstruction.

4Q423 5 6 exhorts the *mebin* to understand his "produce," a reference to agricultural yield. He has crops. "Produce" is in the second person singular. He should reflect theologically upon the growth that takes place in his fields. One can reasonably speculate that he is to understand that any success he has regarding his crops should be attributed to God (see also the discussion of 4Q423 4 below). Compare 4Q416 2 ii 1–2, which praises the deity for making food available to humankind.

The end of 4Q423 5 6 mentions the knowledge of good and evil. Before its deterioration, the text likely stated that the *mebin* should contemplate upon his crops in order to obtain this knowledge. 4Q423 1 portrays the

---

15. Safrai 2010, 246–63.

16. Elgvin in Strugnell and Harrington 1999, 518. See also Kampen 2011, 185.

17. Elgvin in Strugnell and Harrington (1999, 521–22) emphasizes the link between the *mebin* and Noah by pointing out that the beginning of 4QInstruction emphasizes the disclosure of revelation to Noah. See the criticism of this reconstruction in the commentary on 4Q416 1 1.

18. Rey 2009a, 123–24.

19. "My son, from your youth embrace discipline; thus you will gain wisdom with graying hair. As though plowing and sowing, draw close to her (wisdom); then await her bountiful crops, for in cultivating her you will labor but little, and soon you will eat of her fruits."

addressee as tilling the garden of Eden as Adam did. This metaphor can be understood as derived in part from reflection on the fact that some of the members of the intended audience are actual farmers—people with humble agricultural professions who have access to the mystery that is to be. As discussed in the commentary on 4Q423 1 2, the knowledge of good and evil in 4QInstruction signifies comprehension of the natural order and God's deterministic plan that guides it. Understanding the reference to good and evil in 4Q423 5 6 in this way illuminates the pedagogy of this section. 4QInstruction encourages the *mebin* not just to "observe the times of summer" so that he can produce a harvest and be a good farmer. He is to understand the broader theological significance of what he grows. Success with one's crops requires the accurate observation of nature, with its seasons and times for harvest. This is an opportunity to understand how God has structured the cosmos.

Other texts of 4QInstruction support the view that the addressee of 4Q423 5 could be an actual farmer. Sirach 6:18–19 is easily understood as a metaphorical appeal to agriculture because Ben Sira is not a farmer but part of an aristocratic scribal retainer class. He understands scribes as superior to farmers (38:24–34).[20] In 4QInstruction the opposite is the case. The composition understands the members of the intended audience as having a variety of professions, all of which are relatively low in the economic hierarchy of society. Some are craftsmen (4Q418 81 15). Others engage in trade, selling crafts or agricultural surpluses (4Q417 2 i 17–18). Some may be debt slaves (4Q416 2 ii 7–17). Understanding some members of the intended audience as farmers is consistent with the social level of these other professions. Also, a farmer could fall into indebtedness easily, and this is consistent with the prominence of this theme in 4QInstruction.[21]

Several other texts of 4QInstruction assume an addressee who grows crops. 4Q423 4 tells the *mebin* to "[tak]e care [lest] she honor you more than him" (l. 1). The next line states that he will be cursed in all his crops (cf. l. 3 [par. 1Q26 1 6]). If one posits that the woman is the addressee's wife, the text states that she should understand that whatever agricultural success they experience should ultimately be attributed to God, not her husband.[22]

---

20. Sir 38:24–25: "The scribe's profession increases wisdom; whoever is free from toil (ה]סר עסק) can become wise. How can one become wise who guides the plow?"

21. See the second excursus in chapter 3.

22. Elgvin in Strugnell and Harrington 1999, 517.

If she does not understand this, the crops may be cursed. The mystery that is to be is mentioned in 1Q26 1 1 and 4 and thus was attested in a portion of 4Q423 4 that has not survived. This suggests that the text encourages the *mebin* to comprehend the natural order of things not simply by examining the regular cycle of seasons and crops, but also through the study of the *raz nihyeh*. Like 4Q423 5 5–6, the text urges the addressee to understand his farming in the context of God's dominion over the natural order. This may also be the case in 4Q423 3 2, a fragmentary text that mentions both the mystery that is to be and crops.[23] 4Q418 103 ii 3–4 gives instruction on the harvesting of crops.[24] The humble social standing of the envisioned addressee of 4QInstruction and the composition's multiple references to crops and agriculture suggest, *contra* Rey, that 4Q423 5 5–6 was written to a *mebin* who is a farmer. As one who relies upon the productivity of the land, he should understand the natural order of things and God's control over the world.

4Q423 5 7–8

Very little of lines 7–10 survives. They were apparently pedagogical in nature. Line 7 makes a distinction between a "[m]an of understanding" and a fool, literally a "master of folly" (בעל אולת).[25] The expression איש שכל ("man of understanding") was apparently prominent in this section, perhaps also occurring at the end of line 7 and the beginning of line 8. The word "intelligence" is at the end of line 8 (cf. l. 6). The phrase "man of understanding" (איש שכל) is also in 4Q424 3 7. There such a person is praised as an ideal type who accepts instruction. The contrast in 4Q423 5 7 between the intelligent man and the fool evokes traditional wisdom. Lines 7–10 probably encouraged the *mebin* to study and acquire wisdom. Perhaps the farmer-addressee who understands the role of God in the production of his crops (see above on l. 6) is hailed in these lines as an intelligent man. The emphasis on judgment in the column also provides an incentive to follow the right path and to adhere to the instruction provided by the composition. An ideal student who does so may be described in line 7. Another possibility, which would be in keeping with line 4, is that

---

23. The line states "[by the mystery] that is to be. Thus you shall walk and al[l your] c[rops will multiply]."

24. Note also the phrase "in the da[y]s of your h[arv]esting" in 4Q423 12 2.

25. This phrase occurs nowhere else in 4QInstruction, but אולת is frequent (4Q415 9 5; 4Q416 2 ii 3; 4Q417 1 i 7; 4Q418 220 3; 4Q418 243 2).

the line stated originally that God will judge both the wise person and the fool.[26] One can speculate that the suffix in the phrase "[in the abun]dance of his intelligence" of line 8 denotes either the "intelligence" of God or perhaps an ideal type of person whom the addressee is to emulate.

4Q423 5 9

Line 9, if reconstructed correctly, mentions "his entire [pa]th." The antecedent of the suffix is unclear and, as with "his intelligence," the line could refer to the path of God or that of the model student who is correctly following the teachings of the composition.[27] "Path" terminology is central to the pedagogy of the book of Proverbs, supporting the latter suggestion.[28]

4Q423 5 10

The remnants of this line suggest that the text switched to the second person plural to begin the next section of the column, which has not survived.

---

26. Rey 2009a, 125.

27. Kampen 2011, 185, reconstructs the phrase *raz nihyeh* in this line. The suggestion is interesting, but the line is too fragmentary to endorse this reading.

28. E.g., Prov 3:17; 8:20. See Fox 2000, 128–31.

BIBLIOGRAPHY

Adams, Samuel L. 2008. *Wisdom in Transition: Act and Consequence in Second Temple Instructions.* JSJSup 125. Leiden: Brill.

———. 2010. Rethinking the Relationship between 4QInstruction and Ben Sira. *RevQ* 24:555–83.

Aitken, James K. 2002. Divine Will and Providence. Pages 282–301 in *Ben Sira's God: Proceedings of the International Ben Sira Conference, Durham—Ushaw College 2001.* Edited by R. Egger-Wenzel. BZAW 321. Berlin: de Gruyter.

Andrews, Stephen. 2007. What's the Matter with Eve? The Woman and Her Sentence in Ancient Judaism. Pages 1–22 in *Divine Creation in Ancient, Medieval, and Early Modern Thought: Essays Presented to the Rv'd Dr Robert D. Crouse.* Edited by R. Treschow, W. Otten, and W. Hannam. BSIH 151. Leiden: Brill.

Aune, David. 1997. *Revelation 1–5.* WBC 52a. Dallas: Word.

Baker, David L. 2006. Safekeeping, Borrowing, and Rental. *JSOT* 31:27–42.

———. 2009. *Tight Fists or Open Hands? Wealth and Poverty in Old Testament Law.* Grand Rapids: Eerdmans.

Balla, Ibolya. 2011. *Ben Sira on Family, Gender, and Sexuality.* DCLS 8. Berlin: de Gruyter.

Barthélemy, Dominique, and Józef T. Milik, eds. 1955. *Qumran Cave 1.* DJD 1. Oxford: Clarendon.

Bartlett, John R. 1998. *1 Maccabees.* Sheffield: Sheffield Academic Press.

Barzilai, Gabriel. 2007. Incidental Biblical Exegesis in the Qumran Scrolls and Its Importance for the Study of the Second Temple Period. *DSD* 14:1–24.

Baumgarten, Joseph M. 1990. The 4QZadokite Fragments on Skin Disease. *JJS* 41:153–65.

———. 1996. *Qumran Cave 4.XIII: The Damascus Document (4Q266–273).* DJD 18. Oxford: Clarendon.

Baumgarten, Joseph M., Torleif Elgvin, Esther Eshel, Erik Larson, Manfred R. Lehmann, Stephen Pfann, and Lawrence H. Schiffman. 1999. *Qumran Cave 4.XXV, Halakhic Texts.* DJD 35. Oxford: Clarendon.

Baynes, Leslie. 2011. *The Heavenly Book Motif in Judeo-Christian Apocalypses, 200 BCE–200 CE*. JSJSup 152. Leiden: Brill.

Benoit, Pierre, Józef T. Milik, and Roland de Vaux. 1961. *Les Grottes de Murabbaʿat*. DJD 2. Oxford: Clarendon.

Bergmann, Claudia. 2008. *Childbirth as a Metaphor for Crisis: Evidence from the Ancient Near East, the Hebrew Bible, and 1QH XI, 1–18*. BZAW 382. Berlin: de Gruyter.

Berlin, Adele. 2008. *The Dynamics of Biblical Parallelism*. Rev. ed. Grand Rapids: Eerdmans.

Bernstein, Moshe. 2004. Women and Children in Legal and Liturgical Texts from Qumran. *DSD* 11:191–211.

Berthelot, Katell. 1999. La Notion de גר dans les textes de Qumrân. *RevQ* 19:171–216.

———. 2010. Hecataeus of Abdera. Pages 718–19 in *The Eerdmans Dictionary of Early Judaism*. Edited by John J. Collins and Daniel C. Harlow. Grand Rapids: Eerdmans.

Beyerle, Stefan. 2008. "A Star Shall Come out of Jacob": A Critical Evaluation of the Balaam Oracle in the Context of Jewish Revolts in Roman Times. Pages 163–88 in *The Prestige of the Pagan Prophet Balaam in Judaism, Early Christianity and Islam*. Edited by G. H. van Kooten and J. T. A. G. M. van Ruiten. TBN 11. Leiden: Brill.

Blenkinsopp, Joseph. 2000. *Isaiah 1–39*. AB 19. New York: Doubleday.

———. 2003. *Isaiah 56–66*. AB 19B. New York: Doubleday.

Botta, Alejandro F. 2009. *The Aramaic and Egyptian Legal Traditions at Elephantine: An Egyptological Approach*. LSTS 65. London: T&T Clark.

Brewer, David Instone. 1999. Jewish Women Divorcing Their Husbands in Early Judaism: The Background to Papyrus Ṣeʾelim 13. *HTR* 92:349–57.

Brin, Gershon. 1996. Studies in 4Q424, Fragment 3. *VT* 46:271–95.

Bro Larsen, Kasper. 2002. Visdom og apokalyptik i Musar leMevin (1Q/4QInstruction). *DTT* 65:1–14.

Brody, Robert. 1999. Evidence for Divorce by Jewish Women? *JJS* 50:230–34.

Brooke, George J. 2002. Biblical Interpretation in the Wisdom Texts from Qumran. Pages 201–20 in *The Wisdom Texts from Qumran and the Development of Sapiential Thought*. Edited by Charlotte Hempel, Hermann Lichtenberger, and Armin Lange. BETL 159. Leuven: Leuven University Press.

Brooten, Bernadette. 1983. Zur Debatte über das Scheidungsrecht der jüdischen Frau. *EvT* 43:466–78.

Broshi, Magen. 1992. *The Damascus Document Reconsidered.* Jerusalem: The Israel Exploration Society.

Bunta, Silviu. 2006. The Likeness of the Image: Adamic Motifs and צלם Anthropology in Rabbinic Traditions about Jacob's Image Enthroned in Heaven. *JSJ* 37:55–84.

Burns, Joshua Ezra. 2004. Practical Wisdom in 4QInstruction. *DSD* 11:12–42.

Calduch-Belanges, Nuria. 2008. "Cut Her Away from Your Flesh": Divorce in Ben Sira. Pages 81–95 in *Studies in the Book of Ben Sira.* Edited by G. G. Xeravits and J. Zsengellér. JSJSup 127. Leiden: Brill.

Camp, Claudia V. 1991. Understanding A Patriarchy: Women in Second-Century Jerusalem through the Eyes of Ben Sira. Pages 1–39 in *"Women Like This": New Perspectives on Women in the Greco-Roman World.* Edited by A-J. Levine. SBLEJL 1. Atlanta: Scholars Press.

Caquot, André. 1996. Les textes de sagesse de Qoumrân (Aperçu préliminaire). *RHPR* 76:1–34.

Carmichael, Calum M. 1995. Forbidden Mixtures in Deuteronomy XXII 9–11 and Leviticus XIX 19. *VT* 45:433–48.

Cartledge, Tony W. 1992. *Vows in the Hebrew Bible and the Ancient Near East.* JSOTSup 147. Sheffield: Sheffield Academic Press.

Charlesworth, James, et al. 2000. *Miscellaneous Texts from the Judean Desert.* DJD 38. Oxford: Clarendon.

Chazon, Esther G. 1997. The Creation and Fall of Adam in the Dead Sea Scrolls. Pages 13–24 in *The Book of Genesis in Jewish and Oriental Christian Interpretation: A Collection of Essays.* Edited by J. Frishman and L. van Rompay. Leuven: Peeters.

Chirichigno, Gregory C. 1993. *Debt-Slavery in Israel and the Ancient Near East.* JSOTSup 141. Sheffield: Sheffield Academic Press.

Christensen, Duane L. 2002. *Deuteronomy 21:10–34:12.* WBC 6B. Nashville: Thomas Nelson.

Cohen Stuart, G. H. 1984. *The Struggle in Man between Good and Evil: An Inquiry into the Origin of the Rabbinic Concept of Yeṣer Haraʾ.* Kampen: J. H. Kok.

Collins, John J. 1997a. A Herald of Good Tidings: Isaiah 61:1–3 and its Actualization in the Dead Sea Scrolls. Pages 225–40 in *The Quest for Context and Meaning: Studies in Biblical Intertextuality in Honor of James A. Sanders.* Edited by C. A. Evans and S. Talmon. BInS 28; Leiden: Brill.

———. 1997b. *Apocalypticism in the Dead Sea Scrolls.* London: Routledge.

———. 1997c. *Jewish Wisdom in the Hellenistic Age.* OTL. Louisville: Westminster John Knox.

———. 1997d. Marriage, Divorce and Family in Second Temple Judaism. Pages 104–62 in *Families in Ancient Israel.* Edited by Leo G. Perdue, Joseph Blenkinsopp, John J. Collins, and Carol L. Meyers. Louisville: Westminster John Knox.

———. 1997e. Wisdom, Apocalypticism, and Generic Compatibility. Pages 385–404 in *Seers, Sibyls, and Sages in Hellenistic-Roman Judaism.* Edited by John J. Collins. JSJSup 54. Leiden: Brill.

———. 1997f. Wisdom Reconsidered, in Light of the Scrolls. *DSD* 4:265–81.

———. 1998. *The Apocalyptic Imagination.* 2nd ed. Grand Rapids: Eerdmans.

———. 1999. In the Likeness of the Holy Ones: The Creation of Humankind in a Wisdom Text from Qumran. Pages 609–18 in *The Provo International Conference on the Dead Sea Scrolls.* Edited by D. W. Parry and E. Ulrich. STDJ 30. Leiden: Brill.

———. 2001. The Afterlife in Apocalyptic Literature. Pages 119–39 in *Judaism in Late Antiquity, Part 4: Death, Life-after-Death, Resurrection and the World-to-Come in the Judaisms of Antiquity.* Edited by Alan J. Avery-Peck and Jacob Neusner. Leiden: Brill.

———. 2003. The Mysteries of God: Creation and Eschatology in 4QInstruction and the Wisdom of Solomon. Pages 287–305 in *Wisdom and Apocalypticism in the Dead Sea Scrolls and in the Biblical Tradition.* Edited by Florentino García Martínez. BETL 168. Leuven: Leuven University Press.

———. 2004. The Eschatologizing of Wisdom in the Dead Sea Scrolls. Pages 49–65 in *Sapiential Perspectives: Wisdom Literature in Light of the Dead Sea Scrolls: Proceedings of the Sixth International Symposium of the Orion Center, 20–22 May 2001.* Edited by John J. Collins, Gregory E. Sterling, and Ruth A. Clements. STDJ 51. Leiden: Brill.

———. 2010. *The Scepter and the Star: Messianism in Light of the Dead Sea Scrolls.* 2nd ed. Grand Rapids: Eerdmans.

Cook, Johann. 2007. The Origin of the Tradition of the יצר הטב and the יצר הרע. *JSJ* 38:81–92.

Cotton, Hannah M., and Ada Yardeni. 1997. *Aramaic, Hebrew, and Greek Document Texts from Naḥal Ḥever and Other Sites.* DJD 28. Oxford: Clarendon.

Crenshaw, James L. 2010. *Old Testament Wisdom: An Introduction.* 3rd ed. Louisville: Westminster John Knox.

Cross, Frank Moore. 1961. The Development of the Jewish Scripts. Pages 133–202 in *The Bible and the Ancient Near East: Essays in Honor of William Foxwell Albright*. Edited by G. E. Wright. New York: Doubleday.

———. 1995. *The Ancient Library of Qumran*. 3rd ed. Minneapolis: Fortress.

Diamond, James A. 2009. Nahmanides and Rashi on the One Flesh of Conjugal Union: Lovemaking vs. Duty. *HTR* 102:193–224.

Di Lella, Alexander A., and Patrick W. Skehan. 1987. *The Wisdom of Ben Sira*. AB 39. New York: Doubleday.

Dochhorn, Jan. 2002. "Sie wird dir nicht ihre Kraft geben"—Adam, Kain und der Ackerbau in 4Q423 2_3 und Apc Mos 24. Pages 351–64 in *The Wisdom Texts from Qumran and the Development of Sapiential Thought*. Edited by Charlotte Hempel, Hermann Lichtenberger, and Armin Lange. BETL 159. Leuven: Leuven University Press.

Doering, Lutz. 2009. Marriage and Creation in Mark 10 and CD 4–5. Pages 133–63 in *Echoes from the Caves: Qumran and the New Testament*. Edited by Florentino García Martínez. STDJ 85. Leiden: Brill.

Dušek, Jan. 2007. *Les manuscrits araméens du Wadi Daliyeh et la Samarie vers 450–332 av. J.-C.* CHANE 30. Leiden: Brill.

Eisenman, Robert H., and Michael O. Wise. 1992. *The Dead Sea Scrolls Uncovered: The First Complete Translation and Interpretation of 50 Key Documents Withheld for Over 35 Years*. New York: Penguin.

Elgvin, Torleif. 1995a. The Reconstruction of Sapiential Work A. *RevQ* 16:559–80.

———. 1995b. Wisdom, Revelation, and Eschatology in an Early Essene Writing. Pages 440–63 in *Society of Biblical Literature Seminar Papers 1995*. SBLSP 34. Atlanta: Scholars Press.

———. 1996. Early Essene Eschatology: Judgment and Salvation according to Sapiential Work A. Pages 126–65 in *Current Research and Technological Development on the Dead Sea Scrolls: Conference on the Texts from the Judean Desert, Jerusalem, 30 April 1995*. Edited by D. W. Parry and S. D. Ricks. STDJ 20. Leiden: Brill.

———. 1997a. An Analysis of 4QInstruction. PhD diss., Hebrew University of Jerusalem.

———.1997b. "To Master His Own Vessel": 1 Thess 4:4 in Light of New Qumran Evidence. *NTS* 43:604–19.

———. 1998. The Mystery to Come: Early Essene Theology of Revelation. Pages 113–50 in *Qumran between the Old and New Testaments*. Edited by F. H. Cryer and T. L. Thompson. JSOTSup 290. Sheffield: Sheffield Academic Press.

———. 2000a. Wisdom and Apocalypticism in the Early Second Century BCE—The Evidence of 4QInstruction. Pages 226–47 in *The Dead Sea Scrolls Fifty Years after Their Discovery: Proceedings of the Jerusalem Congress, July 20–25, 1997*. Edited by L. H. Schiffman, Emanuel Tov, James C. Vanderkam, and Joy Ungerleider-Mayerson. Jerusalem: Israel Exploration Society.

———. 2000b. Wisdom with and without Apocalyptic. Pages 15–38 in *Sapiential, Liturgical, and Poetical Texts from Qumran: Proceedings of the Third Meeting of the International Organization for Qumran Studies, Oslo 1998: Published in Memory of Maurice Baillet*. Edited by Daniel K. Falk, Florentino García Martínez, and Eileen M. Schuller. STDJ 35. Leiden: Brill.

———. 2001. Wisdom at Qumran. Pages 147–69 in vol. 3 of *Judaism in Late Antiquity, Part 5, Section 2: World View, Comparing Judaism*. Edited by J. Neusner and A. J. Avery-Peck. 3 vols. Leiden: Brill.

———. 2004. Priestly Sages? The Milieus of Origin of 4QMysteries and 4QInstruction. Pages 67–87 in *Sapiential Perspectives: Wisdom Literature in Light of the Dead Sea Scrolls: Proceedings of the Sixth International Symposium of the Orion Center, 20–22 May 2001*. Edited by John J. Collins, Gregory E. Sterling, and Ruth A. Clements. STDJ 51. Leiden: Brill.

———. 2009. From Secular to Religious Language in 4QInstruction. *RevQ* 24:155–63.

Elgvin, Torleif, et al. 1997. *Qumran Cave 4.XV: Sapiential Texts, Part 1*. DJD 20. Oxford: Clarendon.

Ellis, Teresa Ann. 2011. Is Eve the "Woman" in Sirach 25:24? *CBQ* 73:723–42.

Eshel, Esther. 1997. Hermeneutical Approaches to Genesis in the Dead Sea Scrolls. Pages 1–12 in *The Book of Genesis in Jewish and Oriental Christian Interpretation: A Collection of Essays*. Edited by J. Frishman and L. van Rompay. Leuven: Peeters.

Eshel, Esther, and Hanan Eshel. 2007. A Preliminary Report on Seven New Fragments from Qumran [Hebrew]. *Megilloth* 5–6:271–78.

Eshel, Esther, Hanan Eshel, and Gregor Geiger. 2008. Mur 174: A Hebrew I.O.U. Document from Wadi Murabbaʻat. *LASBF* 58:313–26.

Fabry, Heinz-Josef. 2003. Die Armenfrömmigkeit in den qumranischen Weisheitstexten. Pages 145–65 in *Weisheit in Israel: Beiträge des Sym-*

posiums "*Das Alte Testament und die Kultur der Moderne*" *anlässlich des 100. Geburtstags Gerhard von Rads (1901–1971), Heidelberg, 18.–21. Oktober 2001.* Edited by D. J. A. Clines, Hermann Lichtenberger, and Hans-Peter Müller. ATM 12. Münster: Lit-Verlag.

Fee, Gordon D. 2009. *The First and Second Letters to the Thessalonians.* Grand Rapids: Eerdmans.

Fidler, Ruth. 2006. A Wife's Vow—the Husband's Woe? The Case of Hannah and Elkanah (1 Sam 1,21.23). *ZAW* 118:374–88.

Fields, Weston W. 2009. *The Dead Sea Scrolls: A Full History.* Vol 1. Leiden: Brill.

Fishbane, Michael. 1985. *Biblical Interpretation in Ancient Israel.* Oxford: Clarendon.

———. 1992. The Well of Living Water: A Biblical Motif and its Ancient Transformations. Pages 3–16 in *Sha'arei Talmon: Studies in the Bible, Qumran, and the Ancient Near East Presented to Shemaryahu Talmon.* Edited by M. Fishbane and E. Tov. Winona Lake, Ind.: Eisenbrauns.

Fitzmyer, Joseph A. 1958. "Peace upon Earth among Men of His Good Will" (Lk 2:14). *TS* 19: 225–27.

———. 1997. *The Semitic Background of the New Testament.* Grand Rapids: Eerdmans.

Fletcher-Louis, Crispin H. T. 2002. *All the Glory of Adam: Liturgical Anthropology in the Dead Sea Scrolls.* STDJ 42. Leiden: Brill.

Fox, Michael V. 2000. *Proverbs 1–9: A New Translation with Introduction and Commentary.* AB 18A. New York: Doubleday.

———. 2009. *Proverbs 10–31.* AB 18B. New Haven: Yale University Press.

Fraade, Steven D. 1984. *Enosh and His Generation: Pre-Israelite Hero and History in Post-biblical Interpretation.* SBLMS 30. Chico, Calif.: Scholars Press.

———. 1998. Enosh and His Generation Revisited. Pages 59–86 in *Biblical Figures Outside the Bible.* Edited by M. E. Stone and T. A. Bergen. Harrisburg, Pa.: Trinity Press International.

Frey, Jörg. 1999. Die paulinische Antithese von "Fleisch" und "Geist" und die palästinisch-jüdische Weisheitstradition. *ZNW* 90:45–77.

———. 2000. The Notion of "Flesh" in 4QInstruction and the Background of Pauline Usage. Pages 197–226 in *Sapiential, Liturgical, and Poetical Texts from Qumran: Proceedings of the Third Meeting of the International Organization for Qumran Studies, Oslo 1998: Published in Memory of Maurice Baillet.* Edited by Daniel K. Falk, Florentino García Martínez, and Eileen M. Schuller. STDJ 35. Leiden: Brill.

———. 2002. Flesh and Spirit in the Palestinian Jewish Sapiential Tradition and in the Qumran Texts: An Inquiry into the Background of Pauline Usage. Pages 367–404 in *The Wisdom Texts from Qumran and the Development of Sapiential Thought*. Edited by Charlotte Hempel, Hermann Lichtenberger, and Armin Lange. BETL 159. Leuven: Leuven University Press.

———. 2007. Die Bedeutung der Qumrantexte für das Verständis der Apokalyptik im Frühjudentum und im Urchristentum. Pages 11–62 in *Apokalyptik und Qumran*. Edited by J. Frey and M. Becker. Paderborn: Bonifatius.

Friedman, Mordechai A. 1969. Termination of the Marriage upon the Wife's Request: A Palestinian *ketubba* Stipulation. *PAAJR* 37:29–55.

———. 1981. Divorce upon the Wife's Demand as Reflected in Manuscripts from the Cairo Geniza. *JLA* 4:103–26.

Furnish, Victor Paul. 2007. *1 Thessalonians, 2 Thessalonians*. Nashville: Abingdon.

García Martínez, Florentino. 2003. Wisdom at Qumran: Worldly or Heavenly? Pages 1–15 in *Wisdom and Apocalypticism in the Dead Sea Scrolls and in the Biblical Tradition*. Edited by Florentino García Martínez. BETL 168. Leuven: Leuven University Press.

———. 2006. Marginalia on 4QInstruction. *DSD* 13:24–37.

García Martínez, Florentino, and Eibert J. C. Tigchelaar. 1997–1998. *The Dead Sea Scrolls Study Edition*. 2 vols. Leiden: Brill.

Garfinkle, Steven J. 2004. Shepherds, Merchants, and Credit: Some Observations on the Lending Practices in Ur III Mesopotamia. *JESHO* 47:1–30.

Gese, Hartmut. 1962. Kleine Beiträge zum Verständis des Amosbuches. *VT* 12:417–38.

Ginzberg, Louis. 1976. *An Unknown Jewish Sect*. New York: Ktav. First published 1922.

Glass, Zipporah G. 2000. Land, Slave Labor, and Law: Engaging Ancient Israel's Economy. *JSOT* 91:27–39.

Goff, Matthew J. 2003a. The Mystery of Creation in 4QInstruction. *DSD* 10:163–86.

———. 2003b. *The Worldly and Heavenly Wisdom of 4QInstruction*. STDJ 50. Leiden: Brill.

———. 2004. Reading Wisdom at Qumran: 4QInstruction and the Hodayot. *DSD* 11:263–88.

———. 2005a. Discerning Trajectories: 4QInstruction and the Sapiential Background of the Sayings Source Q. *JBL* 124:657–73.

———. 2005b. Wisdom, Apocalypticism, and the Pedagogical Ethos of 4QInstruction. Pages 57–67 in *Conflicted Boundaries in Wisdom and Apocalypticism*. Edited by L. Wills and B. G. Wright. SBLSymS 35. Atlanta: Society of Biblical Literature.

———. 2007. *Discerning Wisdom: The Sapiential Literature of the Dead Sea Scrolls*. VTSup 116. Leiden: Brill.

———. 2009a. Genesis 1–3 and Conceptions of Humankind in 4QInstruction, Philo and Paul. Pages 114–25 in *Exegetical Studies*. Vol. 2 of *Early Christian Literature and Intertextuality*. Edited by C. Evans and H. D. Zacharias. London: T&T Clark.

———. 2009b. Recent Trends in the Study of Early Jewish Wisdom Literature: The Contribution of 4QInstruction and Other Qumran Texts. *CBR* 7:376–416.

———. 2010a. Adam, the Angels, and Eternal Life: Genesis 1–3 in 4QInstruction and the Wisdom of Solomon. Pages 1–21 in *Studies in the Book of Wisdom*. Edited by G. G. Xeravits and J. Zsengellér. JSJSup 142. Leiden: Brill.

———. 2010b. Looking for Sapiential Dualism at Qumran. Pages 20–38 in *Dualism at Qumran*. Edited by G. G. Xeravits. LSTS 76. London: T&T Clark.

———. 2010c. Qumran Wisdom Literature and the Problem of Genre. *DSD* 17:286–306.

———. 2011. Being Fleshly or Spiritual: Anthropological Reflection and Exegesis of Genesis 1–3 in 4QInstruction and 1 Corinthians. Pages 41–59 in *Christian Body, Christian Self: Essays on Early Christian Concepts of Personhood*. Edited by C. Rothschild and T. Thompson. WUNT 1/284. Tübingen: Mohr Siebeck.

Goldin, Judah. 1983. *The Fathers according to Rabbi Nathan*. YJS 10. New York: Yale University Press. First published 1955.

Golitzin, Alexander. 2003. Recovering the "Glory of Adam": "Divine Light" Traditions in the Dead Sea Scrolls and the Christian Ascetical Literature of Fourth-Century Syro-Mesopotamia. Pages 275–308 in *The Dead Sea Scrolls as Background to Postbiblical Judaism and Early Christianity: Papers from an International Conference at St. Andrews in 2001*. Edited by J. R. Davila. STDJ 46. Leiden: Brill.

Goodman, Martin. 1982. The First Jewish Revolt: Social Conflict and the Problem of Debt. *JJS* 33:417–27.

———. 1987. *The Ruling Class of Judea: The Origins of the Jewish Revolt Against Rome, A.D. 66–70*. Cambridge: Cambridge University Press.

Görg, Manfred. 1980. Eine rätselhafte Textilbezeichnung im Alten Testament. *BN* 12:13–17.

Goshen-Gottstein, Moshe H. 1958. "Sefer Hagu"—The End of a Puzzle. *VT* 8:286–88.

Gropp, Douglas M. 2001. *Wadi Daliyeh II: The Samaria Papyri from Wadi Daliyeh.* DJD 28. Oxford: Clarendon.

Hamel, Gildas. 1990. *Poverty and Charity in Roman Palestine, First Three Centuries C.E.* NES 23. Berkeley: University of California Press.

Harrington, Daniel J. 1994. Wisdom at Qumran. Pages 137–53 in *The Community of the Renewed Covenant: The Notre Dame Symposium on the Dead Sea Scrolls.* Edited by E. Ulrich and J. C. VanderKam. Notre Dame, Ind.: University of Notre Dame Press.

———. 1996a. The Raz Nihyeh in a Qumran Wisdom Text (1Q26, 4Q415–418, 423). *RevQ* 17:549–53.

———. 1996b. *Wisdom Texts from Qumran.* London: Routledge.

———. 1997a. Ten Reasons Why the Qumran Wisdom Texts Are Important. *DSD* 4:245–55.

———. 1997b. Two Early Jewish Approaches to Wisdom: Sirach and Qumran Sapitential Work A. *JSP* 16:25–38.

———. 2003. Wisdom and Apocalyptic in 4QInstruction and 4 Ezra. Pages 343–55 in *Wisdom and Apocalypticism in the Dead Sea Scrolls and in the Biblical Tradition.* Edited by Florentino García Martínez. BETL 168. Leuven: Leuven University Press.

———. 2006. Recent Study of 4QInstruction. Pages 105–23 in *From 4QMMT to Resurrection: Mélanges qumraniens en hommage à Émile Puech.* Edited by Annette Steudel, Eibert Tigchelaar, and Florentino García Martínez. STDJ 60. Leiden: Brill.

Harrington, Daniel, and John Strugnell. 1993. Qumran Cave 4 Texts: A New Publication. *JBL* 112:491–99.

Hempel, Charlotte. 1998. *The Laws of the Damascus Document: Sources, Tradition, and Redaction.* STDJ 29. Leiden: Brill.

———. 2002. The Qumran Sapiential Texts and the Rule Books. Pages 277–95 in *The Wisdom Texts from Qumran and the Development of Sapiential Thought.* Edited by Charlotte Hempel, Hermann Lichtenberger, and Armin Lange. BETL 159. Leuven: Leuven University Press.

Hengel, Martin. 1974. *Judaism and Hellenism.* 2 vols. Philadelphia: Fortress.

Hezser, Catherine. 2005. *Jewish Slavery in Antiquity.* New York: Oxford University Press.

Hill, Andrew. 1998. *Malachi*. AB 25D. New York: Doubleday.

Holloway, Paul A. 2008. "Beguile your Soul" (Sir XIV:16; XXX:23): An Epicurean Theme in Ben Sira. *VT* 58:219–34.

Horst, Pieter W. van der. 1978. *The Sentences of Pseudo-Phocylides*. Leiden: Brill.

Hughes, Julie A. 2006. *Scriptural Allusions and Exegesis in the Hodayot*. STDJ 59. Leiden: Brill.

Hyman, Ronald. 2009. Four Acts of Vowing in the Bible. *JQR* 37:31–38.

Ilan, Tal. 1996a. *Jewish Women in Greco-Roman Palestine*. Peabody, Mass.: Hendrickson.

———. 1996b. On a Newly Published Divorce Bill from the Judean Desert. *HTR* 89:195–202.

———. 1999. *Integrating Women into Second Temple History*. TSAJ 76. Tübingen: Mohr Siebeck.

Japhet, Sara. 1993. *I and II Chronicles*. OTL. Louisville: Westminster John Knox.

Jefferies, Daryl. 2002. *Wisdom at Qumran: A Form-Critical Analysis of the Admonitions in 4QInstruction*. GDNES 3. Piscataway, N.J.: Gorgias Press.

———. 2008. Scripture, Wisdom, and Authority in 4QInstruction: Understanding the Use of Numbers 30:8–9 in 4Q416. *HS* 49:87–98.

Joüon, Paul, and Takamitsu Muraoka. 2008. *A Grammar of Biblical Hebrew*. 2nd ed. SB 27. Rome: Pontifical Biblical Institute. Editrice Pontificio Istituto Biblico.

Jungbauer, Harry. 2002. *"Ehre Vater und Mutter": Der Weg des Elterngebots in der biblischen Tradition*. WUNT 146. Tübingen: Mohr Siebeck.

Kampen, John. 1998. The Diverse Aspects of Wisdom at Qumran. Pages 211–43 in vol. 1 of *The Dead Sea Scrolls after Fifty Years: A Comprehensive Assessment*. Edited by P. W. Flint and J. C. VanderKam. 2 vols. Leiden: Brill.

———. 2011. *Wisdom Literature*. Grand Rapids: Eerdmans.

Kister, Menahem. 2003. A Qumranic Parallel to 1 Thess 4:4? Reading and Interpretation of 4Q416 2 II 21. *DSD* 10:365–70.

———. 2004. Wisdom Literature and Its Relation to Other Genres: From Ben Sira to Mysteries. Pages 13–47 in *Sapiential Perspectives: Wisdom Literature in Light of the Dead Sea Scrolls: Proceedings of the Sixth International Symposium of the Orion Center, 20–22 May 2001*. Edited by John J. Collins, Gregory E. Sterling, and Ruth A. Clements. STDJ 51. Leiden: Brill.

————. 2005. Physical and Metaphysical Measurements Ordained by God in the Literature of the Second Temple Period. Pages 153–76 in *Reworking the Bible: Apocryphal and Related Texts at Qumran: Proceedings of a Joint Symposium by the Orion Center for the Study of the Dead Sea Scrolls and Associated Literature and the Hebrew University Institute for Advanced Studies Research Group on Qumran, 15–17 January, 2002.* Edited by Esther G. Chazon, Devorah Dimant, and Ruth A. Clements. STDJ 58. Leiden: Brill.

————. 2009a. Divorce, Reproof, and Other Sayings in the Synoptic Gospels: Jesus Traditions in the Context of "Qumranic" and Other Texts. Pages 195–229 in *Text, Thought, and Practice in Qumran and Early Christianity: Proceedings of the Ninth International Symposium of the Orion Center for the Study of the Dead Sea Scrolls and Associated Literature, Jointly Sponsored by the Hebrew University Center for the Study of Christianity.* Edited by R. A. Clements and D. R. Schwartz. STDJ 84. Leiden: Brill.

————. 2009b. *The Qumran Scrolls and Their World* [Hebrew]. 2 vols. Jerusalem: Yad Izhak Ben-Zvi.

Knibb, Michael A. 2003. The Book of Enoch in the Light of the Qumran Wisdom Literature. Pages 193–210 in *Wisdom and Apocalypticism in the Dead Sea Scrolls and in the Biblical Tradition.* Edited by Florentino García Martínez. BETL 168. Leuven: Leuven University Press.

Knobloch, Frederick W. Adoption. Pages 76–79 in vol. 1 of *Anchor Bible Dictionary.* Edited by D. N. Freedman. 6 vols. New York: Doubleday, 1992.

Kugel, James. 2001. Some Instances of Biblical Interpretation in the Hymns and Wisdom Writings of Qumran. Pages 155–69 in *Studies in Ancient Midrash.* Edited by J. L. Kugel. Cambridge: Harvard University Center for Jewish Studies.

Lambdin, Thomas O. 1953. Egyptian Loan Words in the Old Testament. *JAOS* 73:145–55.

Lange, Armin. 1995. *Weisheit und Prädestination: Weisheitliche Urordnung und Prädestination in den Textfunden von Qumran.* STDJ 18. Leiden: Brill.

————. 1996. Kognitives *lqh* in Sap A., im Tenak und Sir. *ZAH* 9:190–95.

————. 1998. In Diskussion mit dem Tempel: Zur Auseinandersetzung zwischen Kohelet und weisheitlichen Kreisen am Jerusalemer Tempel. Pages 113–59 in *Qohelet in the Conext of Wisdom.* Edited by A. Schoors. BETL 136. Leuven: Leuven University Press; Peeters.

———. 2000. The Determination of Fate by the Oracle of the Lot in the Dead Sea Scrolls, the Hebrew Bible, and Ancient Mesopotamian Literature. Pages 39–48 in *Sapiential, Liturgical, and Poetical Texts from Qumran: Proceedings of the Third Meeting of the International Organization for Qumran Studies, Oslo 1998: Published in Memory of Maurice Baillet.* Edited by Daniel K. Falk, Florentino García Martínez, and Eileen M. Schuller. STDJ 35. Leiden: Brill.

———. 2002. The Weisheitstexte aus Qumran: Eine Einleitung. Pages 3–30 in *The Wisdom Texts from Qumran and the Development of Sapiential Thought.* Edited by Charlotte Hempel, Hermann Lichtenberger, and Armin Lange. BETL 159. Leuven: Leuven University Press.

———. 2003. Die Bedeutung der Weisheitstexte aus Qumran für die hebräische Bibel. Pages 129–44 in *Weisheit in Israel: Beiträge des Symposiums "Das Alte Testament und die Kultur der Moderne" anlässlich des 100. Geburtstags Gerhard von Rads (1901–1971), Heidelberg, 18.–21. Oktober 2001.* Edited by D. J. A. Clines, Hermann Lichtenberger, and Hans-Peter Müller. ATM 12. Münster: Lit-Verlag.

———. 2008. Sages and Scribes in the Qumran Literature. Pages 271–93 in *Scribes, Sages, and Seers in the Eastern Mediterranean World.* Edited by Leo G. Perdue. Göttingen: Vandenhoeck & Ruprecht.

———. 2010. Wisdom Literature and Thought in the Dead Sea Scrolls. Pages 454–78 in *The Oxford Handbook of the Dead Sea Scrolls.* Edited by T. H. Lim and J. J. Collins. New York: Oxford University Press.

Leibner, Uzi. 2010. Arts and Crafts, Manufacture and Production. Pages 264–96 in *The Oxford Handbook of Jewish Daily Life in Roman Palestine.* Edited by Catherine Hezser. New York: Oxford University Press.

Lelli, Fabrizio. 1999. Stars. Pages 809–15 in *Dictionary of Deities and Demons in the Bible.* 2nd ed. Edited by Karel van der Toorn, Bob Becking, and Pieter W. van der Horst. Leiden: Brill.

Lemaire, André. 2006. Les Écrits de sagesse à Qoumrân et l'interprétation du site. *JA* 294:53–65.

Levine, Baruch A. 2000. *Numbers 21–36.* AB 4A. New York: Doubleday.

Levison, John R. 2010. Adam and Eve. Pages 300–2 in *The Eerdmans Dictionary of Early Judaism.* Edited by John J. Collins and Daniel C. Harlow. Grand Rapids: Eerdmans.

Lewis, Naphtali. 1989. *The Documents from the Bar Kokhba Period in the Cave of Letters.* Jerusalem: Israel Exploration Society.

Lichtenberger, Hermann. 2008. Schöpfung und Ehe in Texten aus Qumran sowie Essenerberichten und die Bedeutung für das Neue Testament.

Pages 279–88 in *Judaistik und neutestamentliche Wissenschaft. Stand-orte—Grenzen—Beziehungen*. Edited by Lutz Doering, Hans-Günther Waubke, and Florian L. Wilk. FRLANT 226. Göttingen: Vandenhoeck & Ruprecht.

Macaskill, Grant. 2007. *Revealed Wisdom and Inaugurated Eschatology in Ancient Judaism and Early Christianity*. JSJSup 115. Leiden: Brill.

———. 2008. Creation, Eschatology, and Ethics in 4QInstruction. Pages 217–45 in *Defining Identities: We, You, and the Other in the Dead Sea Scrolls: Proceedings of the Fifth Meeting of the IOQS in Groningen*. Edited by Florentino García Martínez and Mladen Popović. STDJ 70. Leiden: Brill.

Magness, Jodi. 2002. *The Archaeology of Qumran and the Dead Sea Scrolls*. Grand Rapids: Eerdmans.

Milgrom, Jacob. 2000. *Leviticus 17–22*. AB 3A. New York: Doubleday.

———. 2001. *Leviticus 23–27*. AB 3B. New York: Doubleday.

Miller, Patrick D. 1973. *The Divine Warrior in Early Israel*. Cambridge: Harvard University Press.

Moore, Carey A. 1996. *Tobit*. AB 40A. New York: Doubleday.

Morgenstern, Matthew. 2000. The Meaning of בית מולדים in the Qumran Wisdom Texts. *JJS* 51:141–44.

Murphy, Catherine M. 2002. *Wealth in the Dead Sea Scrolls and the Qumran Community*. STDJ 40. Leiden: Brill.

Nickelsburg, George W. E. 2001. *1 Enoch 1: A Commentary on the Book of 1 Enoch, Chapters 1–36, 81–108*. Hermeneia. Minneapolis: Fortress.

———. 2006. *Resurrection, Immortality, and Eternal Life in Intertestamental Judaism and Early Christianity*. Expanded ed. HTS 56. Cambridge: Harvard University Press.

Niehr, H. 2002. Die Weisheit des Achikar und der *musar lammebin* im Vergleich. Pages 173–86 in *The Wisdom Texts from Qumran and the Development of Sapiential Thought*. Edited by Charlotte Hempel, Hermann Lichtenberger, and Armin Lange. BETL 159. Leuven: Leuven University Press.

Niskanen, Paul. 2009. The Poetics of Adam: The Creation of אדם in the Image of אלהים. *JBL* 128:417–36.

Nitzan, Bilhah. 2003. Prayers for Peace in the Dead Sea Scrolls and the Traditional Jewish Liturgy. Pages 113–32 in *Liturgical Perspectives: Prayer and Poetry in Light of the Dead Sea Scroll: Proceedings of the Fifth International Symposium of the Orion Center for the Study of the Dead Sea Scrolls and Associated Literature, 19–23 January, 2000*.

Edited by Esther G. Chazon with the collaboration of Ruth A. Clements and Avital Pinnick. STDJ 48. Leiden: Brill.

———. 2005a. The Ideological and Literary Unity of 4QInstruction and Its Authorship. *DSD* 12:257–79.

———. 2005b. Key Terms in 4QInstruction: Implications for Its Ideological Unity [Hebrew]. *Megilloth* 3:101–24.

Novick, Tzvi. 2008. The Meaning and Etymology of אוש. *JBL* 127:339–43.

Pastor, Jack. 1997. *Land and Economy in Ancient Palestine*. London: Routledge.

———. 2010. Trade, Commerce, and Consumption. Pages 297–307 in *The Oxford Handbook of Jewish Daily Life in Roman Palestine*. Edited by Catherine Hezser. New York: Oxford University Press.

Paul, Shalom. 1973. Heavenly Tablets and the Book of Life. *JANESCU* 5:345–53.

———. 1991. *Amos*. Hermeneia. Minneapolis: Fortress.

———. 2010. Gates of the Netherworld. Pages 163–69 in *A Woman of Valor: Jerusalem Ancient Near Eastern Studies in Honor of Joan Goodnick Westenholz*. Edited by Wayne Horowitz, Uri Gabbay, and Filip Vukosavović. Madrid: Consejo Superior de Investigaciones Científicas.

Perdue, Leo G. 2003. Wisdom and Apocalyptic: The Case of Qoheleth. Pages 231–58 in *Wisdom and Apocalypticism in the Dead Sea Scrolls and in the Biblical Tradition*. Edited by Florentino García Martínez. BETL 168. Leuven: Leuven University Press.

———. 2008. *The Sword and the Stylus: An Introduction to Wisdom in the Age of Empires*. Grand Rapids: Eerdmans.

Peters, Dorothy M. 2008. *Noah Traditions in the Dead Sea Scrolls*. SBLEJL 26. Atlanta: Society of Biblical Literature.

Pfann, Stephen J., et al. 2000. *Qumran Cave 4.XXVI: Cryptic Texts and Miscellanea, Part 1*. DJD 36. Oxford: Clarendon.

Pike, Dana M., and Andrew C. Skinner. 2001. *Qumran Cave 4.XXIII: Unidentified Fragments*. DJD 33. Oxford: Clarendon.

Pleins, J. David. 2001. *The Social Visions of the Hebrew Bible: A Theological Introduction*. Louisville: Westminster John Knox.

Popović, Mladen. 2007. *Reading the Human Body: Physiognomics and Astrology in the Dead Sea Scrolls and Hellenistic-Early Roman Period Judaism*. STDJ 67. Leiden: Brill.

Porten, Bezalel. 2011. *The Elephantine Papyri in English: Three Millennia of Cross-Cultural Continuity and Change*. 2nd rev. ed. DMOA 22. Atlanta: Society of Biblical Literature.

Porten, Bezalel, and Jonas C. Greenfield. 1969. The Guarantor at Elephantine-Syene. *JAOS* 89:153–57.

Porten, Bezalel, and Ada Yardeni. 1986–1999. *Textbook of Aramaic Documents from Ancient Egypt.* 4 vols. Jerusalem: Department of the History of the Jewish People, Hebrew University.

Puech, Émile. 1993. *La croyance des Esséniens en la vie future: Immortalité, résurrection, vie éternelle? Histoire d'une croyance dans le judaïsme ancien.* EBib 21–22. 2 vols. Paris: Gabalda.

2003a. Apports des textes apocalyptiques et sapientiels de Qumrân à l'eschatologie du judaïsme ancien. Pages 133–70 in *Wisdom and Apocalypticism in the Dead Sea Scrolls and in the Biblical Tradition.* Edited by Florentino García Martínez. BETL 168. Leuven: Leuven University Press.

———. 2003b. La Conception de la vie future dans le livre de la sagesse et les manuscrits de la Mer Morte: Un Aperçu. *RevQ* 21:209–32.

———. 2004a. La Croyance à la résurrection des justes dans un texte qumranien de sagesse. Pages 427–44 in *Sefer Moshe: The Moshe Weinfeld Jubilee Volume: Studies in the Bible and the Ancient Near East, Qumran, and Post-Biblical Judaism.* Edited by Chaim Cohen, Avi Hurvitz, Shalom M. Paul, and Moshe Weinfeld. Winona Lake, Ind.: Eisenbrauns.

———. 2004b. Review of Matthew J. Goff, *The Worldly and Heavenly Wisdom. RevQ* 21:649–52.

———. 2005. Les Fragments eschatologiques de *4QInstruction* (4Q416 1 et 4Q418 69 ii, 81–81a, 127). *RevQ* 22:89–119.

———. 2006. Apports des manuscrits de Qoumrân à la croyance à la résurrection dans le judaïsme ancien. Pages 81–110 in *Qoumrân et le judaïsme du tournant de notre ère. Actes de la Table Ronde, Collège de France, 16 novembre 2004.* Edited by A. Lemaire and S. C. Mimouni. Leuven: Peeters.

———. 2008a. Ben Sira and Qumran. Page 79–118 in *The Wisdom of Ben Sira: Studies on Tradition, Redaction, and Theology.* DCLS 1. Edited by A. Passaro and G. Bellia. Berlin: de Gruyter.

———. 2008b. Les Identités en présence dans les scènes du jugement dernier de *4QInstruction* (4Q416 1 et 4Q418 69 ii). Pages 147–73 in *Defining Identities: We, You, and the Other in the Dead Sea Scrolls: Proceedings of the Fifth Meeting of the IOQS in Groningen.* Edited by Florentino García Martínez and Mladen Popović. STDJ 70. Leiden: Brill.

Puech, Émile, and Annette Steudel. 2000. Un Nouveau Fragment du manuscrit 4QInstruction (XQ7 = 4Q417 ou 4Q418). *RevQ* 19:623–27.

Qimron, Elisha. 2008. *The Hebrew of the Dead Sea Scrolls.* HSS 29. Winona Lake, Ind.: Eisenbrauns.

Qimron, Elisha, and John Strugnell. 1994. *Qumran Cave 4.V: Miqsat Ma'aśe ha-Torah.* DJD 10. Oxford: Clarendon.

Rabinowitz, Isaac. 1961. The Qumran Authors' *spr hhgw/y. JNES* 20:109–14.

Rad, Gerhard von. 1965. *Old Testament Theology.* 2 vols. New York: Harper & Row.

Radner, Karen. 2001. The Neo-Assyrian Period. Pages 265–88 in *Security for Debt in Ancient Near Eastern Law.* Edited by Raymond Westbrook and Richard Jasnow. CHANE 9. Leiden: Brill.

Rey, Jean-Sébastien. 2008. Quelques particularités linguistiques communes à 4Q*Instruction* et à Ben Sira. Pages 155–73 in *Conservatism and Innovation in the Hebrew Language of the Hellenistic Period: Proceedings of a Fourth International Symposium on the Hebrew of the Dead Sea Scrolls and Ben Sira.* Edited by J. Joosten and J.-S. Rey. STDJ 73. Leiden: Brill.

———. 2009a. *4QInstruction: Sagesse et eschatologie.* STDJ 81. Leiden: Brill.

———. 2009b. Family Relationships in 4QInstruction and Eph 5:21–6:4. Pages 231–55 in *Echoes from the Caves: Qumran and the New Testament.* Edited by Florentino García Martínez. STDJ 85. Leiden: Brill.

Reymond, Eric D. 2006. The Poetry of 4Q416 2 III 15–19. *DSD* 13:177–93.

———. 2011. *New Idioms within Old: Poetry and Parallelism in the Non-Masoretic Poems of 11Q5 (=11QPs^a).* SBLEJL 31. Atlanta: Society of Biblical Literature.

Rosen-Zvi, Ishay. 2008. Two Rabbinic Inclinations? Rethinking a Scholarly Dogma. *JSJ* 39:1–27.

———. 2009. Sexualising the Evil Inclination: Rabbinic "Yetzer" and Modern Scholarship. *JJS* 60:264–81.

———. 2011. *Demonic Desires: Yetzer Hara and the Problem of Evil in Late Antiquity.* Philadelphia: University of Pennsylvania Press.

Rosenberg, Stephen Gabriel. 2006. *Airaq al-Amir: The Architecture of the Tobiads.* Oxford: John and Erica Hedges Ltd.

Roth, Martha. 2003. The Laws of Hammurabi. Pages 335–53 in vol. 2 of *The Context of Scripture: Canonical Compositions, Monumental Inscriptions and Archival Documents from the Biblical World.* 3 vols. Edited by W. W. Hallo and K. Lawson Younger. Leiden: Brill.

Ruiten, J. T. A. G. M. van. 2000. The Creation of Man and Woman in Early Jewish Literature. Pages 34–62 in *The Creation of Man and Woman*. Edited by G. P. Luttikhuizen. TBN 3. Leiden: Brill.

Safrai, Zeev. 1994. *The Economy of Roman Palestine*. London: Routledge.

———. 2010. Agriculture and Farming. Pages 246–63 in *The Oxford Handbook of Jewish Daily Life in Roman Palestine*. Edited by Catherine Hezser. New York: Oxford University Press.

Sandoval, Timothy J. 2006. *The Discourse of Wealth and Poverty in the Book of Proverbs*. BInS 77. Leiden: Brill.

Satlow, Michael L. 2001. *Jewish Marriage in Antiquity*. Princeton: Princeton University Press.

———. 2010. Marriage and Divorce. Pages 344–61 in *The Oxford Handbook of Jewish Daily Life in Roman Palestine*. Edited by Catherine Hezser. New York: Oxford University Press.

Schiffman, Lawrence H. 1991. The Laws of Vows and Oaths (Num 30, 3–16) in the Zadokite Fragments and the Temple Scroll. *RevQ* 15:199–214.

———. 2004. Halakhic Elements in the Sapiential Texts. Page 89–100 in *Sapiential Perspectives: Wisdom Literature in Light of the Dead Sea Scrolls: Proceedings of the Sixth International Symposium of the Orion Center, 20–22 May 2001*. Edited by John J. Collins, Gregory E. Sterling, and Ruth A. Clements. STDJ 51. Leiden: Brill.

Schmid, Konrad, and Christoph Riedweg, eds. 2008. *Beyond Eden: The Biblical Story of Paradise (Genesis 2–3) and Its Reception History*. FAT 2.34. Tübingen: Mohr Siebeck.

Schmidt, Francis. 2006. Recherche son thème de geniture dans le mystère de ce qui doit être. Astrologie et prédestination à Qoumrân. Pages 51–62 in *Qoumrân et le judaïsme du tournant de notre ère. Actes de la Table Ronde, Collège de France, 16 novembre 2004*. Edited by A. Lemaire and S. C. Mimouni. Leuven: Peeters.

Schofer, Jonathan Wyn. 2005. *The Making of a Sage: A Study in Rabbinic Ethics*. Madison: University of Wisconsin Press.

Schoors, Anton. 2002. The Language of the Qumran Sapiential Works. Pages 61–95 in *The Wisdom Texts from Qumran and the Development of Sapiential Thought*. Edited by Charlotte Hempel, Hermann Lichtenberger, and Armin Lange. BETL 159. Leuven: Leuven University Press.

Schremer, Adriel. 1998. Divorce in Papyrus Ṣe'elim 13 Once Again: A Reply to Tal Ilan. *HTR* 91:193–202.

Schuller, Eileen. 2011. Women in the Dead Sea Scrolls: Research in the Past Decade and Future Directions. Pages 571–88 in *The Dead Sea Scrolls and Contemporary Culture: Proceedings of the International Conference held at the Israel Museum, Jerusalem (July 6–8, 2008).* Edited by Adolfo Daniel Roitman, Lawrence H. Schiffman, and Shani Tzoref. STDJ 93. Leiden: Brill.

Scott, James M. 2001. Korah and Qumran. Pages 182–202 in *The Bible at Qumran: Text, Shape, and Interpretation.* Edited by Peter W. Flint. Grand Rapids: Eerdmans.

Segal, Moshe T. 1953. *The Complete Book of Ben Sira* [Hebrew]. Jerusalem: Bialik.

Seow, Choon-Leong. 1997. *Ecclesiastes.* AB 18C. New York: Doubleday.

Shanks, Hershel. 2002. Chief Scroll Editor Opens Up: An Interview with Emanuel Tov. *BAR* 28:32–35, 62.

Shemesh, Aharon. 1998. 4Q271.3: A Key to Sectarian Matrimonial Law. *JJS* 49:244–63.

———. 2001. דימויי זיווגים אסורים לכלאיים ושעטנז בספרות כת מדבר יהודה [Two Principles of the Qumranic Matrimonial Law]. Pages 181–203 in *Fifty Years of Dead Sea Scrolls Research: Studies in Memory of Jacob Licht.* Edited by Gershon Brin and Bilhah Nitzan. Jerusalem: Yad Izhak Ben-Zvi.

Shimoff, Sandra R. 1995. Gardens: From Eden to Jerusalem. *JSJ* 26:145–55.

Sivertsev, Alexei. 2010. The Household Economy. Pages 229–45 in *The Oxford Handbook of Jewish Daily Life in Roman Palestine.* Edited by Catherine Hezser. New York: Oxford University Press.

Sly, Dorothy. 1990. *Philo's Perceptions of Women.* BJS 209. Atlanta: Scholars Press.

Smith, Jay E. 2001. Another Look at 4Q416 2 ii.21, a Critical Parallel to First Thessalonians 4:4. *CBQ* 63:499–504.

Stegemann, Hartmut. 1998. *The Library of Qumran: On the Essenes, Qumran, John the Baptist, and Jesus.* Leiden: Brill.

Stegemann, Harmut, Eileen Schuller, and Carol Newsom. 2009. *Qumran Cave 1.III: 1QHodayot^a with Incorporation of 1QHodayot^b and 4QHodayot^{a–f}.* DJD 40. Oxford: Clarendon.

Steinmetz, Devora. 2001. Sefer HeHago: The Community and the Book. *JJS* 52:40–58.

Strugnell, John. 1956. Le travail d'édition des fragments de Qumrân: Communication de John Strugnell. *RB* 63:64–66.

———. 1996. More on Wives and Marriage in the Dead Sea Scrolls (4Q416 2 ii 21 [Cf. 1 Thess 4:4] and 4QMMT, B). *RevQ* 17:537–47.

———. 1999. The Sapiential Work 4Q415ff. and the Pre-Qumranic Works from Qumran: Lexical Considerations. Pages 595–608 in *The Provo International Conference on the Dead Sea Scrolls*. Edited by D. W. Parry and E. Ulrich. STDJ 30. Leiden: Brill.

Strugnell, John, and Daniel J. Harrington. 1999. *Qumran Cave 4.XXIV: Sapiential Texts, Part 2. 4QInstruction (Mûsār Lĕ Mēbîn): 4Q415ff. With a Re-edition of 1Q26*. DJD 34. Oxford: Clarendon.

Stuckenbruck, Loren T. 2002. 4QInstruction and the Possible Influence of Early Enochic Traditions: An Evaluation. Pages 245–61 in *The Wisdom Texts from Qumran and the Development of Sapiential Thought*. Edited by Charlotte Hempel, Hermann Lichtenberger, and Armin Lange. BETL 159. Leuven: Leuven University Press.

———. 2004. "Angels" and "God": Exploring the Limits of Early Jewish Monotheism. Page 45–70 in *Early Jewish and Christian Monotheism*. Edited by Loren T. Stuckenbruck and Wendy E. S. North. JSNTSup 263. London: T&T Clark.

Sullivan, Kevin P. 2004. *Wrestling with Angels: A Study of the Relationship between Angels and Humans in Ancient Jewish Literature*. AGJU 55. Leiden: Brill.

Tcherikover, Victor. 1999. *Hellenistic Civilization and the Jews*. Peabody, Mass.: Hendrickson.

Tcherikover, Victor, and Alexander Fuks, eds. 1959. *Corpus Papyrorum Judaicarum*. 3 vols. Cambridge: Harvard University Press.

Thomas, Samuel I. 2009. *The Mysteries of Qumran: Mystery, Secrecy, and Esotericism in the Dead Sea Scrolls*. SBLEJL 25. Atlanta: Society of Biblical Literature.

Tigchelaar, Eibert J. C. 1998. הבא ביחד in *4QInstruction (4Q418 64 + 199 + 66 par 4Q417 1 i 17–19)* and the Height of the Columns of *4Q418*. *RevQ* 18:589–93.

———. 1999. Eden and Paradise: The Garden Motif in Some Early Jewish Texts. Pages 37–57 in *Paradise Interpreted: Representations of Biblical Paradise in Judaism and Christianity*. Edited by G. P. Luttikhuizen. TBN 2. Leiden: Brill.

———. 2000. The Addressees of 4QInstruction. Pages 62–75 in *Sapiential, Liturgical, and Poetic Texts from Qumran: Proceedings of the Third Meeting of the International Organization for Qumran Studies, Oslo 1998. Published in Memory of Maurice Baillet*. Edited by Daniel K.

Falk, Florentino García Martínez, and Eileen M. Schuller. STDJ 35. Leiden: Brill.

———. 2001. *To Increase Learning for the Understanding Ones: Reading and Reconstructing the Fragmentary Early Jewish Sapiential Text 4QInstruction*. STDJ 44. Leiden: Brill.

———. 2002. Towards a Reconstruction of the Beginning of 4QInstruction (4Q416 Fragment 1 and Parallels). Pages 99–126 in *The Wisdom Texts from Qumran and the Development of Sapiential Thought*. Edited by Charlotte Hempel, Hermann Lichtenberger, and Armin Lange. BETL 159. Leuven: Leuven University Press.

———. 2003. Your Wisdom and Your Folly: The Case of 1–4QMysteries. Pages 69–88 in *Wisdom and Apocalypticism in the Dead Sea Scrolls and in the Biblical Tradition*. Edited by Florentino García Martínez. BETL 168. Leuven: Leuven University Press.

———. 2007. Wisdom and Counter-Wisdom in 4QInstruction, Mysteries and 1 Enoch. Pages 41–63 in *The Early Enoch Literature*. Edited by G. Boccaccini and J. J. Collins. JSJSup 121. Leiden: Brill.

———. 2009. "Spiritual People," "Fleshly Spirit," and "Vision of Meditation": Reflections on 4QInstruction and 1 Corinthians. Pages 103–18 in *Echoes from the Caves: Qumran and the New Testament*. Edited by Florentino García Martínez. STDJ 85. Leiden: Brill.

———. 2011. Gleanings from the Plates of Unidentified Fragments: Two PAM 43.674 Identifications (4Q365 and 4Q416). Pages 317–22 in *"Go Out and Study the Land" (Judges 18:2): Archaeological, Historical, and Textual Studies in Honor of Hanan Eshel*. Edited by Aren M. Maeir, Jodi Magness, and Lawrence H. Schiffman. JSJSup 148. Leiden: Brill.

Tiller, Patrick A. 1997. The "Eternal Planting" in the Dead Sea Scrolls. *DSD* 4:312–35.

Tobin, Thomas H. 1983. *The Creation of Man: Philo and the History of Interpretation*. CBQMS 14. Washington, D.C.: Catholic Biblical Association.

Toorn, Karel van der. 2007. *Scribal Culture and the Making of the Hebrew Bible*. Cambridge: Harvard University Press.

Tosato, Angelo. 1990. On Genesis 2:24. *CBQ* 52:389–409.

Tov, Emanuel. 2004. *Scribal Practices and Approaches Reflected in the Texts Found in the Judean Desert*. STJD 54. Leiden: Brill.

Trenchard, Warren C. 1982. *Ben Sira's View of Women: A Literary Analysis*. BJS 38. Chico, Calif.: Scholars Press.

Turner, John D. 1998. The Gnostic Seth. Pages 33–58 in *Biblical Figures Outside the Bible*. Edited by M. E. Stone and T. A. Bergen. Harrisburg, Pa.: Trinity Press International.

Tuschling, R. M. M. 2007. *Angels and Orthodoxy: A Study in their Development in Syria and Palestine from the Qumran Texts to Ephrem the Syrian*. STAC 40. Tübingen: Mohr Siebeck.

Urbach, Ephraim. 1979. *The Sages*. Cambridge: Harvard University Press.

VanderKam, James C. 1999. *From Revelation to Canon: Studies in the Hebrew Bible and Second Temple Literature*. JSJSup 62. Leiden: Brill.

———. 2010. *The Dead Sea Scrolls Today*. 2nd ed. Grand Rapids: Eerdmans.

Vattioni, Francesco. 1968. *Ecclesiastico: Testo ebraico con apparato critico e versioni greca, latina e siriaca*. Napoli: Istituto Orientale di Napoli.

Wacholder, Ben Z., and Martin G. Abegg. 1992. *A Preliminary Edition of the Unpublished Dead Sea Scrolls: The Hebrew and Aramaic Texts from Cave Four. Fascicle Two*. Washington, D.C.: Dead Sea Scrolls Research Council; Biblical Archaeological Society.

Werman, Cana. 2004. What is the *Book of Hagu*? Pages 125–40 in *Sapiential Perspectives: Wisdom Literature in Light of the Dead Sea Scrolls: Proceedings of the Sixth International Symposium of the Orion Center, 20-22 May 2001*. Edited by John J. Collins, Gregory E. Sterling, and Ruth A. Clements. STDJ 51. Leiden: Brill.

Wernberg-Møller, Preben. 1961. A Reconsideration of the Two Spirits in the Rule of the Community (1QSerek III, 13–IV, 26). *RevQ* 3:413–41.

Westbrook, Raymond. 2001a. Introduction. Pages 1–3 in *Security for Debt in Ancient Near Eastern Law*. Edited by Raymond Westbrook and Richard Jasnow. CHANE 9. Leiden: Brill.

———. 2001b. The Old Babylonian Period. Pages 63–90 in *Security for Debt in Ancient Near Eastern Law*. Edited by Raymond Westbrook and Richard Jasnow. CHANE 9. Leiden: Brill.

Westbrook, Raymond, and Richard Jasnow, eds., 2001. *Security for Debt in Ancient Near Eastern Law*. CHANE 9. Leiden: Brill.

Wise, Michael O. 2003. Dating the Teacher of Righteousness and the *Floruit* of His Movement. *JBL* 122:53–87.

Wold, Benjamin G. 2004. Reconsidering an Aspect of the Title *Kyrios* in Light of Sapiential Fragment 4Q416 2 iii. *ZNW* 95:149–60.

———. 2005a Reading and Reconstructing 4Q416 2 II 21: Comments on Menahem Kister's Proposal. *DSD* 12:205–11.

———. 2005b. *Women, Men and Angels: The Qumran Wisdom Document "Musar leMevin" and Its Allusions to Genesis Creation Traditions.* WUNT 2/201. Tübingen: Mohr Siebeck.

———. 2007. Metaphorical Poverty in "Musar leMevin." *JJS* 58:140–53.

———. 2008. Family Ethics in *4QInstruction* and the New Testament. *NovT* 50:286–300.

Wolters, Al. 1994. Anthropoi Eudokias (Luke 2:14) and *'ansy rswn* (4Q416). *JBL* 113: 291–97.

Wright, Benjamin G. III. 2004a. The Categories of Rich and Poor in the Qumran Sapiential Literature. Pages 101–23 in *Sapiential Perspectives: Wisdom Literature in Light of the Dead Sea Scrolls: Proceedings of the Sixth International Symposium of the Orion Center, 20–22 May 2001.* Edited by John J. Collins, Gregory E. Sterling, and Ruth A. Clements. STDJ 51. Leiden: Brill.

———. 2004b. Wisdom and Women at Qumran. *DSD* 11:240–61.

Yardeni, Ada. 2002. *The Book of Hebrew Script: History, Palaeography, Script Styles, Calligraphy, and Design.* New Castle: Oak Knoll Press.

Yardeni, Ada, and Jonas C. Greenfield. 1996. A Receipt for a *Ketubba.* Pages 197–208 in *The Jews in the Hellenistic-Roman World: Studies in Memory of Menahem Stern* [Hebrew]. Edited by Daniel R. Schwartz, Aharon Oppenheimer, and Isaiah Gafni. Jerusalem: The Zalman Shazar Center for Jewish History and the Historical Society of Israel.

INDEX OF ANCIENT SOURCES

THE DEAD SEA SCROLLS AND THE
DAMASCUS DOCUMENT

INDEX OF MODERN AUTHORS